Prior
Analytics

ARISTOTLE

Prior Analytics

translated, with introduction,
notes, and commentary, by

Robin Smith

Hackett Publishing Company

Indianapolis / Cambridge

Aristotle: 384–322 B.C.

Copyright © 1989 by Robin Smith
Printed in the United States of America

Cover and interior design by L. Daniel Kirklin

For further information, please address the publisher

Hackett Publishing Company, Inc.
P.O. Box 44937
Indianapolis, Indiana 46204

Library of Congress Cataloging-in-Publication Data

Aristotle.
    [Prior analytics. English]
    Prior analytics / Aristotle ; translated, with introduction,
notes, and commentary by Robin Smith.
       p.   cm.
    Bibliography: p.
    Includes index.
    ISBN 0-87220-064-7
    1. Logic—Early works to 1800.   I. Title.
B440.A5S65   1989
160—dc19   88-39877
                                      CIP

The paper used in this publication meets the minimum re-
quirements of American National Standard for Information
Sciences—Permanence of Paper for Printed Library
Materials, ANSI Z39.48-1984.

Contents

In Memoriam

Charles Allen Carson
1928–1989

PREFACE

No other treatise on formal logic is comparable to Aristotle's *Prior Analytics*. This is true in the first place because no other logician occupies a position in history at all comparable to Aristotle. He was not only the first formal logician, he was also one of the greatest: the most compelling evidence for this assessment is his startling appearance on the stage of history, with no real predecessor. But historical accident has added much to the importance of the *Prior Analytics*. For many generations, Aristotelian logic (or at least what passed for Aristotelian logic) was identically logic: thus, Kant could say, in the *Critique of Pure Reason*, that the entire field of logic had not made a single advance since Aristotle's great treatise. Few would concur in such an opinion today, but the effect of the *Prior Analytics* in forming our philosophical heritage is difficult to exaggerate.

At the same time, it might be argued that the work has little philosophical interest today. During the last century, formal logic has reached extremely high levels of technical sophistication, and philosophical discussion of its underlying concepts has advanced commensurately. As a result, it might be suggested that whatever admiration we may have today for Aristotle's achievement, nevertheless he has little to teach us that we cannot learn better from our contemporaries. When we consider the effort that is required to study a system in many respects awkward and unfamiliar from a modern point of view, the difficulties occasioned by Aristotle's ignorance of much of what we have since learned about deductive systems, and the many problems of interpretation which arise with any work produced in another language and in another culture at a distance of over two millennia, the *Prior Analytics* may seem to be of value only to the philosophical antiquary.

I do not think this is a fair assessment. In part, I would respond with the same defense many historians of philosophy give for the practice of their craft: Aristotle is a major part of our philosophical ancestry, and we come to understand ourselves better by studying our ideal origins. In larger part, however, I would suggest that we still may have something to learn from this old Greek. If he is ignorant of our vast body of

metalogic, he is also unencumbered by our many newly-born prejudices. Sometimes, we find his approach to a question, once we come to
understand it in our own terms, is a fresh one: occasionally, he might
even be right. The proof, of course, must be in the experiencing.

The Translation. Translation is almost by nature arrogant: the translator acts as a kind of impersonator of the author, and the reader has no
good means of defense against a false representation. In the case of a
work like the *Prior Analytics*, there is a temptation to even further
arrogance. Aristotle's Greek is frequently clipped, difficult of construction, awkward, ambiguous, or obscure. The translator is sorely
tempted to give him a hand in coming across better in English: to
resolve the ambiguities, clean up the messy constructions, fill out what
is abbreviated (or even absent), smooth out the awkward parts. While
about it, one could also give the reader a bit of help with a few rather
full renderings of difficult terms or phrases, creating a text that em-
bodies a certain amount of commentary in its interstices.

There are occasions when this sort of translation is appropriate, but
it is not what I have aimed at. I have tried instead to give the philosophically informed reader who does not know Greek a vehicle for the
study of Aristotle's *Prior Analytics*. To that end, I have attempted to
leave as much of the interpretative work as possible undone. One way
to do that is to follow the model of Robert Grosseteste and construct a
sort of functional mapping of Aristotle's Greek into English (or rather
into a barbarous sort of construction made of English words). But this,
I believe, is in many cases just not to translate at all. The Greekless
reader, presented with such a subliteral string of English vocabulary, is
often prompted to ask: Well, whatever *could* that mean?

What I have tried to do instead is to strike a compromise. The
English of my translation is intended to be English, though I have
sought to avoid making it more elegant than Aristotle's Greek. When
Aristotle is hard to construe, I have undertaken to translate him with
difficult English. However, I have made intelligibility take precedence
over the goal of reproducing the character of Aristotle's Greek in
English, something which probably cannot be done. When alternative
interpretations of the text are possible, I have, of course, chosen the
one I find most likely (though in some fortunate cases, I have been
able to reproduce an ambiguity of Greek syntax in English); however,
in the Notes I alert the reader to those possibilities which I have

closed off in the translation itself. When a certain translation of a technical term is well-established, I have more often than not opted for it, even though these traditional renderings are sometimes less than optimal, simply to make my version useful: readers must otherwise have a glossary converting my renderings into the established ones in order to make sense of the secondary literature. I have, however, avoided one unnecessary barbarism: I usually translate *huparchei panti* as 'belongs to every' rather than 'belongs to all' (which, in the present sense, has no English use outside discussions of the syllogistic: see Geach *1972*, 69).

The Text.   The translation is generally based on Ross's text; variations from his readings, where they are important, are discussed in the Notes (a list of variations from Ross is given as Appendix II). In virtually every such case, my differences with Ross lean towards editorial conservatism: I have tried to find a coherent sense for the best-attested reading, and I have taken the position that Aristotle sometimes nods. I retain the traditional division into Chapters, which (though completely without ancient authority) is a convenient and generally reasonable way of subdividing the text. Line references in the margin are to the standard edition (Bekker). Square brackets enclose passages which, although well-attested in the manuscripts, nevertheless seem to be spurious. I use angle brackets to mark both editorial additions to Aristotle's text (i.e., corrections to the manuscripts) and interpretative additions to the translation.

The Notes.   The Notes are not intended as a comprehensive commentary, but rather as an aid to the reader with more knowledge of logic and philosophy than of Greek. My goal has been to provide others with a *Prior Analytics* that can actually be used for serious study. Accordingly, I have tried to make clear what is controversial or problematic about the text and, to the extent possible, to get out of the reader's way. This has sometimes led me to include rather lengthy discussions of the grammatical and textual problems surrounding certain passages, which may seem odd in a work intended to be intelligible to those who do not know Greek. But it is precisely for that sort of reader that these points require the fullest discussion. Such a reader has no text beyond the translation and cannot see through the finished product to its often murky origins. What I have done is reconstruct some of the messy, even tendentious process whereby renderings come to be chosen; I hope that I have at the same time managed to undermine my own appearance of authority.

I have also tried to alert the reader to difficulties in understanding the text and to give some broad picture of the range of opinion among scholars, although this is necessarily selective and omits mention of many issues. In some cases, I do not take a position myself, but in others I do: the reader is better armed against my prejudices by being informed of what they are. On one point, I have argued for a rather specific line of interpretation. I see the *Prior Analytics* as organized in a certain way to support the goals of the *Posterior*. The nature of my view is spelled out in the Introduction, and the details are defended in various places, as appropriate, throughout the Notes. Once again, I believe that if my readers are aware of my own exegetical hobby-horses, they will be in a better position to defend themselves against any distorting effects.

The Introduction. The *Prior Analytics* is a technical work, and a difficult one. Some framework for viewing its theories is necessary, and we must (as Aristotle says) begin with what is familiar to us. I have therefore offered, in the Introduction, a model for Aristotle's deductive system in the style of mathematical logic. This may be regarded as a bit of temporal provincialism: perhaps in a century or two, it may seem as quaint to future readers as mid-nineteenth century accounts do to us. But at the least, it offers a point of departure from which to begin.

I cite the two Books of the *Prior Analytics* simply as A and B ('A 23' means 'Book A, Chapter 23'). Other works of Aristotle are given English (rather than Latin) titles. References to commentaries and other translations are identified by the commentator's name and page number only; other literature is cited by author and year. The details, in each case, are found in the Bibliography. As for the Bibliography, it should be regarded simply as the list of works I mention (though I also include a few general works on Aristotle).

Acknowledgments. A grant from the Bureau of General Research of Kansas State University provided support for the acquisition of materials and expenses of manuscript preparation; I acknowledge this with thanks. A number of persons have generously helped me with various stages of the work. Robert Turnbull offered advice and encouragement as the project was taking initial shape. John Corcoran has for many years tried to keep my thoughts about Aristotle's logic coherent; he read through the entire manuscript in draft and suggested several corrections in the Notes. As if that were not generosity enough, he and Woosuk Park each took it on themselves to read the whole book in page proofs, suggesting still further changes and finding any number of errors I had overlooked. Allan Bäck kindly allowed me to see parts of the manuscript of his book *On Reduplication* while it was still in press. I prevailed rather heavily on Charles M. Young to transmit me the results of searches of the *Thesaurus Linguae Graecae* by way of electronic mail. Any number of my colleagues in ancient philosophy have tolerated my badgering them about whether they thought this or that construal to be possible. Paige Nichols assisted with the preparation of the manuscript (one result of which is that she is now, I am quite sure, the only living human being to have read aloud the whole of the *Prior Analytics* in any language). James Hullett, Frances Hackett, Dan Kirklin, and the staff of Hackett Publishing Company have exceeded any author's reasonable expectations of what a publisher ought to be.

I am especially indebted to Michael Frede, who, as the second reader of the manuscript for Hackett Publishing Company, made a far more significant contribution to the final work than that office would suggest. He read through the Notes in two drafts and the translation in three. The wealth of careful and detailed comments he provided saved me from many errors and bad decisions and kept this book from being much worse: the force of the typical declaration of modesty by which an author retains only the responsibility for a work's faults and ascribes credit for its virtues to others is perhaps attenuated from overuse, but in this case I can think of no other way to express the truth.

As this book was in its final stages, my brother, Dr. Charles A. Carson, succumbed in a lengthy struggle with cancer. Charles was always a great lover of words (though his language was Latin, not Greek); I would like my book to serve as a small memorial to his exemplary life.

INTRODUCTION

The Content of the Prior Analytics. From Aristotle's viewpoint, the
Prior Analytics is simply the first part of the *Analytics*: the second part is
the work known to us as the *Posterior Analytics*. The subject of the
latter is proof or demonstration (*apodeixis*), that is, argumentation
which produces scientific understanding (*epistēmē*). Aristotle makes it
clear from the start that this is also the subject of the entire *Analytics*,
and thus of its first part, the *Prior*. Aristotle conceives of a demonstrative science as a system of demonstrations, which in turn are a type of
deduction (*sullogismos*). Accordingly, the *Prior Analytics* gives an account of deductions in general and the *Posterior* discusses the specific
character of those deductions which are demonstrations.

Although the relationship of the two parts of the *Analytics* appears to
be straightforward enough on this account, controversies have arisen
about its details and its history. In many respects, the *Prior Analytics* is
the more highly developed work: in the *Posterior*, Aristotle often seems
ignorant of technical results contained in it. Some scholars have argued
that the philosophical environments of the two parts are also different.
To mention the most important such study, Friedrich Solmsen under-
took to recover the course of historical development of Aristotle's logical doctrines using Jaeger's view that Aristotle evolved from an early
Platonic stance in philosophy to a mature position hostile to Platonism.
He concluded that the *Posterior Analytics* was the earlier work and that
it reflected a more primitive stage of the theory of deduction than that
found in the *Prior*. Controversy about this point is still not ended.

At issue here are two points. One is the historical question of when
the various parts of the *Analytics* were composed and how they ultimately took shape in the form preserved for us. The other is how
closely the *Posterior Analytics* depends on the theories of the *Prior*. I
cannot discuss these issues adequately here, but neither do I wish to
ignore them. Instead, let me alert the reader to my own interpretation,
which is to some extent defended in the Notes. I take the *Prior
Analytics* to be what Aristotle says it is: a theoretical preliminary to the
Posterior. It almost follows from this that the doctrines of the *Prior*
were developed after those in the *Posterior* had taken at least initial

XIII

shape. In fact, I believe the connection takes a more interesting form. Aristotle's purpose in the *Posterior Analytics* is not simply to present a view of scientific understanding but also, even primarily, to show that it is the correct one. This leads him to what I would regard as the most original and brilliant insight in the entire work: Aristotle made proofs themselves an object of study in order to answer questions about the possible structures of demonstrative sciences. This is what led him to develop the theory of deductions in the *Prior Analytics*, rather in the same way that Hilbert's desire to resolve certain mathematical questions led to his concept of proof theory. The result is that the contents of the *Prior Analytics* are in large measure designed throughout with the proof-theoretic concerns of the *Posterior* in mind.

Prior Analytics A describes itself more than once as having a tripartite goal: to determine 'how every deduction comes about,' to define a 'route' (*hodos*) whereby deductions may be found, and to explain how to transform any given deduction into a deduction 'in the figures.' The first of these projects is accomplished in Chapters 1−26 and the second in 27−31 (with 31 a comment on the inadequacy of Platonic Division as an alternative procedure). The third project occupies 32−45 (its completion is announced at the beginning of 46, 51b3−5): Chapter 46 appears to be a largely independent study with no obvious relation to the rest of the *Prior Analytics*.

Prior Analytics B is more difficult to characterize with confidence. The internal structure of Book A makes it appear that Aristotle has achieved all his announced goals, with the exception of a few areas (most notably concerning arguments from assumptions) which he has indicated as needing further study. Book B, therefore, has been seen as a collection of afterthoughts. It also lacks the periodic statements of goals and summaries of accomplishments which make the organization of Book A relatively easy to see. In addition, some of the contents of B (for instance B 5−7, 15) seem to be formal or technical studies with no real connection to the analysis of arguments. Influenced by a remark in the *Topics* (VIII.14, 163a29−30), commentators have sometimes favored the opinion that Aristotle's purpose in much of B is a sort of logical 'gymnastics,' offering exercises to develop the student's facility.

As an explanation for the studies in Book B, this is very unsatisfying; it is also unnecessary, for there are better alternatives. I try to show in the Notes that each section of Book B serves one of two purposes: either it tries to explain existing technical notions from the study of dialectic in terms of the theory of the figures of Book A (and thus furthers the project of A 32−44), or it uses the theory of figures to answer some proof-theoretic question raised in the *Posterior Analytics* (and thus contributes to the overall goal of the *Prior Analytics*). The first of these purposes is best illustrated by the final Chapters (22−27), but it also applies to B 16−18 and the short notes on argumentative practice in B 19−20. The second purpose is in evidence throughout the abstract metalogical studies in B 2−15. For instance, B 5−7 provides the background for resolving a question raised in *Posterior Analytics* A 3, while B 2−4 is inspired by *Posterior Analytics* I.12. (There are also internal relations of dependency within Book B itself: B 2−4, for instance, provides part of the basis for B 15, and both these, in turn, are important to B 21). A particularly striking case is B 21, which is parallel to *Posterior Analytics* I.16−17 but clearly reflects a higher level of development of Aristotle's theory of deduction. (See the Notes for detailed suggestions concerning specific passages.)

Aristotle's Theory of Deduction. There was once a time when Aristotle's logic was perceived (both by its adherents and by its detractors) as a serious rival to modern mathematical logic. Those times are for the most part past. Interpreters now invoke the techniques and results of symbolic logic as a matter of course in trying to understand Aristotle's deductive system and his views on logical questions. This is not to say that Aristotle has turned out to be a mathematical logician: to the contrary, much recent work has shown just how different he is from his twentieth-century counterparts in many respects. However, the dispute whether logicians ought to take as their model *Principia Mathematica* or the *Prior Analytics*—or rather, some reformulation of its doctrines in the style of 'traditional' logic—has now been replaced in most quarters by the project of understanding just what Aristotle accomplished.

The great richness and power of modern formal theories, together with the substantial understanding of their natures and properties which has been accumulated over the last century, often permit us to see more clearly the properties of Aristotle's own construction. Of course, caution is necessary in any such interpretation: Aristotle's ways of thinking are often alien to major philosophical currents of the twentieth century, sometimes much more so than at first appears. I will try to offer a serviceable view of Aristotle's deductive system through a twentieth-century lens.

The centerpiece of that theory is the *sullogismos*: the deduction. (I

avoid the English cognate 'syllogism' for a host of reasons, most cen-
trally that it has come to have a set of associations quite out of place in
translating or interpreting Aristotle.) Aristotle defines this term quite
generally in a way that would apply to a wide range of valid arguments.
However, *Prior Analytics* A 4–22 deals only with a much narrower class
of arguments, corresponding (at least in some approximate way) to the
'syllogisms' of traditional logic texts: a *sullogismos* contains two premises and a conclusion, each of which is a 'categorical' sentence, with a
total of three *terms*, one of which (the *middle*) occurs in each premise
but not in the conclusion. This restriction is not a matter of change in
definition, since Aristotle later takes some pains to argue that every
sullogismos is in some way reducible to an argument from this narrower
class. (One of the reasons I avoid translating *sullogismos* as 'syllogism' is
to prevent giving this important claim the appearance of triviality.)

The question just what a *sullogismos* is in modern terms has been a
matter of controversy since Łukasiewicz's pioneering study *Aristotle's
Syllogistic from the Standpoint of Modern Formal Logic*. Traditional logic
had taken syllogisms to be arguments composed of several statements;
Łukasiewicz argued instead that a syllogism is actually a certain type of
conditional propositional form, having as its antecedent the conjunction of the premises and as its consequent the conclusion. His conception differs from the traditional notion in two ways: first, in regarding
the syllogism as a single statement, and second, in regarding it as
utterly devoid of material content, consisting only of free term variables and logical constants. He then interpreted Aristotle's theory as an
axiomatized deductive system in which the syllogistic moods are
theorems.

Łukasiewicz's interpretation has not lacked either for strong adherents
(including Bocheński and Patzig) or for determined critics. Some of
these critics, while generally accepting the appropriateness of rein-
terpreting Aristotle in modern terms, have nevertheless rejected certain aspects of his view. John Corcoran and Timothy Smiley have
proposed that an Aristotelian syllogism is better understood as a deduction than as a proposition. Corcoran in particular has shown quite
clearly how, taking syllogisms to be deductions and representing the
syllogistic as a natural deduction system, it is possible to give a formal
model not only for Aristotle's system but also for the proofs he offers
for his results. Łukasiewicz does the former, but not the latter: instead,
he presupposes the whole of the propositional calculus as part of his
formal model and then faults Aristotle for failing to recognize this as
necessary.

I will not attempt to resolve this controversy here: readers who want a fuller picture of just what is at issue should consult the works in the Bibliography. Instead, I will present an interpretation that essentially follows Corcoran. One principal virtue of Corcoran's approach, which is especially important in the context of a translation of the *Prior Analytics*, is that it permits a formal model which stays very close to Aristotle's actual text, since it allows us to read formally precise natural deductions straight out of it.

Categorical Sentences. Aristotle's theory of deductions relies on a theory of statements which is only given in brief terms in the *Analytics* (it is found in more complete form in *On Interpretation*, although Aristotle does not actually refer us to that account). According to that theory, every declarative sentence (*logos apophantikos*), or sentence capable of being true or false, is either an *affirmation* (*kataphasis*) or a *denial* (*apophasis*) or the combination of several such sentences. An affirmation is a sentence in which a *predicate* is affirmed of a *subject*, for instance, 'Socrates is wise,' 'Plato walks'; a denial is a sentence in which a predicate is denied of a subject, for instance, 'Socrates is not wise,' 'Plato does not walk.' Unlike modern formal logic, which would treat denials as sententially compound (i.e., the negations of affirmations), Aristotle regards them as structurally parallel to affirmations.

In the sentences just described, the predicate and the subject are of different logical type (the predicate must be a general term, whereas the subject is a singular term). But Aristotle extends this same analysis to another class of sentences, in which both subject and predicate are general terms and certain additional syntactic elements appear. In these *categorical sentences*, as they are traditionally called (though not by Aristotle), the subject may be affirmed or denied either of the whole of the subject (expressed by the use of 'every' or 'no') or of part of it (expressed by the use of 'some' or 'not every'). For instance, if 'mortal' is affirmed of the whole of 'man,' we have the affirmation 'Every man is mortal'; if it is denied of the whole, we have 'No man is mortal'; if affirmed of a part, 'Some man is mortal'; and if denied of a part, 'Some man is not mortal.' (This extension is by no means philosophically unproblematic from a modern point of view: see Geach *1972*, 44–61.) In accordance with tradition, we may replace 'of the whole' with 'universal' and 'of a part' with 'particular' and call affirmations and denials *affirmative* and *negative* sentences, respectively. This then gives us four new types of categorical sentences: universal affirmative, universal negative, particular affirmative, and particular negative. I will avail myself of another venerable tradition and refer to these four types respectively as *a*, *e*, *i*, and *o* sentences.

An important thesis of *On Interpretation* is that categorical sentences may be associated into pairs in a unique way, such that exactly one member of each pair is true and one false. Aristotle calls such a pair a 'contradiction' (*antiphasis*); following modern usage, I will say that each member of such a pair is *the contradictory* of the other. In general, the contradictory of a categorical sentence is a categorical sentence having the same subject and predicate and differing only in type. Specifically, an *a* sentence has as its contradictory the corresponding *o* sentence, and an *e* sentence an *i* sentence. For example, the *a* sentence 'Every man is mortal' is the contradictory of the *o* sentence 'Some man is not mortal,' while the *e* sentence 'No man is mortal' and the *i* sentence 'Some man is mortal' are contradictories of one another. It should also be noted that Aristotle regards corresponding *a* and *e* sentences as inconsistent, though not contradictories: both cannot be true together, though both may be false.

The examples given so far reflect Aristotle's analysis in *On Interpretation*. However, in the *Prior Analytics*, he normally makes use of a different (and quite artificial) idiom for expressing categorical sentences. In place of 'Every X is Y,' he says 'Y belongs to every X' (and similarly for the remaining categoricals). It should also be noted that he regularly uses two forms for particular negatives: 'not to every' and 'not to some.' Even though he treats these as equivalent forms, Aristotle sometimes carries an argument through twice, first involving one of the forms and then with the other form substituted for it.

The Figures.   The system which Aristotle studies investigates deductions having as premises two categorical sentences which share one term. This can happen in three ways: the term in common may be subject of one premise and predicate of the other, predicate of both premises, or subject of both. Aristotle refers to each of these as a *figure* (*schēma*) and calls the term which both premises share the *middle* (*meson*) and the other two terms *extremes* (*akra*). If the middle is subject of one premise and predicate of the other, the premises are in the *first figure*; if it is predicate of both, in the *second figure*; if it is subject of both, the *third figure*.

As described, these three figures represent an exhaustive classification of premise pairs: if two categorical sentences share exactly one term, then that term must be predicate of both, subject of both, or predicate of one and subject of the other. However, there is a complication. For those cases in which there is a conclusion, Aristotle normally states the premises in a fixed order: that premise which contains the predicate of the conclusion is first. Consequently, he has special designations for each of the extremes and each of the premises: the extreme which appears as predicate of the conclusion, and therefore in the first premise, is the *major* extreme (*meizon akron*), or simply the *first* (*prōton*), and the corresponding premise is the *major premise*, while the other term is the *minor extreme* (*elatton akron*), or the *third* (*triton*) or *last* (*eschaton*). The precise way in which Aristotle defines these terms is unclear and perhaps confused (see the discussions in the Notes concerning the definition of each figure).

In A 4−6, Aristotle examines various combinations of two premises having exactly one term in common and determines for each pair whether a deduction having a third categorical sentence as conclusion is possible. When a deduction is possible, he proves this fact by telling us how to construct one. When a deduction is not possible, he proves this fact by offering a countermodel, that is, concrete examples to show that premises of the relevant types are consistent with any conceivable type of conclusion. Let us first consider the structure of his deductive system, using a formal model in the style of mathematical logic, and then turn to his countermodel technique.

A Formal Model.   A simple model for Aristotle's theory may be constructed as follows. Take as the primitive symbols the constants a, e, i, o and a supply of variables A, B, C, . . . (it makes no difference for this exposition whether the supply of variables is finite or infinite: Aristotle would argue that it must be finite). A *sentence* of the system is a string consisting of a variable, a constant, and a (distinct) variable, for example, *AaC*, *DiA*. The first variable in a sentence is its *predicate*, the second its *subject* (obviously, these formulas have as their intended interpretation the categorical sentences discussed above). We also need a definition of *the contradictory of*, as follows:

1. The contradictory of *AaB* is *AoB*
2. The contradictory of *AeB* is *AiB*
3. The contradictory of the contradictory of a sentence is that sentence itself.

Finally, we need a set of *conversion inference rules*:

   4. *BeA* => *AeB*
   5. *BiA* => *AiB*
   6. *BaA* => *AiB*

We may now define a *deduction* as follows. First, we define *complete deduction*. A complete deduction is any substitution instance of any of the following (I use '⊢' to separate the conclusion of a deduction from its premises):

   7. *AaB*, *BaC* ⊢ *AaC*   (*Barbara*)
   8. *AeB*, *BaC* ⊢ *AeC*   (*Celarent*)
   9. *AaB*, *BiC* ⊢ *AiC*   (*Darii*)
10. *AeB*, *BiC* ⊢ *AoC*   (*Ferio*)

7−10 are of course the four first-figure moods (I have added the traditional medieval mnemonic names for convenience: see the discussion in Appendix I). We now define *completed deduction*: A completed deduction is a sequence $S_1 \ldots S_n$ of sentences which meets either of the following conditions:

  I. For each i such that $2 < i < n$, either (a) for some j, $k < i$, S_j, S_k, S_i is a complete deduction or (b) for some $j < i$, S_i follows from S_j by 4, 5, or 6.

  II. Either S_1, S_3, . . . S_n is a deduction satisfying I and S_2 is the contradictory of S_n, or S_2, S_3, . . . S_n is a deduction satisfying I and S_1 is the contradictory of S_n.

These may be more readily understood if graphically displayed. A probative or direct deduction has the following structure:

  Premise 1
  Premise 2
  Step 1
  . . .
  Step $n − 1$
  Step n = Conclusion

A deduction through impossibility has the following structure (for 'the contradictory of *s*' I write 'Cont(*s*))':

Premise 1
Premise 2
Cont(Conclusion)
Step 1
. . .
Step *n* = Cont(Premise 1) or Cont(Premise 2)

Proofs for Deductions.   Aristotle takes the four deductions in the first figure as complete deductions and gives proofs for the existence of deductions in the case of ten more pairs, as follows (here '⊢' is a meta-linguistic symbol asserting the existence of a deduction: '*p*, *q* ⊢ *r*' means 'there is a deduction of *r* from premises *p*, *q*'). Again, I give the traditional names for purposes of reference:

Figure II		*Figure III*	
MaN, MeX ⊢ *NeX*	(*Camestres*)	*PaS, RaS* ⊢ *PiR*	(*Darapti*)
MeN, MaX ⊢ *NeX*	(*Cesare*)	*PeS, RaS* ⊢ *PoR*	(*Felapton*)
MeN, MiX ⊢ *NoX*	(*Festino*)	*PaS, RiS* ⊢ *PiR*	(*Datisi*)
MaN, MoX ⊢ *NoX*	(*Baroco*)	*PiS, RaS* ⊢ *PiR*	(*Disamis*)
		PoS, RaS ⊢ *PoR*	(*Bocardo*)
		PeS, RiS ⊢ *PoR*	(*Ferison*)

The proofs he gives may readily be modelled in terms of the system suggested. For example, here is his proof of *Camestres* (A 5, 27a9−14), accompanied by a deduction in the model, indicating the straightforward manner in which his text can be translated into formal notation:

Formal Deduction	*Aristotle's Text*
1. *MaN* (premise)	if M belongs to every N
2. *MeX* (premise)	but to no X,
3. *NeX* (to be deduced)	then neither will N belong to any X.
4. *XeM* (2, conversion)	For if M belongs to no X, neither does X belong to any M;
5. *MaN* (premise 1)	but M belonged to every N;

6. *XeN* (4 + 5 = *Celarent*)   therefore, X will belong to no N
                                      (for the first figure has again
                                      come about).

7. *NeX* (6, conversion)   And since the privative con-
                                      verts, neither will N belong to
                                      any X, so that there will be the
                                      same deduction.

Deductions through impossibility are equally simple to model, as illustrated by this proof for *Baroco* (A 5, 27a36−b1):

Formal Deduction	*Aristotle's Text*
1. *MaN* (premise)	if M belongs to every N
2. *MoX* (premise)	but does not belong to some X.
3. *NoX* (to be deduced)	it is necessary for N not to be-
	long to some X.
4. *NaX* (assumption =	(For if it belongs to every X
Cont(3))	
5. *MaN* (premise 1)	and M is also predicated of
	every N,
6. *MaX* (4 + 5 = *Barbara*)	then it is necessary for M to be-
	long to every X:
7. *MoX* (6 = Cont (2))	but it was assumed not to belong
	to some.)

Rejection Proofs. For the remaining premise-combination possibilities, Aristotle also proves the nonexistence of deductions. He
does this in exactly the same way as is standard in modern logical
theory: he gives countermodels. That is, he shows that a conclusion
does not follow by offering a substitution instance of a premise-pair of
the relevant form such that the premises are true but a putative conclusion false. To show that *no* conclusion follows, of course, he must
give a *set* of countermodels, one for each possible conclusion: since
there are four categorical-sentence types, this would appear to require
four different models.

Instead, Aristotle uses a more efficient, and rather ingenious, procedure. He selects two triplets of terms for a premise combination he
wishes to reject. If we substitute the terms of one triplet into the
relevant premise combination, we get true premises and a true *a* 'conclusion'; with the other triplet, we get true premises and a true *e*

'conclusion.' Since, for Aristotle, an *a* sentence is inconsistent with the corresponding *e* and *o* sentences and an *e* sentence with the corresponding *a* and *i*, the first triplet rules out an *e* or *o* conclusion and the second an *a* or *i*. For good measure (and perhaps a sort of perspicuity), Aristotle regularly selects triplet-pairs which have two terms in common.

An example will help make this clear. To show that the combination *ae* in the first figure yields no conclusion, Aristotle says,

> . . . it is possible for the first extreme to belong to all as well as to none of the last. Consequently, neither a particular nor a universal conclusion becomes necessary; and, since nothing is necessary because of these, there will not be a deduction. Terms for belonging to every are animal, man, horse; for belonging to none, animal, man, stone. (26a5−9)

Aristotle lists the terms in the triplets in the same order in which he normally gives the terms for that figure. In the case of the first figure, that order is major-middle-minor. Accordingly, 'animal, man, horse' instructs us to make 'animal' the major term, 'man' the middle, and 'horse' the minor in a first-figure premise pair of the form *ae*. The result is 'Animal belongs to every man; man belongs to no horse.' We then observe that these premises are true and that the *a* sentence 'animal belongs to every horse' is also true. The next triplet yields the premises 'Animal belongs to every man; man belongs to no stone'; this pair of sentences is again true, but now the *e* sentence 'animal belongs to no stone' is evidently true. (For more on this subject see the Notes on 26a5−9.)

In certain cases, Aristotle must modify his technique slightly (or at least modify the usual interpretation he places on *o* and *i* sentences). For the details, see the Notes on 27b20−23.

The Procedure of 'Ekthesis'.   In a few places, Aristotle mentions an alternate proof procedure for completing deductions which commentators usually refer to as 'ekthesis' (from the Greek word *ekthesis*, 'setting out'). The procedure in question rests on a pair of theses about *i* and *o* statements, which we might state roughly as follows:

I1. If AiB, then there is some S such that AaS and BaS.
I2. If AoB, then there is some S such that AeS and BaS.

Theses I1 and I2 are natural enough: if some Bs are As, then there is some class of things—call it *S*—which are both As and Bs. Similarly, if some Bs are not As, then there is some group of things *S* which are Bs and not As. In addition to these two theses, Aristotle's procedure makes two further assumptions:

I3. If there is some *S* such that *AaS* and *BaS*, then *AiB*.
I4. If there is some *S* such that *AeS* and *BaS*, then *AoB*.

Once again, these are intuitively plausible claims. To add 'ekthetic' deductions to the system, we add new rules (11–14) governing the proof procedure:

11. *AiB* ⊢ *AaS*, *BaS*   (where *S* does not occur previously)
12. *AoB* ⊢ *AeS*, *BaS*   (where *S* does not occur previously)
13. *AaS*, *BaS* ⊢ *AiB*
14. *AeS*, *BaS* ⊢ *AoB*

We also must now modify the definition of a deduction to require that the conclusion not contain any term introduced as a result of rules 11 or 12.

Ekthetic deduction permits relatively straightforward completions of third-figure deductions. Here is such a completion of third-figure *Bocardo*, which avoids the need for a completion through impossibility (I follow Aristotle's letter-usage, as in A 6):

1. *PoS* (premise)
2. *RaS* (premise)
3. *PeN* (1, ekthesis: Rule 12)
4. *SaN* (1, ekthesis: Rule 12)
5. *RaN* (2, 4, *Barbara*)
6. *PoR* (3, 5, ekthesis: Rule 14)

In fact, this is a fleshed-out version of a very brief sketch Aristotle gives in 28b20–21: all he actually says is, "This can also be proved without the leading-away [sc. proof through impossibility], if some one of the Ss should be chosen to which P does not belong."

The interpretation I offer of ekthetic proof is not without its problems. To begin with, Rules 13 and 14 seem (as the ancient commentators noted) to be identical to the two third-figure deductive forms *Darapti* and *Felapton*. Since Aristotle regards these as incomplete deductions, in need of proof, then these rules themselves would appear to be in need of justification. But in A 2, Aristotle seems, instead, to use ekthetic proofs to justify the rules of conversion, which are basic to all his completions (see the Notes on 25a14−26). He therefore seems open to a charge of circularity. Apart from this, the nature of the procedure is not fully clear. Some commentators treat it as merely an expository device, of no probative value, intended to assist the 'student' in seeing that a given form is valid. But in A 6, Aristotle mentions ekthetic proofs as *alternatives* to his other proofs, implying that he took them to be real proofs. Moreover, in at least two places, ekthesis is Aristotle's only means of proof: the justification of the conversion rules in A 2, and the completion of two deductions with necessary premises in A 8 (30a3−14: see the Note on that passage). Consequently, the question of the logical correctness of this procedure is important for our evaluation of his system.

These issues are somewhat complex and cannot be discussed adequately here (for a fuller treatment see Smith *1982b*). Let me note only the following points. Rule 12 in effect says that if *AoB*, then we can 'take some part of B to which A does not belong.' Now, this recalls the definition Aristotle offers of 'predicated of every' in 24b28−29: *AaB* is true when 'none of the subject [B] can be taken of which the other term [A] cannot be said.' In fact, it is in effect just the negation of that definition, just as *AoB* is the negation of *AaB*. Similarly, ekthetic rule 11 is just the negation of the definition (implicit in 24b28−29) of 'predicated of none.' Aristotle may therefore have regarded ekthesis as resting on *definitions* of the particular categorical sentence types, and thus as not in need of further justification.

An Interpretation of the Theory.   In order to form a judgment of the correctness of Aristotle's theory, we must decide how his categorical sentences are to be interpreted. A number of difficult questions arise in this connection, most notably the problem of 'existential import': Aristotle assumes that 'Something which is B is A' follows from 'Everything which is A is B,' and this implies that the subject terms of true universal affirmative sentences cannot be empty. This leads to difficulties, not only in the case of true statements about things that do not exist, but also with respect to how the contradictory of a given sentence should be interpreted: if

(1) Everything A is a B

implies that there are As, then its denial should be

(2) Either something A is not a B or nothing is A.

But since Aristotle regards

(3) Something A is not a B

as the contradictory of (1), this in turn implies that (2) and (3) are equivalent, so that the second disjunct of (2) is otiose. As a result, particular negative sentences should be true when their subjects are empty.

The simplest solution to these problems is to separate the philosophical questions concerning the interpretation of categoricals from the question what the best interpretation of the theory of deductions is. In fact, Aristotle in practice assumes that *no* term in his system is empty. One straightforward model for his theory is thus a system of non-empty classes. We may then interpret the categorical relations set-theoretically:

> AaB is true if and only if the class A contains the class B
> AeB is true if and only if the classes A and B are disjoint
> AiB is true if and only if the classes A and B are not disjoint
> AoB is true if and only if the class A does not contain the class B

So interpreted, Aristotle's theory can be shown to be both sound and complete (see Corcoran *1974*).

The Modally Qualified Deductions. In A 8–22, Aristotle extends his theory to include deductions involving modally qualified categorical sentences. In contrast to the account of assertoric deductions—i.e., those without modal qualifiers—this theory is problematic in the extreme: it appears to be both internally inconsistent and indefensible on several substantial points. Commentators have devoted an extraordinary amount of labor to the tasks of making sense of Aristotle's theory of modal deductions or, failing that, explaining why he comes to the results he does. It would be neither possible nor desirable to treat this question in detail here. Instead, I offer a brief survey of the results

Aristotle does establish and note some of the principal difficulties to which they give rise.

To begin with, we must introduce additional categorical sentence forms. *AaB*, *AeB*, *AiB*, and *AoB* may be used as above for nonmodal ('assertoric') sentences. We add two further sets of forms by prefixing **N** ('necessary') and **P** ('possibly') to them: **N***AaB*, **P***AoC*, etc. These prefixes may be interpreted in more than one way, from a modern viewpoint. They might be seen as sentential operators, like the familiar modal operators of modern logic. So interpreted, **N** and **P** are in effect predicates of sentences or propositions: **N***AaB*, for instance, asserts that the sentence *AaB* is necessary. Since Abelard, this has been known as the *de dicto* interpretation. Alternatively, they may be interpreted as modifiers of predicate terms, so that **N***AaB*, for instance, is seen as an ordinary *a* categorical with predicate **N***A*: '"Necessarily *A*" belongs to every *B*.' This is the *de re* interpretation.

Although Aristotle himself does not elaborate anything comparable to a *de dicto*—*de re* distinction, it can be helpful in clarifying certain details of his account of modal deductions, especially in connection with possibility. In A 13, he defines 'possibly' as 'neither necessarily nor impossibly': '*A* is possibly *B*,' for instance, means '*A* is neither necessarily *B* nor necessarily not *B*.' This definition sits very well with a *de re* interpretation of the modalities, since it can be associated with a notion of possibilities as potentialities present in things. However, in a number of places, Aristotle derives a possible conclusion for a deduction by way of argument through impossibility, taking as assumption a necessary or impossible premise. He is aware that the denial of 'possibly,' according to his official definition, is disjunctive: 'either necessarily or impossibly.' Therefore, an argument through impossibility could never establish a conclusion possible in this sense unless the assumption made were of that disjunctive form. Instead, what Aristotle does in these cases is to derive a 'possible' conclusion and then specify that it is 'not according to the definition.' Thus, he will assume **N***AaB*, deduce a contradiction, and then announce that the conclusion '*A* possibly does not belong to every *B*' follows; however, he specifies that the latter is to be interpreted not as **P***AoB*, but only as a way of denying **N***AaB*. This sense of 'possible' can only be given a *de dicto* interpretation.

Even though Aristotle uses the same verbal forms to express both types of possible conclusion, he is sometimes careful to indicate those cases of possibility 'not according to the definition.' In giving a formal representation of his arguments, therefore, it is necessary to use a distinct representation for these latter cases. Since 'possibly' here functions as a *de dicto* operator, I will represent it as 'P()', as in 'P(*AaB*)'.

Aristotle's account of modal deductions is both too complex and too difficult of interpretation to allow any useful presentation here as a formal system (and in any event I am inclined to agree with Hintikka that a formal model is probably impossible because of internal inconsistencies). A brief tabular listing of the deductive forms Aristotle establishes is found in Appendix I.

Note on the Translation. The *Prior Analytics* is in some respects unusually difficult to translate among Aristotelian treatises, but in other respects comparatively easy. Its language is heavy with technical terms and constructions often quite rare in the remainder of the *corpus*, and the style itself is often extraordinarily compressed and abbreviated, even for Aristotle. However, these compressions are often the result of repetition. Much of the *Prior Analytics* is occupied with proofs, and these proofs and their subparts often have similar structures and treat similar cases. Therefore, Aristotle is forced to repeat himself, and as he does so, he tends to become terser with each repetition. At the limit of such abbreviation is a very forbidding style which actually consists of *nothing but* the variable elements in some basic invariant matrix. This sometimes produces language which is both abbreviated to the point of unintelligibility, if taken in isolation, and yet completely clear in meaning, in its context. This combination of characteristics is almost impossible to reproduce in English, since it depends heavily on such devices as case and grammatical gender.

A close look at an example will be useful. In B 2, 54a4–6, we find the following sentence:

> *legō d' holēn pseudē tēn enantian, hoion ei mēdeni huparchon panti eilēptai ē ei panti mēdeni huparchein.*

Word for word, in subliteral fashion, this says:

> I mean <by> wholly false the contrary, that is, if belonging to none it is taken to belong to every, or if to every to none.

Now, in this sentence, Aristotle is defining the expression 'wholly false,' which he says is exemplified by two cases. One case is 'if, belonging to none, it is taken to belong to every' (*ei mēdeni huparchon panti eilēptai huparchein*), or, adding a few words for clarity, 'if what belongs to none is taken to belong to every.' The second case is 'if what belongs to every is taken to belong to none.' Now, this exactly resembles the first case except that the words 'to every' and 'to none' are interchanged. Accordingly, Aristotle abbreviates the whole case by giving us *just those words*: 'if to every to none' (*ei panti mēdeni*). For added measure, he puts the infinitive 'to belong' (*huparchein*), which is in both statements, only once, at the end of the sentence (a device almost ubiquitous in the *Prior Analytics*). In its context, then, this highly abbreviated string can confidently be translated:

> By 'wholly false' I mean the contrary premise, i.e., if what belongs to none is taken to belong to every, or if what belongs to every is taken to belong to none.

In the Notes, I sometimes call attention to instances in which I have fleshed out such highly abbreviated language, especially when my reconstruction is more speculative.

Discussions of individual points of vocabulary are found scattered through the Notes. However, one general problem deserves mention here: Aristotle's locutions for introducing a premise, supposition, or assumption. To understand this aspect of his usage, let us distinguish two types of ways premises and statements may enter into arguments and the discussion of arguments. First, every actual argument begins with certain starting points which are agreed to by the participants, or assumed as obvious by the person presenting the argument, or conceded for the sake of the argument, or however else we might wish to characterize a particular case. In these cases, the argumentative role of the premises is to act as absolute starting points within the scope of the argument: they are taken as established, treated as true. Let us call statements used in this way *genuine premises*.

Second, some statements find their way into an argument solely because the person developing the argument wishes to note what the consequences *would* be if such a statement *were* to be accepted. The typical case here is what we refer to as a '*reductio* hypothesis': a statement introduced into an argument in order to deduce absurd or self-contradictory results from it and thereby establish its falsity. Other types of assumptions may also be distinguished, however. To take an example from modern formal logic, in order to establish a conclusion, one might show that it follows when each of the components of a disjunctive premise (which has already been accepted) is assumed in turn. Let us call statements used in this way *assumptions*.

Throughout the *Prior Analytics*, Aristotle makes arguments themselves his objects of discussion. To do this requires, not that we actually take certain statements as genuine premises or as assumptions, but that we consider what would happen if we were to do so. Aristotle's interest in such cases is of course not in establishing the conclusions of the arguments in question, but in establishing that the arguments (or more correctly argumentative forms) are valid, i.e., that if we *were* to suppose premises of the sort in question, then we *would be* committed to accepting the associated conclusion. Therefore, strictly speaking, the language we find in the *Prior Analytics* is (in modern terms) metalogical. However, the distinction between genuine premises and assumptions is reflected at this metalogical level with the same distinctions of vocabulary.

Now, Aristotle has a variety of idioms with which to indicate the supposition of a genuine premise. The verb *tithenai* (together with *keisthai*, which usually functions as its passive voice) is very frequent for this purpose: its basic meaning is 'put,' but it has a wide range of signification, including 'suppose' or 'take to be true.' Of comparable frequency is *lambanein*, 'take' (which can also mean 'understand'). A third common locution is the use of the third-person imperatives *estō*, and *estōsan* ('let it be'). I have generally distinguished among these idioms in translation, even though they are probably about equivalent in function. At the same time, I have avoided a uniform rendering for the flexible *tithenai/keisthai*, sometimes using 'suppose' and sometimes 'put' (especially when Aristotle's sentence might be read as 'let the first premise be put in this way,' or even 'let these terms be put in the premises').

The distinction between genuine premises and assumptions, however, is much more critical. Aristotle almost always uses one of the prefixed verbs *hupotithenai*, *hupokeisthai* for assumptions; when he does use *keisthai* or *tithenai* alone, it usually is within a context (for example B 11) of discussing a long sequence of arguments each of which involves an assumption (and there he frequently uses *lambanein* for the genuine premises and *hupokeisthai* for the assumptions; *keisthai* then sometimes appears as a careless shortening of *hupokeisthai*). I have accordingly reserved 'assume' and 'assumption' for these expressions.

A final point about language deserves mention. In my own prose, I avoid the generic use of masculine pronouns. In the translation of

Aristotle, this is somewhat more problematic. Masculine forms are commonly used by ancient Greek writers with a generic sense, and they are frequent enough in the *Prior Analytics*: indeed, on its first page, we find *ho apodeiknuōn* at 24a24. In most cases, no purpose is served by attempting to carry this grammatical gender over into English, and as a rule I have not done so (thus, in the case mentioned, I translate 'someone who is demonstrating'). However, for Aristotle the generic use of the masculine almost certainly corresponds to a tacit assumption that the audience *is* male: there is scholarly debate about the detail of Aristotle's views on the differences between men and women, but there is no real doubt that he was in some sense a male supremacist. I have accordingly permitted myself an occasional generic 'he' in translation, even when there is no actual indication of gender in Greek (as e.g. at 37a20).

PRIOR ANALYTICS
BOOK A

We must first state what our inquiry is about and what its object is, saying that it is about demonstration and that its object is demonstrative science. Next, we must determine what a premise is, what a term is, and what a deduction is, and what sort of deduction is complete and what sort incomplete; and after these things, what it is for something to be or not be in something as a whole, and what we mean by 'to be predicated of every' or 'predicated of none.'

A *premise*, then, is a sentence affirming or denying something about something. This sentence may be universal, particular, or indeterminate. I call belonging 'to every' or 'to none' *universal*; I call belonging 'to some,' 'not to some,' or 'not to every,' *particular*; and I call belonging or not belonging (without a universal or particular) *indeterminate* (as, for example, 'the science of contraries is the same' or 'pleasure is not a good').

A demonstrative premise is different from a dialectical one in that a demonstrative premise is the taking of one or the other part of a contradiction (for someone who is demonstrating does not ask for premises but takes them), whereas a dialectical premise is the asking of a contradiction. However, this will make no difference as to whether a deduction comes about for either man, for both the one who demonstrates and the one who asks deduce by taking something either to belong or not to belong with respect to something. Consequently, a deductive premise without qualification will be either the affirmation or the denial of one thing about another, in the way that this has been explained. It will be demonstrative if it is true and has been obtained by means of the initial assumptions; a dialectical premise, on the other hand, is the posing of a contradiction as a question (when one is getting answers) and the taking of something apparent and accepted (when one is deducing), as was explained in the *Topics*.

1

What a premise is, then, and how deductive, demonstrative, and dialectical premises differ, will be explained more precisely in what follows; let the distinctions just made be sufficient for our present needs.

15

I call that a *term* into which a premise may be broken up, i.e., both that which is predicated and that of which it is predicated (whether or not 'is' or 'is not' is added or divides them).

A *deduction* is a discourse in which, certain things having been supposed, something different from the things supposed results of necessity because these things are so. By 'because these things are so', I mean 'resulting through them,' and by 'resulting through them' I mean 'needing no further term from outside in order for the necessity to come about.'

20

I call a deduction *complete* if it stands in need of nothing else besides the things taken in order for the necessity to be evident; I call it *incomplete* if it still needs either one or several additional things which are necessary because of the terms assumed, but yet were not taken by means of premises.

25

For one thing to be in another as a whole is the same as for one thing to be predicated of every one of another. We use the expression 'predicated of every' when none of the subject can be taken of which the other term cannot be said, and we use 'predicated of none' likewise.

30

A 2

25a

Now, every premise expresses either belonging, or belonging of necessity, or being possible to belong; and some of these, for each prefix respectively, are affirmative and others negative; and of the affirmative and negative premises, in turn, some are universal, some are in part, and some indeterminate.

5

It is necessary for a universal privative premise of belonging to convert with respect to its terms. For instance, if no pleasure is a good, neither will any good be a pleasure. And the positive premise necessarily converts, though not universally but in part. For instance, if every pleasure is a good, then some good will be a pleasure. Among the particular premises, the affirmative must convert partially (for if some pleasure is a good, then some good will be a pleasure), but the privative premise need not (for it is not the case that if man does not belong to some animal, then animal will not belong to some man).

10

First, then, let premise AB be universally privative. Now, if A belongs to none of the Bs, then neither will B belong to any of the As. For if it does belong to some (for instance to C), it will not be true that

15

A belongs to none of the Bs, since C is one of the Bs. And if A belongs
to every B, then B will belong to some A. For if it belongs to none,
neither will A belong to any B; but it was assumed to belong to every
one. And similarly if the premise is particular: if A belongs to some of
the Bs, then necessarily B belongs to some of the As. (For if it belongs
to none, then neither will A belong to any of the Bs.) But if A does not
belong to some B, it is not necessary for B also not to belong to some A
(for example if B is animal and A man: for man does not belong to
every animal, but animal belongs to every man).

It will also be the same way in the case of necessary premises: the
universally privative premise converts universally, while each kind of
affirmative premise converts partially. For if it is necessary for A to
belong to no B, then it is necessary for B to belong to no A (for if it is
possible for it to belong to some, then it would be possible for A to
belong to some B). And if A belongs to every or to some B of necessity, then it is necessary for B to belong to some A (for if it is not
necessary, then neither would A belong to some B of necessity). But
a particular privative premise does not convert, for the same reason as
that which we also stated earlier.

When it comes to possible premises, since 'to be possible' is said in
several ways (i.e., we say of what is necessary, of what is not necessary,
and of what is potential that it is possible), the situation with respect to
conversion will be the same in all these cases with the affirmatives. For
if it is possible for A to belong to every or to some B, then it will be
possible for B to belong to some A: for if it is possible for it to belong to
none, then neither will it be possible for A to belong to any B (this has
been shown earlier).

It is not the same way in the case of the negatives, though it is
similar for those which are said to be possible in virtue of belonging of
necessity or not of necessity not belonging, as, for example, if someone were to say that it is possible for a man not to be a horse or for
white to belong to no coat: the first of these of necessity does not
belong, while the other does not necessarily belong, and the premise
converts similarly. (For if it is possible for horse to belong to no man,
then it is possible for man to belong to no horse; and if it is possible for
white to belong to no coat, then it is possible for coat to belong to
nothing white. For if belonging to some is necessary, then white belonging to some coat will be of necessity: for this has been proved
earlier.) It is also the same way with the negative particular premise.

But those which are said to be possible because of being so for the

20

25

A 3

30

35

40

25b

5

10

15

most part or being naturally so (which is the way that we define what is possible) will not be the same in privative conversions. Instead, the universally privative premise does not convert, and the particular premise does convert. This will be evident when we discuss the possible. For the present, however, we may take this much to be clear in

20

addition to what has been said: that being possible to belong to none or not to some has an affirmative form. For 'is possible' is arranged similarly to 'is', and 'is' always and in all ways makes what it is added to in predication an affirmation, as in 'is not-good' or 'is not-white', or simply 'is not-this' (this too will be proved through what follows); and

25

with respect to their conversions, they will be like other <affirmative> premises.

A 4

Having made these determinations, let us now say through what premises, when, and how every deduction comes about. (We will need to discuss demonstration later. Deduction should be discussed before

30

demonstration because deduction is more universal: a demonstration is a kind of deduction, but not every deduction is a demonstration.)

Whenever, then, three terms are so related to each other that the last is in the middle as a whole and the middle is either in or not in the first as a whole, it is necessary for there to be a complete deduction of

35

the extremes. (I call that the *middle* which both is itself in another and has another in it—this is also middle in position—and call both that which is itself in another and that which has another in it *extremes*.) For if A is predicated of every B and B of every C, it is necessary for A to

40

26a

be predicated of every C (for it was stated earlier what we mean by 'of every'). Similarly, if A is predicated of no B and B of every C, it is necessary that A will belong to no C. However, if the first extreme follows all the middle and the middle belongs to none of the last, there will not be a deduction of the extremes, for nothing necessary results

5

in virtue of these things being so. For it is possible for the first extreme to belong to all as well as to none of the last. Consequently, neither a particular nor a universal conclusion becomes necessary; and, since nothing is necessary because of these, there will not be a deduction. Terms for belonging to every are animal, man, horse; for belonging to

10

none, animal, man, stone. Nor when neither the first belongs to any of the middle nor the middle to any of the last: there will not be a deduction in this way either. Terms for belonging are science, line, medicine; for not belonging, science, line, unit.

Thus, it is clear when there will and when there will not be a deduction in this figure if the terms are universal; and it is also clear both that if there is a deduction, then the terms must necessarily be related as we have said, and that if they are related in this way, then there will be a deduction.

If one of the terms is universal and the other is particular in relation to the remaining term, then when the universal is put in relation to the major extreme (whether this is positive or privative) and the particular is put in relation to the minor extreme (which is positive), then there will necessarily be a complete deduction; when, however, the universal is put in relation to the minor extreme, or when the terms are related in any other way, this is impossible. (I call that extreme the 'major' which the middle is in and that extreme the 'minor' which is under the middle.) For let A belong to every B and B to some C. Then, if to be predicated of every is what was said in the beginning, it is necessary for A to belong to some C. And if A belongs to no B and B to some C, then it is necessary for A not to belong to some C. (For it has also been defined what we mean by 'predicated of no,' so that there will be a complete deduction.) Similarly also if BC should be indeterminate, provided it is positive (for it will be the same deduction whether an indeterminate premise or a particular one is taken).

But if the universal is put in relation to the minor extreme (whether positive or privative), then there will not be a deduction, neither when the indeterminate or particular is affirmative nor when it is negative (for instance, if A belongs or does not belong to some B and B belongs to every C). Terms for belonging are good, condition, wisdom; terms for not belonging, good, condition, ignorance. Next, if B belongs to no C and A belongs or does not belong to some B, or does not belong to every B, then neither in this way will there be a deduction. Terms are white, horse, swan; white, horse, raven. And also the same terms if AB is indeterminate.

Nor will there be a deduction when the term in relation to the major extreme is universally either positive or privative, and the term in relation to the minor is partially privative (as, for instance, if A belongs to every B and B does not belong to some C, or if it does not belong to every C). For whatever part <of the last extreme> it may be that the middle does not belong to, the first extreme could follow all as well as none of this part. For let the terms animal, man, and white be assumed, and next let swan and snow also be selected from among those

15
20
25
30
35
26b
5

white things of which man is not predicated. Then, animal is predicated of all of one but of none of the other, so that there will not be a deduction.

10   Next, let A belong to no B and B not belong to some C, and let the terms be inanimate, man, white. Then, let swan and snow be selected from among those white things of which man is not predicated (for inanimate is predicated of all of one and of none of the other). More-
15   over, since 'B does not belong to some C' is indeterminate, that is, it is true if B belongs to none as well as if it does not belong to every (because it does not belong to some), and since a deduction does not come about when terms are taken such that B belongs to none (this was said earlier), then it is evident that there will not be a deduction on account of the terms being in this relationship either (for there
20   would also be one in the case of these terms). It may be proved similarly if the universal is put as privative.

Nor will there be a deduction in any way if both the intervals are particular, whether positively or privatively, or if one is stated positively and the other privatively, or if one is indeterminate and the other determinate, or both are indeterminate. Common terms for all
25   cases are animal, white, horse; animal, white, stone.

It is evident from what has been said, then, that if there is a particular deduction in this figure, then it is necessary for the terms to be related as we have said (for when they are otherwise, a deduction comes about in no way). It is also clear that all the deductions in it are
30   complete (for they are all brought to completion through the premises initially taken), and that all the problems are proved through this figure, including belonging to every and to none and to some and not to some. I call this sort of figure the *first*.

A 5
35   When the same thing belongs to all of one term and to none of the other, or to all of each or none of each, I call such a figure the *second*. In it, I call that term the *middle* which is predicated of both and call those of which this is predicated *extremes*; the *major* extreme is the one lying next to the middle, while the *minor* extreme is the one farther from the middle. (The middle is placed outside the extremes and is first in
27a   position.) There cannot be a complete deduction in this figure in any way, but there can be a potential one, both when the terms are universal, and when they are not universal.

When the terms are universal, there will be a deduction when the middle belongs to all of one term and none of the other, no matter

which one the privative is in relation to, but otherwise in no way. For   *5*
let M be predicated of no N but of every X. Then, since the privative
converts, N will belong to no M. But M was assumed to belong to
every X, so that N belongs to no X (for this has been proved earlier).
Next, if M belongs to every N but to no X, then neither will N belong
to any X. For if M belongs to no X, neither does X belong to any M;   *10*
but M belonged to every N; therefore, X will belong to no N (for the
first figure has again come about). And since the privative converts,
neither will N belong to any X, so that there will be the same deduction. (It is also possible to prove these results by leading to an impossibility.) It is evident, then, that a deduction comes about when the   *15*
terms are related in this way. But it is not complete, for the necessary
result is brought to completion not from the initial premises alone, but
from others in addition.

But if M is predicated of every N and of every X, there will not be a
deduction. Terms for belonging are substance, animal, man; for not
belonging, substance, animal, number (the middle is substance). Nor   *20*
is there a deduction when M is predicated neither of any N nor of any
X. Terms for belonging are line, animal, man; for not belonging, line,
animal, stone.

It is evident, then, that if there is a deduction with the terms universal, then it is necessary for the terms to be related as we said in
the beginning. For if they are otherwise, a necessary result does not   *25*
come about.

If the middle is universal only in relation to one term, then when it
is universal in relation to the major extreme (whether positively or
privatively) but particularly with respect to the minor and oppositely to
the universal (by 'oppositely' I mean that if the universal is privative
then the particular is affirmative, while if the universal is positive then   *30*
the particular is privative), then it is necessary for a privative particular
deduction to come about. For if M belongs to no N and to some X, it is
necessary for N not to belong to some X. (For since the privative
converts, neither will N belong to any M; but M was assumed to   *35*
belong to some X; consequently, N will not belong to some X, for a
deduction through the first figure comes about.) Next, if M belongs to
every N but does not belong to some X, it is necessary for N not to
belong to some X. (For if it belongs to every X and M is also predicated of every N, then it is necessary for M to belong to every X: but it   *27b*
was assumed not to belong to some.) And if M belongs to every N but
not to every X, then there will be a deduction that N does not belong

to every X. (The demonstration is the same.) But if it is predicated of every X and not of every N, then there will not be a deduction (terms are animal, man, raven; animal, white, raven); nor will there be one when it is predicated of no X but of some N (terms for belonging are animal, substance, unit; for not belonging, animal, substance, science).

When the universal premise is opposite to the particular, then, it has been stated when there will and when there will not be a deduction. But when the premises are the same in form (that is, both are privative or both affirmative), then in no way will there be a deduction. For let the premises first be privative, and let the universal be put in relation to the major extreme (that is, let M belong to no N and not to some X). It is then possible for N to belong to every X as well as to none. Terms for not belonging are black, snow, animal. We cannot get terms for belonging if M belongs to some X and does not belong to some (for if N belongs to every X and M to no N, then M will belong to no X: but it was assumed to belong to some). It is not possible to get terms in this way, then, but it must be proved from the indeterminate. For since 'M does not belong to some X' is also true even if M belongs to no X and there was not a deduction when it belonged to none, then it is evident that there will not be one in the present case either.

Next, let the premises be positive, and let the universal be supposed in the same way as the particular (that is, let M belong to every N and to some X). It is then possible for N to belong to every X as well as to none. Terms for belonging to none are white, swan, stone. We will not be able to get terms for belonging to every through the same cause as before; it must instead be proved from the indeterminate. And if the universal is in relation to the minor extreme (that is, M belongs to no X and does not belong to some N), then it is possible for N to belong to every X as well as to none. Terms for belonging are white, animal, raven; for not belonging, white, stone, raven. And if the premises are positive, terms for not belonging are white, animal, snow; for belonging, white, animal, swan.

It is evident, then, that when the premises are of the same form and one is universal and one particular, a deduction comes about in no way. But neither does a deduction come about if the middle term belongs or does not belong to some of each extreme, or belongs to one and does not belong to the other, or not to all of either, or indeterminately. Common terms for all these are white, animal, man; white, animal, inanimate.

From what has been said, then, it is evident both that a deduction comes about of necessity if the terms are related to one another as was stated, and that if there is a deduction, then it is necessary for the terms to be so related. It is also clear both that all the deductions in this figure are incomplete (for they are all brought to completion by taking in addition certain things which either are implicit in the terms of necessity or are supposed as assumptions, as when we prove through an impossibility) and that an affirmative deduction does not come about through this figure, but rather all the deductions, universal as well as particular, are privative.

A 6

10

If one term belongs to all and another to none of the same thing, or if they both belong to all or none of it, I call such a figure the *third*. By the *middle* in it I mean that term of which they are both predicated, and by *extremes* the things predicated: by *major* extreme I mean the one farther from the middle and by *minor* the one closer. The middle is placed outside the extremes and is last in position. Now, a complete deduction does not come about in this figure either, but a potential one may, both when the terms are universal in relation to the middle and when they are not universal.

When they are universal, then when both P and R belong to every S, it results of necessity that P will belong to some R. For since the positive premise converts, S will belong to some R; consequently, since P belongs to every S and S to some R, it is necessary for P to belong to some R (for a deduction through the first figure comes about). It is also possible to carry out the demonstration through an impossibility or through the setting-out. For if both terms belong to every S, then if some one of the Ss is chosen (for instance N), then both P and R will belong to this; consequently, P will belong to some R.

And if R belongs to every S but P to none, then there will be a deduction that P of necessity does not belong to some R (for the manner of demonstration is the same if premise RS is converted, and it could also be proved through an impossibility as in the previous cases). But if R belongs to no S and P to every S, then there will not be a deduction (terms for belonging are animal, horse, man; for not belonging, animal, inanimate, man). Nor will there be a deduction when both are said of no S (terms for belonging are animal, horse, inanimate; for not belonging, man, horse, inanimate; the middle is 'inanimate').

It is then also evident in this figure when there will and when there will not be a deduction with universal terms. For when both terms are positive, then there will be a deduction that one extreme belongs to some of the other extreme, but when they are privative there will not be. And when one term is privative and the other affirmative, then if the major term should be privative and the other term affirmative, there will be a deduction that one extreme does not belong to some of the other; but if it is the other way around, there will not be one.

If one term is universal in relation to the middle and the other term is particular, then when both terms are positive it is necessary for a deduction to come about, no matter which of the terms is universal. For if R belongs to every S and P to some, then it is necessary for P to belong to some R. For since the affirmative converts, S will belong to
some P; consequently, since R belongs to every S and S to some P, R will also belong to some P, and consequently P to some R. Next, if R belongs to some S and P to every S, then it is necessary for P to belong to some R. For the manner of demonstration is the same, and it can also be demonstrated through the impossible or by means of the setting-out, just as in the previous cases.

But if one term is positive, the other privative, and the positive term is universal, then when the minor term is positive, there will be a deduction. For if R belongs to every S and P does not belong to some, then it is necessary for P not to belong to some R. For if it belongs to every R and R to every S, then P will also belong to every S; but it did
not belong. (This can also be proved without the leading-away, if some one of the Ss should be chosen to which P does not belong). But when the major term is positive (for instance, if P belongs to every S and R does not belong to some S), there will not be a deduction. Terms for belonging to every are animate, man, animal. We cannot get terms for
belonging to none, if R belongs to some S and does not belong to some S (for if P belongs to every S and R to some S, then P will belong to some R: but it was assumed to belong to none). We must rather take it as in the previous cases. For since 'does not belong to some' is indeterminate, it is true to say that what belongs to none does not belong to
some, and when it belonged to none there was not a deduction. It is evident, then, that there will not be a deduction in this case either.

If the privative term is universal, then when the major term is privative and the minor positive there will be a deduction. For if P belongs to no S and R belongs to some S, then P will not belong to
some R (for it will again be the first figure when premise RS has been converted). But when the minor term is privative, there will not be a deduction (terms for belonging are animal, man, wild; for not belong-

ing, animal, science, wild; the middle in both is 'wild'). Nor will there be a deduction when both terms are put as privative but one is universal and the other particular. Terms for the case when the minor extreme is universal in relation to the middle are animal, science, wild; animal, man, wild. When the major extreme is universal, terms for not belonging are raven, snow, white. We cannot get terms for belonging if R belongs to some S and does not belong to some: for if P belongs to every R and R to some S, then P will belong to some S: but it was assumed to belong to none. Instead, it must be proved from the indeterminate. Nor will there be a deduction in any way if each term belongs or does not belong to some of the middle, or if one belongs and the other does not belong, or if one belongs to some and the other not to every, or if they belong indeterminately. Common terms for all these are animal, man, white; animal, inanimate, white.

29a

5

10

It is also evident in this figure, then, when there will and when there will not be a deduction, and <it is evident> both that if the terms are related as was said, then a deduction comes about of necessity, and that if there is a deduction, then it is necessary for the terms to be so related. It is also evident that all the deductions in this figure are incomplete (for all are completed by taking certain things in addition) and that it is not possible to deduce a universal conclusion, whether privative or affirmative, through this figure.

15

It is also clear that in all the figures, whenever a deduction does not come about, then when both the terms are positive or privative no necessary result comes about at all; but when one term is positive and the other privative, then when the privative is taken as universal, a deduction of the minor extreme in relation to the major always comes about. For example, if A belongs to every or to some B and B to no C: if the premises are converted, it is necessary for C not to belong to some A. And similarly also in the case of the other figures, for a deduction always comes about through conversion. It is also clear that putting an indeterminate premise in place of a positive particular will produce the same deduction in every figure.

A 7
20

25

It is furthermore evident that all the incomplete deductions are completed through the first figure. For they all come to a conclusion either probatively or through an impossibility, and in both ways the first figure results. For those completed probatively, this results because they all come to a conclusion through conversion, and conversion

30

35 produces the first figure. And for those proved through an impossibility, it results because, when a falsehood is supposed, the deduction comes about through the first figure. (As, for instance, it is proved in the last figure that if both A and B belong to every C, then A will belong to some B: for if it belongs to none and B to every C, then A will belong to no C: but it belonged to every C. And similarly in the other cases.)

29b It is also possible to lead all the deductions back into the universal deductions in the first figure. It is evident that those in the second figure are completed through these deductions, although not all in the same way: the universal deductions are completed when the privative *5* premise is converted, but each of the particular deductions is completed through leading away to an impossibility.

The particular deductions in the first figure are brought to completion through themselves, but it is also possible to prove them through the second figure, leading away to an impossibility. For instance, if A belongs to every B and B to some C, we can prove that A belongs to *10* some C. For if it belongs to no C and to every B, then B will not belong to any C (for we know this through the second figure). The demonstration will also proceed similarly in the case of the privative deduction. For if A belongs to no B and B to some C, then A will not belong to some C. For if it belongs to every C but to no B, then neither will B *15* belong to any C (this was the middle figure). Consequently, since the deductions in the middle figure are all led back into the universal deductions in the first, while the particular deductions in the first figure are led back into the deductions in the middle figure, it is evident that the particular deductions can also be led back to the universal deductions in the first figure.

20 The deductions in the third figure are brought to completion directly through those universal deductions in the first figure when their terms are universal, and through the particular deductions in the first figure when their terms are taken as particular. But the latter were led back to the former, so that the particular deductions in the third figure are also led back to them. It is evident, then, that they all may be led *25* back into the universal deductions in the first figure.

It has been stated, then, how those deductions that prove something to belong or not to belong are related: both how those from the same figure are related among themselves, and how those from different figures are related to each other.

Since to belong and to belong of necessity and to be possible to belong are different (for many things belong, but nevertheless not of necessity, while others neither belong of necessity nor belong at all, but it is possible for them to belong), it is clear that there will also be different deductions of each and that their terms will not be alike: rather, one deduction will be from necessary terms, one from terms which belong, and one from possible terms.

35

In the case of necessary premises, then, the situation is almost the same as with premises of belonging: that is, there either will or will not be a deduction with the terms put in the same way, both in the case of belonging and in the case of belonging or not belonging of necessity, except that they will differ in the addition of 'belonging (or not belonging) of necessity' to the terms (for the privative premise converts in the same way, and we can interpret 'being in as a whole' and 'predicated of all' in the same way).

30a

In the other cases, then, the conclusion will be proved to be necessary through conversion in the same way as in the case of belonging. But in the middle figure, when the universal is affirmative and the particular is privative, and again in the third figure, when the universal is positive and the particular privative, the demonstration is not possible in the same way. Instead, it is necessary for us to set out that part to which each term does not belong and produce the deduction about this. For it will be necessary in application to each of these; and if it is necessary of what is set out, then it will be necessary of some part of that former term (for what is set out is just a certain 'that'). Each of these deductions occurs in its own figure.

5

10

It sometimes results that the deduction becomes necessary when only one of the premises is necessary (not whatever premise it might be, however, but only the premise in relation to the major extreme). For instance, if A has been taken to belong or not to belong of necessity to B, and B merely to belong to C: for if the premises have been taken in this way, then A will belong or not belong to C of necessity. For since A belongs or does not belong of necessity to every B and C is some of the Bs, it is evident that one or the other of these will also apply to C of necessity.

20

However, if AB is not necessary but BC is necessary, the conclusion will not be necessary. For if it is, it will result that A belongs to some B

25

of necessity, both through the first and through the third figure. But this is incorrect: for it is possible for B to be the sort of thing to which it is possible for A to belong to none of. It is, moreover, also evident from terms that the conclusion can fail to be necessary, as, for instance, if A were motion, B animal, and C stood for man. For a man is of necessity an animal, but an animal does not move of necessity, nor does a man. It would also be similar if AB were privative (for the demonstration is the same).

In the case of particular deductions, if the universal is necessary then the conclusion will also be necessary; but if the particular premise is, the conclusion will not be necessary, whether the universal premise is privative or positive. First, then, let the universal be necessary, and let A belong to every B of necessity, but let B merely belong to some C. Then it is necessary for A to belong to some C of necessity (for C is under B, and A belonged to every B of necessity). It will also be similar if the deduction is privative, for the demonstration will be the same. But if the particular premise is necessary, the conclusion will not be necessary (for nothing impossible results), just as it was not in the case of universal deductions; and similarly also in the case of privatives. Terms are motion, animal, white.

A 10   In the case of the second figure, if the privative premise is necessary, then the conclusion will also be necessary; but if the positive premise is, the conclusion will not be necessary. For first let the privative be necessary, and let it not be possible for A to belong to any B, but let A merely belong to C. Then, since the privative converts, neither is it possible for B to belong to any A. But A belongs to every C; consequently, it is not possible for B to belong to any C, for C is below A. And likewise also if the privative is put in relation to C. For if it is not possible for A to belong to any C, then neither will it be possible for C to belong to any A. But A belongs to every B; consequently, it will not be possible for C to belong to any of the Bs, for it becomes the first figure again. Therefore, neither will it be possible for B to belong to C, for it converts similarly.

But if the positive premise is necessary, the conclusion will not be necessary. For let A belong to every B of necessity but merely belong to no C. Then, when the privative premise is converted, it becomes the first figure; and it has been proved that in the first figure, when a privative premise in relation to the major term is not necessary, the conclusion will not be necessary either. Consequently, neither will it be of necessity in this case. Moreover, if the conclusion is necessary, it results that C of necessity does not belong to some A. For if B belongs of necessity to no C, then C will also belong to no B of necessity. But, in fact, it would be necessary for B to belong to some A, given that A belonged to every B of necessity. Consequently, it would be necessary for C not to belong to some A. But nothing prevents the A having been chosen in such a way that it is possible for C to belong to all of it. And moreover, it would be possible to prove by setting out terms that the conclusion is not necessary without qualification, but only necessary when these things are so. For instance, let A be animal, B man, C white, and let the premises have been taken in the same way (for it is possible for animal to belong to nothing white). Then, man will not belong to anything white either, but not of necessity: for it is possible for a man to become white, although not so long as animal belongs to nothing white. Consequently, the conclusion will be necessary when these things are so, but not necessary without qualification.

The situation will also be similar in the case of the particular deductions. For when the privative premise is both universal and necessary, the conclusion will also be necessary; but when the positive premise is universal and the privative premise is particular, the conclusion will not be necessary. First, then, let the privative premise be both universal and necessary, and let it not be possible for A to belong to any B, but let A belong to some C. Then, since the privative converts, neither would it be possible for B to belong to any A. But A belongs to some one of the Cs, so that B will of necessity not belong to some one of the Cs. Next, let the positive premise be both universal and necessary, and let the positive be put as applying to B. So if A belongs to every B of necessity, but does not belong to some C, then it is evident that B will not belong to some C, but not of necessity. (For the same terms will serve for the proof as in the case of the universal deductions.) But neither will the conclusion be necessary if the privative, taken as particular, is necessary (the demonstration is through the same terms).

A 11

In the last figure, when the terms are universal in relation to the middle and both the premises are positive, then if either one is necessary the conclusion will also be necessary. However, if one is privative and the other positive, then when the privative is necessary the conclusion will also be necessary, but when the positive is necessary, the conclusion will not be necessary. For let both premises first be positive, and let both A and B belong to every C, but let AC be necessary.

25

30

35

40

31a

5

10

15

20

25

Then, since B belongs to every C, C will also belong to some B because the universal converts into a particular. Consequently, if A belongs to every C of necessity, and C belongs to some B, then it is
30   also necessary for A to belong to some B (for B is under C). The first figure therefore comes about. And it will also be proved in the same way if BC is necessary. For C converts to some A; consequently, if B belongs to every C of necessity, then it will also belong to some A of
35   necessity. Next, let AC be privative, BC affirmative, and the privative necessary. Then, since C converts to some B and A belongs of necessity to no C, A will also of necessity not belong to some B: for B is below C.

But if the positive premise is necessary, the conclusion will not be necessary. For let BC be positive and necessary and AC privative and
40   not necessary. Then, since the affirmative converts, C will belong to some of the Bs of necessity. Consequently, if A belongs to no C and C
31b   to some of the Bs, then A will not belong to some of the Bs, but not of necessity: for it was proved that when the privative premise is not necessary in the first figure, the conclusion will not be necessary either. Moreover, this would also be evident through terms. For let A be
5   good, B stand for animal, and C horse. It is possible, then, for good to belong to no horse, while it is necessary for animal to belong to every horse; however, it is not necessary for some animal not to be good, since it is possible for every one to be good. (Or if this is not possible, then being awake or sleeping should be put as a term instead, since
10   every animal is receptive of these.)

It has been stated, then, when the conclusion will be necessary if the terms are universal in relation to the middle. But if one term is universal, the other is particular, and both are positive, then the conclusion will be necessary whenever the universal is necessary. The
15   demonstration is the same as the previous one, for the positive particular also converts. Thus, if it is necessary for B to belong to every C and A is below C, then it is necessary for B to belong to some A. But if it is necessary for B to belong to some A, then it is also necessary for A to belong to some B (for it converts). It would also be similar if AC were
20   necessary and universal (for B is below C).

But if the particular premise is necessary, the conclusion will not be necessary. For let BC be both particular and necessary, and let A belong to every C, but not, however, of necessity. Then when BC is
25   converted it becomes the first figure, and the universal premise is not necessary while the particular premise is necessary. But when the premises were like this, the conclusion was not necessary; conse-

quently, it will not be in this case either. Moreover, this is also evident from terms. For let A be wakefulness, B biped, and C stand for animal. Then, it is necessary for B to belong to some C, it is possible that A belongs to C, and it is not necessary that A belongs to B (for it is not necessary for some biped to be asleep or awake). It can also be proved in the same way, through the same terms, if AC should be both particular and necessary.

30

But if one of the terms is positive and the other privative, then when the universal is both privative and necessary, the conclusion will also be necessary. For if it is not possible for A to belong to any C and B belongs to some C, then it is necessary for A not to belong to some B. But when the affirmative is put as necessary (whether it is universal or particular), or when the privative is particular, the conclusion will not be necessary. The proofs for the rest are the same as those we stated concerning the previous cases; terms for the case in which the positive necessary premise is universal are wakefulness, animal, man (with man the middle), and for the case in which the positive necessary premise is particular they are wakefulness, animal, white. For it is necessary for animal to belong to something white, but it is possible for wakefulness to belong to nothing white, and it is not necessary for wakefulness not to belong to some animal. When the privative premise is particular and necessary, the terms are biped, moving, animal (with animal the middle).

35

40

32a

5

A 12

It is evident, then, that there is no deduction of belonging unless both the premises express belonging; a deduction of belonging of necessity is possible, however, even when only one premise is necessary. But in both cases, with either affirmative or privative deductions, it is necessary for one or the other premise to be like the conclusion. By 'like' I mean that if the conclusion is belonging, the premise must be belonging, and if the conclusion is necessary, the premise must be necessary. Consequently, this also is clear, that the conclusion will not be either necessary or belonging unless a necessary or a belonging premise has been taken.

10

A 13

About enough has been said, then, concerning what is necessary, how it comes about and what differentiates it in relation to what belongs. After these things, let us discuss when, and how, and through what premises there can be a deduction of what is possible.

I use the expressions 'to be possible' and 'what is possible' in ap-

15

20

plication to something if it is not necessary but nothing impossible will result if it is put as being the case (for it is only equivocally that we say that what is necessary is possible). [That this is what is possible is evident from opposed pairs of denials and affirmations. For 'it is not possible to belong' and 'it is impossible to belong' and 'it is necessary not to belong' are either the same or follow one another, and thus their

25

opposites 'it is possible to belong,' 'it is not impossible to belong,' and 'it is not necessary not to belong' will also either be the same or follow from one another (for either the affirmation or the denial is true of everything). Therefore, what is possible will not be necessary and what is not necessary will be possible.]

30

It follows that all premises about being possible convert with each other. I do not mean that affirmative premises convert with negatives, but rather that such as have an affirmative form convert with respect to their opposite: that is, 'possible to belong' converts to 'possible not to belong,' 'possible to belong to every' converts to 'possible to belong to no' (or 'not to every'), and 'it is possible to belong to some' converts to

35

'it is possible not to belong to some.' It is also the same way in the other cases. For since what is possible is not necessary, and it is possible for what is not necessary not to belong, it is evident that, if it is possible for A to belong to B, then it is also possible for it not to belong; and, if it is possible for it to belong to every one, then it is also

40

possible for it not to belong to every one. And it will also be the same in the case of particular affirmations (for the demonstration is the

32b

same). Premises of these sorts are positive and not privative: for 'to be possible' is arranged similarly to 'to be,' as was stated earlier.

Having made these distinctions, let us next explain that 'to be pos-

5

sible' has two meanings. One meaning is what happens for the most part and falls short of necessity, as for a man to turn gray or grow or shrink, or in general what is natural to belong (for this does not have continuous necessity because a man does not always exist; however,

10

when there is a man, it is either of necessity or for the most part). The other meaning is the indefinite, which is capable of being thus as well as not thus, as, for instance, for an animal to walk or for there to be an earthquake while one is walking, or, in general, what comes about by chance (for it is no more natural for this to happen in one way than in the opposite). Now, each of these kinds of possible premise also con-

15

verts in relation to its opposite premise, but not, however, in the same way. A premise concerning what is natural converts because it does not belong of necessity (for it is in this way that it is possible for a man not to turn gray), whereas a premise concerning what is indefinite converts because it is no more this way than that. Science and demonstrative deduction are not possible concerning indefinite things because the middle term is disorderly; they are possible concerning what is natural, however, and arguments and inquiries would likely be about what is possible in this sense. A deduction might possibly arise about the former, but it is, at any rate, not usually an object of inquiry.

Now, these things will be better determined in what follows, but for the present let us say when and how there will be a deduction from possible premises, and what it will be. Now, the expression 'it is possible for this to belong to that' may be understood in two ways: it may mean either 'to that to which this belongs' or 'to that to which it is possible for this to belong.' For 'of what B is true, it is possible that A' signifies one or the other of the following: 'of what B is said' or 'of what it is possible for B to be said'. But 'it is possible that A <is said> of what B is' is no different from 'it is possible for A to belong to every B'. Therefore, it is evident that 'it is possible for A to belong to every B' might have two meanings. First, then, let us state which and what kind of deduction there will be if the premises mean that it is possible that B of what C, and possible that A of what B. For in this way, the premises are both taken in the sense of being possible. But when the premise means that it is possible that A of that of which B is the case, then one premise is belonging and the other is possible. Thus, we should begin from those the same in form, just as also in the other cases.

Now, when it is possible for A to belong to every B and B to every C, there will be a complete deduction that it is possible for A to belong to every C. This is evident from the definition: for this is how we explained 'to be possible to belong to every.' And similarly also if it is possible for A to belong to no B and B to every C, then there will be a complete deduction that it is possible for A to belong to no C (since for it to be possible that not A of that of which it is possible that B just was for it not to leave out any of the things possibly under B).

When it is possible for A to belong to every B and possible for B to belong to no C, then no deduction comes about through the premises taken; but if premise BC is converted in accordance with possibility, then the same deduction comes about as previously. For since it is possible for B to belong to no C, it is also possible for it to belong to every C (this was stated earlier). Thus, if B to every C and A to every B, the same deduction comes about again.

It is also similar if a negation is added along with 'is possible' in both

20

25

30

35

A 14

40

33a

5

10

of the premises (I mean, for instance, if it is possible for A to belong to
none of the Bs and B to none of the Cs). For no deduction comes about
through the premises taken, but if they are converted it will again be
the same deduction as before.

It is evident, then, that when a negation is added to the minor
extreme, or to both the premises, then either no deduction comes
about, or one does come about but it is not complete (for the necessity
is reached from a conversion).

But if one of the premises is taken as universal and the other as
particular, then when the universal premise is the one in relation to
the major extreme there will be a complete deduction. For if it is
possible for A to belong to every B and B to some of the Cs, then it is
possible that A belongs to some C (this is evident from the definition
of being possible). Next, if it is possible for A to belong to no B and for
B to belong to some C, then it must be possible for A not to belong to
some of the Cs (the demonstration is the same).

But if the particular premise is taken as privative, the universal
premise as affirmative, and they are similarly related in position (i.e., it
is possible for A to belong to every B and it is possible for B not to
belong to some C), then an evident deduction does not come about
through the premises taken; but when the particular premise is
converted and it is put that it is possible for B to belong to some C,
then there will also be the same conclusion as before, just as in the
initial cases.

If the premise in relation to the major extreme is taken as particular
and the premise in relation to the minor as universal, then whether
both are put as affirmatives, or both as privatives, or they are not put as
the same in form, or both as indeterminates or particulars, there will
not be a deduction in any way. For nothing prevents B from extending
beyond A and not being predicated of equally many things. Let C be
taken to be that by which B extends beyond A: it will not be possible
for A to belong to all of this, or to none, or to some, or not to some,
since premises according to possibility convert and it is possible for B
to belong to more things than A does.

Moreover, this is also evident from terms. For in the case of premises like this, it is not possible for the first term to belong to any of the
last and it is also necessary that the first necessarily belongs to all of
the last. Terms in common for all cases, for belonging of necessity, are
animal, white, man; for not being possible, animal, white, coat. Since
there are terms of this sort, then, it is evident that no deduction comes
about. For every deduction is of belonging, or of belonging of neces-

sity, or of being possible. Now, it is evident that there is not a deduction of belonging or of belonging necessarily: for the affirmative deduction is taken away by the privative conclusion and the privative deduction by the affirmative conclusion. So there remains for the deduction to be of being possible. But this is impossible: for it has been proved that with terms so related, it can be necessary for the first to belong to all the last, as well as not possible for the first to belong to any of the last. Thus, there will not be a deduction of being possible (for what is necessary was not possible).

It is evident, then, that when the terms are universal in possible premises, a deduction always comes about in the first figure, both when the terms are positive and when they are privative (except that when they are positive it is complete, while when they are privative it is incomplete). 'To be possible' must be taken not in the sense which applies to what is necessary, but rather according to the determination stated (this is sometimes not noticed).

A 15

If one of the premises is taken as belonging and the other as possible, then, when the premise in relation to the major extreme signifies being possible, all the deductions will be both complete and of being possible according to the stated determination. However, when the premise in relation to the minor extreme is possible, then not only are the deductions all incomplete, but also the privative deductions among them are not of what is possible according to the determination, but rather of what belongs of necessity to none or not to every (for if something belongs of necessity to none, or not to every, we also say it is possible for it to belong to none or not to every).

For let it be possible for A to belong to every B and let B be put as belonging to every C. Then, since C is below B and it is possible for A to belong to every B, it is evident that it is also possible for A to belong to every C. A complete deduction comes about, then. And similarly, if premise AB is privative, premise BC is affirmative, and one premise is taken as possible while the other is taken as belonging, there will also be a complete deduction that it is possible for A to belong to no C.

It is evident, then, that when belonging is put with the minor extreme, the deductions are complete. But that there will be deductions when it is contrariwise must be proved through an impossibility. At the same time, it will also be clear that they are incomplete, since the proof is not from the premises taken.

It must first be explained that if it is necessary for B to be when A is, then when A is possible B will of necessity also be possible. For with the terms like this, let what A is applied to be possible and what B is applied to be impossible. If, then, what is possible, when it is possible for it to be, could happen, and what is impossible, when impossible, could not happen, and if A were possible and B impossible at the same time, then it would be possible for A to have come about without B; and if to have come about, then to be (for what has come about, when it has come about, is).

And we must take 'impossible' and 'possible' not only as they apply to coming about, but also as they apply to being true, and to belonging, and however many other ways 'possible' is used (for it will be similar in all of them).

Next, one must not take 'when A is, B is' as if it meant that B will be when some single thing A is. For nothing is of necessity when a single thing is, but instead only if at least two things are, that is, when the premises are so related as was stated concerning deductions. For if C is predicated of D, and D of E, then C will also be predicated of E of necessity; and if each is possible then the conclusion will also be possible. Consequently, if someone were to put the premises as A and the conclusion as B, it would result not only that when A is necessary altogether B is also necessary, but also that when A is possible B is possible.

This having been proved, it is evident that when something false but not impossible is assumed, then what results through that assumption will also be false but not impossible. For instance, if A is false but yet not impossible, and if B is when A is, then B will also be false, but not impossible. For since it has been proved that if B is when A is, then B will also be possible when A is possible; and since A was assumed to be possible, therefore B will also be possible (for if it is impossible, the same thing will be possible and impossible at the same time).

Now, with these determinations made, let A belong to every B and let it be possible for B to belong to every C. Then it is necessary for it to be possible for A to belong to every C. For let it not be possible, and put B as belonging to every C (this is false although not impossible). Therefore, if it is not possible for A to belong to every C and B belongs to every C, then it will not be possible for A to belong to every B (for a deduction comes about through the third figure). But it was assumed that it is possible for A to belong to every B. Therefore, it is necessary for it to be possible for A to belong to every C (for when something false but not impossible was supposed, the result is impossible).

[It is also possible to produce an impossibility through the first figure, putting as a premise that B belongs to C. For if B belongs to every
C and it is possible for A to belong to every B, then it would be
possible for A to belong to every C: but it was assumed not to be
possible for it to belong to every one.]

One must take 'belonging to every' without limiting it with respect
to time (e.g., 'now' or 'at this time') but rather without qualification.
For it is also by means of these sorts of premises that we produce
deductions, since there will not be a deduction if the premise is taken
as holding only at a moment. For perhaps nothing prevents man from
belonging to everything in motion at some time (for example, if
nothing else should be moving), and it is possible for moving to belong
to every horse, but yet it is not possible for man to belong to any horse.
Next, let the first term be animal, the middle term moving, the last
term man. The premises will be in the same relationship, then, but
the conclusion will be necessary, not possible (for a man is of necessity
an animal). It is evident, then, that the universal should be taken
as holding without qualification, and not as determined with respect
to time.

Next, let AB be a universally privative premise, and let A be taken
to belong to no B, but let it be possible for B to belong to every C.
With these put as premises, then, it is necessary for it to be possible
for A to belong to no C. For let it not be possible, and let B be put as
belonging to C, just as before. Then, it is necessary for A to belong to
some B (for a deduction comes about through the third figure). But
this is impossible; consequently, it would be possible for A to belong to
no C (for when that was put as false, the result was impossible).

This deduction, then, is not of what is possible according to our
determination, but rather of what belongs to none of necessity (for that
is the contradictory of the assumption that was made: A was put as
belonging to some C of necessity, and a deduction through an impossibility is of the opposite assertion).

Moreover, it is also evident from terms that the conclusion will not
be a possible one. For let A be raven, B stand for reasoning, and C
stand for man. Then, A will belong to no B (for nothing that reasons is
a raven), while it is possible for B to belong to every C (for reasoning is
possible for every man). However, A belongs of necessity to no C;
therefore, the conclusion is not a possible one. Yet neither is it always
necessary. For let A be moving, B science, C stand for man. Then A
will belong to no B, while it is possible for B to belong to every C, and

5

10

15

20

25

30

35

40

the conclusion will not be necessary (for it is not necessary that no man be moving, nor necessary that some one be). It is clear, then, that

35a

the conclusion is of belonging to none of necessity. (The terms should be better chosen.)

If the privative is put in relation to the minor extreme and signifies being possible, then there will be no deduction from the actual prem-

5

ises taken, but there will be one if the possible premise is converted accordingly, just as in the previous cases.

For let A belong to every B and let it be possible for B to belong to none of the Cs. Now, when the terms are in this relationship, nothing will be necessary. However, when BC is converted and it is taken to be

10

possible for B to belong to every C, then a deduction comes about just as before (for the terms are similarly related in position).

And in the same manner, also, when both intervals are privative, if AB signifies not belonging and BC signifies being possible to belong to none. For a necessity in no way comes about from the actual premises

15

taken, but when the possible premise is accordingly converted there will be a deduction. For let A have been taken to belong to no B and B to be possible to belong to no C. Through these, then, nothing is necessary; but if it is taken to be possible for B to belong to every C (which is true) and premise AB is the same, then there will again be

20

the same deduction.

But if it is put that B does not belong to every C, and not just that it is possible for it not to belong, then there will in no way be a deduction, whether premise AB is privative or positive. Terms in common for belonging of necessity are white, animal, snow; terms for not being possible are white, animal, pitch.

25

It is evident, then, that if the terms are universal and one of the premises is taken as belonging, the other as possible, then whenever the premise in relation to the minor extreme is taken to be possible, a deduction always comes about (except that sometimes it is from the actual premises and sometimes with a premise converted). We

30

have said when each of these sorts of deduction comes about and for what reason.

If one of the intervals is taken as universal and the other as particular, then when the interval in relation to the major extreme is put as universal and possible (whether negative or affirmative), and the particular interval is put as affirmative and belonging, there will be a complete deduction, just as when the terms are universal. (The dem-

35

onstration is the same as before.) And when the interval in relation to

the major extreme is universal, but belonging rather than possible, and the other interval is particular and possible, then whether both premises are put as negative, or both affirmative, or one negative and the other affirmative, in all these ways there will be an incomplete deduction. Some deductions, however, will be proved through an impossibility, and others through the conversion of a premise expressing possibility, just as in the previous cases.   *40*
35b

There will be a deduction through conversion when the universal premise is put in relation to the major extreme and signifies belonging or not belonging and the particular premise is privative and takes something to be possible, for instance, if A belongs or does not belong   *5* to every B and it is possible for B not to belong to some C. For a deduction comes about when BC is converted in accordance with possibility. But when the premise put as particular takes something not to belong, there will not be a deduction. Terms for belonging are white, animal, snow; for not belonging, white, animal, pitch (the dem-   *10* onstration must be gotten through the indeterminate).

If the universal is put in relation to the minor extreme and the particular in relation to the major, then there will in no way be a deduction, regardless of whether either term is privative or positive, possible or belonging.

And when the premises are put as particular or indeterminate   *15* (whether they take something to be possible, or to belong, or in alternation), there will not be a deduction in this way either. The demonstration is the same as that with respect to the previous cases. Common terms for belonging of necessity are animal, white, man; terms for not being possible are animal, white, coat. It is evident, then,   *20* that when the premise in relation to the major extreme is put as universal a deduction always comes about, but when the premise in relation to the minor extreme is, then there is never a deduction of anything.

When one of the premises signifies belonging of necessity and the   **A 16** other premise signifies being possible, there will be a deduction when the terms are related in the same manner, and a complete one when-   *25* ever the necessary term is put in relation to the minor extreme. With the terms positive, the conclusion will be of being possible and not of belonging, whether the terms are put as universal or not universal. If one is affirmative and the other privative, then when the affirmative is necessary, the conclusion will be of being possible, and not of not   *30* belonging; but when the privative is necessary, then the conclusion is both of being possible not to belong and of not belonging, whether the terms are universal or not universal (but 'is possible' in the conclusion must be taken in the same way as in the previous cases). There will be no deduction of not belonging of necessity (for 'does not of necessity belong' is different from 'of necessity does not belong').

It is evident, then, that a necessary conclusion does not come about when the terms are affirmative. For let A belong to every B of necessity, and let it be possible for B to belong to every C. There will then be an incomplete deduction that it is possible for A to belong to every C. That it is incomplete is clear from the demonstration; it will be proved in the same way as in the previous cases.

Next, let it be possible for A to belong to every B and let B belong to every C of necessity. There will then be a deduction that it is possible for A to belong to every C, but not that it belongs; and it will be complete rather than incomplete (for it is brought to completion at once by means of the initial premises).

If the premises are not the same in form, first let the privative premise be necessary, and let it not be possible for A to belong to any B, but let it be possible for B to belong to every C. Then it is necessary for A to belong to no C. For let A be put as belonging either to every or to some C. But it was assumed to be possible for A to belong to no B. Therefore, since the privative converts, neither is it possible for B to belong to any A. But A was put as belonging either to every or to some C. Consequently, it would not be possible for B to belong to any C, or to every C: but it was initially assumed to be possible for B to belong to every C. And it is evident that a deduction of being possible not to belong also comes about, given that there is one of not belonging.

Next, let the affirmative premise be necessary: let it be possible for A to belong to no B, and let B belong to every C of necessity. The deduction, then, will be complete, but its conclusion will be of being possible not to belong rather than of not belonging. For the premise from the side of the major extreme was also taken in this way, and we cannot lead into an impossibility (for if A should be assumed to belong to some C and also put as possible to belong to no B, nothing impossible results through these).

If the privative is put in relation to the minor extreme, then when it signifies being possible there will be a deduction through conversion, as in the previous cases; but when it signifies not being possible, there will not be one, nor again when both are put as privative and the premise in relation to the minor extreme is not possible. The terms are the same: for belonging, white, animal, snow; for not belonging, white, animal, pitch.

The situation will also be the same in the case of particular deductions. For when the privative premise is necessary, then the conclusion will also be of not belonging. For example, if it is not possible for A to belong to any of the Bs and possible for B to belong to some of the Cs, then it is necessary for A not to belong to some of the Cs. For if it belongs to every C but it is not possible for A to belong to any B, then neither is it possible for B to belong to any A. Consequently, if A belongs to every C, then it is not possible for B to belong to any of the Cs. But it was assumed to be possible to some.

And when the particular affirmative premise in the privative deduction (that is, BC) is necessary, or the universal premise in the positive deduction (that is, AB), then there will not be a deduction of belonging. (The demonstration is the same as that in the previous cases.) And if the universal premise, whether affirmative or privative, is put as possible in relation to the minor extreme, and the particular premise as necessary in relation to the major extreme, there will not be a deduction. (Terms for belonging of necessity are animal, white, man; for not being possible, animal, white, coat.)

But when the universal is necessary and the particular is possible, then, if the universal is privative, terms for belonging are animal, white, raven, and for not belonging, animal, white, pitch; but if it is affirmative, terms for belonging are animal, white, swan, and terms for not being possible are animal, white, snow. Nor when the premises are taken as indeterminate, or both as particular, will there be a deduction in this way either. Common terms for belonging are animal, white, man; and for not belonging, animal, white, inanimate (for animal both necessarily belongs to something white and possibly does not belong to something white, and <similarly> white to something inanimate; and it is the same with being possible, so that the terms are usable with respect to all cases).

It is evident from what has been said, then, that both in the case of belonging and in the case of necessary things, a deduction either does or does not come about with the terms in the same relationships except that when the privative premise is put as belonging, the deduction is of being possible, whereas if the privative is put as expressing necessity the deduction is both of being possible and of not belonging.

[It is also clear that all these deductions are incomplete and that they
25   are completed through the aforementioned figures.]

A 17   In the second figure, when both premises take something to be
possible, there will be no deduction, whether they are put as positive
or as privative, as universal or as particular. However, when one
30   premise signifies belonging and the other signifies being possible, then
when it is the affirmative premise which signifies belonging, there will
never be a deduction, but when it is a privative universal premise
which does, there will always be one. And in the same way also when
one of the premises is taken as necessary and the other as possible. (In
these deductions also, one must take 'possible' in the conclusions as in
the previous cases.)

35   First, then, it must be proved that a privative premise of possibility
does not convert: that is, if it is possible for A to belong to no B, it is
not also necessary for it to be possible for B to belong to no A. For let
this be assumed, and let it be possible for B to belong to no A. Then,
since affirmations in being possible convert with their denials (con-
40   traries as well as opposites), and it is possible for B to belong to no A,
37a   then evidently it would also be possible for B to belong to every A. But
this is incorrect: for if it is possible for this to belong to every that, it is
not necessary for it to be possible for that to belong to every this.
Consequently, a privative universal does not convert.

And moreover, nothing prevents it being possible for A to belong to
5   no B and yet B of necessity not belonging to some of the As, as for
instance it is possible for white not to belong to every man (since it
may also belong), though it is not true to say that it is possible for man
not to belong to anything white. For man of necessity does not belong
to many white things, and the necessary was not possible.

10   But neither can it be proved from an impossibility to convert, that is,
if someone should claim: "Since 'It is possible for B to belong to no A'
is false, then 'It is not possible for B to belong to none' is true (for they
are an assertion and its denial); and if this is true, then it is true that B
belongs of necessity to some of the As, so that it is also true that A
belongs of necessity to some of the Bs. But this is impossible." For it is
15   not the case that if it is not possible for B to belong to no A, it is then
necessary for it to belong to some. For 'is not possible to no' is used in
two ways: in one way if it applies to what belongs of necessity to some,
and in the other way if it applies to what of necessity does not belong
to some. For it is not true to say, of that which of necessity does not

belong to some of the As, that it is possible for it not to belong to every one, just as it is not true either to say of what belongs of necessity to some that it is possible for it to belong to every.

If, then, someone were to claim that since it is not possible for C to belong to every D, it of necessity does not belong to some, he would be understanding it incorrectly. For <perhaps> it belongs to every one but, because it belongs to certain ones of necessity, we say, for this reason, that it is not *possible* to every one. Consequently, both 'belongs of necessity to some' and 'of necessity does not belong to some' are opposed to 'is possible to belong to every' (and similarly also opposed to 'is possible to belong to none').

It is clear, then, that as the opposite of what is possible or not possible in the way in which we originally determined it, one must not only take 'of necessity belongs to some' but also 'of necessity does not belong to some.' But if this is taken <as an assumption>, nothing impossible results, so that no deduction comes about. It is evident from what has been said, then, that a universally privative possible premise does not convert.

With this proved, let it be put as possible for A to belong to no B and to every C. There will not then be a deduction through conversion (for it has been explained that this sort of premise does not convert). But neither will there be one through an impossibility. For if we put it <not> to be possible for B <not> to belong to every C, nothing false follows (for it would be possible for A to belong to every C as well as to none).

In general, it is clear that if there is a deduction, it would be of being possible because neither of the premises has been taken as belonging. And this deduction would be either affirmative or privative: but in neither way can that happen. For if we put the conclusion as affirmative, it can be proved through the terms that it is not possible for B to belong to C; while if we take it to be privative, it can be proved through the terms that the conclusion is not possible but necessary. For let A be white, B man, C stand for horse. Then it is possible for A (white) to belong to all of one and none of the other. But it is not possible for B either to belong or not to belong to C. Now, that it is not possible for it to belong is evident, for no horse is a man. Yet neither is it possible for it not to belong: for it is necessary for no horse to be a man, and what is necessary was not possible. Therefore, no deduction comes about.

It will also be proved similarly if the privative is put the other way

20

25

30

35

40
37b

5

10

around, or if both premises are taken as affirmative or privative (the demonstration will be through the same terms), or when one premise is universal and the other particular, or both premises are particular or indeterminate, or in whatever other ways it is possible to replace the premises (the demonstration will always be through the same terms). It is evident, then, that when both premises are supposed as possible, no deduction comes about.

A 18   If one premise signifies belonging and the other signifies being pos-
20   sible to belong, then there will never be a deduction if the positive premise is put as belonging and the privative premise as being possible, whether the terms are taken as universal or as particular (the demonstration is the same and through the same terms). But when the affirmative premise signifies being possible and the privative premise signifies belonging, there will be a deduction.

25   For let A have been taken to belong to no B and to be possible to belong to every C. Then, if the privative premise is converted, B will belong to no A. But it was possible for A to belong to every C, so a deduction that it is possible for B to belong to no C comes about through the first figure. And similarly also if the privative premise is put in relation to C.

30   But if both premises are privative and one signifies not belonging and the other being possible, then nothing necessary results through the actual premises taken; but when the possible premise is accordingly converted, a deduction that it is possible for B to belong to no C
35   comes about, as in the previous cases (for it will again be the first figure). But if both premises are put as positive, there will not be a deduction. Terms for belonging are health, animal, man; terms for not belonging are health, horse, man.

The situation will also be the same in the case of the particular
40   deductions. For when the affirmative premise is belonging, whether
38a   taken as universal or as particular, there will be no deduction (this is also proved similarly to the previous cases, and through the same terms); but when the privative premise is belonging, there will be a deduction through conversion, as in the previous cases. Next, if both
5   intervals are taken as privative and the interval of not belonging is universal, then there will not be a necessity from the actual premises, but when the premise of being possible is converted as in the previous cases, there will be a deduction. And if the privative is belonging and is taken as particular, then there will not be a deduction, no matter

whether the other premise is affirmative or privative. Nor when both *10*
premises are taken as indeterminate (whether affirmative or negative) or as particular. The demonstration is the same and through the
same terms.

A 19

If one of the premises signifies belonging of necessity and the other
premise signifies being possible to belong, then when the privative
premise is necessary there will be a deduction, not only that it is *15*
possible for something not to belong, but also that it does not belong;
but when the affirmative premise is necessary, there will not be a
deduction.

For let A be put as belonging of necessity to no B and as possible to
belong to every C. Then, if the privative premise is converted, neither
will B belong to any A. But it was possible for A to belong to every C,
so a deduction that it is possible for B to belong to no C comes about *20*
again through the first figure. And at the same time, it is clear that B
will also not belong to any of the Cs. For put it as belonging. Then, if it
is possible for A to belong to no B, and B belongs to some of the Cs,
then it will not be possible for A to belong to some of the Cs. But it
was assumed that it is possible for it to belong to every one. It can also *25*
be proved in the same way if the privative is put in relation to C.

Next, let the positive premise be necessary and the other premise
possible, and let it be possible for A to belong to no B, but let A belong
of necessity to every C. If the terms are like this, then, there will be
no deduction, for it results that B of necessity does not belong to C. *30*
For let A be white, B stand for man, C stand for swan. Then white
belongs to swan of necessity, but it is possible for it to belong to no
man, and man belongs to no swan of necessity. It is evident, then, that
there is no deduction of being possible, for what is of necessity was not *35*
possible. But neither is there a deduction of a necessary conclusion, for
something necessary resulted either from both premises being necessary or from the privative premise being so. Moreover, it is also possible for B to belong to C when these things are supposed. For nothing
prevents C being under B, it being possible for A to belong to every B, *40*
and A belonging of necessity to C, as for instance if C is awake, B is
animal, and A stands for motion: for motion belongs of necessity to
what is awake, it is possible that it belongs to every animal, and every- *38b*
thing awake is an animal. It is evident, then, that neither is there a
deduction of not belonging, given that when the terms are like this it is
necessary for B to belong to C. But neither is there a deduction of the

opposite affirmations, either. Consequently, there will be no deduction. It can also be proved similarly if the negative premise is put the
other way around.

If the premises are the same in form, then when they are privative
there will always be a deduction if the possible premise is converted
accordingly, just as in the previous cases. For let A be taken not to
belong to B of necessity and to be possible not to belong to C. Then,
when the premises are converted, B belongs to no A and it is possible
for A to belong to every C; so the first figure comes about. Likewise
also if the privative is put in relation to C.

However, if the premises are put as positive, there will not be a
deduction. For it is evident that there will not be one of not belonging
or of not belonging of necessity, because a privative premise has not
been taken, either as expressing belonging or as expressing belonging
of necessity. But neither will there be a deduction of being possible
not to belong. For with the terms in this relationship, B may of necessity not belong to C (for example, if A is put as white, B stands for
swan, C is man). Nor, indeed, will there be a deduction of the opposite affirmations, since B has been shown as of necessity not belonging to C. Therefore, no deduction comes about at all.

It will be similar in the case of the particular deductions. For whenever the privative premise is both universal and necessary, there will
always be a deduction both of being possible and of not belonging (the
demonstration is through conversion); but when the affirmative
premise is universal and necessary, there never will be one (for this can
also be proved in the same way as in the case of the affirmatives and
with the same terms). Nor when both premises are taken as affirmatives (for the demonstration of this too is the same one as before). But
when both premises are privative and the one signifying not belonging
is both universal and necessary, then a necessary result will not come
about by means of the actual premises taken, but there will be a
deduction when the possible premise is converted accordingly, as in
the previous cases. And if both premises are put as indeterminate or as
particular, then there will not be a deduction (the demonstration is the
same and through the same terms).

It is evident from what has been said, then, that when it is a privative universal premise which is put as necessary, a deduction always
comes about, not only of being possible not to belong, but also of not
belonging, but that a deduction never comes about when it is the
affirmative premise that is put as necessary. It is also evident that

deductions both do and do not result with the terms in the same
relationships in the cases of necessary premises and premises of belonging, respectively. It is also clear that all these deductions are incomplete and that they are completed through the aforementioned
figures.

In the last figure, there will be a deduction either when both premises are possible or when only one of them is. When the premises
signify being possible, then, the conclusion will also be possible, and
also when one premise signifies being possible and the other premise
signifies belonging. However, when one premise is put as necessary,
then if it is affirmative the conclusion will not be either necessary or
belonging, but if it is privative there will be a deduction of not belonging just as in the previous case. In these deductions also, we must take
'possible' in the conclusions similarly.

Let the premises first be possible, then, and let it be possible for
A and B to belong to every C. Then, since the affirmative premise
converts in part and it is possible for B to belong to every C, it would
also be possible for C to belong to some B. Consequently, if it is
possible for A to belong to every one of the Cs and C to some B, then
it is also necessary for it to be possible for A to belong to some of the
Bs (for the first figure comes about). And if it is possible for A to belong
to no C and for B to belong to every C, then it is necessary for it to be
possible for A not to belong to some C (for it will be the first figure
again through conversion). And if both premises are put as privative,
then there will not be a necessary result from the actual premises
taken, but there will be a deduction when the premises have been
converted, as in the previous case. For if it is possible for A and B not
to belong to C, then if 'is possible to belong' is substituted, it will
again be the first figure through conversion.

And if one of the terms is universal and the other is particular, then
there will either be or fail to be a deduction when the terms are in the
same relationships as in the case of belonging. For let it be possible for
A to belong to every C and B to some C. Then it will be the first figure
again if the particular premise is converted. For if it is possible for A to
belong to every C and C to some of the Bs, then it is possible for A to
belong to some B. Likewise if the universal is put in relation to BC.
And similarly also if AC should be privative and BC affirmative (for it
will again be the first figure through conversion). But if both premises
should be put as privative, one as universal and the other as particular,

39a

A 20
5

10

15

20

25

30

35

39b

then there will not be a deduction through the actual premises taken, but when they are converted there will be, as in the previous cases.

5

When both premises are taken as indeterminate or as particular, there will not be a deduction (for it is necessary for A to belong to every as well as to no B). Terms for belonging are animal, man, white; for not belonging, horse, man, white (white is the middle term).

A 21

10

If one of the premises signifies belonging and the other signifies being possible, then the conclusion will be that it is possible and not that it belongs, and there will be a deduction when the terms are in the same relationships as in the previous cases.

15

20

25

For first of all let the terms be positive, and let A belong to every C, but let it be possible for B to belong to every C. Then, when BC is converted, it will be the first figure, and the conclusion will be that it is possible for A to belong to some of the Bs. For when one or the other of the premises in the first figure signifies being possible, then the conclusion was also possible. And similarly also, if BC signifies belonging and AC signifies being possible, or if AC is privative and BC positive (and either one is belonging), in both ways the conclusion will be possible. For the first figure comes about again, and it was proved that in it, if one or the other premise signifies being possible, then the conclusion will also be possible. And if the privative premise should be put in relation to the minor extreme, or again if both premises should be taken as privative, then there will not be a deduction through the actual things put, but there will be one when they have been converted, as in the previous cases.

30

And if one of the premises is universal and the other is particular, then when both premises are positive, or when the universal premise is privative and the particular premise is affirmative, the manner of the deductions will be the same. For they all come to a conclusion through the first figure; consequently, it is evident that the deduction will be of being possible and not of belonging.

35

However, if the affirmative premise is universal and the privative premise is particular, then the demonstration will be through an impossibility. For let B belong to every C, and let it be possible for A not to belong to some C. Then it must be possible for A not to belong to some B. For if A belongs of necessity to every B and B is put as belonging to every C, then A will belong to every C of necessity (this was proved earlier): but it was assumed to be possible for A not to belong to some C.

When both premises are taken as indeterminate or as particular, there will not be a deduction. The demonstration is the same one as in the previous cases and through the same terms.

If one of the premises is necessary and the other is possible, then when the terms are positive there will always be a deduction of being possible. But when one is positive and the other privative, then if the affirmative is necessary, the deduction will be of being possible not to belong, while if the privative is necessary, the deduction will be both of being possible to belong and of not belonging. But there will not be a deduction of not belonging of necessity, just as there also was not in the other figures.

First, then, let the terms be positive, and let A belong to every C of necessity, but let it be possible for B to belong to every C. Then, since it is necessary that A belongs to every C and it is possible for C to belong to some B, then also that A belongs to some C will be possible, but not belonging (for that is the way it turned out in the case of the first figure). If BC is put as necessary and AC as possible, it can also be proved similarly.

Next, let one term be positive, the other privative, and the positive necessary, that is, let it be possible for A to belong to no C and let B belong to every C of necessity. Now, it will again be the first figure; and since the privative premise signifies being possible, it is therefore evident that the conclusion will be possible (for when the premises are like this in the first figure, the conclusion was also possible). But if the privative premise is necessary, then the conclusion will be both that it is possible not to belong to some, and that it does not belong. For let A be put as not belonging to C of necessity, and let it be possible for B to belong to every C. Then, when the affirmative BC is converted, it will be the first figure with the privative premise necessary. But when the premises are like this, it turned out both that it is possible for A not to belong to some B and that it does not belong, so that also necessarily A does not belong to some B.

But when the privative is put in relation to the minor extreme, then if it is possible there will be a deduction when the premise is replaced, as in the previous cases; but if it is necessary there will not be a deduction, for it <may> both belong necessarily to all and also be possible to belong to none. Terms for belonging to all are sleep, sleeping horse, man; for belonging to none, sleep, waking horse, man.

It will also be similar if one of the terms is universal and the other

40
40b particular in relation to the middle. For when both are affirmative, then the deduction will be of being possible, but not of belonging; and also when one is taken as privative and the other as affirmative and the affirmative is necessary. But when the privative is necessary, the con-
5 clusion will also be of not belonging. For the manner of proof will be the same whether the terms are universal or not universal (for the deductions must be completed through the first figure; consequently, it necessarily turns out just the same way in these cases as it did in those). But when the privative premise, taken as universal, is put in
10 relation to the minor extreme, then if it is possible there will be a deduction through conversion, but if it is necessary there will not be. This will be proved in the same way as in the universal cases and through the same terms.

It is also evident in this figure, then, both when and how there will be a deduction and when it will be of being possible and when of
15 belonging. It is clear too that the deductions are all incomplete and that they are completed by means of the first figure.

A 23   It is clear from what has been said, then, that the deductions in these figures are both completed through the universal deductions in the first figure and led back into them. But it will now be evident that
20 this holds for every deduction without qualification, when every one has been proved to come about through some one of these figures.

Now, every demonstration, and every deduction, must prove something either to belong or not to belong, and this either universally or
25 particularly, and in addition either probatively or from an assumption (for deduction through an impossibility is a part of deduction from an assumption). First, then, let us discuss probative cases: for when these have been proved, it will also be evident both for those which lead into an impossibility and, generally, for those which are from an assumption.

30 Now, if someone should have to deduce A of B, either as belonging or as not belonging, then it is necessary for him to take something about something. If, then, A should be taken about B, then the initial thing will have been taken. But if A should be taken about C, and C about nothing nor anything else about it, nor some other thing about
35 A, then there will be no deduction (for nothing results of necessity through a single thing having been taken about one other). Consequently, another premise must be taken in addition. If, then, A is taken about something else, or something else about it or about C, then nothing prevents there being a deduction, but it will not be in

relation to B through the premises taken. Nor when C is taken to
belong to something else, that to another thing, and this to something
else, but it is not connected to B: there will not be a deduction in
relation to B in this way either. For, in general, we said that there
cannot ever be any deduction of one thing about another without some
middle term having been taken which is related in some way to each
according to the kinds of predications. For a deduction, without
qualification, is from premises; a deduction in relation to this term is
from premises in relation to this term; and a deduction of this term in
relation to that is through premises of this term in relation to that. And
it is impossible to take a premise in relation to B without either predicating or rejecting anything of it, or again to get a deduction of A in
relation to B without taking any common term, but <only> predicating or rejecting certain things separately of each of them. As a result,
something must be taken as a middle term for both which will connect
the predications, since the deduction will be of this term in relation to
that. If, then, it is necessary to take some common term in relation to
both, and if this is possible in three ways (for it is possible to do so by
predicating A of C and C of B, or by predicating C of both A and B, or
by predicating both A and B of C), and these ways are the figures
stated, then it is evident that every deduction must come about
through some one of these figures. (The argument will also be the
same if A is connected with B through more things: for the figure will
be the same even in the case of many terms.)

It is evident, then, that probative deductions are brought to a conclusion through the figures stated previously. But it will be clear
through these next considerations that this holds for deductions which
lead into an impossibility as well. For all those which come to a conclusion through an impossibility *deduce* the falsehood, but *prove* the original thing from an assumption when something impossible results when
its contradiction is supposed, <proving,> for example, that the diagonal is incommensurable because if it is put as commensurable, then
odd numbers become equal to even ones. It *deduces* that odd numbers
become equal to even ones, then, but it *proves* the diagonal to be
incommensurable from an assumption since a falsehood results by
means of its contradiction. For this is what deducing through an impossibility was: proving something impossible by means of the initial
assumption. Consequently, since a probative deduction of the falsehood comes about in those cases which lead away to an impossibility
(while the original thing is proved from an assumption), and we ex-

35   plained earlier that probative deductions are brought to a conclusion through these figures, it is evident that deductions through an impossibility will also be through these figures.

And likewise also all the other kinds of deduction that are from an assumption. For in all of them, the deduction comes about in relation
40   to what is substituted, while the initial thing is concluded through an
41b   agreement or some other kind of assumption. But if this is true, then every demonstration and every deduction must necessarily come about through the three figures stated before. With this proved, it is clear that every deduction is both brought to completion through the first
5   figure and led back into the universal deductions in it.

A 24   Moreover, in every deduction one of the terms must be positive and one of them must belong universally. For without a universal, either there will not be a deduction, or it will not be in relation to what was proposed, or the original thing will be asked for. For let it be proposed
10   to show that musical pleasure is good. Then, if someone should claim that pleasure is good, without adding 'every,' there will not be a deduction; but if <he should claim that> some pleasure is good, then if it is another pleasure, that is nothing towards what was proposed, whereas if it is this very pleasure, then he is taking the original thing.

This becomes more evident in geometrical proofs, for instance, the
15   proof that the angles at the base of an isosceles triangle are equal. Let the lines AB be drawn towards the center. Then, if someone should take angle AC to be equal to angle BD without claiming that in general the angles of semicircles are equal, or next should take C to be equal to D without taking this in addition for every angle of a segment, or in addition should take <the premise> that if equal angles are taken
20   away from the whole angles, which are equal, the remainders E and F are equal, without taking equal things to remain when equals are subtracted from equals—<in all these cases,> he will be asking for the original thing.

It is evident, then, that every deduction must include belonging universally, and also that the universal is proved from all the terms being universal, while the particular is proved both in this latter way
25   and in the former. As a result, if the conclusion is universal, then the terms must also be universal, while if the terms are universal it is possible for the conclusion not to be universal. It is also clear that in every deduction either both premises, or one of them, must become like the conclusion (I do not mean only in respect of being affirmative

or privative, but also in respect of being necessary or belonging or be- *30*
ing possible). The other kinds of predications must also be examined.

It is evident, then, both when there will and when there will not be
a deduction without qualification, and when it will be potential and
when perfect, and also that if there is a deduction it is necessary for
the terms to be related in accordance with one of the ways stated.   *35*

A 25

It is also clear that every demonstration will be through three terms,
and no more, unless the same conclusion comes about through different groups of premises, for example E through A and B and also
through C and D, or through A and B and also through A, C and D (for
nothing prevents there being several middles for the same terms; but   *40*
when there are, then there is not one deduction but several), or next *42a*
when each one of A and B is obtained through a deduction, for example A through D and E and next B through F and G, or one through
induction and the other through deduction. (But in this way also there
are several deductions, for the conclusions are many, i.e., not only A   *5*
but also B and C.)

If the deductions are not many but one, then, it is in this way
possible for the same conclusion to come about through more than
three terms; however, it is impossible for this to happen in the way
that C comes about through A and B. For suppose that E has been
concluded from A, B, C and D. Then some one of them must have
been taken in relation to another, one as whole and the other as part   *10*
(for this was proved earlier, viz., that if there is a deduction it is
necessary for some of the terms to be related in this way). Then let A
be so related to B. Therefore, there is some conclusion from them.
Now, it will be either E, or one of C and D, or something else besides
these. But if it is E, then the deduction would be from A and B alone.
And if C and D are so related as to be one a whole and the other a   *15*
part, then there will also be some conclusion from them, and it will be
either E or one of A and B or something else besides these. If it is E or
one of A and B, then either there will be several deductions, or it will
turn out as it was possible for the same thing to be concluded through
multiple terms. But if it is something else besides these, then the   *20*
deductions will be multiple and not connected to one another. And if C
should not be so related to D as to make a deduction, then these
premises will have been taken to no purpose (unless for the sake of
induction, or concealment, or something else of that sort). If it is not E
but some other conclusion which comes about from A and B, and if the   *25*

conclusion from C and D is either one or the other of these or something else besides them, then the deductions become both multiple and not of what was assumed (for the deduction was assumed to be of conclusion E). And if no conclusion comes about from C and D, then it results both that they were taken pointlessly and that the deduction is not about the original thing. Consequently, it is evident that every demonstration and every deduction will be through only three terms.

And since this is evident, it is clear that it will also be from two premises and no more (for three terms are two premises), unless something should be taken in addition for the purpose of completing the deductions, as was explained in our initial remarks. It is evident, then, that if the premises in a deductive argument through which the main conclusion comes about are not even in number (for some of the upper conclusions must be premises) then that argument either has not deduced, or has asked for more things than are necessary for its position.

Counting deductions by their main premises, then, every deduction will be from an even number of premises and an odd number of terms (for the terms are more in number by one than the premises). Also, the conclusions will be half as many as the premises. And when the conclusion is reached by means of prior deductions or several continuous middle terms (for instance if premise AB is concluded through terms C and D), then the number of terms will likewise exceed the premises by one (for the term inserted will be put either outside or in the middle; but in both ways it results that the intervals are one fewer than the terms, and the premises are equal to the intervals). However, the premises will not always be even and the terms odd; rather, in alternation, when the premises are even, the terms will be odd, and when the terms are even, the premises will be odd. (For a single premise is added at the same time as a term, no matter from what side the term may be added, so that since the premises were even and the terms odd, this will necessarily alternate when the same addition has been made.)

But the conclusions will never have the same arrangement either in relation to the terms or in relation to the premises. For when one term is added, conclusions will be added one fewer in number than the terms which were already present: for only in relation to the last term does it fail to produce a conclusion, while it produces one in relation to all the rest. For example, if D is added to A, B and C, then two conclusions are also added immediately, the one in relation to A and also the one in relation to B (and similarly in the other cases). It will also be the same way if the term is inserted into the middle (for it will only fail to produce a deduction in relation to one of them). Consequently, the conclusions will be much greater in number than either the terms or the premises.   *25*

Since we now know what deductions are about, and what sort of problem is proved in each figure and in how many ways, it is also evident to us what kind of problem is difficult and what kind easy to approach. For that kind which is concluded in more figures and by means of more cases is easier to approach, whereas that which is concluded in fewer figures and by means of fewer cases is more difficult to approach.   **A 26**   *30*

An affirmative universal problem, then, is proved by means of the first figure alone, and by means of this in only one way. A privative universal is proved both by means of the first figure and by means of the middle: by means of the first in one way, by means of the middle in two. A particular affirmative is proved by means of the first and by means of the last: in one way by means of the first and in three ways by means of the last. A privative particular problem is proved in all the figures; in the first figure it is proved in one way, while in the middle and in the last figures it is proved in two ways and in three, respectively.   *35*   *40*

It is evident, then, that a universal positive problem is most difficult to establish but easiest to refute. And in general, universal problems are easier to refute than particulars. For if it either belongs to none or does not belong to some, it has been refuted; and of these, not belonging to some is proved in all the figures, while belonging to none is proved in two of them. And it is also the same way in the case of privative universals. For if it belongs either to every or to some, then the initial problem has been refuted; and this was proved in two figures. But in the case of the particulars, the problem is refuted only in one way, i.e., by proving to belong either to all or to none.   *43a*   *5*

But in establishing, the particular problems are easier, for they are proved in more figures and through more cases. And in general, it must not be overlooked that it is possible to refute problems by means of one another, i.e., both universals by means of particulars and particulars by means of universals, but that it is not possible to establish universals by means of particulars, although it is possible to establish the latter by means of the former. At the same time, it is also clear that it is easier to refute than to establish.   *10*   *15*

A 27
20

From what has been said, then, it is clear how every deduction comes about, both through how many terms and premises and what relationships they are in to one another, and furthermore what sort of problem is proved in each figure, and what sort in more and what in fewer figures. Now it is time to explain how we may ourselves always be supplied with deductions about what is set up, and the route by which we may obtain the principles concerning any particular subject. For surely one ought not only study the origin of deductions, but also have the power to produce them.

25

Now, of all the things that are, some are such as to be predicated of nothing else truly universally (for example, Kleon and Kallias and what is individual and perceptible) but to have other things predicated of them (for each of these is both a man and an animal); some are them-

30

selves predicated of others but do not have other things predicated previously of them; and some are both predicated of others and have others predicated of them (for example, man is predicated of Kallias and animal of a man).

It is clear, then, that there are some things which are not naturally said of anything. For, indeed, each perceptible thing is such as not to be predicated of anything except as incidentally (for we do sometimes

35

say that this white thing is Socrates, or that what is approaching is Kallias). And that it also comes to a stop at some point proceeding in the upwards direction we will explain later: for the present, let this be supposed. Of these <primary things>, then, it is not possible to dem-onstrate anything else to be predicated (except as a matter of opinion), but they are predicated of others. Neither can individuals be predi-

40

cated of other things, but instead other things are predicated of them. But it is clear that for those in between, predication is possible in both ways (for they can be said of other things, and other things can also be said of them). And arguments and inquiries are almost always chiefly concerned with these things.

43b

So one must select the premises about each subject in this way, assuming first the subject itself, and both its definitions and whatever is peculiar to the subject; next after this, whatever follows the subject; next, whatever the subject follows; and then, whatever cannot belong

5

to it. (Those to which it is not possible for the subject to belong need not be selected, because the privative converts). The terms which follow the subject must also be divided into those which are predicated of it essentially, those which are peculiar to it, and those which are predicated incidentally. And these, again, <should be divided> into such as are matters of opinion and such as are according to the truth.

For to the extent that someone is supplied with more of these, he will more quickly hit on a conclusion; but to the extent that he is supplied *10* with more true things, the more will he demonstrate.

One must select those things which follow the subject as a whole, not those which follow some of it (for instance, not what follows some man, but what follows every man), for a deduction is through universal premises. Now, if it is indeterminate, it is unclear whether the premise *15* is universal, whereas if it is determinate this is evident. Similarly, one must also select those things which it follows as wholes, for the reason stated. However, one must not take that which follows to follow as a whole (I mean, for instance, taking every animal to follow man or every science to follow music), but only to follow without qualification, just as we also propose premises. For the other way, e.g., for every man *20* to be every animal or justice every good, is both useless and impossible. Instead, 'to every' should be put with that which the subject follows.

And when the subject for which one must take the things that follow is contained under something, the things following or not following the <containing> universal need not be selected for inclusion in these (for they were already included in the former terms: whatever follows *25* animal also follows man, and likewise for those which do not belong). But those which are peculiar concerning each subject must be taken (for there are certain things which are peculiar to a species in comparison with its genus, since it is necessary for some things to belong peculiarly to the various species). Nor, again, should those which the thing contained follows be selected for the <containing> universal, for example, taking what man follows in the selection for animal (for if *30* animal follows man, then it is necessary for it to follow all of these, but they are more appropriate to the selection for man).

Those things which follow or are followed for the most part must also be taken. For deductions of problems which are for the most part are also from premises which are for the most part (either all or some of *35* them), since the conclusion of each deduction is like its premises.

In addition, things which follow everything are not to be selected, for there will not be a deduction from them (the reason why will be clear in what follows).

A 28

Those who want to establish something about the whole of something, then, must look to the subject terms of which the predicate that *40* is to be established is in fact said, and to those which follow the term of which this term must be predicated. For if there should be something the same among these groups, then the one term must belong to the other.

And if someone wants to establish, not that it belongs to every, but that it belongs to some, then he must look to those which each term follows. For if some one of these is the same, the predicate must belong to some of the subject.

When someone needs to establish that it belongs to none, then he must look to those following the term to which the predicate must be shown not to belong, and to those which cannot be present in the term which must be shown not to belong to it; or, in reverse, he must look to those things which cannot be present in the term to which it must be shown not to belong, and to those which follow what must be shown not to belong to it. For if either of these pairs has something the same, it will not be possible for the one term to belong to any of the other. (Sometimes the deduction in the first figure comes about, sometimes the one in the middle figure.)

And if someone needs to establish that the predicate does not belong to some, he must look to those which the term it must not belong to follows and those which are not capable of belonging to the term which must not belong to it. For if some one of these should be the same, then the predicate proposed must not belong to some of the subject.

Perhaps each of these statements will be clearer in the following way. Let the things which follow A be labelled B, let those which A follows be labelled C, and let those which cannot belong to A be labelled D. Next, let those which belong to E be labelled F, those which it follows be labelled G, and those which cannot belong to it be labelled H. Accordingly, if one of the Cs should be the same as one of the Fs, then it is necessary for A to belong to every E (for F belongs to every E and A to every C, so that A belongs to every E). But if a C and a G are the same, then it is necessary for A to belong to some one of the Es (for A follows every C and E every G). And if an F and a D are the same, then A will belong to none of the Es, from a prior deduction (for since the privative converts and the F is the same as the D, A will not belong to any of the Fs, but the F belongs to every E). Next, if a B and an H are the same, then A will not belong to any of the Es (for the B will belong to every A but to none of the term labelled E: for the B was the same as the H, and the H belonged to none of the Es). And if a D and a G are the same, then A will not belong to some of the Es (for it will not belong to the G, because it does not belong to the D either;

44a

5

10

15

20

25

but the G is below E, so that it will not belong to some of the Es). But   *30*
if a B is the same as a G, then there will be a converted deduction. For
E will belong to every A (for the B will belong to A, and E to the B
since it was the same as the G); and though it is not necessary for A to
belong to every E, it is necessary for it to belong to some because a
universal predication converts into a particular.   *35*

It is evident, then, that with respect to each type of problem one
must look to what was previously explained in relation to each of its
terms (for all the deductions are through these).

In addition, among both those things which follow each term and
those which are followed by it, one must look to the primary and most
universal. For instance, when it comes to E, one ought to look more to   *40*
KF than to F alone, or, when it comes to A, look more to KC rather   *44b*
than to C alone. For if A belongs to KF, it also belongs to F and to E,
whereas if it does not follow the latter, it still is possible for it to follow
F. One ought also to examine those which the subject itself follows in
the same way. For if something follows the first terms, then it follows
those below them, although if it does not follow the latter, it is still   *5*
possible for it to follow those below the former.

It is also clear that the inquiry is by means of the three terms and
the two premises, and that all the deductions are through the previously stated figures. For A is proved to belong to every E when we
get some same term from among the Cs and the Fs (but this will be
the middle term, and A and E the extremes; the first figure comes   *10*
about, then). And A is proved to belong to some E when we get a C
and a G that are the same (but this is the last figure, for the G becomes
the middle term). And A is proved to belong to no E when we get a D
and an F that are the same. But in this way, both the first figure and
the middle come about: the first because A belongs to no F (since the
privative converts) and F belongs to every E, and the middle because   *15*
the D belongs to no A and to every E. And A is proved not to belong to
some E when a D and G are the same (but this is the last figure, for A
will belong to no G and E to every G). It is evident, then, that all the
deductions are through the figures stated before.

And it is also evident that one should not select such things as follow   *20*
everything because no deduction comes about from them: for it was
not possible at all to establish from the terms which follow something,
and it is not possible to refute by means of what follows everything (for
it must belong to one thing and not belong to another).

It is also evident that the other inquiries in accordance with these   *25*

selections are useless for producing a deduction (for instance, whether
things following each term are the same, or whether things which A
follows and things which are not possible to belong to E are the same,
or next whether things which cannot belong to each term are the
same): for no deduction comes about through these. For if things

30   which follow each term are the same (that is, a B and an F), it will
become the middle figure with the premises positive; if things which A
follows and things which are not possible to belong to E are the same
(that is, a C and an H), then it will be the first figure with the premise
in relation to the minor extreme negative; and, if things which cannot

35   possibly belong to each are the same (that is, a D and an H), then both
premises will be negative, either in the first or in the middle figure.
But in none of these ways is there a deduction.

It is also clear that one must take things which are the same, not
things which are different or contrary, as the terms selected for the
investigation. This is because, in the first place, the examination is for

40   the sake of a middle term, and one must take as middle something the
45a   same, not something different. Moreover, those cases in which there
does turn out to be a deduction through taking contraries or things
which cannot belong to the same thing can all be led back to the ways
stated previously. For example, suppose a B and an F are contraries or

5   that it is not possible for them to belong to the same thing. Now, if we
get these, then there will be a deduction that A belongs to none of the
Es. However, it will not be from these things themselves, but rather
out of the way previously explained: that is, B will belong to every A
and to no E, so that B must be the same as some one of the Hs.

[Next, if it is not possible for a B and a G to be present in the same

10   thing, then there will be a deduction that A will not belong to some of
the Es. For in this way also it will be the middle figure. For B will
belong to every A but to no E, so that it is necessary for the B to be the
same as some one of the Hs (for there is no difference between it not
being possible for a B and a G to belong to the same thing and the B

15   being the same as some one of the Hs, since all the things that cannot
belong to E were taken).]

It is evident, then, that no deduction comes from these examina-
tions themselves; however, if a B and an F are contraries, then the B
must be the same as some one of the Hs, and the deduction must

20   come about by means of these terms. So it turns out that those who
examine in this way are carrying out a superfluous examination of a
different route from the one needed, because they overlook the identity of the Bs and the Hs.

Deductions which lead into an impossibility are also in the same condition as probative ones: for they too come about by means of what each term follows or is followed by, and there is the same inquiry in both cases. For whatever is proved probatively can also be deduced through an impossibility by means of the same terms, and whatever is proved through an impossibility can also be deduced probatively, as for example that A belongs to none of the Es. For let it be supposed to belong to some. Then, since B belongs to every A and A to some of the Es, B will belong to some of the Es: but it belonged to none. Next, <consider a proof> that it belongs to some. For if A belongs to none of the Es and E to every one of the Gs, then A will belong to none of the Gs: but it belonged to them all. And similarly also in the case of the other problems: for always and in every case, the proof through an impossibility will be from what each of the terms follows or is followed by.

And the inquiry is the same, with respect to each problem, whether someone wants to deduce probatively or to lead to an impossibility. For both demonstrations are from the same terms, as, for example, in a case in which A has been proved to belong to no E because it results that B also belongs to some of the Es, which is impossible: if B should be taken to belong to no E and to every A, it is evident that A will belong to no E. Next, if it has been deduced probatively that A belongs to no E, then by assuming it to belong to some it will be proved to belong to none through an impossibility. And it is similar in the other cases. For in them all, it is necessary to take something common (other than the subjects) which the deduction of the falsehood will be in relation to; consequently, if this premise is converted while the other premise remains the same, the deduction will be probative through the same terms. For the probative deduction differs from the one into an impossibility in that both the premises are put in accordance with the truth in the probative deduction, whereas in the deduction into an impossibility, one premise is put falsely.

Now, these things will be more evident in the course of the following remarks, when we come to discuss proof through an impossibility, but for now let this much be clear to us: that one must look to the same things whether one wants to deduce probatively or to lead into an impossibility. In other deductions from an assumption, for instance, those according to substitution or according to quality, the search will concern the subject terms—not the initial ones, but those substituted—and the manner of the examination will be the same. We must examine arguments from an assumption and divide up how many ways <they can come about>.

Each of the problems can be proved in this way, but it is also possible to deduce some of them in another way, as in deducing universal problems from an assumption by means of the examination for a particular. For if a C and a G were the same and E were taken to belong only to Gs, then A would belong to every E. And next, if a D and a G were the same and E were predicated only of Gs, then it results that A will belong to none of the Es. It is evident, then, that one should also examine in this way.

And in the same way also in the cases of necessary and of possible problems: the inquiry is the same, and the deduction of being possible will be through terms the same in arrangement as the deduction of belonging. But in the case of possible problems, one must also select things which do not belong but are capable of belonging, for it was proved that a deduction of being possible also comes about through these. (And similarly in the cases of the other kinds of predication.)

It is evident from what has been said, then, not only that it is possible for all deductions to come about through this route, but also that this is impossible through any other. For every deduction has been proved to come about through some one of the figures stated previously, and these cannot be constructed except through the things each term follows or is followed by (for the premises and the selection of a middle is from these, so that it is not even possible for a deduction to come about through other things).

A 30

The route is the same with respect to all things, then, whether concerning philosophy or concerning any kind of art or study whatever. For one must discern the things which belong to each term and the things to which it belongs, and be provided with as many of them as possible, and examine these things through the three terms, refuting in this way and establishing in that: <when arguing> in accordance with truth, <this must be> from things that have been strictly proved to belong in accordance with truth, but in dialectical deductions it is from premises according to opinion.

The principles of deductions have been discussed in general, both how they are related and in what way one ought to hunt for them, in order that we might not look to all the statements made about a subject, or to the same things when establishing as when refuting, or to the same things when establishing a predicate of every as of some, or when refuting a predicate of every as of some, but rather that we should look to a smaller, definite class of things.

But we must make a selection about each thing that there is (for instance, about the good or science). The majority of principles for each science are peculiar to it. Consequently, it is for our experiences concerning each subject to provide the principles. I mean, for instance, that it is for astronomical experience to provide the principles of the science of astronomy (for when the appearances had been sufficiently grasped, in this way astronomical demonstrations were discovered; and it is also similar concerning any other art or science whatsoever).

Consequently, if the facts concerning any subject have been grasped, we are already prepared to bring the demonstrations readily to light. For if nothing that truly belongs to the subjects has been left out of our collection of facts, then concerning every fact, if a demonstration for it exists, we will be able to find that demonstration and demonstrate it, while if it does not naturally have a demonstration, we will be able to make that evident.

[The way one ought to select premises has been sufficiently explained in general, then. We have gone through this in detail, however, in our treatise concerning dialectic.]

A 31

It is easy to see that division by means of kinds is only a small part of the procedure that has been described. For division is a sort of weak deduction: it asks for what it ought to be proving and always deduces something higher up. But first of all, this very point had escaped the notice of all those who made use of it, and, moreover, they tried to convince us that it is possible for a demonstration concerning substance, or what something is, to come about. Thus, they understood neither what it is possible to deduce by dividing, nor that it was possible to deduce in the way which we have explained.

Now, in demonstrations, when one must deduce something to belong, the middle term through which the deduction comes about must always be both less than the first of the extremes and not universally true of it. Division, however, tries to do just the opposite: it takes the universal as a middle term. Let A stand for animal, B for mortal, and C for immortal, and let man, the definition of which we must get, be labelled D. Division, then, takes every animal to be either mortal or immortal, and this is to take everything which is A to be either B or C. And next, as the division continues, it takes a man to be an animal, so that it takes A to belong to D. The deduction, then, is that every D will be either B or C; consequently, it is necessary for a man to be either mortal or immortal. <For a man> to be a mortal animal, however, is not necessary, but rather is asked for: yet this was what needed to be deduced. And next (putting A to be mortal animal, B to stand for footed, C to stand for footless, and D to be man), the division likewise takes A to be either in B or in C (for every mortal animal is either footed or footless) and A to be predicated of D (for it took man to be a mortal animal). Consequently, it is necessary for man to be either a footed or a footless animal. For a man to be a footed animal, however, is not necessary, and the division takes it instead: but this was again what it needed to prove.

So it results that those who continue to divide in this way take the universal as their middle term, and that subject about which it was required to prove and its differences as their extremes. And as for the goal—that this is man, or whatever it might be that is being sought—they do not explain at all clearly how this is necessary. For indeed, they follow out their different route in its entirety without even thinking that the possible solutions exist.

And it is evident that one cannot either refute through this procedure, or deduce something concerning an accident or a peculiarity, or concerning a genus, or deduce in those cases in which it is not known whether it is this way or that (for example, whether the diagonal of a square is incommensurable or commensurable with its side). For if someone takes that every length is either commensurable or incommensurable and that the diagonal is a length, then it has been deduced that the diagonal is either commensurable or incommensurable. However, if it is taken to be incommensurable, then what needed to be deduced will be taken. Therefore, it cannot be proved: for this is the route, and by means of this route it cannot be done. (Let A stand for incommensurable or commensurable, B length, C diagonal.) It is evident, then, that this way of investigation is neither suitable for every inquiry, nor even useful in those very cases in which it appears to be most appropriate.

It is evident from the things which have been said, then, what all demonstrations come from, and how, and what things one should look to in the case of each problem. But after these things, we must explain how we can lead deductions back into the figures stated previously, for this part of our inquiry still remains. For if we should study the origin of deductions, and also should have the power of finding them, and if, moreover, we could resolve those which have already been produced into the figures previously stated, then our initial project would have

15

20

25

30

35

A 32
40
47a

5

reached its goal. It will also result at the same time that what we have said previously will be rendered more secure, and it will be clearer that this is how things are, by what we are now about to say: for all that is true must in all ways be in agreement with itself.

First, then, one must try to pick out the two premises of the deduction (for it is easier to divide into larger parts than smaller ones, and composite things are larger than what they are made from); next, one must see which is universal and which is particular; and, if both should not have been taken, one must put the other premise in oneself. For sometimes people who propose a universal premise do not take the premise included in it, either in writing or in speech. Or, they propose these premises but leave out what they are concluded through and instead ask for other useless things. One must therefore see whether something superfluous has been taken, and whether one of the necessary premises has been left out; and the one should be put in and the other taken away, until the two premises are reached. For without these, it is not possible to lead back arguments which have been asked in this way.

It is easy to see what is missing from some arguments, then, but others escape notice and appear to deduce because something necessary results from what is supposed, as for instance if it were taken that a substance is not destroyed by the destruction of what is not a substance and that if the things out of which something is composed are destroyed then what is made from them must also perish. For when these have been put, it is necessary for a part of a substance to be a substance; yet it has not been deduced by means of the things taken, but rather premises have been left out. As a next example, if it is necessary for an animal to be if a man is, and a substance if an animal is, then it is necessary for a substance to be if a man is, but it has not yet been deduced (for the premises are not related as we have said).

We are misled in cases like these by the fact that something necessary results from what is supposed, because a deduction is also necessary. But 'necessary' is more extensive than 'deduction': for every deduction is necessary, but not everything necessary is a deduction. Consequently, if something does result when certain things have been put, one should not try straight-off to lead it back <into the figures>. Instead, one must first get the two premises and next divide them in this way into terms, and that term which is stated in both the premises must be put as the middle (for the middle must occur in both of them in all of the figures).

If, then, the middle is predicated and a subject of predication, or if

10

15

20

25

30

35

40

47b

it is predicated and something else is denied of it, then the figure will be the first; if it is both predicated of something and denied of something, then the figure will be the middle; and if others are predicated
5 of it, or one is denied and another is predicated, then the figure will be the last. (For this is how the middle was in each figure.) And similarly also if the premises should not be universal (for the determination of the middle term will be the same). It is evident, then, that a deduction cannot come about in any argument in which the same thing is not stated several times (for no middle term has been taken).
10 And since we know what kind of problem is concluded in each figure, and in which one a universal and in what sort a particular, it is evident that one ought not look to all the figures, but only to the one appropriate to each problem (and for those problems which are concluded in several figures, we may recognize the figure by the position of the middle).

A 33

15 It often happens, then, that we are led astray about deductions because of something necessary resulting, as was said earlier, but sometimes it is as a result of the resemblance of the position of the terms, which must not escape our attention. For instance, if A is said of B and B of C: now someone might think that if the terms are so
20 related there is a deduction, though nothing necessary at all comes about, nor any deduction. For let A stand for being always, B stand for thinkable Aristomenes, and C stand for Aristomenes. Then it is true that A belongs to B, for thinkable Aristomenes always is. But also B
25 belongs to C, for Aristomenes is thinkable Aristomenes. However, A does not belong to C: for Aristomenes is perishable. For a deduction did not come about with the terms related in this way; rather, it was necessary to take premise AB as universal. But this is false (i.e., to claim that every thinkable Aristomenes always is) if Aristomenes is perishable.
30 Again, let C stand for Mikkalos, B for musical Mikkalos, and A for perishing tomorrow. Then, it is true to predicate B of C, for Mikkalos is musical Mikkalos. But it is also true to predicate A of B, for musical Mikkalos might perish tomorrow. However, to predicate A of C is
35 false. So this is in fact the same as the preceding case: for the statement that musical Mikkalos will perish tomorrow is not true universally, and when this is not taken there was not a deduction. This error,

then, arises in a small point. For we are led to agree as if there were no
difference between saying that this belongs to that and that this be-   *40*
longs to *every* that.

Mistakes frequently will happen because the terms in the premise
have not been well set out, as, for example, if A should be health, B
should stand for illness, and C for man. For it is true to say that it is
possible for A to belong to no B (for health belongs to no illness), and   *5*
again that B belongs to every C (for every man is susceptible of illness). It might seem to result, then, that it is not possible for health to
belong to any man. The cause of this is that the terms are not set out
well as a matter of language, since there will not be a deduction if
terms applying to the conditions are substituted (i.e., if 'healthy' is put   *10*
in place of 'health' and 'ill' in place of 'illness'). For it is not true to say
that being healthy cannot belong to someone who is ill. But if this
premise is not taken, a deduction does not come about, except if it is
one of being possible. (And that is not impossible: for it is possible for
health to belong to no man.)   *15*
    Next, there can be a similar mistake in the case of the middle figure:
for it is possible for health to belong to no illness but to every man, so
that it is possible for illness to belong to no man. But in the third
figure, the mistake results in connection with being possible, for it is
possible for both health and illness, or both knowledge and ignorance,
and, in general, for contraries to belong to the same thing, but impos-   *20*
sible for them to belong to one another. (But this is not in agreement
with what was said earlier: for when it was possible for several things to
belong to the same thing, it was also possible for them to belong to
each other.)
    It is evident, then, that in all these cases the error arises as a result
of the setting out of the terms. For when terms applying to the condi-   *25*
tions are substituted, no mistake arises. Thus, it is clear that in the
case of such premises the expression which applies to the condition
must always be substituted for the condition and put as the term.

One must not always seek to set out a term with a word, for there
will often be phrases to which a name cannot be put. It is for this   *30*
reason difficult to lead such deductions back. Sometimes, errors can
also happen as a result of this sort of search. For example, we may

mistakenly think that a deduction is from unmiddled things. Let A be
two right angles, B stand for triangle, C stand for isosceles. Then, A
belongs to C through B, but it belongs to B through nothing else (for
the triangle possesses two right angles of itself); consequently, there
will be no middle term of AB, although it is demonstrable. For it is
evident that one must not always take the middle term as a particular
'this' but rather sometimes as a phrase, which is just what happens in
the example given.

A 36

One must not take the statement that the first belongs to the middle, or this to the extreme, as always implying that they can be predicated of one another, or that the first can be predicated of the middle
and it of the last in the same way (and likewise in the case of not
belonging). Rather, one must think that 'to belong' also has as many
meanings as the ways in which 'to be' is said, or the very phrase 'true
to say.' Take as an example the statement that there is a single science
of contraries. For let A be there being a single science, and let B stand
for things contrary to each other. Then, A belongs to B, not in the
sense that contraries are a single science of them, but because it is true
to say of them that there is a single science of them.

Sometimes it happens that the first is said of the middle but the
middle is not said of the third; for example, if wisdom is a science and
wisdom is of the good, the conclusion is that a science is of the good.
(So the good is not a science, but wisdom is a science.) And sometimes, the middle is said of the third, but the first is not said of the
middle. For example, if there is a science of every quality or contrary
and the good is both a contrary and a quality, the conclusion is that
there is a science of the good (but the good is not a science, nor is a
quality or a contrary, though the good is these). And it is possible for
neither the first to be said of the middle nor this of the third, with the
first sometimes being said and sometimes not being said of the third.
For example, if there is a genus of that of which there is a science, and
there is a science of the good, the conclusion is that there is a genus of
the good: and nothing is predicated of anything. And if that of which
there is a science is itself a genus, and there is a science of the good,
the conclusion is that the good is a genus: so the first is predicated of
the <last> extreme, but the terms are not said of one another.

So, we must also take it in the same way in the case of not belonging. For 'this does not belong to that' does not always signify that this

is not that, but sometimes 'this is not *of* that' or 'this is not *to* that.' For   *30*
example, 'There is no motion of a motion or coming-to-be of a coming-
to-be, but there is a coming-to-be of pleasure; therefore, pleasure is
not a coming-to-be,' or again, 'There is a sign of laughter, but there is
no sign of a sign; consequently, laughter is not a sign.' It would also be
similar in those other cases in which a problem is rejected through the
genus being said about it in some certain way. Again: 'Opportunity is   *35*
not the time needed, for there is opportunity for a god, but not a time
needed, because nothing is needful to a god.' Opportunity, time
needed, and god should be put as terms and the premise should be
taken in accordance with the inflections of the words. For we state this
without qualification about them all: that terms must always be put in   *40*
accordance with their nominative forms (as 'man' or 'good' or 'contraries', not 'man's' or 'of the good' or 'of contraries'), while premises   *49a*
must be taken in accordance with the inflected form of each term. For
it might be 'to this' (as 'equal'), or 'of this' (as 'double'), or 'this' in the
accusative case (as 'hitting' or 'seeing'), or 'this' in the nominative (as
'a man is an animal'), or the word might be inflected in some other way   *5*
in the premise.

'This belongs to that' and 'this is true of that' should be taken in as   **A 37**
many senses as the ways in which predications have been divided, and
these either in some way or without qualification, and, moreover, either simple or compound; and similarly also with not belonging.
(These things must be studied and better determined.)   *10*

Something extra duplicated in the premises should be put with the   **A 38**
first extreme, not with the middle. I mean, for instance, if there should
be a deduction that there is knowledge in that it is a good of justice,
then 'in that it is a good' or 'insofar as it is a good' should be put with
the first extreme. For let A be knowledge in that it is a good, B stand   *15*
for good, C stand for justice. Then it is true to predicate A of B: for of
the good there is science in that it is a good. But it is also true to
predicate B of C: for justice is just a good. In this way, then, a resolution comes about. However, if 'in that it is a good' is put with B, then a
resolution will not be possible. For A will be true of B, but B will not   *20*
be true of C: for to predicate 'good in that it is a good' of justice is
incorrect and not intelligible. And similarly also if it should be proved
that the healthful is knowable insofar as it is good, or a goat-stag is

25
knowable insofar as it is nonexistent, or that a man is perishable insofar as perceptible: for in all these cases of extra predication, the extra duplication should be put with the <first> extreme.

The setting of the terms is not the same when something is deduced without qualification as when it is deduced as this something, or in some respect, or somehow (I mean, for example, when the good has been proved to be knowable and when it has been proved to be knowable in that it is good). Rather, if it has been proved to be
30
knowable without qualification, then 'being' should be taken as the middle term, whereas if it has been proved knowable in that it is good, then 'being so-and-so' should be taken. For let A be knowledge in that it is something, B stand for being so-and-so, and C stand for good. Then, it is true to predicate A of B: for there was knowledge of what is so-and-so in that it is so-and-so. But it is also true to predicate B of C:
35
for what C stands for is being so-and-so. Consequently, it is also true to predicate A of C. Therefore, there will be knowledge of the good in that it is good (for 'being so-and-so' was a symbol for its peculiar being). On the other hand, if 'being' were put as the middle term, and 'being' without qualification were said in relation to the <first> extreme rather than 'being so-and-so,' then there would not be a deduction that there is knowledge of the good in that it is good, but rather in
49b
that it *is* (e.g., A stands for knowledge in that it is, B stands for being, C stands for good). It is evident, then, that the terms should be taken in this way in particular deductions.

A 39

5
One ought also to substitute things which have the same value for one another (words in place of words, phrases in place of phrases), whether a word or a phrase, and always to take the word instead of the phrase: for the setting out of terms will be easier. For example, if there is no difference between saying that the believable is not the genus of the opinable and that what is opinable is not just a certain kind of believable (for what is signified is the same), then 'believable' and 'opinable' should be put as terms in place of the phrase stated.

A 40

10
Since it is not the same thing for pleasure to be *a* good and for pleasure to be *the* good, the terms should not be put in the same way; rather, if the deduction is that pleasure is *the* good, then 'the good' should be put as the term, while if the deduction is that pleasure is *a* good, then 'a good' should be put. And this way also in the other cases.

It is not the same thing either to say, or for it to be the case, that whatever B belongs to, A belongs to all of it, and to say that what B belongs to all of, A also belongs to all of. For nothing prevents B belonging to C, but not to every C. For instance, let B be beautiful and C white. Then, if beautiful belongs to something white, it is true to say that beautiful belongs to the white, but perhaps not to everything white. If A belongs to B, then, but not to everything of which B is said, then whether B belongs to *every* C, or merely belongs to it, then not only is it not necessary for A to belong to *every* C, but also it is not even necessary for it to belong at all. But if it belongs to all that of which B is truly said, then it will result that whatever B is truly said of all of, A will be said of all of that. However, if A is said of whatever B is said of all of, then nothing prevents B from belonging to C while A does not belong to every C, or even does not belong to C at all. So putting it in the three terms, it is clear that 'A is said of what B is said of all of' is this: 'such things as B is said of, A is also said of all those.' And if B is said of all of something, then A is also thus; but if B is not said of all of something, then A need not be said of it all.

One should not think that any absurdity results from setting something out. For we do not make use of it insofar as it is a particular thing; instead, it is like the geometer who calls this a foot-long line, this a straight line, and says that they are breadthless, though they are not, but does not use these things as though he were deducing from them. For in general, in the case of whatever is not as a whole in relation to a part, with something else related to it as a part in relation to a whole, the man who proves does not prove from any such things: consequently, neither does any deduction come about from these. We use 'setting out' in just the same way as we use 'perceiving' when we mean someone who understands. For it is not as if the conclusion could not be demonstrated without such things, as it is in the case of the premises which a deduction is from.

Let us not fail to notice that not all the conclusions in the same deduction are from a single figure, but rather one is through this figure and one is through another. It is clear, then, that resolutions are also to be produced in this way. And since not every problem is proved in all the figures, but rather an ordered group of problems in each figure, it is evident from the conclusion in which figure one should seek.

A 41
15

20

25

30

35

50a

A 42
5

10

A 43   In reference to arguments aimed towards a definition which happen
to draw a conclusion about one of the terms in the definition, that
about which a conclusion has been drawn should be put as the term in
the deduction, and not the entire definition (for confusion is less likely
to result because of length). For instance, if someone proved that
15   water is a drinkable liquid, then drinkable and water should be put as
the terms.

A 44   Moreover, one must not try to lead back deductions from an assumption, for it is not possible to lead them back from the things
supposed (for they have not been proved by means of a deduction but
instead are all consented to by means of an agreement). For example,
if someone assumed that if there is not a single potentiality for con-
20   traries then there is not a single science either, and next were to argue
that not every potentiality is for contraries (for example, of what is
wholesome and what is unwholesome: for the same thing would be at
the same time wholesome and unwholesome). Now, it has been established by proof that there is not a single capacity of all contraries, but it
has not been proved that there is not a single science of them. Indeed,
25   to agree is necessary; not from a deduction, however, but from an
assumption. This deduction, then, cannot be led back; but the deduction that there is not a single potentiality for the contraries can be (for
the latter was doubtless a deduction, though the former was an
assumption).
    And similarly also in the case of those deductions brought to a
30   conclusion through an impossibility. For it is not possible to resolve
these either; rather, it is possible to resolve the leading away to an
impossibility (for it is proved by a deduction), but not possible to
resolve the other part (for it is concluded from an assumption). These
deductions differ from the ones discussed previously because in those
earlier ones, it is necessary for someone to have made an agreement in
advance whether he is going to consent (for example, that if it is
proved that there is a single capacity of contraries, then he will consent
35   that the science of them is also the same); in these latter cases,
however, people consent even without having made an agreement
in advance because the falsehood is obvious (as, for instance, that
odd numbers are equal to even, when the diagonal is put as
commensurable).
    Many other deductions are also brought to a conclusion from an
40   assumption, and these must be examined and marked off in a clear

fashion. We will state later what the differences among these are and
in how many ways something can be from an assumption. But for the
present, let this much be evident to us: that it is not possible to resolve
these sorts of deductions into the figures. (And we have explained
through what cause this is so.)

  In the case of those problems which are proved in several figures, if
they have been deduced in one of those figures, then it is possible to
lead the deduction back into the other figure. For instance, the privative deduction in the first figure can be led back into the second, and
the privative deduction in the middle figure can be led back into the
first. Not all of the deductions can be led back, however, but only
some (this will be evident in what follows).
  For if A belongs to no B and B to every C, then A belongs to no C: in
this way, then, it is the first figure, but if the privative is converted it
will be the middle figure (for B belongs to no A but to every C). And
similarly also if the deduction is not universal but particular, for example, if A belongs to no B but B belongs to some C (for if the privative is
converted it will be the middle figure).
  The universal deductions in the second figure can be led back into
the first figure, but only one of the particular deductions can be. For let
A belong to no B but to every C. Then, when the privative is converted it will be the first figure (for B will belong to no A and A to
every C). But if the positive should be in relation to B and the privative in relation to C, then C must be put as the first term: for this
belongs to no A and A belongs to every B; consequently, C belongs to
no B, and therefore neither does B belong to any C (for the privative
converts). And if the deduction is particular, then when the privative is
in relation to the major extreme, the deduction can be led back into
the first figure, for example, if A belongs to no B and to some C. For
when the privative is converted it will be the first figure (for B belongs
to no A and A to some C. But when the positive is in relation to the
major extreme, the deduction cannot be resolved (for example, if A
belongs to every B and not to every C: for AB does not admit of
conversion, nor would there be a deduction if it did).

the first, but the deductions in the first can all be resolved into the
third. For let A belong to every B and B to some C. Then, since the
particular positive converts, C will belong to some B. But A belonged

to every B, so that the third figure comes about. And likewise if the
deduction is privative (for the particular positive converts, so that A
will belong to no B and C will belong to some).

Only one of the deductions in the last figure is not resolved into the
first (i.e., when the privative is not put as universal), while all the other
deductions are resolved into it. For let A and B be predicated of every
C. Then, C will convert partially in relation to each term: therefore, it
will belong to some B. Consequently, it will be the first figure, if A
belongs to every C and C to some B. And if A belongs to every C and
B to some C, then the argument is the same (for C converts in relation
to B). But if B belongs to every C and A to some C, then B must be
put as the first term (for B belongs to every C and C to some A, so that
B belongs to some A; and, since the particular converts, A will also
belong to some B). And if the deduction is privative, then, when the
terms are universal, it must be taken in the same way. For let B belong
to every C and A to none; then, C will belong to some B and A to no
C, so that C will be the middle term. And similarly also if the privative
is universal and the positive is particular (for A will belong to no C and
C to some of the Bs). However, if the privative is taken as particular,
then no resolution will be possible (that is, if B belongs to every C and
A does not belong to some C: for when BC is converted both the
premises will be particular).

It is also evident that in order to resolve the figures into one another,
the premise in relation to the minor extreme must be converted in
both the figures (for it was when this premise was replaced that the
transition to the other figure took place).

One of the deductions in the middle figure can be resolved into the
third, but the other cannot be resolved. For when the universal is
privative, the deduction can be resolved: if A belongs to no B and to
some C, both convert alike in relation to A, so that B belongs to no A
and C to some (the middle, therefore, is A). However, when A belongs
to every B and does not belong to some C, a resolution will not be
possible (for neither of the premises resulting from the conversion is
universal).

And the deductions from the third figure can be resolved into the
middle if the privative is universal, that is, if A belongs to no C and B
belongs to some or to every C (for C will also belong to no A and to
some B). However, if the privative is particular, then the deduction
cannot be resolved (for a particular negative does not admit of
conversion).

It is evident, then, that the same deductions are not resolved in these figures as were also not resolved into the first, and that when deductions are led back into the first figure, these deductions alone are brought to a conclusion through an impossibility.

From what has been said, then, it is evident how one must lead deductions back, and that the figures are resolved into one another.

A 46

It makes a certain difference in establishing and refuting whether one believes 'not to be this' and 'to be not this' signify the same thing or different things (for example, 'not to be white' and 'to be not white'). For these do not signify the same thing, nor is 'to be not white' the denial of 'to be white': instead, 'not to be white' is. And here is the account of this. Now, 'is able to walk' has the same relationship to 'is able to not walk' as 'is white' to 'is not-white,' or as 'knows the good' to 'knows the not good.' For 'knows the good' is no different from 'is one knowing the good,' and 'is able to walk' is no different from 'is one being-able to walk.' Consequently, their opposites 'is not able to walk', 'is not one being-able to walk' are also no different. If, therefore, 'is not one being-able to walk' signifies the same thing as 'is one being-able to not walk' (or <as we say it> 'one being-able not to walk'), these can even belong to the same thing at the same time (for the same man is able to walk and not walk, and is one knowing the good and the not good): but an assertion and the denial opposed to it do not belong at the same time to the same thing. Therefore, just as 'not to know the good' and 'to know the not good' are not the same, neither are 'to be not good' and 'not to be good' the same: for with terms in analogous relationships, if those in one pair are different, then also those in the other pair are different.

Nor are 'to be not equal' and 'not to be equal' the same: for there is a certain subject for 'to be not equal,' that is, the thing which is unequal, whereas there is not any subject for the other. It is for this reason that not everything is equal or unequal, though everything is equal or not equal.

Next, 'it is a not white log' and 'it is not a white log' do not belong to something at the same time. For if it is a not white log it will be a log; whereas it is not necessary for what is not a white log to be a log.

Consequently, it is evident that 'is not-good' is not the denial of 'is good.' If, therefore, 'affirmation' or 'denial' is true about every single <predicate>, then if 'is not-good' is not a denial, it is evident that it

must be a sort of affirmation. But there is a denial of every affirmation,
and, therefore, the denial of this affirmation is 'is not not-good.'

They stand in this order in relation to one another. Let A stand for
'to be good,' B stand for 'not to be good,' C stand for 'to be not good'
(which is below B), and D stand for 'not to be not good' (which is
below A). Now, either A or B will belong to everything but not
<both> to any same thing; and also either C or D will belong to
everything, but not <both> to any same thing. And it is necessary for
B to belong to everything to which C belongs: for if it is true to say
that something is not-white, then it is true to say that it is not white
(for it is impossible to be white and to be not-white at the same time,
or to be a not-white log and to be a white log), so that if the affirmation
does not belong then the denial will. But C does not always belong to
B (for what is not a log at all will not be a not-white log). Therefore, in
reverse order, D belongs to everything to which A belongs: for either C
or D belongs to everything, and since it is not possible to be at once
not-white and white, D will belong to A (for of that which is white it is
true to say that it is not not-white). But A will not be true of every D
(for it is not true to say A—that it is a white log—of what is not a log at
all; consequently, it is true to say D, but it is not true to say A, i.e.,
that it is a white log). It is also clear that A and C cannot belong to
anything the same, and that B and D can belong to the same thing.

Privations also have the same relationship to their predications
when put in this arrangement. Let A stand for equal, B stand for not
equal, C stand for unequal, D stand for not unequal.

In the case of a group of things, where the same term belongs to
some of them and not to others, the denial might similarly be true
either in that they are not all white or in that each of them is not white,
though it is false that each is not-white or that all are not-white. In the
same way also, the denial of 'every animal is white' is not 'every animal
is not-white' (for both are false), but 'not every animal is white.'

And since it is clear that 'is not-white' and 'is not white' signify
something different, and that one is an affirmation and the other a
denial, it is evident that the way of proving each is not the same (i.e.,
proving that whatever is an animal is not white, or that it is possible for
it not to be white, and proving that it is true to call it not-white—for
this is to be not-white). But 'it is true to call it white' and '<it is true to
call it> not-white' *are* proved in the same way. For both are proved in
the manner of establishing through the first figure, since 'is true' is

arranged similarly to 'is.' ('It is true to call it not white' is not the denial of 'it is true to call it white,' but rather 'it is not true to call it white' is.) So if <the thing to be proved> is 'it is true to say that whatever is a man is musical' (or 'not musical'), then whatever is an animal should be taken to be musical or to be not musical, and it has been proved. But 'whatever is a man is not musical' is proved refutatively through the three ways stated. *35*

Without qualification, whenever A is so related to B that it is not possible for them to belong to the same thing at the same time but of necessity one or the other of them belongs to everything, and C and D, in turn, are likewise related, and A follows C and does not convert with it, then D will follow B and will not convert with it. Also, it is possible for A and D to belong to the same thing but not possible for B and C. *40* *52b*

First, then, it is evident from the following argument that D follows B. Since one or the other of C and D belongs to everything of necessity, but it is not possible for C to belong to what B does (because C brings along with it A, and it is not possible for A and B to belong to the same thing), it is evident that D will follow B. *5*

Next, since C does not convert with A, but either C or D belongs to everything, it is possible for A and D to belong to the same thing. However, this is not possible for B and C, because A follows along with C (for something impossible results). It is evident, then, that B does not convert with D either, since it is possible for D and A to belong to something at the same time. *10*

Sometimes, it also happens that we are deceived in the case of this arrangement of terms because of failure to take correctly the opposites, one or the other of which must necessarily belong to everything. As an example, if it is not possible for A and B to belong to the same thing at the same time, but it is necessary for one of them to belong to what the other does not, and C and D, in turn, are likewise related, but A follows everything to which C belongs. For it will result <from the error in question> that B belongs of necessity to whatever D does, which is incorrect. For <we might reason as follows:> "take what F stands for to be the denial of A and B, and next take what H stands for to be the denial of C and D. Then, it is necessary for either A or F to belong to everything (for either the assertion or the denial belongs to everything). And next, either C or H belongs to everything, for they are an assertion and denial. But A was assumed to belong to *15* *20*

25

everything to which C belongs. Consequently, H belongs to everything to which F does. Next, since one or the other of F and B belongs to everything, and one or the other of H and D likewise, and H follows F, then B will also follow D (for we know this). Therefore, if A belongs to C, then B belongs to D." But this is incorrect, for the consequence was in reverse order for terms related in this way. For it is surely not

30

necessary for either A or F to belong to everything, nor necessary for either F or B to (for F is not the denial of A: for 'not good' is the denial of 'good,' but 'not good' is not the same as 'neither good nor not good'). And in the same way also in the case of C and D; for the denials which were taken are two.

PRIOR ANALYTICS
BOOK B

Chapter 1

We have already gone through the number of figures a deduction **B 1**
comes about in, and the kinds and numbers of premises through which
a deduction comes about, and when and why this occurs; and in addi- *40*
tion, we have gone through what sorts of things one must look to when
refuting or establishing, and how one must search for premises con- *53a*
cerning whatever is proposed <for proof>, in the case of any discipline whatever, and finally the route through which we may obtain the
principles concerning each subject.

Now, seeing that some deductions are universal and others are particular, all the universals always deduce several results; among particu- *5*
lar deductions, positive deductions deduce several things, but negatives only deduce their conclusions. For, although the privative
<particular> premise does not convert, the other premises convert;
and the conclusion is one thing predicated about another, so that the
other deductions deduce several things. For example, if A has been
proved to belong to every B or to some, then it is also necessary for B *10*
to belong to some A; and if A has been proved to belong to no B, then
neither does B belong to any A (and this conclusion is different from
the previous one). However, if A does not belong to some B, it is not
also necessary for B not to belong to some A, since it is possible for it
to belong to every.

This cause <of deducing more than one result>, then, is common *15*
to all deductions, universals as well as particulars. However, it is also
possible to give another account concerning universal deductions. For
the same deduction will be possible for all of those which are either
under the middle or under the conclusion-term, if the former are put
in the middle and the latter in the conclusion-term. For example, if AB
is the conclusion deduced through C, then, whatever things are below *20*
B or C, it will be necessary for A to be said of all of them. For if D is in
B as a whole, and B is in A, then D will also be in A. Next, if E is in C

as a whole, and C in A, then E will also be in A. And similarly also if
the deduction is privative.

25   But in the case of the second figure, for example, when A belongs to
no B and to every C, we can only deduce what is below the conclusion-
term (the conclusion is that B belongs to no C). Now, if D is below C,
it is evident that B will not belong to it. However, it is not clear by
30   means of the deduction that it does not belong to those below A. To be
sure, B does not belong to E if E is below A. But that B belongs to no
C has been proved through the deduction, while that B does not
belong to A was taken as undemonstrated; consequently, that B does
not belong to E does not result by means of the deduction.

And in the case of particular deductions, no necessary result will be
35   possible for things below the conclusion-term (for a deduction does not
come about when this premise is taken as particular); one will be
possible for all those below the middle term, except that it does not
result by means of the deduction. For example, if A belongs to every B
and B to some C: no deduction will be possible for something put
below C, but one will be possible for what is put below B, although it is
40   not by means of the deduction already formed.

And similarly also in the case of the other figures: a conclusion will
not be possible for something below the conclusion-term, but one will
53b1   be possible for what is below the other term, except that it results not
by means of the deduction, but in the way that those below the middle
were also proved from the undemonstrated premise in the case of the
universals. Consequently, either there will not be a deduction in the
former case, or there is also one in the latter case.

B 2   Now, it is possible for circumstances to be such that the premises by
5   means of which the deduction comes about are true, or that they are
false, or that one premise is true and the other false. The conclusion,
however, is either true or false of necessity. It is not possible, then, to
deduce a falsehood from true premises, but it is possible to deduce a
truth from false ones (except that it is not a deduction of the 'why' but
of the 'that,' for a deduction of the 'why' is not possible from false
10   premises). The reason why this is so will be explained in what follows.

First, then, it is clear from the following that it is not possible to
deduce a falsehood from truths. For if it is necessary for B to be when
A is, then when B is not it is necessary for A not to be. Thus, if A is
true, then it is necessary for B to be true, or else it will result that the
15   same thing both is and is not at the same time: but this is impossible.

But let it not be believed, because A is set out as a single term, that it is possible for something to result of necessity when a single thing is, for that cannot happen: for what results of necessity is a conclusion, and the fewest through which this comes about are three terms and two intervals or premises. If it is true, then, that A belongs to everything to which B belongs, and B to what C belongs, then it is necessary for A to belong <to what C belongs to>, and this cannot be false (for the same thing would belong and not belong at the same time). Therefore, A is put as if a single thing, the two premises being taken together. And similarly also in the case of privative deductions. For it is not possible to prove a falsehood from truths.

It is possible, however, to deduce a truth from falsehoods, either when both premises are false or when only one is (this cannot be either premise indifferently, if it is taken to be wholly false, but only the second; however, if it is not taken as wholly false, then it can equally well be either premise). For let A belong to the whole of C and to no B, and B not belong to any C. (This is possible: for instance, animal does not belong to any stone, nor stone to any man.) Then, if A should be taken to belong to every B and B to every C, A will belong to every C; consequently, from premises both false the conclusion is true (for every man is an animal). The privative deduction is also likewise. For it is possible for neither A nor B to belong to any C and yet A to belong to every B, for example, if the same terms are taken but man is put as the middle (for neither animal nor man belongs to any stone, but animal belongs to every man). Thus, if <the deduction> takes one term to belong to none of that to which it does belong and the other to belong to all of that to which it does not belong, the conclusion will be true from both premises false. This can also be proved in the same way if each premise is taken to be false in part.

But if only one premise is put as false, then when the first premise (that is, premise AB) is wholly false the conclusion cannot be true, but when premise BC is wholly false it can be. (By 'wholly false' I mean the contrary premise, i.e., if what belongs to none is taken to belong to every, or if what belongs to every is taken to belong to none.) For let A belong to no B and B to every C. Now, if I take premise BC as true and AB as wholly false (that is, take A to belong to every B), then it is impossible for the conclusion to be true (for A did not belong to any of the Cs, if it belongs to none of that to which B belongs and B belongs to every C). And similarly, if A belongs to every B and B to every C, and BC was taken as a true premise but AB as a wholly false one (i.e.,

20

25

30

35

40

54a

5

10

A was taken to belong to none of that to which B belongs), then the
conclusion will be false: for A will belong to every C, if A belongs to
everything to which B belongs and B to every C. It is evident, then,
that when the first premise is taken as wholly false (whether it is
affirmative or privative) and the other premise as true, then the conclusion cannot be true.

However, when the first premise is taken as not wholly false, the
conclusion may be true. For if A belongs to every C and to some B and
B belongs to every C (as, for instance, animal belongs to every swan
and to something white, and white belongs to every swan), then if A is
taken to belong to every B and B to every C, A will belong to every C
truly (for every swan is an animal). And similarly also if AB should be
privative. For it is possible for A to belong to some B and to no C and
for B to belong to every C, as, for example, animal belongs to something white and to no snow, and white belongs to all snow. Therefore,
if A should be taken to belong to no B and B to every C, then A will
belong to no C.

But if premise AB is taken as wholly true and premise BC as wholly
false, then a true deduction will be possible. For nothing prevents A
from belonging to every B and every C and yet B belonging to no C,
as, for example, such species of the same genus as are not under one
another. For animal belongs both to horse and to man, but horse belongs to no man. If, then, A is taken to belong to every B and B to
every C, then the conclusion will be true when premise BC is wholly
false. And similarly also if premise AB is privative. For it is possible for
A to belong neither to any B nor to any C, nor B to any C, as the genus
does to species from another genus. For animal belongs neither to
music nor to medical knowledge, nor does music belong to medical
knowledge. Taking A to belong to no B, then, and B to belong to every
C, the conclusion will be true.

And if premise BC is not false wholly, but only in part, in this way
also the conclusion can be true. For nothing prevents A from belonging
to the whole both of B and of C and yet B belonging to some C, as the
genus does to the species and the difference. For animal belongs to
every man and to everything footed, but man belongs to something
footed, not everything. Therefore, if A should be taken to belong to
every B and B to every C, then A will belong to every C, which was
true. And similarly also if premise AB is privative. For it is possible for
A to belong neither to any B nor to any C but yet B to some C, as the
genus does to a species and a difference from another genus. For

animal belongs neither to any wisdom nor to any theoretical science, but wisdom belongs to some theoretical science. If, then, A should be taken to belong to no B and B to belong to every C, then A would belong to no C (and this was true).   *15*

In the case of particular deductions, it is possible for the conclusion to be true when the first premise is wholly false and the other premise true, or when the first premise is in part false and the other premise is   *20*   true, or when the first premise is true and the other premise in part false, or when both premises are false. For nothing prevents A from belonging to no B and to some C and B belonging to some C, as animal belongs to no snow but to something white and snow to something white. Therefore, if snow should be put as the middle term and animal as the first, and A should be taken to belong to the whole of B and B to   *25*   some C, then premise AB is wholly false, premise BC is true, and the conclusion is true.

And similarly also if premise AB is privative. For it is possible for A to belong to the whole of B and not to belong to some C, and yet for B to belong to some C, as animal belongs to every man but does not   *30*   follow something white and man belongs to something white. Consequently, putting man as the middle term, if A should be taken to belong to no B and B to some C, the conclusion will be true when premise AB is wholly false.

And the conclusion can also be true if premise AB is false in part.   *35*   For nothing prevents A from belonging both to some B and to some C and B belonging to some C, as animal belongs to something beautiful and to something large and beautiful belongs to something large. Therefore, if A is taken to belong to every B and B to some C, then   *55a*   premise AB will be in part false, premise BC true, and the conclusion true. And similarly also when premise AB is privative (the terms will be the same, and positioned likewise, for the demonstration).

Next, if premise AB is true and premise BC false, it will be possible   *5*   for the conclusion to be true. For nothing prevents A from belonging to the whole of B and to some C and B belonging to no C, as animal belongs to every swan and to something black and swan belongs to nothing black. Consequently, if A should be taken to belong to every B and B to some C, then the conclusion will be true when BC is false.   *10*   And similarly also when premise AB is taken as privative. For it is possible for A to belong to no B and not belong to some C and yet for B to belong to no C, as a genus does to a species from another genus and to an accident of its own species. For animal belongs to no number and   *15*

to something white, and number to nothing white. Therefore, if number is put as the middle term and A is taken to belong to no B and B to
some C, then A will not belong to some C (which was true), and
premise AB is true and premise BC false.

20   And if premise AB is false in part and premise BC is also false, then
the conclusion can be false. For nothing prevents A from belonging
both to some B and to some C and B belonging to no C, for example, if
B is contrary to C and both are accidents in the same genus. For animal
belongs to something white and to something black, but white belongs
25   to nothing black. Therefore, if A is taken to belong to every B and B
to every C, then the conclusion will be true. And likewise if premise
AB is taken as privative (the same terms, arranged likewise, may be
put for the demonstration).

It will also be possible for the conclusion to be true when both
premises are false. For it is possible for A to belong to no B and to
30   some C and yet for B to belong to no C, as a genus does to a species
from another genus and to an accident of its own species. For animal
belongs to no number and to something white, and number belongs to
nothing white. Therefore, if A is taken to belong to every B and B to
35   belong to some C, then the conclusion is true but the premises are
both false. And similarly also when premise AB is privative. For
nothing prevents A belonging to the whole of B and not belonging to
some C, nor B to any C, as animal belongs to every swan and does not
belong to something black and swan belongs to nothing black. Conse-
40   quently, if A should be taken to belong to no B and B to some C, then
55b   A will not belong to some C (the conclusion, then, is true, and the
premises are false).

B 3   In the middle figure it is possible to deduce a true conclusion by
means of false premises in all ways: when both premises are taken
5   as wholly false, or when either one is taken as in part false, or when
one is true and the other is [wholly] false (no matter which one is put
as false), [or if both are in part false, or if one is true without qualification and the other false in part, or if one is wholly false and the other in
part true,] in the case of universal as well as particular deductions.

10   For if A belongs to no B and to every C, as animal belongs to no
stone and to every horse, then if the premises are put contrariwise and
A is taken to belong to every B and to no C, the conclusion will be true
from wholly false premises. And similarly also if A belongs to every B
15   and to no C (for it will be the same deduction).

And next, the conclusion may be true if one premise is wholly false and the other wholly true. For nothing prevents A belonging both to every B and to every C and yet B to no C, as a genus does to species which are not under one another. For animal belongs both to every horse and to every man, and no man is a horse. Therefore, if animal is taken to belong to all of one and none of the other, then one premise will be wholly false, the other premise will be wholly true, and the conclusion will be true, no matter which one the privative is put in relation to.

And <similarly> if one premise is partly false and the other wholly true. For it is possible for A to belong to some B and to every C and yet for B to belong to no C, as animal belongs to something white and to every raven, but white belongs to no raven. If, then, A is taken to belong to no B and to the whole of C, then premise AB is in part false, premise AC is wholly true, and the conclusion is true. And likewise also when the privative is put in the other position (for the demonstration is through the same terms).

And also if the affirmative premise is false in part and the privative premise is wholly true. For nothing prevents A belonging to some B and not belonging to the whole of C, and B belonging to no C, as animal belongs to something white and to no pitch, and white belongs to no pitch. Thus, if A is taken to belong to the whole of B and to no C, then premise AB is partly false, premise AC is wholly true, and the conclusion is true.

And it will also be possible for the conclusion to be true if both premises are partly false. For it is possible for A to belong both to some B and to some C and for B to belong to no C, as animal belongs both to something white and to something black and white belongs to nothing black. Therefore, if A is taken to belong to every B and to no C, then both premises are in part false but the conclusion is true. And similarly also if the privative premise is put in the other position (the proof is through the same terms).

And it is also evident in the case of particular deductions. For nothing prevents A belonging to every B and to some C and B not belonging to some C (for example, animal belongs to every man and to something white, but animal may fail to belong to something white). If, therefore, it is supposed that A belongs to no B and belongs to some C, then the universal premise is wholly false, the particular premise is true, and the conclusion is true. And likewise also if premise AB is taken as affirmative. For it is possible for A to belong to no B and not to some C and for B not to belong to some C (for example, animal belongs to nothing inanimate and to something white, but inanimate may fail to belong to something white). Therefore, if it is supposed that A belongs to every B and does not belong to some C, then premise AB (the universal premise) is wholly false, premise AC is true, and the conclusion is true.

And <the conclusion may be true> when the universal premise is put as true and the particular premise as false. For nothing prevents A following neither any B nor any C but yet B not belonging to some C, as animal belongs to no number or anything inanimate and number does not follow something inanimate. If, then, it is supposed that A belongs to no B and to some C, then the conclusion will be true, and also the universal premise, but the particular premise will be false. And it is also likewise when the universal premise is put as affirmative. For it is possible for A to belong to the whole both of B and of C, but yet for B not to follow some C, as a genus in relation to the species and the difference (for animal follows every man and follows footed as a whole, but man does not follow everything footed). Consequently, if A is taken to belong to the whole of B and not to belong to some C, then the universal premise is true, the particular premise is false, and the conclusion is true.

And it is also evident that it is possible for a true conclusion to be from premises both false, since it is possible for A to belong to the whole of B and of C, but yet for B not to follow some C. For if A is taken to belong to no B and to some C, then both premises are false but the conclusion is true. And similarly also if the universal premise is positive and the particular premise is privative. For it is possible for A to follow no B and every C and for B not to belong to some C, as, for example, animal follows no science and every man and science does not follow every man. Therefore, if A is taken to belong to the whole of B and not to follow some C, then the premises are false but the conclusion is true.

B 4

A true conclusion through false premises is also possible in the last figure, either when both premises are wholly false, or when each premise is in part false, or when one premise is wholly true and the other false, or when one is in part false and the other wholly true, or the reverse, or in whatever other ways it is possible to replace the premises. For nothing prevents neither A nor B belonging to any C and yet A belonging to some B. For example, neither man nor footed follows anything inanimate and yet man belongs to something footed. If A and B are taken to belong to every C, then, the premises are wholly false but the conclusion true. And likewise also when one premise is priva-tive and the other is affirmative. For it is possible for B to belong to no *15* C and A to every C and for A not to belong to some B (for example, black belongs to no swan, animal to every swan, and animal does not belong to everything black). Consequently, if B is taken to belong to every C and A to none, then A will not belong to some B; and the con-clusion is true and the premises false. *20*

And the conclusion can also be true if each premise is partly false. For nothing prevents both A and B belonging to some C and A belong-ing to some B (for example, white and beautiful belong to some animal and white belongs to something beautiful). Therefore, if A and B are put as belonging to every C, then the premises are false in part and the *25* conclusion is true. And similarly also when premise AC is put as priva-tive. For nothing prevents A not belonging to some C and B belonging to some, and A not belonging to every B (for example, white does not belong to some animal, beautiful does belong to some, and white does *30* not belong to everything beautiful). Consequently, if A is taken to belong to no C and B to every C, then both the premises are false in part and the conclusion is true.

And likewise also when one premise is taken as wholly false and the other as wholly true. For it is possible for both A and B to follow every C but yet for A not to belong to some B (for example, animal and white *35* both follow every swan, and yet animal does not belong to everything white). Therefore, putting these sorts of things as terms, if B is taken to belong to the whole of C and A not to belong to the whole of it, then premise BC will be wholly true, premise AC wholly false, and the conclusion true. And similarly also if BC is false and AC true (for the *40* terms for the demonstration are the same). And also if both premises *57a* should be taken as affirmative. For nothing prevents B following every C, A not belonging to it as a whole, and A belonging to some B (for example, animal belongs to every swan, black to no swan, and black *5* belongs to some animal). Consequently, if A and B are taken to belong to every C, then premise BC is wholly true, premise AC wholly false, and the conclusion true. And similarly also when a true premise AC is taken (for the proof is by means of the same terms).

Again when one premise is wholly true and the other is in part false. For it is possible for B to belong to every C, for A to belong to some C, *10* and for A to belong to some B (for example, biped belongs to every man, beautiful does not belong to every man, and beautiful belongs to some biped). If, then, both A and B are taken to belong to the whole of C, then premise BC is wholly true, premise AC is in part false, and

15 the conclusion is true. And similarly also when premise AC is taken as true and premise BC as in part false (for there will be a demonstration when the same terms are transposed). And when one premise is privative and the other is affirmative. For since it is possible for B to belong to the whole of C and for A to belong to some C, and <also possible>,

20 when the terms are so related, for A not to belong to every B, consequently if B is taken to belong to the whole of C and A to none, then the privative premise is in part false and the other premise is wholly true, as is the conclusion. Next, since it has been proved that when A belongs to no C and B belongs to some C it is possible for A not to

25 belong to some B, it is evident that when premise AC is wholly true and premise BC in part false, it is also possible for the conclusion to be true. For if A is taken to belong to no C and B to belong to every C, then premise AC is wholly true and premise BC in part false.

And it is also evident in the case of particular deductions that a true

30 conclusion can be deduced through false premises in all ways. For the same terms are to be taken as when the premises are universal: the positive terms in positive deductions, the privative terms in privative deductions (for it makes no difference with respect to the setting out of the terms whether we take what belongs to none to belong to every

35 or take what belongs to some to belong universally). And similarly also in the case of privatives.

It is evident, then, that if the conclusion is false, it is necessary for either all or some of the premises which the argument rests on to be false. However, when the conclusion is true, then it is not necessary either for one or for all of the premises to be true, but instead it is possible for the conclusion to be true all the same (though not of

40 necessity) when none of the premises in the deduction is true. The

57b reason is that when two things are so related to each other that if one is, then the other of necessity is, then when the second is not, the first will not be either, but when the second is, there is no necessity for the first to be. But it is impossible for the same thing to be of necessity both when a certain thing is and when that same thing is not (I mean,

5 for example, for B to be large of necessity when A is white, and for B to be large of necessity when A is not white). For whenever it is the case that if this thing, A, is white, then that thing, B, is necessarily large, and that if B is large then C is not white, then, if A is white, it is necessary for C not to be white. And when there are two things such

that if one of them is, it is necessary for the other to be, then if the   *10*
latter is not, the first necessarily is not. So if B is not large, then A
cannot be white. But if it is necessary for B to be large when A is not
white, then it results of necessity that when B is not large then this
very thing B is large: but that is impossible. For if B is not large, then
A will of necessity not be white; therefore, if B will also be large when   *15*
this is not white, then it results that if B is not large it is large, just as if
by means of three terms.

Proving in a circle, or from one another, is concluding something   **B 5**
which was taken in some other deduction as a premise by means of the
conclusion of that deduction and its other premise taken as reversed in   *20*
predication. As an example of this, if \<someone who\> had been
required to prove that A belongs to every C, and had proved it through
B, should then next prove that A belongs to B, taking A to belong to C
and C to B (previously, he took B to belong to C, in the reverse order).
Or if, because he needs to prove B to belong to C, he should take A as   *25*
predicated of C (which was the conclusion) and B as predicated about
A (previously, A was taken as predicated about B, in the reverse order).
Proving from one another is not possible otherwise. For if another
middle is taken, it will not be in a circle, for none of the same things is
taken. And if some one of these is taken, then only one must be: for   *30*
if both are taken, the conclusion will be the same one, but it must be
different.
    In the case of terms which do not convert with one another, then,
the deduction comes about from one undemonstrated premise (for it
cannot be demonstrated by means of these terms that the third be-
longs to the middle or the middle to the first). But in the case of those   *35*
which do convert, they can all be proved through each other, as for
example, if A, B, and C convert with each other. For let conclusion AC
have been proved by means of middle B, and again AB by means of
the conclusion together with premise BC converted, and likewise also   *40*
BC by means of the conclusion and premise AB converted. Both   *58a*
premise CB and premise BA need to be demonstrated, for we have
used only these premises as undemonstrated. Accordingly, if B is
taken to belong to every C and C to every A, then there will be a
deduction of B in relation to A. Next, if C is taken to belong to every   *5*
A and A to every B, then it is necessary for C to belong to every B.
Now, in both of these deductions, premise CA was taken as undemonstrated (for the others had been proved). Consequently, if we
can demonstrate this premise, then all of the premises will have been

10 proved through one another. Accordingly, if C is taken to belong to every B and B to every A, then both the premises taken have been demonstrated, and also it is necessary for C to belong to A.

It is evident, then, that only in the case of terms which convert is it possible for demonstrations in a circle or from one another to come
15 about; in the case of others, it is as we explained earlier. And it also results in these cases that we use the very thing proved itself for its demonstration. For 'C is said of B' and 'B is said of A' are proved by means of taking 'C is said of A,' but 'C is said of A' is proved by means of these <first two> premises; consequently, we use the conclusion
20 for its <own> demonstration.

In the case of privative deductions, proof from each other is as follows. Let the premises be that B belongs to every C and A to no B (the conclusion is that A belongs to no C). Now, if one next must conclude that A belongs to no B (which <the argument> previously
25 took), then let the premises be that A belongs to no C and C to every B (for in this way the premise is reversed). But if it must be concluded that B belongs to C, then AB is no longer to be converted in the same way (for 'B belongs to no A' and 'A belongs to no B' are the same premise). Instead, one must take B to belong to all of what A belongs
30 to none of. Let it be that A belongs to none of the Cs (which was the conclusion), and let B have been taken to belong to all of what A belongs to none of. It is necessary, then, for B to belong to every C. Consequently, each of the three premises has become a conclusion; and this is what it is to demonstrate in a circle, to take the conclusion
35 and one premise in reverse and deduce the remaining premise.

In the case of the particular deductions, the universal premise cannot be demonstrated by means of the others, but the particular premise can be. Now, it is evident that it is not possible to demonstrate the universal premise: for a universal is proved by means of universals,
40 but the conclusion is not universal, and one must prove from the con-
58b clusion and the other premise. Moreover, no conclusion comes about at all when the <other> premise is converted, for both premises become particular. The particular premise can be demonstrated, however. For let A have been proved true of some C by means of B. If, then, B is
5 taken to belong to every A and the conclusion remains, then B will belong to some C (for the first figure comes about, and A is the middle). But if the deduction is privative, the universal premise cannot be proved, for the reason also given previously. However, the particular premise can be, if AB is converted in the same way as in the case of

the universal deductions (that is, that B belongs to some of what A does not belong to some of). For otherwise, no deduction comes about because the particular premise is negative.   *10*

In the second figure, the affirmative cannot be proved in this manner, but the privative can be. Now, the positive cannot be proved because both the premises are not affirmative (for the conclusion is privative, and a positive was proved from premises both affirmative). But the privative is proved in the following way. Let A belong to every B and to no C (the conclusion is that B belongs to no C). Then, if B is taken as belonging to every A and to no C, then it is necessary for A to belong to no C (for the second figure comes about, and the middle is B). And if AB was taken as privative and the other premise as positive, then it will be the first figure (for C belongs to every A and B to no C, so that B does not belong to any A, nor, therefore, A to any B). A deduction does not come about by means of the conclusion and one premise, then, but there will be one when another premise is taken in addition.

B 6
15

.20

25

If the deduction is not universal, then the universal premise cannot be proved, for the same reason as we have also stated previously; the particular premise can be proved, however, when the universal is positive. For let A belong to every B and not to every C (the conclusion is BC). Therefore, if B is taken to belong to every A and not to every C, then A will not belong to some C (the middle is B). But if the universal premise is privative, then premise AC cannot be proved by converting AB (for it results either that both the premises become negative or that one of them does, so that there will not be a deduction). However, it can be proved in a way similar to the case of the universal deductions if A is taken to belong to some of what B does not belong to some of.

30

35

In the case of the third figure, when both the premises are taken as universal it is not possible to prove by means of one another: for a universal is proved by means of universals, but the conclusion in this figure is always particular, so that it is evident that it is not possible at all to prove the universal premise by means of this figure.

B 7
40

59a

But if one premise is universal and one particular, then sometimes it can be done and sometimes it cannot. When both premises are taken as affirmative, then, and the universal premise is in relation to the minor extreme, it can be done; but when it is in relation to the other extreme, it cannot be. For let A belong to every C and B belong to

5

some C (the conclusion is AB). Therefore, if C is taken to belong to every A, then it has been proved that C belongs to some B, but it has not been proved that B belongs to some C. Of course, if C belongs to some B, then it is necessary for B also to belong to some C: but it is not the same thing for this to belong to that and for that to belong to this. Rather, it must be taken in addition that if this belongs to some of that, then that other also belongs to some of this. But when this premise has been taken, the deduction no longer comes about from the conclusion and the other premise.

And if B belongs to every C and A to some C, then it will be possible to prove AC when C is taken to belong to every B and A to some. For if C belongs to every B and A to some B, then it is necessary for A to belong to some C (B is the middle). And when one premise is positive, the other premise is privative, and the positive premise is universal, then the other premise can be proved. For let B belong to every C, and let A not belong to some (the conclusion is that A does not belong to some B). If, then, it is taken in addition that C belongs to every B, then it is necessary for A not to belong to some C (B is the middle). But when the privative premise is universal, then the other premise cannot be proved, unless, as in the previous cases, it is taken that this one belongs to some of what the other does not belong to some of, as, for instance, if A belongs to no C and B belongs to some C (the conclusion is that A does not belong to some B). Therefore, if it is taken that C belongs to some of what A does not belong to some of, then it is necessary for C to belong to some B. But otherwise, the other premise cannot be proved by converting the universal premise, for there will not be a deduction at all.

[It is evident, then, that in the first figure, proof by means of one another comes about both through the third figure and through the first. For when the conclusion is positive, the proof is through the first figure, but when the conclusion is privative it is through the last (for it is taken that what this belongs to none of, the other belongs to all of). And in the middle figure, when the deduction is universal then proof by means of one another is both through the same figure and through the first; but when the deduction is particular, it is through both the same and the last. And in the third figure, all proofs by means of one another are through the same figure. It is also evident that in the third and the middle figures, the deductions which do not come about through the same figure are either not in accordance with circular proof or are incomplete.]

To convert is to make a deduction either that the <first> extreme *59b*
does not belong to the middle term, or that the middle term does not
belong to the last extreme, by replacing the conclusion <with its
converse>. For if the conclusion is converted and one premise remains, it is necessary for the other premise to be rejected (for if that   *5*
premise should be so, then the conclusion would be also). But it makes
a difference whether we convert the conclusion oppositely or contrarily, for the same deduction does not come about when it is converted in each way (but this will be clear through what follows). I say
that 'to every' is the opposite of 'not to every,' and 'to some' the
opposite of of 'to none,' and I say that belonging 'to every' converts   *10*
contrarily with 'to none, and 'to some' with 'not to some.'

For let A have been proved of C by means of middle term B. Now, if
A is taken to belong to no C and to every B, then B will belong to no
C. And if A is taken to belong to no C and B to belong to every C,
then A will not belong to every B (but not simply to none, for a   *15*
universal was not proved through the last figure). And in general, the
premise in relation to the major extreme cannot be rejected universally
through conversion, since the rejection is always through the third
figure (for it is necessary to take both the premises in relation to the
minor extreme). And likewise if the deduction is privative. For let it   *20*
have been proved by means of B that A belongs to no C. Therefore, if
A is taken to belong to every C and to no B, then B will belong to no
C. And if A and B are taken to belong to every C, then A will belong to
some B (but it belonged to none).

But if the conclusion is converted oppositely, then the deductions   *25*
will also be opposite, not universal (for one premise always becomes
particular, so that the conclusion will also be particular). For let the
deduction be positive, and let it be converted in this way. Then, if A
does not belong to every C but belongs to every B, then B will not
belong to every C; and, if A does not belong to every C but B does,   *30*
then A will not belong to every B. And similarly also if the deduction is
privative. For if A belongs to some C and to no B, then B will not
belong to some C (not without qualification to none); and if A belongs
to some C and B to every C (which was taken originally), then A will   *35*
belong to some B.

In the case of the particular deductions, when the conclusion is
converted oppositely both premises are rejected; but when it is converted contrarily, neither premise is (for a rejection in the manner of

40

60a

5

10

conversion with a conclusion that falls short <of a universal>, as in the case of universal deductions, no longer results, but instead no rejection at all). For let A have been proved of some C. Therefore, if A is taken to belong to no C and B to belong to some, then A will not belong to some B; and if A is taken to belong to no C and to every B, then B will belong to no C. Consequently, the premises are both rejected. But if it is converted contrarily, then neither premise is rejected. For if A does not belong to some C and belongs to every B, then B will not belong to some C, but the original premise has not yet been rejected (for it is possible to belong to some and not to belong to some). But no deduction of AB, the universal premise, comes about at all. For if A does not belong to some C and B does belong to some C, then neither of the premises is universal. And similarly also if the deduction is privative. For if A should be taken to belong to every C, then the premises are both rejected, while if it should be taken to belong to some, then neither premise is (the demonstration is the same).

B 9

15

20

25

30

35

In the second figure, the premise in relation to the major extreme cannot be rejected contrarily, regardless of which type of conversion we use (for the conclusion will always be in the third figure, and a universal deduction was not possible in this). However, we can reject the other premise in a manner similar to the conversion. (By 'similar', I mean <rejecting> contrarily if the conclusion is converted contrarily and oppositely if it is converted oppositely.)

For let A belong to every B and to no C (the conclusion is BC). Therefore, if B is taken to belong to every C and premise AB remains, then A will belong to every C (for the first figure comes about). And if B is taken to belong to every C and A to no C, then A will not belong to every B (the figure is the last). But if BC is converted oppositely, then premise AB can be proved similarly and premise AC oppositely. For if B is taken to belong to some C and A to no C, then A will not belong to some B. Next, if B is taken to belong to some C and A to every B, then A will belong to some C (so that the deduction becomes opposite). And it can also be proved similarly if the premises should be in the reverse relation.

But if the deduction is particular, then when the conclusion is converted contrarily neither of the premises is rejected (just as in the first figure), but when the conclusion is converted oppositely, both premises are rejected. For let A be put as belonging to no B and to some C (the conclusion is BC). Therefore, if B is put as belonging to some C and premise AB remains, then there will be a conclusion that A does not belong to some C, but the initial premise has not been rejected (for it is possible to belong to some and not belong to some). Next, if B is taken to belong to some C and A to some C, then there will not be a *40* deduction (for neither of the things taken is universal). Consequently, AB is not rejected. However, if <the conclusion> is converted op- *60b* positely, then both premises are rejected. For if B is taken to belong to every C and A to belong to no B, then A will belong to no C (but it belonged to some). Next, if B is taken to belong to every C and A to some C, then A will belong to some B. And the demonstration is also *5* the same if the universal premise is positive.

In the case of the third figure, when the conclusion is converted **B 10** contrarily, neither of the premises is rejected in any of the deductions; but when it is converted oppositely, both premises are rejected, and in all of the deductions. For let A have been proved to belong to some B, let C have been taken as middle term, and let the premises be univer- *10* sal. Then, if A is taken not to belong to some B and B to belong to every C, no deduction of A and C comes about. Nor will there be a deduction of B and C if A does not belong to some B and belongs to every C. And it can also be proved similarly if the premises are not *15* universal. For either it is necessary for both premises to be particular as a result of the conversion, or the universal is in relation to the minor extreme (and in this way there was no deduction either in the first figure or in the middle figure).

But if the conclusion is converted oppositely, then both premises are rejected. For if A to no B and B to every C, then A to no C. Next, if A *20* to no B and to every C, then B to no C. And likewise also if one premise is not universal. For if A to no B and B to some C, then A will not belong to some C; and if A to no B and to every C, then B to no C. *25*

And similarly also if the deduction is privative. For let A have been proved not to belong to some B, and let BC be positive and AC negative (for this is the way a deduction came about). Then, when the contrary of the conclusion is taken, there will not be a deduction (for if A to some B and B to every C, there was no deduction of A and C). *30* Nor was there a deduction of B and C if A to some B and to no C. Consequently, the premises are not rejected.

However, when the opposite of the conclusion is taken then they are rejected. For if A to every B and B to every C, then A to every C (but *35* it belonged to none). Next, if A to every B and to no C, then B to no C (but it belonged to every). And it is also proved similarly if the premises are not universal. For AC becomes both universal and privative, while the other <premise> is particular and positive. Therefore, if A

40
61a
to every B and B to some C, then it results that A to some C (but it belonged to none). Next, if A to every B and to no C, then B to no C (but it was put that it belongs to some). But if A to some B and B to some C, no deduction comes about. Nor if A is taken to belong to some B and to no C, not in this way either. Consequently, the premises are rejected in the former way, but not in the latter.

5
It is evident through what has been said, then, how a deduction comes about in each of the figures when the conclusion is converted, and when it is contrary to the premise and when opposite; It is also evident that in the first figure the deductions come about through the middle figure and the last, and that the premise in relation to the

10
minor extreme is always rejected through the middle figure and the premise in relation to the major extreme rejected through the last figure; that in the second figure, the deductions come about through the first and the last figures, and that the premise in relation to the minor extreme is always rejected through the first figure and the premise in relation to the major extreme is rejected through the last figure; and that in the third figure, the deductions come about through the first and the middle figures, and that the premise in relation to

15
the major extreme is always rejected through the first figure and the premise in relation to the minor extreme rejected through the middle figure.

B 11
It is evident, then, what converting is, and how it is possible in each figure, and which deduction comes about.

A deduction through an impossibility is proved when the contradic-

20
tory of the conclusion is put as a premise and one of the premises <of the deduction> is taken in addition; this comes about in all the figures. For it is like conversion but differs to the extent that it is converting when a deduction has already come about and both the premises have been taken, while it is leading away to an impossibility, not when

25
the opposite has previously been agreed to, but when it is obvious that it is true. The terms are similarly related in both, and the way of taking premises is the same for both. For instance, if A belongs to every B and C is the middle, then if A is assumed to belong either not to every B, or to none, and to belong to every C (which was true), then

it is necessary for C to belong either to no B, or not to every B. But this
is impossible; consequently, what was assumed is false. Therefore, its
opposite is true. And similarly also in the case of the other figures (for
whatever deductions admit of conversion also admit of deduction
through an impossibility).

The other problems, then, are all proved through an impossibility in
all the figures. A universal positive conclusion, however, is proved in
the middle and the third figures, but it is not proved in the first. For let
A be assumed not to belong to every B, or to belong to none, and let
another premise be taken in addition, from whichever side, whether
that C belongs to every A or that B belongs to every D (for in this way
it would be the first figure). Then, if A is assumed not to belong to
every B, a deduction does not come about, no matter from which side
the premise is taken; whereas if A is assumed to belong to no B, then
when premise BD is taken in addition there will be a deduction of a
falsehood, but what was proposed is not proved. For if A to no B and B
to every D, then A to no D. But let this be impossible. That A belongs
to no B is therefore false. But it is not the case that if 'to none' is false
then 'to every' is true. And if a premise CA is taken in addition, a
deduction does not come about, nor when A is assumed not to belong
to every B. Consequently, it is evident that 'belongs to every' is not
proved through an impossibility in the first figure.

But 'belongs to some' and 'belongs to none' and 'does not belong to
every' can be proved. For let A be assumed to belong to no B, and let B
be taken to belong to every or to some C. Then it is necessary for A to
belong to no C, or not to every. But this is impossible (for let it be true
and evident that A belongs to every C); consequently, if this is false,
then it is necessary for A to belong to some B. However, if the other
premise is taken in relation to A, then there will not be a deduction,
nor will there be one when the contrary of the conclusion (that is, that
A does not belong to some B) is assumed. It is evident, then, that it is
the opposite of the conclusion which must be assumed.

Next, let A be assumed to belong to some B, and let C have been
taken to belong to every A. It is then necessary for C to belong to
some A. But let this be impossible, so that what was assumed is false.
In that case, to belong to none is true. And similarly also if CA is taken
as privative. But if the premise in relation to B was taken, then there
will not be a deduction. And if the contrary was assumed, then there
will be a deduction and something impossible will result, but what was
proposed is not proved. For let A be assumed to belong to every B, and

let C have been taken to belong to every A. Then, it is necessary for C to belong to every B. But this is impossible; consequently, that A belongs to every B is false. However, to belong to none is not yet

30 necessary if it does not belong to every. And similarly also if the other premise is taken in relation to B (for there will be a deduction and something impossible will result, but the assumption is not rejected). Consequently, it is the opposite which must be assumed.

In order to prove A not to belong to every B, it must be assumed to belong to every. For if A belongs to every B and C to every A, then C

35 will belong to every B; consequently, if this is impossible, then what was assumed is false. And similarly also if the other premise was taken in relation to B. And likewise if CA was privative (for a deduction also comes about in this way). However, if the privative premise should be in relation to B, then nothing is proved. And if A was assumed to

40 belong to some B rather than to every, then it is not proved that it does not belong to every, but rather that it belongs to none. For if A is taken to belong to some B and C to belong to every A, then C will belong to

62a some B. Therefore, if this is impossible, then it is false that A belongs to some B; consequently, it is true that it belongs to none. But when this has been proved, what is true has been rejected in addition (for A belonged to some B and did not belong to some). Moreover, neither

5 does an impossibility follow as a result of the assumption: for the asumption would then be false (since a falsehood cannot be deduced from truths), while as things are, it is true (for A belongs to some B). Consequently, it must not be assumed that it belongs to some, but rather that it belongs to every. And similarly also if we want to prove A not to belong to some B (for if not to belong to some and not to belong

10 to every are the same, then there will be the same demonstration for them both).

It is evident, then, that it is the opposite, not the contrary, which must be assumed in all of the deductions. For in this way there will be a necessary result, and also the claim will be accepted. For if either the assertion or the denial is true of everything, then when it has been

15 proved that the denial is not true, it is necessary for the affirmation to be true. Moreover, if someone does not put the affirmation to be true, then it is accepted to claim the denial. To claim the contrary, however, is not suitable in either way (for neither is it necessary for 'belongs to every' to be true if 'belongs to none' is false, nor is it accepted that if the one is false then the other is true).

It is evident, then, that in the first figure all the other problems are proved through an impossibility, although a universal positive is not so proved. But in the middle and the last figures, this problem is also proved. For let A be assumed not to belong to every B, and let A have been taken to belong to every C. Therefore, if A not to every B and to every C, then C not to every B. But this is impossible (for let it be *25* evident that C belongs to every B), so that the thing assumed is false. Therefore, it is true that A belongs to every B. But if the contrary were assumed, then there would be a deduction and something impossible will result, but yet what was proposed is not proved. For if A to no B and to every C, then C to no B. But this is impossible; consequently, it *30* is false that it belongs to none. However, it is not the case that if this is false, then it is true that it belongs to every.

To prove that A belongs to some B, let A be assumed to belong to no B, and let it belong to every C. Then, it is necessary for C to belong to no B. Consequently, if this is impossible, then it is necessary for A to *35* belong to some B. And if it were assumed not to belong to some B, the results would be the same as in the case of the first figure.

Next, let A be assumed to belong to some B, and let it belong to no C. It is, then, necessary for C not to belong to some B. But it belonged to every one, so that what was assumed is false. Therefore, A will *40* belong to no B.

To prove that A does not belong to every B, let it be assumed to belong to every B and to no C. It is then necessary for C to belong to *62b* no B. But this is impossible; consequently, that it does not belong to every is true. It is evident, then, that all the types of deductions can come about by means of the middle figure.

And similarly, they also can come about by means of the last figure. For let A be assumed not to belong to some B and to belong to every C. Therefore, A does not belong to some C. If this is impossible, then it is false that A does not belong to some B, and consequently true that it belongs to every B. But if A is assumed to belong to no B, then although there will be a deduction and something impossible will result, what was proposed is not proved (for if the contrary were as- *10* sumed, the results would be the same as in the previous cases).

This assumption must be chosen, instead, for proving that A belongs to some B. For if A to no B and C to some B, then A not to every C. Therefore, if this is false, then it is true that A belongs to some B.

15   And to prove that A belongs to no B, let it be assumed to belong to some, and let C also have been taken to belong to every B. Then, it is necessary for A to belong to some C. But it belonged to none; consequently, it is false that A belongs to some B.

However, if A were assumed to belong to every B, then what was proposed is not proved; this assumption must be taken, instead, for *20* proving that it does not belong to every B. For if A to every B and C to every B, then A belongs to some C. But this was not so; consequently, it is false that it belongs to every B. And if this is the case, then it is true that it does not belong to every B. If it were assumed to belong to some, the results would be the same as in the previously stated cases.

25   It is evident, then, that it is the opposite which must be assumed in all deductions through an impossibility. And it is also clear that an affirmative is, in a way, proved in the middle figure, and a universal in the last.

B 14   A demonstration <leading> into an impossibility differs from a pro-
30 bative demonstration in that it puts as a premise what it wants to reject by leading away into an agreed falsehood, while a probative demonstration begins from agreed positions. More precisely, both demonstrations take two agreed premises, but one takes the premises which the deduction is from, while the other takes one of these premises and, as the other premise, the contradictory of the conclusion. Also, in the
35 former case it is not necessary for the conclusion to be familiar or to believe in advance that it is so or not, while in the latter case it is necessary to believe in advance that it is not so. It makes no difference whether the conclusion is an affirmation or a denial, but rather it is similar concerning both kinds of conclusion.

Everything concluded probatively can also be proved through an
40 impossibility, and whatever is proved through an impossibility concluded probatively, through the same terms. For when the deduction
63a of an impossibility comes about in the first figure, then the true conclusion will be in the middle figure or the last (a privative conclusion in the middle figure and a positive conclusion in the last). When the deduction comes about in the middle figure, then the true conclusion will be in the first figure in the case of all the problems. When the
5 deduction of an impossibility comes about in the last figure, then the true conclusion will be in the first or the middle figure (affirmative conclusions in the first figure and privatives in the middle).

For let A have been proved of no B, or not of every B, by means of the first figure. The assumption, therefore, was that A belongs to some B, and C was taken to belong to every A and to no B (for it is in this way that a deduction and an impossibility came about). But this is the middle figure: 'if C belongs to every A and to no B'; and it is evident from these premises that A belongs to no B. And similarly also if it has been proved that it does not belong to every B. For the assumption was that it belongs to every B, and C was taken to belong to every A and not to every B. And likewise if CA should be taken as privative (for in this way also the middle figure comes about). Next, let A have been proved to belong to some B. The assumption, then, was that it belongs to none, and B was taken to belong to every C and A to belong either to every or to some C (for in this way there will be an impossibility). But this is the last figure: 'if A and B to every C'; and it is evident from these premises that it is necessary for A to belong to some B. Similarly also if either B or A should be taken to belong to some C.

Next, in the middle figure: let A have been proved to belong to every B. The assumption, then, was that A does not belong to every B, and A was taken to belong to every C and C to every B (for in this way there will be an impossibility). But this is the first figure: 'A to every C and C to every B.' And similarly also if A has been proved to belong to some B. For the assumption was that A belongs to no B, and A was taken to belong to every C and C to some B. And if the deduction is privative, then the assumption was that A belongs to some B, and A was taken to belong to no C and C to every B, so that the first figure comes about. And likewise if the deduction is not universal, and A has instead been proved not to belong to some B. For the assumption was that A belongs to every B, and A was taken to belong to no C and C to some B (for in this way it is the first figure).

Next, in the third figure: let A have been proved to belong to every B. The assumption, therefore, was that A does not belong to every B, and C was taken to belong to every B and A to belong to every C (for in this way there will be an impossibility). But this is the first figure. And likewise also if the demonstration is particular. For the assumption was that A belongs to no B, and C was taken to belong to some B and A to every C. And if the deduction is privative, then the assumption was that A belongs to some B, and C was taken to belong to no A and to every B (but this is the middle figure). And similarly also if the demonstration is not universal. For the assumption will be that A belongs to every B, and C was taken to belong to no A and to some B (but this is the middle figure).

10

15

20

25

30

35

40

63b

5

10

It is evident, then, that it is also possible to prove each of the problems <which was proved through an impossibility> through the same terms probatively. But similarly, if the deductions <in question> are probative, it will also be possible to lead them away into an impos-

15   sibility, using the terms which were taken, when the premise opposite to the conclusion is taken. For the same deductions come about as by means of conversion; consequently, we also know at once the figure by means of which each one will be possible. It is clear, then, that every problem can be proved in both ways, through an impossibility as well

20   as probatively, and that it is not possible for one of the ways to be separated off.

B 15   In which figures it is possible to deduce from opposite premises, and in which figures it is not, will be evident in the following way.

I say that verbally there are four <pairs of> opposite premises, to

25   wit: 'to every' and 'to no,' 'to every' and 'not to every,' 'to some' and 'to no,' and 'to some' and 'not to some.' In truth, however, there are three, for 'to some' and 'not to some' are only opposites verbally. Of these, I call the universal premises *contraries* ('to every' is contrary to 'to none,' as, for example, 'every science is good' is contrary to 'no

30   science is good') and the other pairs of premises *opposites*.

In the first figure, then, there cannot be a deduction from opposite premises, neither an affirmative one nor a negative one. There cannot be an affirmative deduction because both premises must be affirma- tive, whereas opposite premises are an assertion and denial. There

35   cannot be a privative deduction, on the other hand, because opposite premises predicate and reject the same thing of the same thing: the middle term in the first figure, however, is not said of both extremes, but rather one is denied of it and it is predicated of the other (and these premises are not opposed).

40   But in the middle figure, it is possible for a deduction to come about
64a   both from opposite and from contrary premises. For let A stand for good and B and C for science. Now, if someone took every science to be good, and also no science to be good, then A belongs to every B and to no C, so that B belongs to no C: no science, therefore, is a science.

5   And similarly also if, taking every science to be good, he took medical knowledge not to be good (for A belongs to every B and to no C, so that a particular science will not be a science). And if A to every C and to no B, and B is science, C medical knowledge, and A belief (for while

10   taking no science to be belief, he has taken some science to be belief).

This differs from the previous case in that it is converted in respect of the terms: previously, the affirmative premise was in relation to B, but now it is in relation to C. And likewise also if one or the other premise is not universal (for the middle will always be that which is said negatively of one extreme and affirmatively of the other). Consequently, it is possible for opposites to give a conclusion; not, however, always or in all ways, but rather if the terms below the middle are so related that they are either the same or as a whole to a part. Otherwise, it is impossible, for the premises will in no way be either contraries or opposites.

In the third figure, an affirmative deduction will never be possible from opposite premises for the reason also stated in the case of the first figure, but a negative deduction will be possible both when the terms are universal and when they are not universal. For let B and C stand for science and A for medical knowledge. If, therefore, someone should take all medical knowledge to be a science and no medical knowledge to be a science, then he has taken B to belong to every A and to no C; consequently, some science will not be a science. And similarly also if premise BA is taken as not universal. For if some medical knowledge is a science and, next, no medical knowledge is a science, it results that some science is not a science. When the terms are taken as universal, the premises are contrary, but when one or the other term is particular, the premises are opposites.

We should take note that although it is possible to take opposites in this way (as we have said that every science is good and, next, that none is, or that some is not good), this ordinarily does not escape notice <in an argument>. But it is also possible to deduce one or the other by means of different questions, or to obtain it as was explained in the *Topics*.

And since there are three oppositions of affirmations, it results that opposites can be taken in six ways: 'to every' and 'to no,' or 'to every' and 'not to every,' or 'to some' and 'to no,' and converting this in respect of the terms (for example, taking A to belong to every B and to no C, or (converting the terms) to every C and to no B; or taking it to belong to all of one and not to all of the other, and again converting this with respect to the terms). And similarly also in the case of the third figure. Consequently, it is evident both in how many ways and in which figures it is possible for a deduction through opposite premises to come about.

It is also evident that while it is possible to deduce a true conclusion

15

20

25

30

35

40
64b

5

from falsehoods (as was explained earlier), it is not possible to do so
from opposite premises. For the deduction always comes about con-
10   trary to the subject (for instance, if it is good, the deduction is that it is
not good, or if it is an animal, the deduction is that it is not an animal),
because the deduction is from a contradiction (and the subject terms
are either the same or one is a whole and the other a part).

And it is clear that in trick arguments nothing prevents the contradictory of the assumption following (for instance, that it is not odd if it
15   is odd). For a deduction from opposite premises was contrary: thus, if
one takes such premises, then the contradictory of the assumption will
result.

But one must take note that it is not possible to conclude contraries
from a single deduction in this way (so that the conclusion is that what
is good is not good, or something else of this sort), unless a premise of
20   this kind is taken straightaway (for example, that every animal is white
and not white, and a man is an animal). Instead, one must either take
the contradictory in addition (for example, take in addition the premise that every science is belief; then take the premises that medical
knowledge is a science and that no medical knowledge is belief, in the
25   way that refutations are effected), or else get the contradiction from
two deductions. But to take them so that the things taken are in truth
contraries is not possible in any other way than this, as was said earlier.

B 16   To ask for, or take, the initial thing is (to grasp its family, so to
speak) a kind of failure to demonstrate what is proposed. But this
30   happens in several ways. For it happens if someone has not deduced at
all, or if he has deduced through more unfamiliar things or things
equally unfamiliar, or if he has deduced what is prior through posterior
things (for a demonstration is by means of things both more convincing
and prior). Now, none of these is asking for the initial thing. However,
since some things are of such a nature as to be recognized through
themselves, while others are of such a nature as to be recognized
35   through something else (for the principles are recognized through
themselves, but those below the principles are recognized through
other things), therefore, whenever someone tries to prove through
itself that which is not familiar through itself, he then asks for the
initial thing.

It is possible to do this in such a way as directly to claim what is
proposed; but it is also possible to do so by shifting the argument over

to some other premises from among those which are naturally proved
by what is proposed and to demonstrate the initial statement by means
of these. For example, if someone should prove A through B and B
through C, but C were of such a nature as to be proved by means of A
(for it results that those who deduce in this way prove A through
itself). This is just what those people who think they draw proofs that
there are parallels do: for they do not notice that they themselves take
the sorts of premises which it is not possible to demonstrate if there
are no parallels. Thus, it turns out that those who deduce in this way
are saying that a given thing is so if it is so; but in this way everything
would be familiar through itself, which is impossible.

Therefore, if someone should ask for the premise that A belongs to
B when it is unclear that A belongs to C and also equally unclear that it
belongs to B, then although it is not yet clear whether he is asking for
the initial thing, it is clear that he is not demonstrating (for what is
equally unclear is not the beginning of a demonstration). However, if B
is so related to C as to be the same, or if it is clear that they convert (or
one belongs to the other), then he has asked for the initial thing. For
he could also prove that A belongs to B through those terms, if he
converted it (as it is, this prevents him, but not the type of argument).
But if he did this, he could do what was stated and convert the three of
them. And likewise also if he took B to belong to C, though this was
equally unclear as that A did, then he would not yet be asking for the
initial thing, but he is not demonstrating. However, if A should be the
same as B because A either converts with or follows B, then he is
asking for the initial thing for the same reason. For it has been explained by us what 'asking for the initial thing' means: it is proving
through itself what is not clear through itself.

If, therefore, asking for the initial thing is proving through itself
what is not clear through itself (and this is failing to prove when the
thing being proved and the thing through which someone is proving it
are equally unclear because of either the same things belonging to the
same thing, or the same thing belonging to the same things), then it
would be possible to ask for the initial thing in both ways in the middle
figure and in the third, and in a positive deduction in both the third
figure and the first. And when the conclusion is deduced negatively, it
is possible to ask for the initial thing when the same things are denied
of the same thing; but not possible for both the premises similarly,
because the terms do not convert with respect to negative deductions

40
65a

5

10

15

20

25

30

35

(and likewise also in the middle figure). Asking for the initial thing is a matter of the premises being related in this way in truth in demonstrations, but according to opinion in dialectical arguments.

B 17

40
65b

The phrase 'the falsehood does not follow because of this,' which we are accustomed to make frequent use of in arguments, occurs, first of all, in connection with deductions into an impossibility, when it is intended as the contradiction of something which was being proved by means of a leading away into an impossibility. For unless the argument had come to a contradiction, no one would say 'not as a result of this' (but rather that something false was put among the earlier things); nor will anyone use it of a probative demonstration, since it does not suppose what it contradicts. Moreover, when something is rejected

5

probatively through A, B, and C, it is not possible to say that the deduction has not come about as a result of what was set down. For we say that 'not as a result of this' arises when, although this is taken away, the deduction nonetheless comes to a conclusion, which is not possible in probative deductions (for when the assumption is taken away, then the deduction related to it will not be possible either). It is

10

evident, then, that 'not because of this' is said in connection with deductions into an impossibility, i.e., when the initial assumption is so related to the impossibility that whether this assumption is or is not made, the impossibility nonetheless results.

The most obvious way for the falsehood not to be as a result of the assumption, then, arises when the deduction from the middles to the

15

impossibility is unconnected with the assumption, as has been explained in the *Topics*. For this is what putting a non-cause as the cause is, as, for example, if someone who wished to prove that the diagonal is incommensurable should make use of Zeno's argument that it is not possible to move and should lead away into this impossibility (for the

20

falsehood is not connected in any way at all with the initial assertion).

Another way is if the impossibility should be connected to the assumption but nevertheless should not follow by means of it (for it is possible for this to happen when taking something connected either upwards or downwards). For example, if A is put to belong to B, B to

25

C, and C to D, and this statement, that B belongs to D, should be false. For if B should nonetheless belong to C, and C to D, when A is taken away, then the falsehood would not be by means of the initial assumption. Or again if someone should take something connected upwards, for instance, should take A to belong to B, E to A, and F to E, and it should be false that F belongs to A. For in this way, also, the *30* impossibility would result nonetheless when the initial assumption is taken away.

The impossibility must instead be connected to the initial terms. For this is the way it will be by means of the assumption: in the downwards direction, taking something connected to the term which *35* is predicated (for if it is impossible for A to belong to D, then, when A is taken away there will no longer be a falsehood); or, in the upwards direction, taking something connected to that term of which the other is predicated (for if it is not possible for F to belong to B, then when B is taken away, the impossibility will no longer result). And similarly also when the deductions are privative. *40*

It is evident, then, that when the impossibility is not related to the *66a* initial terms, then the falsehood does not result because of the assumption. Or even in this way, might the falsehood fail always to be by means of the assumption? For if A was put to belong, not to B, but to K, and K to C, and this to D, in this way also the impossibility remains *5* (and similarly also when taking the terms upwards); consequently, since the impossibility results both when this is so and when it is not, it would not be because of the assumption. Or should we take 'when this is not so the falsehood comes about nonetheless' not in this sense, that when something *else* is supposed the impossibility results, but *10* rather that when this is taken away the *same* impossibility is concluded through the remaining premises (since it is really not strange for the same falsehood to result by means of several assumptions, as, for instance, it results that parallels intersect both if the internal angle is greater than the external and if a triangle has more than two right *15* angles)?

A false argument comes about as a result of its first falsehood. For **B 18** every deduction is either from two premises or from more. If it is from two premises, then, it is necessary for one of these (or both) to be false (for a false deduction was not possible from true premises). But if it is from more premises (for example, if C is deduced by means of A and *20* B, and these are deduced by means of D, E, F, and G), then some one of these higher things will be false, and as a result of it, the argument (for A and B are concluded through them). Consequently, the conclusion, that is, the falsehood, follows as a result of some one of these.

B 19

25

In order to avoid being defeated with a deduction, one should take care, when someone is asking for the premises without the conclusion, not to allow the same thing twice in the premises, since we know that a deduction does not come about without a middle and that the middle is what is said several times. And the way one must watch out for the

30 middle with relation to each type of conclusion is evident from a knowledge of what sort of conclusion is proved in each figure. This will not escape our notice because we know what argument we are defending.

But those who are attacking should themselves try to get away with the very thing which we are warning those in the answering role to

35 guard against. This will be possible if, first, the conclusions are not deduced in advance but are still nonevident though the necessary premises have been taken; and next, if the attacker does not ask premises close in order, but as far as possible without middles. For instance, let it be required to conclude A of F (the middle terms are B, C, D, and E). He ought then to ask whether A belongs to B; next, not

40 whether B belongs to C, but whether D belongs to E, and next after that whether B belongs to C, and so on for the rest. And if the deduc-

66b tion should come about from a single middle term, then he should begin from the middle term (for in this way he is most able to escape the notice of the one answering).

B 20

5

Since we know when a deduction comes about, i.e., with what relations of the terms, it is also evident both when a refutation will be possible and when it will not. For it is possible for a refutation to come about either when everything asked gets an affirmative response, or when the answers are given alternately (that is, one negative and another affirmative): there was a deduction when the terms were related both in the latter way and in the former. Consequently, if what is

10 proposed is contrary to the conclusion, then it is necessary for a refutation to come about (for a refutation is a deduction of a contradiction). But if nothing should get an affirmative response, then it is impossible for a refutation to come about. For there was no deduction when all the terms were privative, so that there is not a refutation either (for if there is a refutation, it is necessary for there to be a deduction, though

15 when there is a deduction it is not necessary for there to be a refutation). And likewise also if nothing should be put to belong to something as a whole in the course of the answer (for the determination of a refutation and of a deduction are the same).

Sometimes it happens that, just as we fall into error in connection with the position of the terms, the same error also arises in connection with our beliefs, as, for instance, if it is possible for the same thing to belong to several things primarily and for someone to fail to notice one of these and think the term belongs to none of it, but to know that it belongs to another one. For let A belong to B and to C according to themselves, and these likewise to every D. Now, if someone thinks that A belongs to every B and this to every D, but that A belongs to no C and this to every D, then he will have both knowledge and ignorance about the same thing in the same respect. Next, this is possible if someone should be in error about terms from the same series. For example, if A belongs to B, this belongs to C, and C to D, but he believes that A belongs to every B and next to no C (for he will at the same time both know that it belongs and believe it does not). Based on these premises, then, would he be doing anything but claiming not to believe that very thing which he knows? For in a way he knows that A belongs to C by means of B (that is, as we know the particular by the universal knowledge); consequently, what he knows in a way, that he also claims not to believe at all, which is impossible.

Concerning the case mentioned previously, if the middle term is not from the same series then it is not possible to believe both the premises according to each of the middles (for example, to believe that A belongs to every B and to no C and that these both belong to every D). For it results that the first premise is taken as a contrary, either without qualification or partially. For if someone believes A to belong to everything to which B belongs and knows that B belongs to D, then he also knows that A belongs to D. Consequently, if he thinks, in turn, that A belongs to none of what C belongs to, then he thinks that A does not belong to that which B belongs to some of. But to think that that which he thinks belongs to everything to which B belongs does not, in turn, belong to something to which B belongs is contrary, either without qualification or partially.

It is not possible to believe both the premises in this way, then, but nothing prevents believing only one premise according to each middle term, or both premises according to <only> one, for example, believing that A belongs to every B and B to every D and that A in turn belongs to no C. For this sort of error is similar to the way we are deceived in the case of particular premises. For example, if A belongs to everything to which B belongs and B to every C, then A will belong to every C. Therefore, if someone knows that A belongs to everything to which B belongs, then he also knows that it belongs to C. But nothing prevents him being ignorant that C exists, as, for example, if A is two right angles, B stands for triangle, and C stands for a perceptible triangle: for someone could believe C not to exist, while knowing that

15   every triangle has two right angles, and consequently, he will at the same time know and be ignorant of the same thing. For to know of every triangle that it has angles equal to two right angles is not a simple matter, but rather one <way of knowing it> is in virtue of having universal knowledge, and another way is in virtue of having the particular knowledge. In this way, then, i.e., by means of the universal knowledge, he knows C, that it has two right angles; but he does not

20   know it as by means of the particular knowledge; consequently, he will not possess contrary states of knowledge.

And the argument in the *Meno* that learning is being reminded is also similar: for it never results that people know the particular in advance, but rather that they get the knowledge of the particulars at the same time, by means of the induction, like those who recognize something. For there are some things which we know right away (for

25   example, we know that something <has angles equal> to two right angles, if we see that it is a triangle, and similarly also in the other cases). In virtue of the universal knowledge, then, we contemplate the particulars, but we do not know them in virtue of their peculiar knowledge. Consequently, it is also possible to be in error concerning these, but not contrarily: instead it is possible to have the universal knowl-

30   edge and be in error about the particular.

Similarly also, therefore, in the cases mentioned previously: for error in accordance with a middle term is not contrary to knowledge according to a deduction, nor is the belief according to each of the middles contrary to it. And nothing prevents someone who knows both that A belongs to the whole of B, and that this, in turn, belongs to C, from thinking that A does not belong to C (for example, knowing that every

35   female mule is infertile and that this is a female mule but thinking that this is pregnant): for he does not know that A belongs to C, if he does not simultaneously reflect on the term related to each one. Consequently, it is also clear that if he knows one but does not know the other, then he will be in error.

And this is just what the relation is of universal to particular knowl-

67b   edges. For we do not know any perceptible thing when it is outside our perception, not even if we happen to have perceived it before, except as in virtue of possessing universal knowledge, or in virtue of possess-

ing, but not exercising, its peculiar knowledge. For 'to know' can be used with three meanings: as knowing by means of universal knowledge, knowing by means of the peculiar knowledge of something, or as knowing by means of exercising knowledge; and consequently 'to be   5
in error' also has the same number of meanings. Nothing then prevents someone both knowing and being in error about the same thing (although not contrarily), which is also what happens to the man who knows a premise according to each kind of knowledge and has not previously examined them: for in believing that the female mule is pregnant, he does not have knowledge in the sense of exercising it, nor indeed does he have the error contrary to the knowledge as a re-   10
sult of his belief (for the error contrary to universal knowledge is a deduction).

He who believes the essence of good is the essence of bad will believe that the essence of good is the same as the essence of bad. For let A stand for the essence of good, B stand for the essence of bad, and C again stand for the essence of good. Then, since he believes B and C   15
are the same, he will believe C to be B, and next B likewise to be A, so that he will also believe C to be A. For just as if it were true that B is predicated of what C is predicated of, and A predicated of what B is predicated of, it would also be true that A is predicated of C, thus also in the case of believing. And similarly also in the case of being <the   20
same as>: for if C and B are the same, and again B and A, then C would be the same as A. Consequently, it will be the same also in the case of holding an opinion. Is this then necessary, if someone grants the first thing? But perhaps this is false, that someone believes the essence of good is the essence of bad, unless incidentally (for it is pos-   25
sible to believe this in many ways). This should be examined better.

When the extremes convert, it is necessary for the middle also to   **B 22**
convert in relation to both of them. For if A is proved to belong to C through B, and if it converts, that is, C belongs to everything to which A does, then B also converts with A, that is, B will belong to every-   30
thing to which A belongs through the middle term C. And C will convert with B through A as the middle term.

And likewise in the case of not belonging. For example, if B belongs to C and A does not belong to B, then neither will A belong to C. If B then converts with A, C will also convert with A. For let B not belong   35
to A: therefore, neither will C (for B belonged to every C). And if C converts with B, then it will also convert with A (for of that of all of

which B is true, C is also true). And if C converts in relation to A, then B will also convert with it. For C belongs to that to which B belongs; but C does not belong to what A belongs to. The latter alone begins from the conclusion, while the other cases are not similar to the case of the positive deduction.

68a

Next, if A and B convert, and C and D likewise, and it is necessary for either A or C to belong to everything, then B and D will also be so related that one or the other of them belongs to everything. For since B belongs to that to which A belongs, and D belongs to that to which C belongs, and either A or C belongs to everything but not both together, then it is evident that either B or D also belongs to everything but not both together | (two deductions are combined). Next, if either A or B and either C or D belong to everything, but they cannot belong at the same time, then, if A and C convert, B and D also convert. For if B does not belong to something to which D belongs, it is clear that A belongs to it; and if A belongs, then also C does (for they convert). Consequently, C and D belong to it together: but this is impossible.| For example, if what is ungenerated is imperishable and what is imperishable is ungenerated, then it is necessary for what is generated to be perishable and for what is perishable to be generated. | But when A belongs to the whole of B and of C and is predicated of nothing else, and B belongs to every C, then it is necessary for A and B to convert. For since A is said only of B and C, and B is predicated both of itself and of C, it is evident that B will also be said of all of those things of which A is said except for A itself. Next, when A and B belong to the whole of C and C converts with B, then it is necessary for A to belong to every B (for since A belongs to every C, and C belongs to B because of converting, then A also belongs to every B).

5

8
11

15
16
8

10
16

20

When A and B are two opposites, of which A is preferable to B, and D is preferable in the same way to its opposite C, then if <the combination of> A and C is preferable to <the combination of> B and D, then A is preferable to D. For A is as much to be pursued as B is to be fled (for they are opposites), and C is similarly related to D (for these are also opposed). Therefore, if A is equally desirable as D, then B is equally avoidable as C (for each is similarly related to each, the desirable to the avoidable). Consequently also <the combination of> both, A and C, would be equally desirable as <the combination of> B and D. But since, in fact, it is more desirable, A cannot be equally desirable as D (for then B and D would also be equally desirable <as A and D>). And if D were preferable to A, then B would be less to be

25

30

avoided than C (for the lesser is opposed to the lesser). And the *35*
greater good and lesser evil is preferable to the lesser good and greater
evil; the combination of B and D, therefore, would be preferable to A
and C. But in fact it is not. Therefore, A is preferable to D, and thus C
is less to be avoided than B.

Now, if every lover would choose, when it comes to his love, for
<his beloved> to be of a mind to grant favors (A) and not to grant   *40*
them (which C stands for) rather than to grant favors (which D stands
for) and not to be of a mind to grant them (which B stands for), then it   *68b*
is clear that A, being of such a mind, is preferable to granting favors.
To receive affection, therefore, is preferable to intercourse, when it
comes to his love. Therefore, love is more of affection than of intercourse. But if it is chiefly of this, then this is also its goal. Therefore,   *5*
intercourse is either not the goal at all or is so for the sake of receiving
affection. (The other appetites and arts are also like this.)

It is evident, then, how terms are related with respect to conversions   **B 23**
and with respect to being preferable or more to be avoided. But now, it
should be explained that not only dialectical and demonstrative deduc-   *10*
tions come about through the figures previously mentioned, but also
rhetorical ones, and absolutely any form of conviction whatever, arising
from whatever discipline. For we have conviction about anything either
through deduction or from induction.

Induction, then—that is, a deduction from induction—is deducing   *15*
one extreme to belong to the middle through the other extreme, for
example, if B is the middle for A and C, proving A to belong to B by
means of C (for this is how we produce inductions). For instance, let A
be long-lived, B stand for not having bile, and C stand for a particular   *20*
long-lived thing, as a man, a horse, or a mule. Now, A belongs to the
whole C (for every bileless thing is long-lived); but B (not having bile)
belongs to every C. If, then, C converts with B and the middle term
does not reach beyond the extreme, then it is necessary for A to
belong to B: for it has been proved earlier that if two terms belong to   *25*
the same thing and the extreme converts with one of them, then the
other one of the predicates will also belong to the term that converts
with it. (But one must understand C as composed of every one of the
particulars: for induction is through them all.)

This is the sort of deduction that is possible of a primary and unmid-   *30*
dled premise (for the deduction of those premises of which there is a
middle term is by means of the middle term; but the deduction of

those of which there is not a middle term is by means of induction).
And in a way, induction is the opposite of deduction, for deduction
proves the first extreme to belong to the third term through the middle, while induction proves the first extreme to belong to the middle
35   through the third. By nature, then, the deduction through the middle
term is prior and more familiar, but the deduction through induction is
clearer to us.

B 24   It is an example when the <first> extreme is proved to belong to
the middle by means of something similar to the third extreme. And it
40   must be familiar both that the middle belongs to the third and that the
first belongs to the thing similar to the third. For instance, let A be
69a   evil, B choosing to make war against neighbors, C stand for Athenians
against Thebans, D stand for Thebans against Phocians. If, therefore,
we should wish to prove that making war on the Thebans is evil, it
should be taken that making war against one's neighbors is evil. Conviction about this comes from similar cases, for instance, that the war
5   against the Phocians was evil for the Thebans. Then, since making war
against one's neighbors is evil, and against the Thebans is against
neighbors, it is evident that making war against the Thebans is evil.
The premises that B belongs to C and to D, then, are evident (for both
are waging a war against one's neighbors), and also the premise that
10   A belongs to D (for the war against the Phocians did not go to the
advantage of the Thebans); but that A belongs to B will be proved
through D. And it would be the same way also if conviction about the
middle in relation to the extreme should come about by means of
several similar things.
     It is evident, then, that an example is neither as a part to a whole nor
15   as a whole to a part, but rather as a part to a part, when both are below
the same thing but one of them is familiar. But it differs from induction in that induction proves the extreme to belong to the middle from
all the individuals and does not connect the deduction to the extreme,
while example both does connect it and does not prove from them all.

B 25
20   It is leading away when it is clear that the first term belongs to the
middle and unclear that the middle belongs to the third, though nevertheless equally convincing as the conclusion, or more so; or, next, if
the middles between the last term and the middle are few (for in all
these ways it happens that we are closer to scientific understanding).

For example, let A be teachable, B stand for science, and C justice. *25*
That science is teachable, then, is obvious, but it is unclear whether
virtue is a science. If, therefore, BC is equally convincing as AC, or
more so, it is a leading away (for it is closer to scientific understanding
because of taking something in addition, as we previously did not have
scientific understanding of AC). Or next, it is leading away if the
middle terms between B and C are few (for in this way also it is closer *30*
to scientific understanding). For instance, if D should be 'to be
squared,' E stands for rectilinear figure, F stands for circle. If there
should only be one middle term of E and F, to wit, for a rectilinear
figure together with lunes to become equal to a circle, then it would
be close to knowing. But when BC is not more convincing than AC
and the middles are not few either, then I do not call it leading away. *35*
And neither when BC is unmiddled: for this sort of case is scientific
understanding.

An objection is a premise contrary to a premise. It differs from a   **B 26**
premise in that an objection can be particular, while a premise either
cannot be particular at all, or not in universal deductions. An objection *69b*
is brought in two ways and through two figures: in two ways because
every objection is either universal or particular, and from two figures
because they are brought as premises opposite to a premise, and opposites are concluded only in the first and third figures. For when   *5*
someone claims that it belongs to every, we object either that it belongs to none, or not to some; of these, 'to none' is from the first figure
and 'not to some' from the last.

For instance, let A represent there being a single science and B
stand for contraries. Now, when someone proposes that there is a single science of contraries, someone objects either that in general there *10*
is not the same science of opposites, and contraries are opposites (so
that the first figure comes about); or, he objects that there is not a
single science of the known and the unknown (and this is the third
figure: for of C, known and unknown, being contraries is true but
there being a single science of them is false). Next, it is the same way *15*
in the case of a privative premise. For if someone claims that there is
not a single science of contraries, we say that there is the same science
either of all opposites, or of some contraries (for instance of healthy
and sick): 'of every,' then, is from the first figure, and 'of some' from
the third.

For without qualification in all cases, the person who is objecting

20   universally must state a contradiction in relation to the universal one of the terms proposed (for instance, if someone should claim that there is not the same science of contraries, he must object by saying that there is a single science of all opposites). And in this way, it must be the first figure (for the term that is universal in relation to the original subject becomes the middle term). But someone objecting with a particular statement must state a contradiction in relation to something with respect to which the term the premise is said of is universal, for in-

25   stance, that there is not the same science of known and unknown (for 'contraries' is universal in relation to these). And the third figure comes about, for the middle term is what is taken in part, i.e., 'known and unknown.'

   Those premises from which it is possible to deduce a contrary result are those from which we also try to state objections. For this reason,

30   we also bring them only from these figures, for only in them are there opposite deductions (through the middle figure, it was not possible to deduce affirmatively). And in addition, an objection through the mid- dle figure would require more argument, as, for example, if someone should not grant that A belongs to B because C does not follow it. For

35   this would be clear through other premises; but an objection should not turn aside into other matters, but rather the other premise should be evident at once. [For which reason also a sign is not possible from this figure alone.]

   There should also be an examination concerning other objections (such as those from the contrary, and what is like, and those according

70a   to reputation) and whether it is possible to get a particular objection from the first figure or a privative objection from the middle figure.

B 27   A likelihood and a sign are not the same thing; rather, a likelihood is an accepted premise (for what people know for the most part hap-

5   pens or does not happen thus, or is or is not, this is a likelihood, for example, 'people hate those they envy' or 'people show affection for the ones they love.' A sign, however, is supposed to be either a neces- sary or an accepted demonstrative premise. For whatever is such that if it is, a certain thing is, or if it happened earlier or later the thing in question would have happened, that is a sign of this thing's happening

10   or being. (An enthymeme is a deduction from likelihoods or signs.)

   A sign may be taken in three ways, corresponding to the ways the middle term in the figures is taken: for it is taken either as in the first figure, or as in the middle, or as in the third. For instance, proving that a woman is pregnant because she has milk is from the first figure, for the middle term is having milk (let A stand for being pregnant, B having milk, C for a woman). But 'The wise are good, for Pittakos was good' is through the last figure. A stands for good, B stands for the wise, C stands for Pittakos. So it is true to predicate both A and B of C, except that people do not state the latter premise because they know it, though they do take the former. And 'She is pregnant because she is pale' is intended to be through the middle figure: for since paleness follows pregnant women and also follows this woman, people think it has been proved that she is pregnant. A stands for pale, B stands for being pregnant, C stands for a woman.

If one premise alone is stated, then, it is only a sign, but if the other premise is also taken in addition, it is a deduction. For instance, 'Pittakos is generous, for the ambitious are generous, and Pittakos is ambitious.' Or again, 'The wise are good, for Pittakos was good, but also wise.' In this way, then, they become deductions. However, the one through the first figure is binding if it is true (for it is universal), while the one through the last is nonbinding even if the conclusion is true, because the deduction is neither universal nor directed to the point (for even if Pittakos is good, the other wise men need not be so for this reason). And the deduction through the middle figure is always and in all ways nonbinding, for a deduction never comes about when the terms are related in this way. For it is not the case that if a pregnant woman is pale and this woman here is also pale, then it is necessary for this woman to be pregnant. The truth, then, can occur in all signs, but they have the differences stated.

Now, should signs be divided in this way, so that the <kind of> sign which is a middle term is taken to be evidence (for we say that what makes us know is evidence, and the middle is most like this)? Or should the ones from the extremes be called a sign and those from the middle term be called evidence (for that which is through the first figure is most accepted and most true)?

Recognizing natures is possible, if someone concedes that the body and the soul are altered simultaneously by such affections as are natural (of course, someone who has learned music has altered his soul in a certain way; but this condition is not one of those in us by nature, but instead it is things like passions and appetites that are natural motions). Now, if this be granted, and in addition that there is a single sign of a single thing, and if we are able to grasp the affection and the sign peculiar to each kind of animal, then we will be able to recognize

15

20

25

30

35

70b

5

10

natures. For if there is some affection belonging peculiarly to an indi-
visible kind, as courage to lions, then there must also be some sign (for
body and soul are assumed to be affected together with each other).
Let this be having large extremities (which may also belong, though
not universally, to other kinds of animals: for the sign is peculiar in this
sense, that it is [a] peculiar [affection] for the whole kind, but not a
peculiarity of a single thing, as we usually use this term). Now, this
may be found also in another kind of animal, i.e., a man may be
courageous, or some other animal. Therefore, it will have the sign, for
we assumed there was one sign of one affection. Consequently, if
these things are so, and we are able to collect such signs from those
animals which have only some one peculiar affection (and each has a
sign, since it must have a single sign), then we will be able to recognize natures.

But if the whole kind has two peculiar affections (as, for example,
the lion is courageous and generous), then how can we tell which one
of the signs that follow peculiarly is the sign of which affection? Perhaps if both belong to something else but not as a whole, and among
those cases in which each belongs to something but not entirely, some
have one sign and not the other (for if something is courageous but not
generous and possesses a certain one of the two signs, then it is clear
that this is also the sign of courage in the case of the lion).

Now, recognizing natures is by means of a deduction in the first
figure in which the middle converts with the first extreme but reaches
beyond the third and does not convert with it. For example, courage is
A, B stands for large extremities, C is lion. Now, B belongs to everything to which C belongs, but also to others. But A belongs to everything to which B belongs and to no others, but instead it converts (if it
does not, then there will not be a single sign of a single thing).

NOTES TO BOOK A

Chapter 1

24a10–15. 'Demonstration' (*apodeixis*) is the subject of the first Book of the *Posterior Analytics*; in the *Prior*, especially Book A, the attention is instead on 'deduction' (*sullogismos*). However, at the beginning of A 4 (25b26–31), Aristotle tells us that since a demonstration is a species of deduction, an account of the former should first treat the latter. The entire *Analytics* would then form a single treatise on demonstration, with the *Prior* serving as a prelude to the *Posterior*. This traditional view of the relationship of the parts of the *Analytics* is in my view confirmed by the internal structure of the work, and by the fact that the only treatise in the entire Aristotelian *corpus* which makes any substantive use of the results of the *Prior Analytics* is the *Posterior*.

The Greek commentators find a puzzle in the grammar of the first sentence, which appears to ask two questions: (1) what is his inquiry *about* (*peri ti*), and (2) what is it *of* (*tinos*). Since the pronoun is in the accusative case in the first instance and in the genitive case in the second, these are answered by phrases marked only by their case endings: (1) <about> demonstration (accusative case), (2) <of> demonstrative science (genitive case). The question what faculty an area of inquiry falls under would be an unusual one for Aristotle to raise: the only remotely comparable cases are the discussions in *Metaphysics* III, VI, VII, concerning whether there is such a science as first philosophy. Alexander, who develops this line of interpretation (9.17–23), suggests that the ability with which we understand demonstration in general is the same as the ability with which we understand demonstrations in particular cases. But whatever may be the merits of this approach, I think it goes beyond what we can reasonably be sure of. My translation tries to remain non-committal. See Brunschwig *1981* for a persuasive defense of another interpretation.

24a11. 'science': there are many reasons for objecting to this as a translation of *epistēmē*. I have stuck by it because all the alternatives have even more difficulties. (But the reader should regard it as a translator's term of art; its modern associations, while not wholly irrelevant to Aristotle, are to be resisted.) In ordinary Greek, *epistēmē* can be rendered comfortably as 'knowledge,' 'skill,' or sometimes 'art.' In Plato and Aristotle, it takes on more precise senses laden with epistemic distinctions. The translation 'understanding' has acquired some popularity in recent years (see Barnes *1975*, Burnyeat *1981*), but this is in my judgment even more awkward in some contexts (there is no adjective which stands to it as 'scientific' to 'science,' and it is forced to talk about, for instance, arithmetic as an 'understanding'). In a number of places, where convenient, I adopt the more expansive translation 'scientific

understanding'; in others, when it occurs only as a part of an example, I make
it 'knowledge.'

24a12. 'Deduction' translates *sullogismos*. The English word 'syllogism' ultimately derives, not simply from this Greek word, but from Aristotle's use of it
in the *Prior Analytics*; somewhat paradoxically, it is for this reason a poor
translation. The history of logic has created such a strong association between
'syllogism' and the particular forms of argument studied in A 4–22 that the
modern reader cannot help being confused by its presence. Aristotle does not
intend to *define* the word *sullogismos* to have a sense as narrow as 'syllogism'
(see the notes on the definition in 24b18–22), nor was it his own coinage.
Etymologically, a *sullogismos* is the result of an act of 'syllogizing' (*sullogizesthai*). The latter verb is the compound of *sun-* ('together') and *logizesthai*
('calculate'), so that the nontechnical meaning of *sullogizesthai* is 'reckon up' or
'compute' (a sense found as early as Herodotus), and a *sullogismos* is a 'com-
putation.' Plato uses both *sullogismos* and *sullogizesthai*, sometimes in connection with drawing conclusions in an argument, though often with the broader
sense of reckoning or calculating. I follow Corcoran's suggestion in translating
it 'deduction.'

24a14. 'What we mean by': literally, 'what we call' (*ti legomen*). This is
Aristotle's usual way to introduce the technical senses of terms.

24a16. 'sentence' (*logos*): this term has a range of meaning too broad to be
captured with a uniform English rendering. It can also mean 'discourse' (e.g.,
an entire speech, or even something the length of the *Iliad*).

24a16–b15. The term *protasis*, translated here as 'premise,' is difficult to
render in English without prejudice. It is not found before Aristotle at all,
although he uses it in the *Topics* in a way that suggests that it was at least
current in Academic circles and probably was not his coinage. Translators have
favored two choices: 'proposition' and 'premise.' The first, if interpreted to
mean a sentence with a truth value, would be most consonant with the definition Aristotle gives here; the second, which emphasizes a certain role in an
argument, fits more naturally with the actual use of the term in the bulk of the
Prior Analytics. Since argumentative role is so often in question, I have elected
to use 'premise,' even though this sometimes makes Aristotle talk about premises without arguments (though he never refers to the *conclusion* of an argument as a *protasis*). See also the Note on 42a38.

In fact, what has happened is that Aristotle's terminology has evolved over
time. In the *Topics*, a *protasis* is defined as a type of question (I.10, 104a8–11),
and the etymological connection with the root verb *proteinein* ('hold out,' 'put
forward,' 'propose') is strong: in the context of question-and-answer argument,
a *protasis* is what one offers for acceptance to one's opponent. However, Aristotle came to understand that contained in every such 'premise' there is (at least
implicitly) a declarative sentence (or a pair consisting of a sentence and its
negation: see the note below on 24a25). He also developed a theory according
to which every such sentence either affirms or denies one thing of one thing,

so that a single assertion always contains a single subject and a single predicate. (In *On Interpretation*, he explains more complex sentences either as having complex subjects or predicates or as really equivalent to groups of sentences.) In the *Analytics*, logical form and argumentative role are not entirely separated; in *On Interpretation*, the separation is more complete, and Aristotle defines the expression 'declarative sentence' (*logos apophantikos*) in the way he here defines *protasis*. (See more on this below.)

Aristotle distinguishes three varieties of premise: *universal* (*kath'holou*: literally, 'of a whole'), *particular* (*en merei*, *kata meros*: literally, 'in part,' 'with respect to a part'), and *indeterminate* (*ahoristos*). The definition given here appeals to verbal markers (or their absence, in the case of indeterminates), but Aristotle does not rely exclusively on forms of expression (see, for instance, the remarks about the ambiguities of some of his modal expressions in the Notes on A 14, A 16, A 17). The locutions 'belongs to some,' etc., are peculiar to Aristotle and not at all everyday Greek. (See the Introduction for a brief discussion of Aristotle's language.)

24a20−21. 'without a universal or a particular': Aristotle has just defined 'universal' and 'particular' with certain phrases ('to every,' 'to some'). Thus, here 'a universal' or 'a particular' would just be an occurrence of some one of these phrases.

24a21−22. The two examples of indeterminate premises given here are actually quite different in form. 'Pleasure is not a good' is a straightforward categorical sentence with a simple subject and predicate but no indication of quantity. 'The science of contraries is the same' is more problematic. Aristotle uses this sentence, drawn from philosophical discussions of his time, more than once in the *Prior Analytics* (most extensively in B 26, 69b8−29; see also the Notes on 48b4−7, in which passage Aristotle seems to maintain that this very example is actually not a predication). Its meaning, more fully, is 'The science which has one of a pair of contraries as its object also has the other member of the pair as its object.' From a modern viewpoint, this has a somewhat complex structure: most contemporary logicians would see it as an assertion of the identity of two things each identified by a definite description. However, to judge by B 26, Aristotle sees it as having as its subject 'contraries' and as its predicate 'there is a single science of them' (see 69b8−9). So interpreted, it is presumably regarded here as indeterminate because it does not say 'of every <pair of> contraries' or 'of some <pair of> contraries.'

24a22−b15. This section reflects the complex background of the term *protasis*. Aristotle distinguishes *demonstrative* (*apodeiktikē*), *dialectical* and *deductive* (*sullogistikē*) premises. As in the definition of *protasis* itself, syntactical and pragmatic elements are combined in these distinctions. Underlying them all is the notion of a *contradiction* (*antiphasis*), that is, the contradictory pair consisting of an affirmation and the corresponding denial. Pragmatically, a demonstrative premise is the 'taking' (*lēpsis*) of one or the other member of such a pair (specifically, the 'true and primary' one), while a dialectical premise is the 'asking' (*erōtēsis*) of the contradictory pair itself: in effect, such a pair put as a question. The fundamental point is that the demonstrator and the dialectical arguer do different things: one asserts premises while the other gets them as answers to questions. According to the *Topics*, dialectical premises are questions which are 'proposed in the manner of a contradiction' (*kat' antiphasin proteinomena*), that is, admit a yes-or-no answer (see, e.g., *Top.* I.10, 104a14, 104a21, 104a26). The dialectician's skill includes the ability to take either reply and build an argument from it. Accordingly, in its dialectical origins *protasis* means 'question presented in the course of an argument.' By contrast, the demonstrator 'takes,' or assumes, premises as the basis for a proof. The critical difference between dialectical and demonstrative premises, then, is *how* the dialectician and the demonstrator respectively 'get' (*lambanein*) their premises (Alexander, 13.18—19, says that the difference is 'the way of taking'). In this passage, Aristotle isolates the element both practices have in common, which is 'one of the parts of the contradiction,' i.e., a simple affirmation or denial, and notes that even in the dialectical case, conclusions are drawn by 'taking something either to belong or not to belong'; the deductive premise is then defined in this neutral way. Apart from these argumentative roles, Aristotle also differentiates demonstrative and dialectical premises on semantic and epistemic grounds. Semantically, demonstrative premises must be true, though dialectical premises need not be. Epistemically, dialectical premises must be 'accepted' or 'respected' (*endoxos*) and 'apparent.' Although the present chapter does not describe the epistemic status of demonstrative premises, Aristotle discusses this at length in *Posterior Analytics* I.2 and briefly in *Topics* I.1 (100a27—b22). The notion of deductive premise here is the result of a distillation from all these contexts of a fundamental core meaning, excluding any epistemic properties; this is an important innovation of the *Prior Analytics*.

24a27.   'Something with respect to something' or 'something about something' (*ti kata tinos*) is a common phrase in Aristotle to indicate predication.

24b10—11.   'getting answers . . . deducing': the verb *punthanesthai*, which I translate 'getting answers,' means 'inquire,' 'learn through hearing.' Aristotle uses it in the logical works interchangeably with 'ask' (*erōtan*) and 'attack' (*epicheirein*) to apply to that participant in a formal dialectical exchange who asks questions in order to secure premises from which to refute the thesis which the other participant has undertaken to defend. This other participant is said to 'answer' (*apokrinesthai*) or to 'maintain' (*hupechein*).

24b12.   'in the *Topics*': I.10—11.

24b16—18.   The last phrase of this definition, 'whether or not "is" or "is not" is added or divides them' (*ē prostithemenou ē dihairoumenou tou einai ē mē einai*) is an occasion of difficulty. Some interpreters, appealing to *Metaphysics* VI.4, suppose that Aristotle means that affirmative and negative statements respectively 'combine' (*suntithenai*) and 'divide' (*dihaireisthai*) their predicate and subject terms. But Aristotle does not elsewhere oppose *prostithenai* to *dihaireisthai*: he opposes *dihaireisthai* to *suntithenai* ('put together'), *sunhaptein* ('join together'), *sumplekesthai* ('weave together'), or *sunkeisthai* ('put together'), *dihairesis* to *sunthesis* or *sumplokē* (see *Met*. VI.4, IX.10 for a good sampling). *Prostithenai* always carries the suggestion of adding, rather than combining or joining; it is usually opposed to *aphairein*, which (as far as I know) is never used of the relation between predicate and subject in a denial. The grammar of the whole genitive-absolute phrase is also problematic. If we take the verbs as passive in sense, then it is unclear what it means to talk about 'being' or 'not being' being divided. If, in accordance with the attempt to associate the passage with the views in *Met*. VI.4, we try to associate *prostithemenou* with *einai* and *dihairoumenou* with *mē einai*, then we get something like "if 'being' adds or 'not being' divides," which (even apart from the fact that 'adds' and 'combines' are not synonyms) is grammatically implausible.

Ross takes Aristotle to be talking about the linguistic structure of a *protasis*, so that he only means to call attention to the copula (whether affirmative or negative) as something added to the two terms. If we follow his suggestion of striking out 'or dividing,' the phrase means 'when "is" or "is not" is added' and is then most plausibly taken as modifying 'predicated.' I think this is on the right track, but it would be better to avoid a textual change. The problem is to figure out just what Aristotle thinks of the copula. In fact, a copula is not an essential constituent of a predication in Greek, since one can accomplish the same result by simple concatenation, as in *pasa hēdonē agathon* ('every pleasure a good'), *hēdonē tis agathon* ('some pleasure a good'), to take two random examples from Aristotle (25a9, 25a11). If the copula is present, it might be positioned between subject and predicate, as in English, or added in front (e.g., *esti tis hēdonē agathon*, 'is some pleasure a good'). If the copula comes between the terms, we could plausibly describe it as 'dividing' them; if it is placed in front, we could say it has been 'juxtaposed' or 'added' (both acceptable senses for *prostithenai*). For that matter, in a predication without copula, we could say that one term is 'juxtaposed' or 'put next' (*prostithetai*) to the other. Now, Aristotle hardly ever uses *einai* to express a predication in the exposition of his theory of deductions (A 1-22), though it is somewhat more common later in the *Prior Analytics*. He might, therefore, want to say something at this point about the fact that 'is' and 'is not' may appear in premises in addition to the terms and the indicators of quantity. What he has just said is that a premise 'breaks up' (*dialuetai*) into terms, and thus, by implication, a premise is made up *only* of terms: what then do we say about 'is' and 'is not,' should they be present? Aristotle's response, I think, is that the copula is to be regarded as a purely optional occurrence: the premise still is composed of just its terms, whether or not a copula is present.

24b18-22. This celebrated definition appears in almost exactly the same form in *Topics* I.1, 100a25-27 (cf. *Sophistical Refutations* 1, 164b27-165a2, *Rhetoric* I.2, 1356b16-18). It has been the subject of enormous discussion by commentators ancient and modern, and I cannot summarize the range of these opinions here. (See the notes above on 24a12-13 for the history of the word *sullogismos.*) The definition is clearly intended to apply to a wide range of arguments: Aristotle does not regard *sullogismoi* as merely one species of valid argument. The exact range of the term is less certain, but it is surely less wide than 'valid argument' for most present-day logicians. Alexander points out that, according to the definition, the 'thing which results' (the conclusion) must be distinct from any of the 'things taken' (the premises) and that the plural 'certain things being supposed' implies that there must be more than one premise. Thus, arguments containing the conclusion as a premise and arguments with only one premise would not be *sullogismoi* (As Alexander tells us, the Stoics included such arguments in their logic). Also note in passing that arguments with no premises and arguments with multiple conclusions (both notions which have been used by some modern logicians) seem to fall outside Aristotle's definition. Nothing in the definition, however, requires that a deduction have exactly two premises nor that it fall into one of the figures Aristotle defines in A 4–6. Aristotle does, in fact, hold that every deduction whatsoever can be transformed into argument in one of the forms of A 4–6, or at any rate a compound of such arguments, but this is for him the result of a lengthy proof, not merely a matter of definition.

On the expression 'certain things having been supposed' (*tethentōn tinōn*) see the 'Note on the Translation' in the Introduction (*tethentōn*, 'having been supposed,' is the aorist passive participle of *tithenai*). Given the mathematical flavor of much of the *Prior Analytics*, it is probably worth observing in passing that the phrase 'a discourse in which, certain things having been supposed' (*logos en hōi tethentōn tinōn*) can be given a different interpretation: *logos* might mean 'relationship,' and the phrase might mean 'a relationship such that when some things are put in it.'

Aristotle rather surprisingly glosses 'resulting through them' with 'needing no further *term*': we might expect him to say 'no further *premise*.'

24b22–26.   There has been considerable debate among modern scholars about the notion of a 'perfect' or 'complete' (*teleios*) deduction: good discussions of the problem may be found in Patzig *1968*, 43–87; Corcoran *1973, 1974b*. I translate this term as 'complete' because Aristotle contrasts such deductions with 'incomplete' (*atelēs*) or 'potential' (*dunatos*) ones and speaks of 'completing' (*perainesthai, teleiousthai, epiteleisthai*) the latter (but the honorific associations of 'perfect' would not be out of place here). It is clear enough that Aristotle has in mind the difference between a valid argument and an *evidently* valid argument. Alexander stresses the notion that completing is bringing to light what is 'implicit' (*enhuparchei*) or potential in the premises (23.17–24.18, 24.9–11). In modern terms, Corcoran compares the distinction to that between a valid premise-conclusion argument (that is, a set of premises and a conclusion which they imply) and a deduction (that is, an extended discourse which makes it evident that a certain conclusion is implied by certain premises). Note that once again, Aristotle refers to terms where we would expect him to mention premises.

24b26—30. This passage contains what later became known as the *dictum de omni et nullo*, upon which, according to the traditional interpretation, the theory of deduction (and thus all logic) was supposed to be based. Łukasiewicz dismissed this claim as hopelessly confused. But Aristotle himself appeals to this definition as a justification of perfect deductions (e.g., 25b39—40, 26a24—25). There may appear to be a confusion here: if a complete deduction is *evidently* valid, then what need is there for a proof to make its validity evident? And besides, as Aristotle himself argues in *Posterior Analytics* I.3, any system of proofs must rest on some principles not subject to proof, so that it is a mark of ignorance to look for a principle to support every claim (cf. *Metaphysics* IV.3, 1005b2—5). But what Aristotle is doing here is analogous to a modern formal theorist justifying the axioms of a system by offering a model which makes those axioms evidently true. There is nothing inconsistent about his offering justifications for deductions which he characterizes as perfect.

In fact, 25b26—29 is not the only passage which functions in this way in the *Prior Analytics*. Twice in A 14 (32b40—33a5 and 33a24—25), Aristotle justifies his claims that certain combinations of modally qualified premises yield complete deductions by appealing to a definition of possibility (in this case the definition discussed at length in A 13). If indeed these definitions function as semantical principles of meaning and truth, then it is appropriate that Aristotle should have distinct principles defining the truth of simple assertions and assertions of possibility.

24b27. 'every one': the Greek is just 'of every' (*kata pantos*). I am trying to preserve the parallel in Aristotle's language without resorting to the barbarous and unintelligible 'predicated of every of another.'

24b30. 'likewise': not that 'of every' and 'of none' are synonymous, of course, but that 'of none' is defined like 'of every,' *mutatis mutandis* (presumably something like 'none of the subject . . . of which . . . *can* be said').

Chapter 2

25a1. 'Now': the word used here (*epei*) means 'since,' but Aristotle often begins summaries or enumerations this way.

25a3. 'Prefix' (*prosrhēsis*) (which occurs here for the only time in Aristotle's works) refers to the indicators of the three modalities. In other writers, it means 'designation' or 'form of address.'

25a5—13. This section states the conversion properties of nonmodal premises. A proof of these is offered immediately following, in 25a14—26. It is significant that in this opening statement, Aristotle's language is entirely metalinguistic, even at the cost of some awkwardness of expression: that is, he *describes* classes of premises rather than exemplifying them or exhibiting their structures. By contrast, in the proof which follows, he displays premise *forms*, using letters in place of actual terms. As Frede *1974* suggests, Aristotle almost certainly borrows this latter practice from the mathematics of his time: letters are a proof device, not (as Łukasiewicz thought) part of his logical theory itself. Other similarities to mathematical proof are the use of third-person imperatives in 'setting out' the terms (as at 25a14); the recapitulations of results proved after the proof (noted below); and possibly some appeal to diagrams (on which see Einarson *1936*, Rose *1968*).

25a6–8.   Although Aristotle's initial definitions distinguish premises into 'affirmative' (*kataphatikos*) and 'negative' (*apophatikos*), he regularly varies each of these terms with a synonym: 'positive' (*katēgorikos*) in place of affirmative, 'privative' (*sterētikos*) in place of 'negative.' These pairs of terms appear to be completely synonymous in the *Prior Analytics*, but Aristotle takes care to differentiate 'negative' and 'privative' in other contexts: the latter term is derived from *sterēsis*, 'privation,' which is one of the four types of opposites enumerated in various places (the opposite of a privation is a 'possession,' *hexis*). Since this terminological peculiarity may be of significance for the study of Aristotle's development, I have regularly translated *katēgorikos* as 'positive' and *sterētikos* as 'privative.'

25a14–26.   Aristotle's proofs of the conversion properties rest on the initial proof of the convertibility of *e* sentences. This has, from early times, been challenged as circular since it appears to be an indirect proof with an embedded third-figure deduction (either *Disamis* or *Darapti*), for the proofs of which Aristotle later (A 6) relies in turn on the very conversion properties being proved here. More probably, as Philoponus and Patzig suggest, Aristotle is using the procedure he occasionally calls 'proof through the setting out' (*dia tēs ektheseōs*), which bears a certain resemblance to the existential instantiation of modern predicate logic. Given that *A* belongs to some *B*, we may assign a name (say '*C*') to those *B*s to which *A* belongs; but if *A* belongs to every *C*, then there are some *A*s (viz., *C*) which are *B*s; thus, *B* belongs to some *A*. (Aristotle himself does not mention this procedure until A 6, and he never discusses it in detail. For a survey of interpretations, see Smith *1982b*.) But if this is what he is doing, then it is somewhat odd that he bases his proof of *i*-convertibility on the indirect proof of *e*-convertibility, since, as Alexander notes (33.23ff) a proof of *i*-convertibility by *ekthesis* is almost immediate.

Chapter 3

25a27–36.   Aristotle expresses necessity in several ways: he says that a predicate 'belongs of necessity' (*ex anankēs huparchei*) or that 'it is necessary <for a subject> to belong' (*anankē huparchein*), and he says that a premise or conclusion is necessary (*anankaios*). He also uses negated idioms of possibility for necessary negative premises, e.g., 'it is not possible for A to belong to any B.' As the latter type of expression indicates, Aristotle's usage is somewhat flexible, and one probably ought not make too much of the particular idiom used on a particular occasion. However, I have generally tried to associate a single English idiom with each of his Greek constructions.

25a37—b25. In Aristotle's Greek, 'is possible' is expressed with a single verb (*endechesthai*, or less commonly *enchōrein*: I translate these two verbs identically). It is sometimes difficult to reflect this in idiomatic English. Aristotle expresses possibility by saying 'it is possible for A to belong to B' (*to A endechetai tōi B huparchein*); He also describes premises as 'possible' (*endechomenon*) or 'in possibility' (*en tōi endechesthai*). As in other cases, he frequently abbreviates. For instance, we often find the compressed form 'A to B is possible' (*to A endechetai tōi B*), in which 'to belong' is omitted. I have generally filled these out where the meaning is unambiguous.

This discussion of the conversion of possible premises should be compared with the later discussion in A 13. Despite the prospective reference here and a retrospective reference in that later chapter (32b1—3), Aristotle's doctrine in the two passages seems inconsistent or confused. (See the notes on A 13 for attempts at resolving these problems.)

Chapter 4

This Chapter contains the exposition of the first-figure deductions (although we do not hear of the first figure, or indeed of figures at all, until the very last words of the Chapter).

25b26—28. 'Having made these determinations': Aristotle's announced project is quite grand in scope: to determine 'through what premises, when, and how *every deduction* comes about.' As the remainder of Book A makes clear, Aristotle is using 'deduction' in its officially defined sense, in which it applies to an extremely large class of arguments. The subsequent structure of the treatise reflects the project stated here: Aristotle first undertakes to determine all the ways an argument 'in the figures' can come about (Chapters 4—22) and then argues that every deduction without qualification comes about through an argument in one of these figures (Chapter 23). 'Through what premises': compare 43a16—17, 46b38.

25b32—35. This joint statement of *Barbara* and *Celarent* is couched in almost deliberately awkward terminology. The proof, brief as it is, follows in 25b37—26a1.

25b35—37. Aristotle's definitions of 'major,' 'middle,' and 'minor' have caused commentators great difficulty. The problem is that they rely on two incompatible sorts of criteria: both syntactical (the position of the term in Aristotle's standard form for expressing a deduction in the relevant figure) and semantical (the relative extensions of terms). Since the semantical criterion is sensible only for a deduction in *Barbara* with true premises, much ingenuity has been expended on making Aristotle consistent. It is better to suppose that, here as elsewhere, Aristotle is simply less careful than he should be.

25b39—40. Aristotle explicitly appeals to his definition of 'predicated of every/of no' at 24b27—30, as he does again at 26a24 and 26a27: despite the opinions of some commentators, there is no doubt that he takes that earlier passage as a definitional principle of his system.

26a5−9. 'For it is possible': Here, Aristotle uses for the first time his peculiar countermodel technique of term-triple pairs for showing that a certain pattern of premises does not, of itself, give a conclusion. Simply put, he provides two triples of terms concerning each of which premises of the form in question are true, but such that the 'major' term of the first is universally true of the 'minor,' while the 'major' of the second is universally false of its 'minor.' Given Aristotle's understanding of the categoricals, it follows that for any putative form of conclusion, an example can be constructed which has true premises of the appropriate forms and a false conclusion of that form; thus, no deduction results based on the form alone. In this place, Aristotle precedes the technique with a brief explanation. Łukasiewicz (*1957*, 72) objects to Aristotle's introduction of 'concrete terms' into logic and develops an axiomatized rejection procedure to fill what he regards as a gap here (for a similar point, see Geach *1972*, 298−299). Similarly, Ross complains that the use of counterexamples is not 'completely satisfactory' because it introduces extra-logical knowledge. But there is nothing logically flawed in Aristotle's procedure: in fact, countermodels are the paradigmatic means of proving invalidity for modern logicians. The discussion in Patzig *1968*, 168−192, is extremely useful; see also Lear *1980*, 54−61, 70−75, for criticisms of Geach, Ross, and Łukasiewicz.

26a21−23. This definition of 'major' and 'minor' is purely semantical, unlike the partly syntactical definition at 25b35−37.

26a27−28. 'For it has also been defined': here again, Aristotle associates proof by appeal to a definition with the completeness of a deduction.

26b3. The phrase 'whether an indeterminate . . . is taken' (*adihoristou te kai en merei lēphthentos*), which occurs earlier at 26a30, follows here also in most manuscripts. Ross, noting that it makes no sense in this location, omits it as probably a copyist's error.

26b21. Aristotle sometimes uses 'interval' (*diastēma*) as a synonym for 'premise.' The term apparently derives from the Greek mathematical theory of music, as do many of Aristotle's technical terms in the logical treatises. For a discussion, see Einarson *1936*.

26b26−33. The discussion of the first figure ends with a summary of the results proved, as do all the subsequent discussions. Aristotle regularly stresses three points: (1) which deductions in the figure are complete (here, all of them are); (2) how the deductions are completed (here, since all are complete, it is 'through the premises initially taken,' i.e., through *only* those premises); (3) which 'problems' are 'proved' in the figure, i.e., which types of categorical sentences are found as conclusions. In the *Prior Analytics*, 'problem' invariably has this sense (cf. 43a18, 43b34, 45a34−36, 44a37, 45a34−36, 45b21, 46b39, 47b10−13, 50a8, 50b5, 61a34, 63b13−19). In origin, however, it is a technical term of dialectic (like 'premise'). For a discussion of its background, see the Note on 42b27.

Chapter 5

26b34−39. Aristotle's definitions of the second figure and the meanings within it of 'major,' 'minor,' and 'middle' are clearly syntactical in character, with no mention of the relative extensions of terms (the middle is 'outside the extremes and is first in position' in that it is mentioned first in his standard formulation).

27a1−25. Here, for the first time, Aristotle contrasts a complete deduction with a 'potential' (*dunatos*) one. The phrase suggests that an incomplete deduction is only potentially a deduction. Corcoran *1973* argues that this fits well with the view that a 'completed' or 'perfected' incomplete deduction is a valid premise-conclusion argument supplemented by deductive steps which make its validity evident (see also Smiley *1973*). We also find here the first example of the process of completing an incomplete deduction. For a discussion of his procedure, see the Introduction.

27a10. 'neither will N belong to any X': the manuscripts generally have 'neither will X belong to any N'; Alexander also read this in his text and was puzzled by it. In Greek, the two phrases are very close (*to X tōi N* versus *tōi X to N*), so that a mistake here is easy (as anyone who has attentively read long stretches of this type of prose can affirm). Since Aristotle's practice is almost always to state in advance the conclusion he is about to deduce, I have switched the variables. (But see also Patzig *1968*, 140 n.18.)

27a14−15. Aristotle mentions here for the first time the procedure of 'leading to an impossibility' (*agein/apagein eis to adunaton*) as an alternate way of completing an incomplete deduction (for a discussion of his procedure here, see the Introduction). The technique is introduced and used without explanation or discussion, most probably because Aristotle expected it to be familiar to his audience from its use in Greek mathematics and in philosophical arguments (notably by the Eleatics). There is a problem about the relationship of his *use* of proof through impossibility here to his *discussions* of the technique in A 23 (41a21−37), A 29, and B 11−14. In those later passages, he claims that whatever can be deduced or proved through impossibility can also be deduced or proved 'probatively' (*deiktikōs*), i.e., in modern terms, directly (see especially A 29, B 14, and the associated Notes). This would imply that proof through impossibility is simply a redundant technique, and in these places that appears to be just what Aristotle is urging. But although completions through impossibility are sometimes mentioned as mere alternatives (as here), in other cases they are essential (as in the completion of second-figure *Baroco*, 27a36−b3, or third-figure *Bocardo*, 28b17−20). In A 45, in fact, Aristotle's intent appears to be to establish that proof through impossibility is the *only* means for completing these very cases.

We might try to reconcile these passages with the suggestion that A 23, A 29, and B 11−14 are all concerned with the analysis of actual arguments, using the theory of deductions in the figures as a means for that analysis, whereas in

A 4–22 we are establishing that theory itself. A modern logician might be tempted to see here a distinction between deductions within the system and results proved about the system (in modern terms, *metatheoretical* results). Aristotle could then be seen as holding that, within the system itself and its applications, proof through impossibility is redundant, even though it is essential for the establishment of the system. But however much kinship one may see between Aristotle and his twentieth-century successors in logical theory, it seems to me very difficult to find grounds for imputing such a distinction to him.

27a16–18. 'not from the initial premises alone, but from others': all Aristotle actually says is 'from the initial <things>' (*ek tōn ex archēs*) and 'from others' (*ex allōn*), but he always describes a deduction as 'from' (*ek*) its premises. The 'other premises' are the intermediate steps in the deduction, which Aristotle regards as distinct premises (cf. 28a4–7, and the associated Notes). The 'necessary result' (*to anankaion*: literally, 'the necessary thing' or 'the necessity') is the conclusion: since Aristotle regards the conclusion as necessary because it necessarily results from the premises, he often uses this designation for it. And, since there is a deduction only if there is a conclusion, Aristotle frequently speaks as if the properties of the conclusion of a deduction are properties of the deduction, or conversely, and takes the conclusion as representing or summing up the deduction itself. Thus, here it is the *conclusion* that is 'completed.'

27a36–b3. In this proof of *Baroco* Aristotle gives us an explicit completion through impossibility for the first time (though he does not identify it as such). It is noteworthy that he runs through the proof twice: once with the *o* premise stated in the form 'M does not belong to some X,' and once with it in the form 'M does not belong to every X.' (He does not, however, undertake to show that both forms of *o conclusion* follow when there is no *o premise*, as in the case of *Festino*.) Compare B 11, 62a9–10.

27b20–23. Here Aristotle introduces a sophisticated modification of his countermodel technique, which he calls 'proof from the indeterminate.' The difficulty is that Aristotle usually treats the particular categoricals as strictly particular: 'A belongs to some B' means 'A belongs to some *but not every* B.' But if we apply such an interpretation to the particular affirmative premise here, we in effect have the premises of *Festino*: as a result, it is not possible to find 'terms for belonging' (that is, terms satisfying the premises and with the major universally true of the minor) under this interpretation. Aristotle's response is that: (1) the truth of 'M belongs to no X' is sufficient for the truth of 'M does not belong to some X'; (2) it has already been shown that 'M belongs to no N and to no X' gives no conclusion. He thus invokes the principle that if a set of premises yields no conclusion, then the set that results from it when one of the premises is replaced by a weaker premise also yields no conclusion.

Aristotle's designation of this procedure as 'from the indeterminate' indicates what the fundamental meaning of 'indeterminate' is. Any given particular sentence is made true both by the circumstances under which it is *strictly* true ('some but not every') and by the circumstances under which its corresponding universal sentence is true. Consequently, if we know only that a certain particular sentence is true, then we do not in virtue of that knowledge know which of these circumstances obtains. What is 'indeterminate' about particular sentences in these cases is that the truth of the sentence does not imply that a *unique* state of affairs (as Aristotle sees it) holds. We find a similar use of 'indefinite' (*ahoristos*) in the case of possible premises: see the Notes on 32b4−22.

27b20. 'must be proved' (*deikteon*): The verb *deiknunai* can have the weak sense 'show' (or even 'point out') as well as the strong sense 'prove.' However, in the *Prior Analytics*, Aristotle commonly uses it interchangeably with 'demonstrate' (*apodeiknusthai*). The stronger sense is quite appropriate here: showing that certain types of premises do not yield a conclusion is just as much a matter of proof as showing that others do. (But see the Note on 38b21−22.)

27b21. 'There was not a deduction' (*ouk ēn sullogismos*): i.e., '*as we have seen*, there was not a deduction.' The use of the past (imperfect) tense to indicate a result previously established is extremely common in the *Prior Analytics*.

28a4−7. In explaining why the second-figure moods are incomplete, Aristotle gives us a better idea what it is that must be 'taken in addition' to complete an argument: either intermediate steps which are 'implicit in' the premises or assumptions for proofs through impossibility (*reductio* hypotheses). In either case, it is evidently the appearance of a statement in the completed deduction which counts as 'taking' it. See the notes below on A 23, A 29, B 14 concerning difficulties in Aristotle's understanding of argument through impossibility.

The word I translate 'are implicit in' is *enhuparchei* (literally 'belong in,' 'be present in,' 'exist in'). This word has a number of uses in Aristotle and sometimes has a technical force associated with the constituents of a definition. However, it also is used in the biological works of the incomplete parts of immature animals and in other contexts where it clearly suggests something present but not yet discernible, developed, or brought out.

Chapter 6

28a10−15. These definitions of the third figure and the meanings in it of 'major,' 'minor,' and 'middle' are essentially syntactical, as in the case of the second figure.

28a22−26. Aristotle again alludes to the possibility of a proof through impossibility, though he does not give the details, and introduces his third proof technique: 'through the setting-out' (*tōi ekthesthai*). For a discussion of this procedure see the Introduction.

28a28. 'of necessity does not belong': the position of the phrase 'of necessity' in this sentence appears to indicate, not just that the conclusion follows of necessity, but that it is itself a necessary conclusion (in the discussion of modally qualified deductions in A 8–22, exactly the same sort of phrase would probably have just that meaning). Aristotle does not mean that, of course (see the Notes below on 31a6–7, 36a17–18).

28b17–21. Aristotle explicitly gives a proof through impossibility for *Bocardo* and then notes that this can be avoided by a procedure evidently identical with the proof 'through the setting-out' used for *Darapti* (28a22–26). The present passage suggests that Aristotle may have regarded proof through *ekthesis* as a (preferable?) alternative to proof through impossibility. The two procedures are often mentioned together; later, in A 9, Aristotle appeals to *ekthesis* expressly because an attempted proof through impossibility fails. (In Smith *1983* I show that a formal version of Aristotle's deductive theory lacking proof through impossibility, but containing *ekthesis*, is still complete. Although there is no direct evidence that Aristotle realized this, it is at least conceivable that he saw *ekthesis* as a way of avoiding proof through impossibility.)

Note his characterization of the proof as 'a leading away' (*apagōgē*). This term, which might be Latinized as 'abduction' or 'deduction,' is usually associated in his usage with proof through impossibility, but it is defined in a more general way in B 25 as the substitution of one 'problem' for another (see the Notes on that chapter).

Chapter 7

29a19–29. Aristotle here adds a note that effectively brings the fourth-figure moods *Fesapo*, *Fresison* into his system. His basic point is a simple one: *e* premises are convertible into *e* premises, while any affirmative premise can be converted to yield an *i* premise (which is again convertible), and, therefore, any combination of an *e* premise and an affirmative premise can be worked around by means of conversions into the form of *Ferio*. In all those cases in which no deduction resulted in the three figures, this is because the resulting conversions have the effect of reversing major and minor terms; Aristotle takes note of this fact here.

29a30–39. The result announced here, together with the claim which follows, are among the most important conclusions Aristotle draws from his study of deductions. Briefly, his claim is that if a deduction in one of the figures is possible at all, then it is possible through a first-figure deduction. He appears to take this to mean that every deduction can be *transformed into* a first-figure deduction. This passage contrasts completing a deduction 'probatively' (*deiktikōs*) and completing it through an impossibility. The natural, modern equivalent of *deiktikōs* here is 'directly,' but I have chosen 'probatively' in order to preserve the connection with *deiknunai*, 'prove' (and, in any event, Aristotle has no equivalent for 'indirect'). See further the discussion of A 23, 40b25. The word translated 'come to a conclusion' (*perainesthai*) could also be translated 'come to a goal' or 'be completed,' and thus it could have the same meaning as 'complete' (*teleiousthai*).

29b1−25. Aristotle closes by proving an important result about his system (in modern terminology, a metatheorem): every deduction in the three figures can be completed by means of the two universal deductions of the first figure. The argument is economically organized: (1) this already holds for the second-figure deductions; (2) the first-figure particular deductions can be completed through second-figure universal deductions (which are, in turn, completed by the two universal first-figure deductions); (3) the third-figure deductions are all completed through first-figure deductions (and the particular deductions of the first figure have just been shown to be completable through the universal first-figure deductions). This is a sophisticated result which, in its elegance of presentation, is evidence of Aristotle's level of technical expertise. I argue in Smith *1986* that this result is of crucial importance in one of the central arguments in the *Posterior Analytics*.

Here, for the first time, Aristotle refers to 'leading back' (*anagein*) one deduction into another. The process is indistinguishable from the proofs of Chapters 4−6, but the new verb reinforces the suggestion that the process is one of analysis into elements or principles. Possibly, this passage was added some time after Aristotle originally composed Chapters 1−6, as Łukasiewicz and Bocheński proposed. The traditional translation of *anagein* is 'reduce,' which masks the real sense of the word. On this procedure, see the Notes on 46b40−47a2.

29b26−28. The deductions which 'prove something to belong or not to belong' are those which contain no modal terms (in other words, everything considered so far). The point of the phrase is to contrast these results with those about to be established in the next part of the treatise.

Chapter 8

Chapter 8 begins the exposition of deductions with modally qualified premises. Aristotle first discusses combinations of two necessary premises (8) and of one necessary and one assertoric premise (9−11) in all the figures. He then discusses combinations involving possible premises, treating each figure separately: first two possible premises, then one possible and one assertoric premise, then one possible and one necessary premise. The first figure is studied in 14−16, the second in 17−19, and the third in 20−22. Interspersed in the treatments of individual deductions and inconcludent premise pairs, there are a brief summary note (12), a second and fuller discussion of the conversion of possible premises (13), a lengthy and difficult discussion related to the use of proof through impossibility in modal cases (15, 34a5−18), and an argument that possible *e* premises do not convert analogously to their assertoric and necessary counterparts (17, 36b35−37a26).

For discussion of Aristotle's idioms for expressing the modalities, see the Notes on A 3. He distinguishes assertoric premises (premises without a modal qualifier) as assertions 'of belonging' (*tou huparchein*), and regularly uses 'belonging' (*huparchon*) in parallel with 'necessary' (*anankaios*) and 'possible' (*en-*

dechomenos) to describe the modal status of premises. The verb *huparchein* can mean 'be the case' as well as 'belong,' and therefore there is a certain ambiguity in all these expressions: we might translate 'since to be the case, to be the case of necessity, and to be possible to be the case are all different . . .' However, the use of *huparchein* in connection with the relation of predicate to subject is enormously frequent in the *Prior Analytics*.

29b33−35. This summary rather crudely implies that the conclusion will have the same modality as the premises: the view Aristotle actually espouses is more complex, since he thinks that in some cases an assertoric conclusion can be deduced from a necessary and a possible premise. This may be the result of carelessness or excessive brevity, but Aristotle misdescribes the results of his study of modal deductions elsewhere (see in particular A 12): an alternative explanation, which I would favor, is that these remarks were written before the details of A 8−22 had been worked out.

29b36−30a3. Aristotle asserts that a deduction with necessary premises and a necessary conclusion is possible if and only if a parallel deduction with assertoric premises and conclusion exists. In general, his account of modally qualified deductions rests on the theory of assertoric deductions: he only investigates those premise combinations which he already knows to yield a conclusion in their assertoric forms (this does not quite hold for possible premises because of 'complementary conversions').

30a2−3. Aristotle appears to claim here that two points suffice to establish the parallel between pairs of assertoric and pairs of necessary premises: (1) (universal) negative premises convert in the same way, whether assertoric or necessary, and (2) the definitions of 'in a whole' and 'of every' from 24b26−30 carry over to this case. Presumably, what he has in mind is that all the proofs offered in 4−6 can be duplicated in the case of necessary premises. But two points are puzzling. First, why does he only mention negative premises, since the conversions of affirmatives are also essential to those earlier proofs? Ross supposes him to have in mind the fact that, whereas necessary *e* premises convert analogously to their assertoric counterparts, possible *e* premises (according to A 17) do not (and he suggests that Aristotle simply does not bother to mention the convertibility of affirmatives). This may be the best answer, but it does take Aristotle to be speaking in an extraordinarily elliptical manner. The second puzzle, and a more serious one, is the fact that Aristotle proceeds at once to give a case for which these arguments are insufficient.

30a3−14. *Baroco* and *Bocardo* are the only deductions for which Aristotle cannot give proofs by conversions; thus, the argument of 29b36−30a3 will not do for their case. As A 45 shows, Aristotle realizes that completion through some means other than conversions is unavoidable for the assertoric deductions in these cases. In A 5 and A 6, he gave proofs through impossibility. However, in the present case he evidently believes that he cannot use such an approach. Accordingly, he resorts to proofs by 'setting-out,' parallel to those given earlier for *Darapti* and *Bocardo*. This again reinforces the notion that such proofs were conceived by him as an alternative to proof through impossibility.

The customary explanation why Aristotle cannot use proof through impossibility is that it requires him to appeal to a deduction with mixed premises (since the denial of a necessary premise is not a necessary premise). For instance, in the proof given in A 5 for *Baroco* (27a36—b1), Aristotle uses the denial of the conclusion and the major premise to deduce the denial of the minor premise. In the present case, this would require a deduction in *Barbara* with possible major and necessary minor, yielding a possible conclusion. Ross says that Aristotle cannot use this because he 'has not yet examined the conditions of validity in mixed syllogisms.' But when Aristotle does get around to this case (A 16, 36a2—7), he tells us that it is a complete deduction: why then does he not appeal to that fact here?

30a12—13. 'is just a certain "that"': this phrase is difficult to put into graceful English, though the sense is clear enough. Aristotle means that if the predicate belongs (or does not belong) of necessity to the 'term set out,' then it likewise belongs (or does not) of necessity to *some* of the original term of which the 'thing set out' was taken as a part. The complication is Aristotle's reliance on the Greek convention of using 'that' (*ekeino*) as we use 'the former': the phrase *ei de kata tou ektethentos estin anankaios, kai kat' ekeinou tinos: to gar ektethen hoper ekeino ti estin* might be rendered 'if it is necessary of what is set out, then it will be necessary of some of the former <sc., the original term in the deduction>: for the thing set out is just a certain "former."' Some commentators take *hoper ekeino ti* here as indicating that the term set out is a sensible particular, rather than a universal, and conclude from this that the procedure of 'setting out' relies in some way on sensory perception. But Aristotle most frequently uses *hoper* as a technical locution to indicate the essence or nature of something: saying that X is *hoper* Y is equivalent to saying that X is essentially a Y. Thus, he need only be saying that 'the thing set out is essentially a certain so-and-so.'

30a14—15. Each proof through setting-out relies on a deduction in the same figure (second or third, respectively) as the original deduction.

Chapter 9

30a15—23. The best-known difficulty with Aristotle's account of modal deductions is that he holds that it is sometimes possible to deduce a necessary conclusion from premises not all of which are necessary. Many proposals have been offered for devising an account of necessity which will accommodate this position or, failing such a defense, for explaining why Aristotle is led to take it: see Łukasiewicz *1957*, 181—208; McCall *1963*; Rescher *1964*; Patzig *1968*, 67—69. But Hintikka (*1973*, 135—146) persuasively argues that all attempts at a formal model are doomed to failure by inconsistencies in Aristotle's basic views about modalities. Note that Aristotle's proof procedure again relies on *ekthesis*, as indicated by the reference to 'some of the Bs' in 30a22.

30a25−28.   Aristotle gives a counter-argument for the case of a necessary minor premise: if we accept the validity of such a deduction, we can derive something which clearly does not follow from the premises (in the case given, we start with premises 'A belongs to every B' and 'B belongs of necessity to every C' and deduce 'A belongs of necessity to some B'). Aristotle's technique is sophisticated and flawless: he notes that the entire *inference* from the original premises to 'A belongs of necessity to some B' is invalid by giving (in the abstract) a counterexample, and then he concludes that the inference *rule* which gave rise to this must, therefore, be invalid.

30a27.   'this is incorrect': Aristotle actually says *pseudos* ('false'), but here, as occasionally elsewhere, he applies it to a rejected rule of inference (see 37a2, 37a22, 48a16, 49a18−22, 52b20, 52b28).

30a35.   Although Aristotle actually says 'the conclusion will not be necessary,' it does not actually *follow* in this case (and similar cases) that the conclusion is not necessary but instead only *fails to follow* that it must be. We may take Aristotle to mean that the inference in this case is invalid.

30a40.   'C is under (*hupo*) B': 'under' in this sort of context usually means either 'within the extension of' or 'a subject of predication of.' In the present case, it has to mean something like 'part of C falls under B,' if Aristotle's argument is to work. He must mean his proof to follow the same form as that in 30a21−23, though his expression is perhaps careless.

30b4.   'Nothing impossible results': that is, nothing impossible *would* result from supposing the conclusion not to be necessary. The reference to the case of 'universal deductions' is to 30a28−33, and what Aristotle gives us there is a proof through terms that a non-necessary conclusion is consistent with premises of the relevant types. This should be seen as the complement to the procedure of deducing an impossibility: we show that a set of premises *is* possible by producing a conceivable case in which all its members are true, and we show that a set of premises is *not* possible by deducing a contradiction from it.

Chapter 10

30b10.   Note that Aristotle readily expresses a negative necessary premise as a denial of possibility. Later this gives rise to ambiguities: see the Notes on A 14, 33a3−5; A 16, 36a17−18; A 17, 36b35−37a32.

30b24.   'Of necessity' is ambiguous: it could mean either that the conclusion which follows *cannot* be 'of necessity' (i.e., necessary), or that it is not of necessity (*need* not be) a necessary conclusion.

30b33.   'Necessary when these things are so' (*toutōn ontōn anankaion*) is Aristotle's usual way of expressing 'hypothetical necessity.' His doctrine on this point is alien to modern logicians: Aristotle takes the sentence 'If *A*, then necessarily *B*' as attributing a kind of necessity ('hypothetical' necessity) to *B*. The point which he makes in the present case actually applies to any assertoric deduction, since (according to his definition) the conclusion of a deduction follows of necessity from the premises: thus, the conclusion of any deduction is necessary-if-the-premises-are-true (cf. the Note on 27a16−18).

31a6−7. 'let it not be possible for A to belong to any B': word for word, 'let A to no B be possible' (*to A tōi B mēdeni endechesthō*). Aristotle often expresses a necessary *e* premise this way (the general form is 'to none is it possible for A to B to belong': *oudeni endechetai to A tōi B huparchein*). An almost identical idiom serves for possible *e* premises: 'it is possible for A to no B to belong' (*endechetai to A oudeni tōi B huparchein*). The crucial distinction is the order of 'is possible' (*endechetai*) and 'to no' (*oudeni/mēdeni*): when *oudeni* precedes *endechetai* the meaning is 'necessarily not to any,' while otherwise the meaning is 'possibly not to any.' (See the Note on 36a17−18.)

Chapter 11

31a31−32. 'C converts to some A' (*antistrephei gar to G tōi A tini*): this very elliptical phrase must mean 'by converting the premise AC, we have the premise that C belongs to some A.'

31b8−9. 'Not possible' here is *mē dunaton*, not *ouk endechomenon*. In Aristotle, *dunatos* usually has the stronger sense 'potential,' but in the *Prior Analytics*, we occasionally find it as a synonym for *endechomenos*. Here, it is not actually applied to a premise but to a situation. See the Notes on A 13 and on A 15, 34a5−12, for further remarks.

31b15−16. 'the previous one': at 31a24−37.

31b28. 'wakefulness': this is not an attributive term but (in modern terminology) an abstract singular term; as Aristotle himself notes later in A 34, we do not predicate 'wakefulness' of something, but rather 'awake' (as indeed we find a few lines later in the example). What this indicates, I think, is that Aristotle regards premises and deductions, not as essentially linguistic entities composed of certain words, but as relationships of nonlinguistic terms. On such an understanding, to say that X is awake does indeed predicate wakefulness of X, though it does not predicate 'wakefulness' of X (that would be done by a sentence like 'X is wakefulness'). In the background of this is a theory of the subjects of predication as 'paronymous' with—'named after'—the qualities or properties attributed to them. Thus, things which possess wakefulness are called, not wakefulness, but 'awake,' and things which possess equality are called, not equality, but 'equal.' Aristotle only gives us sketches of this picture in the treatises (*Categories* 8, 10a28−b7; *Topics* II.2, 109a39−b12; *Eudemian Ethics* III.1, 1228a36); it is reminiscent of Plato (compare, e.g., *Parmenides* 130e5−131a2, where things which partake of Forms are said to be 'called after the name' of the Form). See the Notes on A 34 for a fuller discussion.

31b29−30. Aristotle actually expresses the second premise and the conclusion very elliptically here: 'the A to C is possible and the A to B is not necessary' (*to de A tōi G endechetai, kai to A tōi B ouk anankaion*). They can be filled out from the specification of the case at 31b20−23.

31b39–40. 'the proofs': all Aristotle says is 'the rest' but the phrase is parallel to others in which he adds 'proof' (*deixis*) or 'demonstration' (*apodeixis*).

Chapter 12

The results summarized in A 12 complement those of A 24. Aristotle's point is more difficult to state clearly than at first appears; since he has already argued that a number of deductions with one necessary and one assertoric premise have assertoric conclusions, his first claim seems to be false. Commentators usually take him to presuppose an ordering of modalities in terms of strength, with necessity the strongest and possibility the weakest. He would then be asserting here that a necessary conclusion may follow from premises not all of which are *at least* necessary, whereas an assertoric conclusion only follows from premises all of which are *at least* assertoric. But all Aristotle has considered up to this point is necessary and assertoric premises, and to apply this interpretation to his present assertion is strained. Moreover, it is flatly inconsistent with his later claims (A 16, 36a7–17, 34–39; A 19, 38a16–26, 38b8–13, 25–27; A 22, 40a25–32, 40a40–b8) that some combinations of a necessary and a possible premise yield an assertoric conclusion. A more likely view, in my opinion, is that the passage is simply a defense of the claim that a necessary conclusion can follow from one necessary and one assertoric premise. This was challenged by his associate Theophrastus, who argued instead for the rule that in application to modalities, the conclusion always has the weakest modality exhibited in the premises. A 12 may be an attempt to draw a parallel with the facts about quantity and quality summarized in A 24. Every deduction must have one affirmative premise and one (not necessarily distinct) universal premise; a deduction has a negative conclusion if and only if it has a negative premise; and a deduction with a particular premise has a particular conclusion. These rules might be formulated as remarks about 'the other' premise, e.g., a deduction must have an affirmative premise, and *the other* premise must be like the conclusion (in quality). The parallel cannot be made exact, however. Once again (cf. A 8, 29b33–35), either Aristotle is careless or this passage antedates the full study of modal deductions.

It is worth noting that Aristotle refers to this same thesis in the *Rhetoric* (I.2, 1357a27–30) and cites the *Analytics*. If the reference is indeed Aristotle's and not the work of a later reconciling editor, this suggests that the *Rhetoric* antedates the final form of Book A.

Chapter 13

32a18–21. As given in this passage, Aristotle's official definition of the senses of 'to be possible' (*endechesthai*) and 'possible' (*to endechomenon*) is 'not necessary but not entailing anything impossible.' The remark that 'we call the necessary possible only equivocally' is an acknowledgment that there is a sense of 'possible' (to wit, 'not impossible') which applies to what is necessary but that Aristotle is not defining that sense here. (Subsequently, Aristotle often refers to possibility in this sense as possibility 'not according to our definition.') Aristotle's definition seems to be logically equivalent to 'neither necessary nor impossible.' Waterlow *1982* 16−17 explains its prolix form by proposing that it offers a test for possibility rather than a definition of it; she argues further that the test is linked to the notion of 'relative temporalized' possibility which she claims is fundamental for Aristotle.

32a21−29.   These lines, which offer a defense of the preceding definition of 'possible,' are extremely difficult to reconcile with the surrounding text. The style of argument, reminiscent of *On Interpretation* 12, revolves around the determination of the contradictories of expressions (the underlying principle is that the contradictories of equivalent expressions are equivalent). What the argument begins with is plausible enough, but on the definition of 'possible' just given it leads to an absurdity. If what is necessary is not possible, then 'is not possible to belong' follows from 'is necessary to belong.' But if we take Aristotle to mean here that the three expressions he gives entail one another, then 'is necessary not to belong' follows, in turn, from 'is not possible to belong'; therefore, we can derive 'is necessary not to belong,' from its contradictory 'is necessary to belong.' Hintikka *1973* tries to resolve this by interpreting 'follow' (*akolouthein*) as expressing consistency rather than entailment; but even if we accept this (which I think we cannot), we still get the absurd result that 'is necessary to belong' is consistent with its contradictory.

The inference from the equivalence of the three expressions to the equivalence of their contradictories is unproblematic, but it leads only to the conclusion that 'possible' is equivalent to 'not impossible' and 'not necessarily not.' The final conclusion that 'possible' is equivalent to 'not necessary' does not follow from this, nor is it clear how to reconcile it with Aristotle's officially announced definition of possibility. Taken literally, it has the absurd consequence that whatever is impossible is possible (since the impossible is not necessary). However, Aristotle probably means to include the impossible as a species of the 'necessary' in the sense that what is impossible is necessarily *not* the case; so interpreted, the conclusion is a statement of Aristotle's standard doctrine, though its relationship to the premises from which it is supposed to follow is then problematic.

A number of scholars, beginning with Becker *1933*, have argued that these lines are an inept interpolation designed to reconcile Aristotle's definition of possibility here with the wider definition of *On Interpretation* 12. Hintikka, however, defends their authenticity by suggesting that the passage is highly elliptical and 'concise' (*1973* 31−34). On his view, Aristotle is arguing for the definition of 'possible' as 'neither necessary nor impossible' by temporarily discussing some of the consequences of the *alternative* view ('not impossible') in order to show that they are unacceptable. But while this would be an attractive interpretation, it requires us to suppose some very substantive (and in my opinion implausible) ellipses: it is more likely that an interpolator has been at work.

32a29–b1.   Here, Aristotle introduces what Ross calls 'complementary conversion.' As is argued in 32a36–b1, if 'possible' means 'neither necessary nor impossible,' then 'possible to belong' entails 'not necessary to belong,' which, in turn, entails 'possible not to belong.' As a result, we may add or remove 'not' within the scope of 'possible' with preservation of equivalence: 'it is possible for A to belong to B' entails and is entailed by 'it is possible for A not to belong to B.' Aristotle extends this to all the quantified forms of predication. On those which 'have an affirmative form,' cf. the immediately following sentence.

32b1–3.   'as was stated earlier': the reference is to A 3, 25b19–25, where Aristotle asserts that 'is possible,' like 'is,' 'always and in all ways makes an affirmation' of that to which it is added. In that earlier passage, Aristotle said that this claim would be 'proved through what follows': evidently, the present passage is the promised proof.

32b4–22.   Aristotle here distinguishes two cases of 'possible' understood as he has defined it: what generally or naturally happens, and what may equally well happen or not happen. His intent is to defend complementary conversion for both cases. Such a defense would seem to be otiose in view of the simple general argument of 32a36–b1, but Aristotle's method yields an insight into his understanding of logic: he regards the present argument as giving the *reason why* possible premises of each of the two sorts admit complementary conversion. This is probably related to his general position that 'verbal' (*logikos*) arguments cannot actually explain *why* something is so, even though they may establish *that* it is.

The Greek commentators take Aristotle's distinction to have an important statistical component: what is 'for the most part' is what happens more often than not in a given case, whereas what is 'indefinite' is what happens or fails to happen with equal frequency (both Alexander and Philoponus suppose that this category also includes what generally does *not* happen, the complement of what generally happens). But there is evidence, both in the present passage and elsewhere in Aristotle's works, that the distinction rests on very different grounds.

'For the most part' (*hōs epi to polu*) in Aristotle means 'what ordinarily happens in the usual course of events'; his designation of it as 'natural to belong' (*pephukos huparchein*) reflects the fact that for him such things have their origins in the natures of things. The 'indeterminate' (*ahoristos*) type of possibility actually embraces two very different cases. Aristotle first refers to what is 'capable' (*dunaton*) of being thus or not thus. This term reflects a view of capacities as occurrent properties of things (that is, potentialities) and is closely bound up with Aristotle's doctrines concerning potentiality and actuality. He often tells us that capacities of this sort are intrinsically two-sided:

the capacity to walk, for instance, is identically the capacity not to walk. (In some places, e.g., *Metaphysics* IX.5, he distinguishes 'rational' capacities, which are two-sided in this way, from 'irrational' ones, which are not.) His second case, however, is quite distinct: a coincidence of unrelated events. This is often the meaning of 'by chance' (*apo tuchēs*). A fundamental distinction between these two last cases is that whereas the existence of a capacity provides an explanation for its exercise (as an animal's capacity to walk is part of the explanation why it is now walking), coincidences which happen 'by chance' simply have no explanation.

Another important difference could be described as a matter of the semantic basis of the modality. Aristotle tends to regard possibilities strictly so called as matters of the inherence of properties in subjects: 'This man is possibly grey' asserts, of this man, that he possesses the potentiality or capacity of being grey. However, such an analysis does not fit well with logically complex propositions such as 'It is possible that it will thunder while I am walking' or 'It is possible that when I go to the well to get a drink as a result of eating spicy food, I will be killed by passing brigands' (cf. Freeland *1986*). We might put the point by saying that Aristotle tends to think of modalities only in *de re* terms; the *de dicto* analysis required for these latter examples is generally suppressed in his considerations. (For Aristotle's views on chance, see *Metaphysics* VI.3.)

The term 'indefinite' (*ahoristos*) is close in meaning to 'indeterminate' (*adihoristos*). As noted above (27b20–23), Aristotle regards particular premises as 'indeterminate' in the sense that the conditions under which they are true are complex. Similarly, 'indefinite' possibilities here are defined disjunctively: *either* what is potential *or* what is coincidental. In general, faced with a type of sentence which is true under several distinct types of circumstances, Aristotle tends to regard one set of circumstances as the primary truth condition, and others as secondary but not ruled out. Thus, he sometimes says that a deduction leads to a possible conclusion when he means that it leads to a non-impossible one, although it does not lead to one possible in accordance with his official definition. A modern logician (and many a commentator on the *Prior Analytics*) would define two distinct technical terms for these two senses of 'possible' instead of retaining a single one and noting that it sometimes means one thing and sometimes means another.

32b18–22. In the *Posterior Analytics*, the term 'science' (*epistēmē*) is applied to the epistemic state resulting from demonstration or proof (*apodeixis*). On Aristotle's conception, there can be science in this strict sense only of what is necessarily true, not of 'what can be otherwise.' The present point indicates how limited the range of Aristotelian science is when so understood: what happens this way or that without any natural proclivity one way or the other would include a great many of the particular facts about the world. The middle term is 'disorderly' (*ataktos*) in that it fails to have any determinate (and hence knowable) relationship with the extremes. The term *ataktos* has military associations, as do a number of Aristotle's technical terms concerning proof. Compare the use of *tattesthai*, 'be arranged,' at 32b3 above, and the much-discussed military metaphor of the 'rout' in *Posterior Analytics* II.19, 100a12ff.

32b23. 'These things will be better determined': it does not appear that Aristotle ever does so anywhere in his surviving works.

32b24–37. In this passage, Aristotle makes another distinction of sense of possible premises. The ambiguity he intends to call attention to only arises when both terms of the premise are general terms, and even then it is more believable as an ambiguity of Aristotle's preferred locution *kath' hou to B, to A endechetai*—word for word, in roughly equivalent English, 'it is possible that A of what B is of.' Aristotle seems to be concerned by the similarity of this construction to such locutions as 'A is predicated of what B is' (*kath' hou to B, to A katēgoreitai*), which he often uses to express categorical sentences. Here, he rather surprisingly opts for interpreting the sentence in question as 'it is possible that A <is predicated> of what *it is possible* that B <is predicated> of.' One consideration may be the need to have a single middle term in a deduction. If we regard 'it is possible that A to B' as attributing the predicate 'possibly A' to B, and likewise 'it is possible that B to C' as attributing the predicate 'possibly B' to C, then these two premises appear to contain four terms: 'possibly A,' 'B,' 'possibly B,' and 'C.' On the interpretation which Aristotle advocates, there are only three terms, but they are 'possibly A,' 'possibly B,' and 'possibly C.'

Aristotle's reference to 'those the same in form' (*homoioschēmones*) is puzzling. The Greek commentators take him to mean that the interpretation of 'A possibly belongs to B' as 'A possibly belongs to what B actually belongs' leads to a deduction with one possible and one assertoric premise. But there is only one premise here. What Aristotle may be thinking of is something akin to the procedure of *ekthesis*.

32b25–31. 'Now . . . Therefore, it is evident that': The 'therefore' (*epei*) actually occurs at the beginning of this long sentence, in 32b25. I move it, for clarity, to the beginning of the clause it explains, beginning at 32b31.

32b32–33. We could read the text here as saying either 'it is possible that B of what it is *possible* that C' or 'it is possible that B of what it *is* <sc. true> that C.' Owen and Jenkinson explicitly opt for the latter, Tredennick for the former. In view of the preceding discussion, Tredennick probably is right, but I have tried to preserve the ambiguity.

Chapter 14

32b39. 'There will be a complete deduction': as in the case of assertoric first-figure deductions (25b39–40, 26a24), Aristotle defends this claim by asserting that it follows from a definition (here, the definition just offered in 32b25–37).

33a3−5. Aristotle similarly appeals to the definition of possibility to establish the negative case. Here, he gives us a fuller form of the definition he is relying on, which combines the definition at 32b35−37 with the definition of 'belongs to every/to no' at 24b28−30: note the reference to 'not leaving out' (*mēden apoleipein*) anything which is under the subject term. The context clearly requires that the awkward expression 'for it to be possible that not A of that of which it is possible that B' (*kath' hou to B endechetai, to A mē endechesthai*) must mean 'for everything to which it is possible that B belongs, it is possible that A does not belong to it.' However, this is made particularly difficult by the phrase *to A mē endechesthai*: 'A not to be possible' or 'it not to be possible that A.' The 'not' (*mē*) would naturally be taken to go with the infinitive 'to be possible,' giving the phrase the sense 'for it *not to be possible* that A,' which is clearly not what Aristotle intends here. This may explain why some manuscripts omit 'not,' even though this makes Aristotle suddenly revert to discussion of the first deduction (32b38−40). But it is quite in accordance with Aristotle's way of abbreviating premises to let 'A not' mean 'A not to belong' (*to A mē huparchein*). I translate with a modern-sounding 'not A.'

33a12−13. 'negation' (*apophasis*) here clearly means 'sign of negation' (i.e., the word 'not').

33a17−20. Aristotle's remark here implies that at least some combinations of universal premises in the first figure do not yield a conclusion. But he has adopted it as a rule that a possible universal affirmative and its corresponding universal negative are, in effect, equivalent: it follows that *any* combination of universal premises in the first figure entails *both* a universal affirmative *and* a universal negative conclusion. Aristotle only lists four of these eight possible cases: *aaa, eae, aee, eee*. The reason may be that the other four (*aae, eaa, aea, eea*) all contradict the rules he later states (A 24) that an affirmative conclusion follows from two affirmative premises and a negative conclusion from an affirmative and a negative premise. (But that should not disturb him, since he has already maintained that all possible premises are really affirmative in form.) Similarly, in discussing first-figure deductions with particular premises, he should again include all possible combinations (*aii, eii, aoi, eoi, aio, eio, aoo, eoo*): he mentions only *aii, eio, aoo* (and perhaps implies *eoo*).

33a21−22. The text as it stands here claims that *any* combination of a possible universal major premise and a possible particular minor in the first figure yields a complete deduction; but as Waitz and Ross point out, 33a27−34 says that *aoi* is an *incomplete* deduction. These commentators accordingly doubt the authenticity of 'complete' here. But Aristotle justifies the deduction *aii* (and *eao*) by appeal to a definition, which he normally does only for complete deductions (cf. Alexander 169.17−170.16, 173.17−19); it seems more likely that 'complete' is intended only to apply to these two and that Aristotle has simply made an error.

Once again, Aristotle does not list all the deductions his principles imply: he gives *aii, eio, aoi*, and omits *aoo, aio, eii, eoi, eoo*.

33a26–27. 'It must be possible' (*anankē . . . endechesthai*): the 'must' is that which Aristotle regularly attaches to the conclusion of any deduction).

33a29. 'similarly related in position' (*tēi de thesei homoiōs echōsin*): that is, if the major premise is universal (as it was at 33a21–23).

33a31. 'evident': i.e., complete (cf. 24b24).

33a38–40. 'extending beyond (*huperteinein*) . . . predicated of equally many things (*ep' isōn*)': this language, with its stress on the extensions of terms, is relatively uncommon in the presentation of the theory of deductions (but compare its use in B 23, 68b23–29). The proof which follows may be regarded as a variant on *ekthesis*, a technique which also emphasizes the extensions of terms.

33a40–b3. The argument is as follows. Suppose first that A possibly belongs to some B (and therefore, possibly not to some B). It is consistent with this that A not belong (even possibly) to every B; suppose, then, that it does not, and let C belong to just those Bs to which A does not (even possibly) belong (which is consistent with the assumptions). Now, by hypothesis, it is not possible for A to belong to any C; therefore, both 'A possibly to every C' and 'A possibly to some C' are false. Moreover, by the equivalence of complementary converses, both 'A possibly to no C' and 'A possibly not to some C' are false. Thus, in the case imagined, *every* premise expressing possibility with A as predicate and C as subject is false, and thus no such sentence follows from the original premises. If the argument is to work, it is necessary to suppose (as I have) that C is the part of B to which A *necessarily* does not belong.

The argument is presented in a slightly convoluted manner. Aristotle first says 'let C be taken to be . . .' and then begins a clause with 'for' in which he spells out the proof: it is more natural to put 'for' at the beginning, as I have.

33b3–17. Aristotle's text suggests that he gives a countermodel proof by terms as an alternative. In fact, this argument is much more complete than the preceding argument, since it undertakes to show that a necessary and an assertoric conclusion also do not follow. Aristotle now returns to the double-triplet countermodels in application to modal deductions: here, the two 'conclusions' must be a *necessary* universal affirmative and a *necessary* universal negative. Aristotle takes some care in pointing out how such a countermodel rules out every conceivable conclusion: (1) the necessary affirmative rules out an assertoric or necessary negative conclusion, and the necessary negative likewise rules out an assertoric or necessary affirmative one; (2) the necessary affirmative rules out an *affirmative* possible conclusion (because 'what is necessary was not possible'), and the necessary negative similarly rules out a *negative* possible conclusion.

33b4. 'in the case of': what Aristotle means is that we can find premises of this sort in which the 'major' term cannot belong to any of the 'minor,' and *other* premises of this sort in which the 'major' belongs of necessity to all of the 'minor' (cf. 33b14–16).

Chapter 15

33b25—33. Aristotle here invokes, for the first time, a distinction between 'possibility according to the stated determination' (i.e., his usual sense, 'neither necessary nor impossible') and a looser sense of 'nonimpossibility.' As in the present case, he only appeals to this latter sense with respect to the conclusions of deductions. The weaker sense arises, in fact, only as the result of assuming a necessary premise in a proof through impossibility and deducing a contradiction from it.

34a2—3. 'contrariwise' (*enantiōs echontos*): that is, when the major premise is assertoric and the minor possible.

34a5—12. The purpose of the next section (34a5—24) is to clarify the workings of proofs through impossibility in the context of modal deductions. Aristotle's argument is complex and raises more issues than can readily be discussed here: for a related discussion, see *Metaphysics* IX.4. Throughout this passage, 'possible' is *dunatos* ('potential') rather than the usual *endechomenos* or *endechesthai*. Aristotle does sometimes appear to use *dunatos* quite like *endechomenos* (see the Note to 31b8—9), but *dunatos* is used in *Met.* IX.4 and probably has the sense 'potential' there.

34a12—15. Aristotle notes here that 'impossible,' etc., have application not only to states of affairs (*en tēi genesei*) but also to utterances (*en tōi alētheuesthai*) and to predication (*en tōi huparchein*). His point is that his preceding remarks about states of affairs may be extended to statements, in particular the premises and conclusions of deductions.

34a16—24. Although the point that nothing follows from a single premise is one Aristotle frequently makes, his goal here is not to rule out single-premise arguments, but rather to treat the premises of a deduction as a single thing so as to apply the argument of 34a5—12 to deductions. He does this by treating the premises much more like things (substances) than he typically does (this may explain his persistence in using *dunatos* rather than *endechomenos* throughout the passage). The final stage in the argument is perhaps more subtle than convincing, since it rests on labelling the premises with a single letter. 'A is necessary altogether' (*anankaiou tou A ontos hama*) as I translate it, means 'both the premises of which A is composed are necessary' (in Greek, where a neuter plural subject usually takes a singular verb, this is perhaps more readily acceptable than in English).

34a25—33. This passage gives the principle which Aristotle ultimately wishes to defend and on which his subsequent proofs rest: if a false but not impossible supposition is made, then an impossibility cannot follow from it. Aristotle's text, in fact, seems to make the stronger claim that a false but not impossible supposition *will* lead to a false but not impossible conclusion, which (as Aristotle takes some pains to show in B 2—4) is not the case. We might be able to save Aristotle from error by interpreting 'will be' (*estai*) as meaning 'will

be possible' and translating 'it will be possible for what results from the assumption to be false, but not, however, <possible for it to be> impossible.'
This is difficult grammar, however; Aristotle has probably been careless. In
any event, the point he is really interested in, as the remainder of the argument shows, is that an impossible result cannot follow from asumptions which
are not impossible.

Aristotle seems to overlook the case of premises which are individually
possible but jointly impossible (such as 'every animal is awake' and 'some
animals are asleep'). But he probably has in mind only the assignments of
modalities to the various members of premise-pairs already known to yield
deductions in their assertoric forms.

34a34–b2.   This proof shows the application of the principle: Aristotle
constructs a proof from impossibility by supposing both the contradictory
of the desired conclusion and a premise *consistent with* one of the premises,
and from this he deduces (as in the nonmodal cases) the contradictory of the
other premise. But, in fact, his argument contains an equivocation. The assumption 'it is not possible for A to belong to every C,' if taken in the sense of
possibility 'according to the determination,' is equivalent to '*Either* A of necessity belongs to some C *or* A of necessity does not belong to some C.' In some
places, Aristotle takes note of this (see, for instance, 37a15–20). Here,
however, he treats it as equivalent to the second disjunct alone: this is quite in
accord both with ordinary Greek and with his own usage in the exposition of
deductions with necessary premises (*to A ex anankēs ouch huparchei tini tōi B* and
to A ouch endechetai huparchein panti tōi B may be used as equivalents), but to do
so is to use 'possible' in the broader sense of 'not necessarily not.' As Ross
points out, Aristotle should say here, as he does in the case of *eio*, that the only
conclusion which follows from these premises is one of possibility in that
broader sense.

34a40–41.   'it was assumed': the assumption, at 34a34, was 'A *belongs* to
every B.' Waitz takes Aristotle to be making a tacit inference from this to 'It is
possible that A belongs to B.' But such an inference only holds for the broad
sense of 'possible.'

34b2–6.   The sentence in brackets is found in all sources, but it is hard to
get any coherent sense out of it. Ross rejects it as the work of 'a rather stupid
glossator' (but conceivably, it is a garbled version of a direct proof).

34b7–18.   This passage illustrates well how difficult it can be to make sense
of Aristotelian modalities. The distinction between belonging 'at a moment'
(*kata to nun*: compare *Physics* IV.11, VI.3) and belonging 'without qualification'
or 'simply' (*haplōs*) is uncomfortably close to the difference between merely
belonging and belonging of necessity (Alexander works hard to preserve a
distinction: see 189.27–36). Conversely, if this passage does indeed contemplate a distinction between 'always' and 'necessarily,' then it appears to con-
flict with other passages (most prominently *On the Heavens* I.12) in which

Aristotle identifies them. In any event, Aristotle does not follow his own advice elsewhere, but is quite willing to use counterexamples 'according to time' in this way (see 35a20−24). (See Waterlow *1982*, Hintikka *1973* for extensive discussions of these points.)

34b22. 'let it not be possible': Aristotle immediately equates this denial of 'Possibly A to no C' with 'Necessarily A to some C' (compare 34b28−31).

34b31−35a2. The conclusion is 'not a possible one' in the strict sense, though it is in the broad sense; the deduction is 'of belonging to none of necessity' in that the conclusion *may* be necessary, though it need not be. Aristotle is evidently unhappy with his counterexample, perhaps (as Alexander suggests) because the major premises are not assertoric but necessary (or perhaps just because the two triples share only one term instead of his preferred two).

35a4. 'from the actual premises taken': the Greek (*ex autōn men tōn eilēmmenōn protaseōn*) could also be translated 'from the premises taken *themselves*.' However, Aristotle conceives of all completions of incomplete deductions as requiring the introduction of premises not actually taken but implicit in the premises that are taken (compare the similar uses of *autōn* at 37b31−32, 38a5−6, 38b33, 45a7).

35a5−6. 'converted accordingly': Aristotle says literally 'if the premise according to possibility is converted' (*antistrapheisēs tēs kata to endechesthai protaseōs*). But the phrase 'according to possibility' is his usual way of indicating *conversion* of the special sort applicable to possible premises. I have taken it here to be doing double duty, which is conceivable (cf. 35a14−15, 37b32−33, 38a32−33, 38b7−8).

35a8−20. Three times in these lines, Aristotle says that nothing follows through the premises as taken (once that there will 'in no way'—*oudamōs*—be a deduction), when what he means is that there is no *complete* deduction, though there is an incomplete one.

35a19. 'Which is true': that is, which follows by complementary conversion from the minor premise.

35a20−24. The countermodel triple used here takes 'White belongs to every animal' and 'White belongs to no animal' as possible premises: but since Aristotle regards some animals (e.g., swans) as necessarily white, others (e.g., ravens) as necessarily not white, these must be possible *at a time* in the way seemingly forbidden in 34b7−18.

35b2−11. This argument is a compressed but close parallel to that in 35a3−24 (even the countermodel triples for the nonmodal cases are the same). 'Through the indeterminate' has the sense it did in A 4−7: 'some snow is not an animal' is true because no snow is. Following Ross, I omit *kai* in 35b2; but 'or not belonging' (*ē mē huparchein*) in 35b4 is a harmless ambiguity. Even *kai* might be retained if regarded as explanatory ('There will be a deduction . . . *that is*, when the universal premise . . . ').

35b16. 'In alternation' (*enallax*) means 'one possible and the other assertoric.'

35b20–22. As Waitz points out, this summary is inaccurate: Aristotle rejects two combinations of possible major and assertoric minor (*ao*, *eo*) as nonconclusive.

Chapter 16

36a2. 'The same way as in the previous cases': presumably, the proof through impossibility used for *aaa* with possible minor and assertoric major.

36a7–15. Aristotle argues in this and a few other cases for an assertoric conclusion from a necessary and a possible premise. In each case, the proof is through impossibility and (as Alexander notes: 209.4–7, 216.28–32) turns on Aristotle's other, more celebrated modal curiosity: a necessary conclusion sometimes follows from one necessary and one assertoric premise.

36a15–17. According to Aristotle's strict definition of possibility, 'possibly does not belong' does *not* follow from 'does not belong.' We may charitably suppose that he means possibility 'not according to the definition' here, or we may uncharitably suppose that he has been inattentive.

36a17–18. This possible *e* premise and the necessary *e* of the previous example (36a8–9) nicely illustrate the potentially ambiguous expressions mentioned above in the Note on 31a6–7. The *only* difference between the statements of these two premises is the relative order of *mēdeni* and *endechesthō*: *to men A mēdeni endechesthō tōi B* (36a8–9), *to men A endechesthō mēdeni tōi B* (36a18). Waitz (397) and Alexander (136.23–29) recognize the potential these expressions have for ambiguity but do not note Aristotle's simple rule of word order.

36a21–22. 'premise from the side of the major extreme': a variant way of saying 'major premise.'

36b5. 'in relation to the major extreme' (*pros tōi meizoni akrōi*): Ross excises this phrase because it appears to say that the middle term in a first-figure deduction is predicated of the major extreme. Aristotle does make extremely frequent use of the preposition *pros* in this way (so that the predicate of a premise is *pros* its subject). However, he occasionally reverses this order in connection with major premises of first-figure deductions: exact parallels of the present case occur in the initial exposition of the assertoric first figure in A 4 (26a18–19, 26a39–b1).

36b19–21. 'in the case of belonging': that is, with *one* assertoric or necessary premise and one possible premise.

36b24–25. Although this sentence is in all the manuscripts, it contradicts Aristotle's claims that some of the deductions just considered are complete. As Ross points out, it is a verbatim copy of 39a1–3, which is correct in its place; it is, therefore, probably not due to Aristotle.

Chapter 17

36b35−37a32. Aristotle offers a lengthy proof (comprising three separate arguments) that 'it is possible that A to no B' does not imply 'it is possible that B to no A' (thus, possible *e* premises do not convert analogously to their assertoric and necessary counterparts). As noted above, the locution he uses is unfortunately ambiguous, being equivalent on one reading to 'of no B is it possible that it is A' and on the other to 'of every B it is possible that it is not A.' Interpreted in the former way, the sentence is, for Aristotle, a necessary universal negative and therefore converts in the same manner as a universal negative. Interpreted in the latter way, the sentence expresses possibility, and therefore, in the phrase of A 3 and A 13, is really affirmative in form: it is a universal affirmative and thus (as Alexander notes) does not convert.

36b37. 'let this be assumed': that is, assume that it *does* convert. Since this is the assumption of an argument through impossibility, I translate *keisthai* as 'assume': Aristotle occasionally substitutes the unprefixed *keisthai* for *hupo-keisthai* in such contexts (e.g., B 12, 62a23; B13, 62b5).

36b38−40. 'contraries as well as opposites' (*kai hai enantiai kai hai anti-keimenai*): as Alexander explains, this means: (1) 'possibly to every' converts with 'possibly to no' ('contraries'), and (2) 'possibly to some' converts with 'possibly not to some' ('opposites'). Alexander notes that these terms here indicate mere verbal form: the syntactical relationship between 'possibly to every' and 'possibly to no' is analogous to that between 'to all' and 'to no' (221.16−28). Despite what Aristotle says in B 8, 59b8−11, 'opposite' (*anti-keimenos*) need not mean 'contradictory,' but only 'opposite' or 'opposed' in a generic sense.

37a2. 'this is incorrect': as at 30a27, the word is *pseudos*.

37a9. 'was not possible': that is, as determined in A 13.

37a10−14. Aristotle imagines an argument through impossibility which he thinks fails. I have inserted quotes to separate this putative argument from his comments: the 'for' clause beginning in 37a14 gives the reason why he thinks it fails, i.e., that 'not possibly to none' does not imply 'necessarily to some' but rather '*either* necessarily to some *or* necessarily not to some.' The awkward embedded double negative in 'it is not the case that if it is not possible for B to belong to no A' reflects an equally awkward construction in Greek (*ou gar ei mē endechetai mēdeni to B tōi A*).

37a15−17. 'used in two ways' (*dichōs legetai*): Aristotle does not mean that this phrase has two meanings, but that there are two different ways in which 'not possible to no' could be true (cf. the Notes on 27b20−23). This is one of the few places in which he takes express note of the fact that possible premises as he conceives them have (to use modern terminology) disjunctive negations. The negation of 'It is possible that B belongs to A' is really 'either B

necessarily belongs to A or B necessarily does not belong to A.' To apply this
to the quantified sentence 'It is possible that B belongs to no A,' we must first
note that Aristotle considers this equivalent to 'It is possible that B belongs to
every A.' This would be rendered false if there is some A (let us call it S) such
that 'It is possible that B belongs to S' is false; and this, in turn, would be
rendered false, either if S is necessarily B, or if S is necessarily not B. Since all
that is important about S here is that it is some (part of) A, we can express the
conditions for the falsehood of 'It is possible that B belongs to no A' as 'Either
B necessarily belongs to some A or B necessarily does not belong to some A.'

But this last sentence is no longer a categorical sentence. In fact, since it is
not 'one thing either affirmed or denied of one,' Aristotle probably would not
regard it as a single statement at all. Whatever may be the case in that regard,
he certainly makes no room for disjunctive sentences in the deductive theory
of the *Prior Analytics*. Accordingly, what he does here is instead to say, in
effect, that there are two ways in which the *negation* of the possible *e* premise
can be true.

37a22. 'understanding it incorrectly' (*pseudōs an lambanoi*): not 'assuming a
falsehood' but making an incorrect inference (so Tricot: 'commettrait une er-
reur'). Compare 30a27, 48a16, 49a18–22, and the associated Notes.

37a24–26. Since for Aristotle, 'possibly to none' and 'possibly to every' are
equivalent, 'necessarily to some' and 'necessarily not to some' are each inconsistent with each of those. But the latter two are not equivalent: probably,
what Aristotle is calling attention to here is that, in this case, we cannot find a
one-to-one correspondence between premises and their 'opposites' (since we
have two distinct components of the disjunctive negation, each of which is
'opposed' to the universal possible premise).

37a28–29. 'if this is taken': that is, if we take the *second* of the opposites
('of necessity does not belong to some') as the assumption of the attempted
proof through impossibility which Aristotle has been discussing. The point can
be put more precisely by going beyond Aristotle's analysis. If we want to get a
strictly possible conclusion using a deduction through impossibility, then we
need to assume the negation of the desired conclusion. But, as we have just
seen, this assumption would need to be disjunctive ('either of necessity to
some or of necessity not to some'). To make an argument through impossibility
from such an assumption work, we would need to show that *each* of its disjuncts leads to an impossibility; and here, the second disjunct yields no contradiction. Once again, Aristotle's insight into the logical situation outstrips his
own means for analyzing it.

In 37a28, I follow Rolfes and Tricot in reading 'not only . . . but also' (*ou
monon . . . alla kai*), as in manuscripts B, d, and *n*, Philoponus, and Pacius,
rather than Ross's 'not . . . but' (*ou . . . alla*).

37a35–36. The text here reads 'If we put it to be possible for B to belong
to every C' (*tethentos gar tou B panti tōi G endechesthai*). The expected *reductio*

hypothesis would be the *denial* of 'it is possible for B not to belong to every C.' Ross approves Maier's suggestion to insert 'not' (*mē*) twice: '*not* possible <for B> *not* to belong to every C.' I have inserted this in brackets into the text, but it should be regarded as tentative. Aristotle has just discussed at length the fact that the proper contradictory of 'possible not to belong to every' really contains two alternatives; it is not clear how he would reconstruct the putative argument through impossibility in view of that fact.

37a38−b3.   What Aristotle gives here is a general rejection by counter-models of all combinations of two possible premises in the second figure. His language is more verbose and difficult than usual.

37b15.   'replace': i.e., replace them with other premises (compare 210a34, 56b8−9). The word *metalabein* can mean simply 'change,' and most translators so take it. However, elsewhere in the *Prior Analytics* Aristotle clearly uses it to mean 'put in place of,' 'substitute for' (see 39a27, 41a39, 48a9, 48a25−27). Here, it has the sense: 'substitute *something for*.'

Chapter 18

37b22−23.   'the demonstration is the same': that is, as in the case of two (universal) possible premises in the second figure (see 37a32−37). As before, the reason is that the possible *e* premise cannot be converted.

37b32−33.   'accordingly converted': cf. 35a5−6 and Note.

Chapter 19

38a21−22.   'will also not belong': a more literal translation of the Greek (*oud' huparxei*) might be 'will not belong either,' but this fails to bring out Aristotle's point, which is that we *also* get an assertoric conclusion.

38a30.   'it results that B of necessity does not belong to C': Aristotle presumably means that this *may* happen, just as any other categorical relation of B to C may happen (cf. 38a36ff).

38a36−38.   Aristotle's appeal to the requirement that a necessary conclusion can be obtained only from two necessary premises or one necessary and one assertoric premise is illegitimate, since he has not offered any justification for that requirement (or for that matter even asserted it, except in application to the first figure). In the case of the earlier result that an affirmative conclusion only follows from two affirmative premises, Aristotle's proof was just an exhaustive survey of all cases, and there is no evidence that he has any other means of proof for this case: but he is engaged in just that survey here, and, thus, he can hardly appeal to its result.

38b3−4.   The 'opposite affirmations' are 'B belongs/B belongs of necessity/ it is possible for B to belong to every C'.

38b7−8. 'converted accordingly': cf. 35a5−6 and Note.

38b10. 'when the premises are converted': as Alexander points out (239.12−17), the major premise is converted by interchange of terms, the minor by complementary conversion. Aristotle omits 'of necessity' in the converted major premise.

38b13−14. Aristotle rejects any conclusion from two affirmative premises. But Alexander (240.4−11) offers a proof through impossibility that 'B is possible to no C' (in the wide sense) follows from 'A is necessary to every B' and 'A is possible to every C' and wonders why it is not acceptable. Probably, the reason is that Aristotle simply never accepts the deduction of a negative conclusion from affirmative premises. (Alexander makes similar remarks about other combinations of two affirmatives: see 240.32−241.1, 241.5−9.)

38b18−19. 'B may of necessity not belong': here 'may' is expressed with a future tense (*ex anankēs . . . ouch huparxei*).

38b21−22. 'has been shown' (*dedeiktai*): here the verb *deiknunai* does not mean 'prove,' (see the Note to 27b20), but rather 'exhibit' or 'show.' In 38b18−19, just preceding, Aristotle offered a counterexample 'showing' a term B of necessity not belonging to C; while this does constitute a proof that the relevant combination of premises and 'conclusion' is possible, it is not a proof that B of necessity belongs to no C.

38b34. 'converted accordingly': cf. 35a5−6 and Note.

39a3. 'through the aforementioned figures': Alexander argues that 'figures' here may mean 'deductions' ('moods'), since all the proofs Aristotle gives appeal to first-figure deductions. Ross suggests that Aristotle has in mind the fact that some of the first-figure deductions used in this section were earlier proved by arguments through impossibility that appeal to third-figure arguments with one necessary premise. Of course, this can be carried one step further: those deductions in their places were proved by appeal to still other first-figure deductions. All that Aristotle needs to be saying, however, is that nothing *other than* the aforementioned figures is required.

Chapter 20

39a11−13. 'we must take . . . similarly': that is, as before, we must sometimes take 'possible' in the conclusion in the strict sense, and sometimes take it in the wide sense.

39a27. 'if "is possible to belong" is substituted': i.e., if a universal affirmative is substituted for a universal negative (complementary conversion). Presumably Aristotle includes the two deductions which result if this is done either once (for the minor premise) or twice (for both premises).

39a29−31. That is, the deductions are exactly analogous to those with purely assertoric premises (except of course for the additional deductions through complementary conversion that Aristotle mentions at 39a38−b2).

Chapter 21

39b28—29. 'manner of the deductions will be the same': as in 39b9—10, this means that these deductions are analogous to their nonmodal counterparts.
39b31—39. Aristotle does not mention that the conclusion of this deduction will be possible only in the wider sense.
40a2—3. 'in the previous cases': the manuscripts all say 'in the universal cases,' which must be an error. Tredennick and Ross suggest that the reference is to the parallel treatment of cases with two possible premises (39b2—6). I follow Ross's suggestion of replacing 'universal' with 'previous'; in these chapters, Aristotle often says both 'as in the previous cases' and 'as in the universal cases,' so that the mistake is a natural one for a copyist to make.

Chapter 22

40a21—25. Aristotle's language is elliptical here, and I have tried to fill it out. I take *estai de palin to prōton schēma* to mean something like 'at this point, we get the first figure again *by conversion of the minor premise*'. As Ross notes, *gar* in 21 is 'anticipatory' ('since').
40a34—35. 'when the premise is replaced' (*metalēphtheisēs tēs protaseōs*): that is, replaced by its complementary converse. Compare the use of *metalambanein* at 37b15, 56b8.
40a37—38. Although Aristotle says the two term-triplets are for 'belonging to every' and 'belonging to no,' he must mean 'belonging *of necessity* to every/ no.' The examples chosen are also curious. It is, of course, impossible for something to be awake or not asleep and be a sleeping horse. However, on Aristotle's usual understanding of necessity and possibility, no horse is of necessity awake or of necessity asleep: these are, instead, good examples of things that are 'capable of being otherwise' (in fact, Aristotle would elsewhere probably agree that every waking horse is potentially asleep and every sleeping horse potentially awake). The type of necessity involved here is actually closer to that which Aristotle regularly attributes to the conclusions of deductions: 'necessity when certain things are so' (*tinōn ontōn anankē*).

Chapter 23

This Chapter contains an extended argument that every deduction whatsoever can be transformed into a deduction resting only on first-figure universal deductions. As such, it is critical to Aristotle's overall project in the *Prior Analytics*. The argument picks up here precisely where A 7 left off: there is no trace of the account of modal deductions (this is evidence in favor of Bocheński's view that A 8—22 are a later addition to the work).
40b17—20. The opening claim of the Chapter has in no way been established for modal deductions. Aristotle proved many of the results in A 8—22 by

appeal to deductions other than *Barbara* and *Celarent*, and he identified a number of modal deductions as complete and thus not in need of proof. It is not at all clear how to apply the claim made here to these cases. We would, at the least, need an argument corresponding to that in A 7 to show how alternate proofs for these complete deductions could be constructed; such an argument would be quite complex, if possible at all, and there is no reason to suppose Aristotle had attempted it. Once again, the theory of modal deductions appears not to be well integrated with the rest of the text.

40b25. 'either probatively or from an assumption': on the term 'probative' (*deiktikos*), a term of art which may be an Aristotelian coinage, see also the remarks on 29a30–39. Aristotle contrasts probative deductions with those 'from an assumption' (*ex hupotheseōs*), and the latter include not only proofs through impossibility but also other types of arguments which, in his view, rest on assumptions. This contrast is related to a distinction in the *Rhetoric* between probative and 'refutative' (*elenktikos*) arguments (see *Rhetoric* II.22, 1396b22–27). Aristotle's views on the logical foundations of proof through impossibility are notoriously unclear and probably embody some confusions, even though he uses the procedure flawlessly in practice. See his own discussions immediately below, in 41a21–b5, and A 29, together with the associated Notes.

40b32. 'the initial thing' (*to ex archēs*, literally 'that from the beginning'), is the conclusion which it is required to prove. A basic rule of the game of proving is that one may not 'take' this 'initial thing' as a premise, but rather must obtain it by deduction from other premises. The phrase comes from dialectical practice: see B 16–17 and the associated Notes.

40b35–36. The claim that nothing follows from a single premise has indeed been *made*, and even *used*, before (A 14, 34a17–19), but it has not been proved in any way. Alexander says Aristotle must mean 'nothing follows *deductively*' (*sullogistikōs*) and appeals to the definition of *sullogismos*, in which Aristotle says 'certain *things* having been supposed (*tethentōn tinōn*), something else results of necessity': the plural then rules out single-premise deductions as a matter of definition (257.8–13; cf. his discussion of the definition and rejection of one-premise arguments as deductions, 17.10–18.7). Aristotle does not, in fact, believe that nothing can ever follow from a single premise, since he uses conversion inferences in his proofs of deductions: these must, therefore, fail to be deductions. Unfortunately, he never explains what the conversion rules are to be understood as, if not as deductions. Alexander's account, unsatisfying as it is, may be the best we can get.

41a1. 'connected' (*sunhaptei*): Aristotle often uses this verb of a lengthy series of deductions (a 'sorites'), which eventually 'connects' a predicate term with its subject (as at 41a19, a few lines later).

41a2–4. 'there will not be a deduction . . .': Again, this claim is nowhere proved but seems to be a matter of definition for Aristotle. It should be noted, however, that the long discussion beginning in A 32 of how to get arguments into the figures at least serves to make plausible the claim that any argument can be put into figured form.

41a4. 'the kinds of predications' (*tais katēgoriais*): the 'predications' here are simply the types of categorical sentence. In the *Prior Analytics*, Aristotle usually uses the term 'problem' to express this.

41a7−18. The crux of Aristotle's argument is simply the requirement that a deduction have two premises which share one (middle) term. It then follows immediately from the definitions of the figures that every such argument must be in one of them.

41a18−20. 'The argument will also be the same': Exactly what this means is unclear. If we imagine a chain of predications, with A predicated of C, C of C', and so on, ending with B, then we could plausibly claim that the whole series is in the first figure and joins up A with B. But the possible forms of such extended deductions are enormously variable: infinitely so, if we permit them to be arbitrarily long. A more thorough attempt to determine the possible forms of deductions is at least implied by *Posterior Analytics* I.19−22. In Smith *1986*, I argue that the project pursued in those Chapters may have been Aristotle's principal motive for developing the theory of deductions in the *Prior Analytics*; in Smith *1984*, I suggest that his project of classifying the possible structures of proofs recalls Hilbert's concept of proof theory.

41a22−b1. This discussion of arguments through impossibility should be supplemented by comparison with A 29, B 11−14, *Posterior Analytics* I.26, and *Topics* VIII.14. Aristotle undertakes to show that every such argument *contains* a deduction in the figures. Whether this suffices to prove his overall claim that all deductions whatsoever are 'both completed through the universal deductions in the first figure and led back into them' depends on how we interpret 'completed through' and 'led back into.' If it is taken to mean that every deduction can be *replaced by* a deduction containing nothing but first-figure universal deductions, then it is indefensible: Aristotle must treat the hypothesis of a deduction through impossibility as somehow external to the deduction.

Alexander (260.18−261.20) spells out the example given of proving the diagonal and side of a square incommensurable. The proof is found as the (spurious) last proposition (117) of the tenth book of Euclid's *Elements* (see Heath *1908*, III.2).

41a23−26. This description of arguments through impossibility appears to function as a sort of definition or canonical account: see 41a30−32. Note that Aristotle refers to arguments *coming to a conclusion* (*perainontes*) through an impossibility and says that they *prove* (*deiknuousin*) the intended conclusion when they *deduce* (*sullogizontai*) a falsehood or impossibility. According to the analysis presented here, an argument through impossibility is not, strictly speaking, a *deduction* of its intended conclusion, but only of the 'impossibility': the real conclusion is reached 'from an assumption' or 'from an agreement.' On such a view, we should not really speak of *deductions* through an impossibility, but only *arguments* or *proofs* through an impossibility (which will contain deductions *of* an impossibility). Aristotle appears to make some effort to conform his language to this, sometimes using the verb 'come to a conclusion' (*perainein/perainesthai*, as here and at 41a40; see also 51b2) or 'prove' (*deiknunai*, as at 41a25) rather than 'deduce.' However, he is not very consistent about this, and quite frequently reverts to speaking of deductions, or deducing, through an impossibility or from an impossibility (e.g., 45a26−27, 45b9, 61a18−18, 61a33, 62b25−26). The reason, no doubt, is that these expressions are part of the received technical vocabulary of his day, not his own coinage, and thus have an established usage towards which he inclines. See further the Notes on B 11−14.

41a30−32.   'For this is what': if the imperfect 'was' indicates reference to an earlier definition here, then this must refer to 41a23−26 (perhaps to the words 'when something impossible results when its contradiction is supposed'). The match is hardly a close one, however.

41a37.   'all the other kinds of deduction that are from an assumption': later, in A 28, Aristotle gives as examples of these 'those according to substitution or according to quality' (45b16−17). It is clear in that context that his views are not very well formed on this subject.

Chapter 24

41b7.   'belong universally': this includes *not*-belonging universally (i.e., belonging to none) as well.

41b7−13.   In order to prove that there is no deduction without at least one universal premise, Aristotle could simply rely on his survey of all premise combinations in A 4−22 and observe that he has already shown every combination of two particular premises fails to yield a conclusion. What he actually gives us is a more complex argument which is both difficult to make sense of in its own terms, and hard to connect with the preceding account of deductions in the figures: I am inclined to think it is an older discussion of its topic which was composed in ignorance of the *Analytics*' theory of deductions. He presupposes a dialectical situation in which something is proposed for proof and one participant in the argument undertakes to prove it from premises obtained from an opponent by asking questions (see the Notes on 24a22−b15). Aristotle's claim is that if the person arguing does not manage to secure a universal premise, then one of three failings must attach to the argument: (1) there is no deduction, (2) it is not 'in relation to what was proposed,' (3) the person arguing will be 'asking for the original thing.'

His account is closely tied to the case of establishing a universal affirmative conclusion, and it is difficult to see how it should be generalized to other cases. Suppose that we are required to establish the conclusion 'Musical pleasure is good.' Aristotle then lists three mistakes we can make. First, we might try to get the premise 'Pleasure is good,' without adding 'every.' Aristotle says that this is an instance of case (1), although he does not explain why. Presumably, our attempted deduction would *not* have committed the fault in question had we taken the premise 'Every pleasure is good.' But we cannot deduce 'Musical pleasure is good' without taking some other premise in addition, and Aristotle does not indicate what that must be. What we need, of course, is 'Musical pleasure is a pleasure.' This might initially be taken to be a particular premise, but it is really universal, being equivalent to '*Every* [or *all*] musical pleasure is a pleasure.'

The second fault we could commit is to take some pleasure other than musical pleasure to be good. In this case, says Aristotle, 'it will not be in relation to (*pros*) what was proposed.' Does Aristotle mean that there may indeed be a deduction in this case but that it is not 'in relation to what was proposed,' or is he making a totally independent point? We may get some idea by considering what the premise taken in such a case would be like: it would be some premise of the form 'Such-and-such pleasure is good,' where 'such-and-such' is not 'musical.' But this is not really a particular premise, despite the fact that we could describe it as saying that some pleasure is good. Aristotle's way of describing the case suggests that he may, in fact, be thinking along these lines: saying 'if *it* is another' takes the word 'some' not as part of the premise supposed, but (in modern terms) as a metalogical term *describing* the premise taken. That is to say, if the premise taken is 'Mathematical pleasure is good,' then it would be correct to say that it had been taken as a premise that a certain pleasure is good, though not correct to say that the premise taken was 'A certain pleasure is good.'

The third fault is taking as a premise 'Musical pleasure is good,' which is, of course, the very thing we were supposed to be proving. Aristotle indicates that this is an instance of 'asking for the initial thing,' or in the traditional (and somewhat bizarre) translation associated with this phrase, 'begging the question.' For a fuller discussion of this criticism, see the Notes to B 16. Once again, Aristotle evidently regards 'Musical pleasure is good' as somehow not universal.

Alexander suggests that Aristotle's point is, not simply that every deduction must have a universal premise, but that every deduction must include a premise universal *in relation to* the subject term of the conclusion to be proved (266.20–31). If this means that every deduction must include a premise which affirms or denies something universally of its minor term, then it is simply false, as evidenced by *Darii, Ferio, Baroco, Festino*, and the entire third figure. However, it may well be close to what Aristotle has in mind. In many places, Aristotle talks as if every deduction were a first-figure universal deduction (this holds, for instance, in his discussion of extended deductions in A 25). It is at least possible that some of these discussions were originally composed before Aristotle had completely developed the theory of deductions in the figures. If that is the case here, then the overall point may be the claim that in every first-figure deduction of a universal conclusion, we must include some premise which affirms or denies something universally of the subject of the intended conclusion.

41b14. 'geometrical proofs': literally, 'drawings' or 'diagrams' (*en tois diagrammasin*). Aristotle often uses this term of geometrical proofs, which include diagrams. Similarly, the verb *diagraphein* ('draw out' or 'diagram') in Aristotle usually means 'prove by means of a diagram,' 'prove geometrically.' See the Notes on 46a8, 65a4−7.

41b14−22. There is some difficulty about determining just what geometrical proof Aristotle has in mind here: evidently, it is different from the proof of the same theorem found in Euclid (I.5). Alexander gives one reconstruction (268.6−24); Heath suggests that a pre-Euclidean proof, involving angles between straight lines and circles, may be preserved here. See Ross 374−376, Mignucci 429−430 for further discussion.

Whatever the actual proof is, the important problem is to determine what point Aristotle wants to illustrate. The salient factor, I think, is the use of a figure, which might be seen as a *particular* case. Thus, in reasoning about the figure in question, when we say such things as 'angle AC is equal to angle BD,' we must really take as our premise 'All angles of a semicircle are equal to one another.' He identifies three instances of such an error, and at the end says 'he will be asking for the original thing.' Since it appears that each of these is an instance of the same type of mistake, I have assumed that Aristotle means this last remark to apply to all three cases (so that he uses the geometrical example only to illustrate the *third* type of failing). Aristotle may be interpreting the role of the figure in a geometrical proof as somewhat analogous to what he describes in B 24 as an 'example' (*paradeigma*): see the Notes on that section.

41b24. 'both in this latter way and in the former' (*kai houtōs kai ekeinōs*): the 'latter way' is 'from all the terms being universal,' while 'the former way' may be taken as a rather loose reference to the beginning of the sentence ('must include belonging universally'), understood as meaning 'from at least one universal.' As frequently happens in the *Prior Analytics*, the meaning is clear enough but the grammar hard to explain.

41b27−31. The generalization offered here is rather complex. The traditional interpretation would be: (1) if the conclusion is affirmative, both premises must be; (2) if the conclusion is negative, one premise must be; (3) at least one premise must share the modal status of the conclusion. Since Aristotle thinks that an assertoric conclusion may be deduced from a necessary and a possible premise, (3) is inconsistent with what he has already said. The closing line is one of Aristotle's notes to himself to study a question further (cf. 50a39−40, 67b26, 69b38−70a2, and *Posterior Analytics* I.29, 87b16−18); since 'the other kinds of predications' are evidently the various modal relations, we have here further evidence that A 8−22 is later than the rest of A.

Chapter 25

In this Chapter, Aristotle considers for the first time extended deductions in which the conclusions following from pairs of premises may be subsequently used as premises for further conclusions. Much of what he says turns on the distinction between the 'main' (*kurios*) conclusion of an extended argument and the various intermediate conclusions in it. The Chapter is not fully consistent and may not have been fully worked out. Its purpose is almost certainly related to the argument in *Posterior Analytics* I.19–29 (especially 23, 29) concerning the possible structures of demonstrations: in 29, 87b16–18, we may have a demand for just the investigation we find here.

41b36–42a5. It is not fully clear what Aristotle wants to prove here: the assertion that every deduction is through only three terms, and thus two premises, appears to be a strong claim that every argument really rests on a *single* argument in the figures. Yet the Chapter clearly envisions extended deductions with intermediate conclusions, and at its end Aristotle counts up various possible structures of such arguments. It is possible that what Aristotle wants to show is this: whenever there are three or more *true* premises from which a conclusion follows, then there is necessarily some pair of *true* premises from which that conclusion follows.

Throughout this passage, Aristotle uses letters to stand both for terms and for premises. I have tried to leave the translation as ambiguous as (but, I hope, not more so than) the original in this regard.

41b37–42a1. The first exception Aristotle allows to his claim is the case in which the same conclusion follows with deductions having two different middle terms. Compare here *Posterior Analytics* I.29.

41b39. 'and also through A, C and D': the manuscripts give a wide variety of readings here: 'BC,' 'AC,' 'AC and BC,' 'BC and AC.' My translation follows Ross's conjecture 'ACD' (Aristotle often concatenates terms without conjunctions).

42a1–5. The second case is that of a genuine extended deduction. Aristotle actually distinguishes between deducing C from A and B, on the one hand, and deducing each of A and B from further premises, on the other. The sense of the argument must be this: Suppose that we have a case in which C is deduced from (say) D, E, F, and G, in the following manner: A is deduced from D and E, B is deduced from F and G, and C is then deduced from A and B. In such a case, we do not have a single deduction of C from four premises, but rather three separate deductions with three separate conclusions. On 'induction' (*epagōgē*) see B 23 and the associated Notes.

42a6–8. Aristotle concedes that his complex example might be counted as a single deduction but counters that, even if we have a deduction with more than three terms in that case, still the conclusion does not come about in *the same way* as C follows from A and B. The following argument (42a8–31) undertakes to spell out what that same way is. Evidently, Aristotle's real concern is to define what counts as a (minimum) single deduction; thus, as in the case of the claim that nothing can be deduced from a single premise, Aristotle's thesis may simply be true by definition. In 42a7, *dia pleionōn* must be elliptical for 'through more *than three*': cf. 41b36−37, *dia triōn horōn kai ou pleionōn*.

42a10. 'one as whole and the other as part': from the subsequent discussion, *A* and *B* are evidently premises and not terms. The relationship of whole to part for premises used here is not explained by Aristotle, though it is often taken as a reference to the *dictum de omni et nullo* of A 2 (24b28−30). The phrase 'this was proved earlier' is presumably a reference to the argument just given that every deduction must include 'universal belonging' (41b7−27). But as we have seen, the interpretation of that argument and the exact determination of the claim it is intended to establish are problematic, and thus the relationship to the present passage is also uncertain. It might be, instead, that Aristotle means to refer to the entire account of deductions in the figures.

42a23−24. 'induction, or concealment': Aristotle regularly distinguishes *epagōgē* and deduction (cf. *Topics* I.12), which allows him to ignore such arguments for his present purposes. 'Concealment' (*krupsis*) means adding extraneous matter to an argument to make it harder for one's opponent to detect one's purposes. Ross appropriately refers to *Topics* VIII.1, 155b20−24.

42a24−30. As this passage makes clear, Aristotle's strategy is to show, for every putative case of a conclusion from more than two premises, *either* that it is not a single deduction, *or* that the additional premises are deductively superfluous.

42a34−35. 'taken in addition for the purpose of completing': this fits particularly well with the view that Aristotle's concept of completing a deduction is a matter of supplying the necessary steps to get from the premises to the conclusion.

42a35−40. The 'main' (*kurios*) conclusion of an extended deduction differs from the 'upper' or 'anterior' conclusions (*ta anōthen*) in that it is not also used as a premise for a further conclusion. Similarly, Aristotle later refers to those premises which are not also 'upper' conclusions as the 'main' premises (42b1). The claim that the main premises must be even in number is puzzling: not only does it not follow from what Aristotle has said, but also it seems to be contradicted by 42b5−16 (where it is said that the number of premises is odd if the number of terms is even, and *vice versa*). Possibly, what Aristotle has in mind is this: Call a *one-layer* deduction a deduction with two premises. Call a *two-layer* deduction the result of replacing *each* premise of a one-layer deduction with a one-layer deduction of that premise; and, generally, call an *n-layer* deduction the result of replacing each of the highest-level (main) premises of an $(n - 1)$-layer deduction with one-layer deductions of them. In such a deduction, there is always an even number of main premises (and indeed, an *n*-layer deduction has 2^n main premises). Aristotle ignores or neglects complex cases in which main premises may be at different heights.

42a38. 'must be premises': note that *protasis* here indicates an argumentative role (thus, to translate 'proposition' would be seriously misleading).

42a39−40. 'for its position' (*pros tēn thesin*): that is, for the purpose of defending the statement he is required to defend in the exchange.

42b1. 'Counting deductions by [*kata*] their main premises': that is, *counting* or *individuating* deductions by reference to their main premises.

42b4−5. The claim that the conclusions will be half as many as the premises is still more puzzling. In an n−layer deduction, there are half as many 'upper' conclusions at the second highest level as there are main premises (and, in general, half as many conclusions at each level as at the one above); but there are 2^{n-1} conclusions (including both the main conclusion and all intermediates). Aristotle's remark is true strictly only in the case of a one-layer deduction, with two premises and one conclusion.

42b5−26. Aristotle contrasts 'prior deductions' with 'continuous middles.' The latter is related in sense to the notion of deductions 'joined up' (*sunhaptoi*) with each other found in previous sections: each member of a continuous series of middles is predicated of its successor (the case Aristotle has principally in mind is a series of terms each of which is universally true of the next). Arguments with 'prior deductions' are presumably those with intermediate conclusions. It is not clear just how Aristotle conceives these two as related, or what extent either has, since the subsequent discussion entirely concerns continuous terms. The term 'prior deduction' (*prosullogismos*) is not common in Aristotle, but the sense is apparently not confined to the context of extended deductions: see *Topics* VI.10, 148b4−10.

42b6. Note that Aristotle uses letters here to stand for terms, and not (as in 41b36−42a40) premises.

42b8. 'the term inserted': Aristotle distinguishes adding a term to one end of a continuous series from adding a term in the middle. Einarson *1936* argues that the term 'inserted' (*parempiptōn*) probably derives from Greek proportion theory.

42b9−26. To understand Aristotle's argument, suppose that we have a continuous series of terms $A_1 \ldots A_n$ where for each i, A_i is predicated of A_{i+1}. There are then $n - 1$ 'intervals' between adjacent terms in this series, and, thus, we have a series of $n - 1$ 'continuous' premises. From any pair of adjacent premises in this series, we can deduce another premise; this yields another series of $n - 2$ adjacent premises. Proceeding thus through $n - 1$ iterations, there are $(n - 1) + (n - 2) + \ldots + 1 = (n^2 - n)/2$ conclusions. Adding a term to the series, in effect, adds one premise at each of the $n - 1$ levels and moves the original conclusion down one level: thus, the number of conclusions is increased by n, the *initial* number of terms.

42b16−18. 'the conclusions will never have the same arrangement [*taxis*]': all this seems to mean is that there is no fixed *ratio* of number of conclusions, either to number of premises or to number of terms. Again, it is not clear why Aristotle is interested in this. He may have in mind some parallel with Pythagorean *gnōmon*-arithmetic: cf. *Physics* III.4, 203a13−15.

Chapter 26

42b27. 'what deductions are about' (*peri hōn hoi sullogismoi*): Ross explains this as 'what syllogisms aim at doing, viz., at proving propositions of one of the four [categorical forms].' But the phrase has a close parallel in *Topics* I.4, where Aristotle tells us that 'what arguments are from' (*ex hōn hoi logoi*) and 'what deductions are about' are 'equal in number and the same.' He then explains that arguments are 'from' premises and 'about' problems (*problēmata*). The term 'problem' in the *Prior Analytics* means 'type of categorical sentence' (as here, at 42b29; see the Note on 26b31). In the *Topics*, however, both 'premise' and 'problem' carry with them more of a suggestion of argumentative role. As the associated verb *proballein* ('throw out [as an obstacle]'), suggests, a *problēma* in dialectic is the proposition under discussion (which one party to the debate undertakes to defend and the other to attack). In *Top.* I.4, 101b28–36, Aristotle tells us that a premise and a problem differ only in the way they are presented (*tōi tropōi*), so that by a change in this, a problem can be converted to a premise, and conversely. Scholars differ on just how to interpret this, but it seems to me that Aristotle has in mind the fact that the same proposition (to use a modern term) might figure in two argumentative roles: as a premise to argue from or as a 'problem' for debate. In the latter case, Aristotle suggests, it might be expressed in a form beginning with 'whether' (*ara*). This implies that a problem is a two-sided question; but Aristotle also defines a dialectical premise as an 'asking of a contradiction,' so that there is a natural correspondence of the two.

I think we can make a guess as to how 'problem' came to have the sense it does in the *Prior Analytics*. First, we should note that the problems in dialectical arguments actually have less to do with the construction of the arguments themselves than premises: premises are the sources which deductions are built from, whereas problems would only serve to indicate what conclusions one should be aiming at. However, certain features of a problem do matter for the dialectical debater: as the present sections of the *Prior Analytics* make clear, knowing which type of categorical sentence it is influences how one goes about looking for an argument to establish or refute it. Consequently, it is important to determine the *kinds* of problems. It is easy to imagine Aristotle abbreviating 'kinds of problems' into 'problems' with repeated use: compare the more famous abbreviation of 'kinds of predicates' (*ta genē tōn katēgoriōn*) into 'predicates' (i.e., 'categories').

42b29. 'easy to approach' (*euepicheirētos*): this word has as its root *epicheirein*, 'lay hands on,' which elsewhere in Aristotle means 'attack' in dialectical contexts (cf. Note on 24b10–11); here, that is nearly reversed. The sense of the word is 'easy to lay hands on.'

42b30–31. 'in more figures and by means of more cases' (*en pleiosi schēmasi kai dia pleionōn ptōseōn*): it seems clear enough that 'case' (*ptōsis*) means 'mood,' in traditional terminology. (In the *Topics*, arguments from 'cases' are those

relying on parallel substitutions of certain inflected forms: see especially II.9.)
Aristotle has no settled way of saying 'mood': most commonly, when referring
to deductive patterns, he does so through metalogical comments about the
figures, e.g., 'we saw that in the first figure when the major premise was
universal and affirmative . . .'

43a10. 'more cases': Ross reads 'more ways' (*tropōn*), and his apparatus
implies that this is the reading of all his sources; Waitz reads 'cases' (*ptōseōn*),
and his apparatus implies that *this* is the universal reading. According to
Williams, Ross simply reports the manuscript testimony incorrectly. Nothing is
very surprising about 'case' appearing here in this sense, since it has just been
used in 42b30. However, it is at least of some historical significance if *tropos*
does not occur here. The word 'mood' (as a technical term in connection with
syllogisms) ultimately descends from *tropos* used in this sense (as in the Greek
commentators), by way of the Latin *modus*. If *ptōseōn* is the right reading here,
then it appears that Aristotle himself never referred to a mood as a mood.

Chapter 27

43a20−24. Several details of Aristotle's vocabulary in this sentence merit
comment. 'Being supplied' (*euporein*) is the opposite of 'being at a loss' (*apo-
rein*). The reference to a 'route' or 'way' (*hodos*) recalls the beginning of the
Topics, which sets as the goal of that treatise 'finding a way of pursuit (*methodos*)
by means of which we may be able to deduce about any problem proposed
from things accepted' (100a18−22); the goal of discovering a 'way' is an old one
in Greek philosophy. The term 'principle' (*archē*) literally means 'beginning':
its sense here is that found in the *Posterior Analytics*, where principles are the
first premises on which all scientific demonstrations depend. The expression
'the principles concerning any particular subject' is a common one in Aristotle,
especially in the *Posterior Analytics*. Aristotle often distinguishes between 'common principles,' which serve among the principles of many or even all sciences, and the principles 'peculiar' or 'proper' to each given science. This
doctrine represents a rejection of the Platonic view of all science as forming a
unity resting on a single set of highest principles (or even a single highest
principle). The details of Aristotle's views on this subject are much too complex to enter into here, but it is probably in order to mention that by the
'principles concerning any particular subject' Aristotle could mean the principles *peculiar to* that subject.

43a25−43. Aristotle's procedure rests on a division of 'things that are' (*ta
onta*) into three classes: those which are subjects of predication but never
predicates, those which are predicates but never subjects, and those which can
be both. The first class is exemplified by Aristotle as 'the individual and
perceptible' (*to kath' hekaston kai aisthēton*), though he does not here address the
question whether it includes other types of things as well. The second class is
regularly identified by commentators as the categories, but, in fact, Aristotle

says only that he will 'explain later' (*palin eroumen*) that 'it comes to a stop at some point proceeding in the upwards direction' (*epi to anō poreuomenois histatai pote*). The phrase 'it comes to a stop' almost certainly has the quasi-technical sense it does in *Posterior Analytics* I.3 (72b11, 72b22) and I.19–22 (81b32–33, 36; I.20, 82a22; I.21, 82a36–37, 82b11–12, 25-28, 32, 35; I.22, 83b30, 39–84a1, 84a28, 39–b1), where it is associated with his argument that there are premises not susceptible of proof; he establishes this by arguing that there cannot be an infinite chain of predicates each of which has a higher predicate true of it. (Thus, the chain 'comes to a stop eventually.')

The third class consists of everything else. Curiously, having made what appears to be an important distinction, Aristotle promptly disregards the first two classes. One explanation, offered by Łukasiewicz and Patzig, is that the rules of conversion can be given unrestricted scope only if every term is able to function both as subject and as predicate, which only holds of terms in the third class.

(Concerning this section, see also the Note on 65a10–25.)

43a26. 'predicated of nothing else truly universally' (*kata mēdenos allou katēgoreisthai alēthōs katholou*): here, 'universally' is not a term of quantity (opposed to 'particular') but has its metaphysical sense (opposed to 'individual'). In Aristotle, the term 'universal' functions grammatically as an indeclinable noun, adjective, or adverb, as the context may require. I have taken it as adverbial, but it could conceivably be adjectival ('truly predicated of nothing else universal'). The phrase 'truly universally' (*alēthōs katholou*) means 'genuinely as a universal,' not 'universally true' or 'truly and universally.' Perceptible individuals are not merely not predicated of anything *universally*, they are also not predicated of anything *at all* (except 'incidentally,' as Aristotle says). Mignucci comes close to this sense by translating *katholou* as 'absolutely' ('assolutamente'), but unfortunately I do not think Aristotle ever uses the word in this way.

43a34–35. Being predicated 'incidentally' (*kata sumbebēkos*) is illustrated well enough by Aristotle's examples. For a discussion of the meaning of this problematic expression, see Barnes *1975*, 118–119.

43a40. 'other things are predicated of them': the Greek is just 'these of others' (*tauta kat' allōn*), which could equally well mean 'other things are demonstrated to be predicated of them.'

43b1–11. Aristotle's procedure for finding principles consists in collecting all the premises one can find about a given term S and classifying their predicates into three groups: those which follow S, those which S follows, and those which are inconsistent with S. Obviously, the selection is to be made from among *true* premises. What Aristotle gives us is a way to take a collection of all the truths about some subject, and then determine both what can be proved from those truths and how to construct those proofs. In the terminology of modern logic, his method is comparable to a *decision procedure* for deductive systems. It has been suggested that the procedure is ultimately derived from

Plato's *Phaedo*; but even if this should be true, Aristotle's justification of it in the following Chapter is fundamentally dependent on his theory of deductions. (See the Notes on 46a17−27.)

As later becomes evident, the selection process defined here is to be applied to both the subject and the predicate of the proposition one wants to prove. Aristotle refers to the term to which the process is being applied as the *pragma*, a word with a rather loose range of meanings; I translate it 'subject' in the sense 'subject of discussion,' but it might also be rendered as 'thing.'

43b5−6. 'need not be selected' (*ouk eklēpteon*): this could mean either 'need not' or 'must not,' but I think the former better fits the context.

43b6−8. 'predicated . . . essentially' (*en tōi ti esti*: literally, 'in the what it is') may roughly be translated 'predicated in the definition': see *Posterior Analytics* I.4. 'Peculiar' predicates (*idia*) are those true coextensive with a given subject. This division resembles the fourfold division given in the *Topics* (I.4), where it is asserted that every predicate true of a subject is true of it as its definition, its peculiar property, its genus, or its incidental characteristic.

43b9−11. This sentence contrasts 'more quickly hitting on the conclusion' (*thatton entunchanesthai sumperasmati*) with 'demonstrating more' (*mallon apodeiknunai*). According to the *Posterior Analytics*, true premises are a necessary condition for demonstrating at all, and at any rate, demonstration does not seem to admit of degrees: Aristotle's phrase might be taken to mean 'demonstrate more often' (i.e., produce more demonstrations). My rather unattractive translation tries to preserve the unclarity.

43b19−20. 'we also propose premises': the Greek is 'we propose' (*proteinometha*). The verb *proteinein* ('stretch out,' 'hold out,' 'offer'), is cognate with 'premise': a premise is 'that which is held out' (i.e., for acceptance or rejection in an argument). Noun and verb are closely associated in the *Topics* (for a good picture of the relation, see 104a3−7), but this is one of the relatively few appearances of *proteinein* in the *Prior Analytics* (for another see 47a15). Its association with *protasis* is strong enough that the noun may be supplied (the only thing Aristotle ever speaks of proposing is a premise). The phrase 'both useless and impossible' (*achrēston . . . kai adunaton*) embraces both a methodological point (such relationships of terms contribute nothing to the search for premises) and a syntactical point (sentences like 'every man is every animal' are not grammatically well formed).

43b22−32. The rationale behind the various restrictions given in this section on what predicates should be selected is evident once we see the purposes to which it is put. In discussing the relationships of selections for a term contained under another and that term containing it, Aristotle refers to the containing term as 'the universal' (*to katholou*): his language is compressed and difficult. The reference to 'those which do not belong' means 'those which do not belong *to any.*'

43b24. 'need not be selected' (*ouk eklekteon*): as at 43b5, this fits the context better than 'must not.' The subject of 'have been taken' is 'the things following or not following the <containing> universal.' These *need* not be added to the selection of terms which follow the contained universal because they will already have been included. To use Aristotle's example, if we are selecting terms in connection with 'man,' then all those which follow 'animal' will automatically be selected among those which follow 'man.' Similarly, whatever 'does not follow' (is inconsistent with) animal also 'does not follow' man in this sense.

43b36−38. 'Things which follow everything' are terms such as 'being' (*on*). This practical recommendation recalls the view common in the logical works that there is neither a genus nor a science of everything. Aristotle gives the reason why in 44b20−24.

Chapter 28

Aristotle now proceeds to spell out the procedure for finding true premises from which to deduce a given proposition. In fact, in the course of his argument he argues not only that his procedure can find deductions if they are possible, but that it is the *only* procedure needed.

43b39−44a11. Aristotle's presentation of his method recalls certain features of his proofs of deductions in A 4−22. He first states the result which he is going to prove: here, that result consists of a set of rules for finding premises from which to deduce a given conclusion by looking for common terms in the sets defined by the procedure of A 27. As in the earlier proofs, these results are stated entirely without benefit of letters. In highly abbreviated language, a proof of the result follows (44a11−35), in the course of which Aristotle introduces letters.

44a11−17. Aristotle uses letters here, not to stand for terms, but to stand for sets of terms. However, in the course of his proofs, he treats these letters as a sort of formal predicate: B, for instance, is used to mean 'a term from class B.'

44a17−35. Aristotle now shows that each rule is correct by showing how to construct a deduction with the desired conclusion in each case. Some details of his reasoning suggest that this passage antedates the account of A 4−7. He presents a third-figure deduction of a particular affirmative conclusion (*Darapti*) with essentially no justification (44a19−21). By contrast, in the treatment of universal negatives, he spells out a completion through conversion of second-figure *Cesare*, calling it an argument 'from a prior deduction' (*ek prosullogismou*) (44a20−24). The subsequent discussion of second-figure *Camestres* (44a25−27) makes no mention of conversion. At no time does he appeal to what was established earlier in the account of deductions. The deductions given for particular conclusions are both third-figure (*Darapti*, 19−21; *Felapton*, 28−30); this is a result of the procedure, which admits only universal premises into the selected sets, but the treatments of these cases resemble the proofs through *ekthesis* in A 7. Aristotle also adds what amounts to a fourth-figure deduction (*Bramantip*) in 30−35, calling it a 'converted deduction' (*antestrammenos sullogismos*).

It is significant that Aristotle's procedure makes use only of universal premises. Since he later claims that it is also sufficient to find any premises for a deduction that can be found, he must hold that anything that can be proved at all can be proved from only universal premises. This can be shown to be equivalent to the two assumptions on which the procedure of *ekthesis* rests.

44a38−b5. Here Aristotle makes yet another use of letters. He continues to use *A*, *C*, *E*, and *F* as they are defined in 44a11−17, and '*KC*' evidently indicates (in modern terms) the *union* of *K* and some particular member of *C*. Such a clearly extensional conception of terms is unusual in the *Analytics*. The point Aristotle wants to make is obscure. Ross suggests that he is recommending the choice of that middle term which is widest in extension of all possible middles. This may be correct, but: (1) if '*KF*' is true of every *E*, then it should already have been counted among the terms in *F*; (2) it is quite unclear how this could be applied to anything but universal affirmative deductions (this is a difficulty with many of Aristotle's remarks: see the Notes on A 24).

44b4−5. The 'first terms' here are not the 'primary' terms of A 27, 43a25−43, but simply the first terms (in order) *which the subject follows*, i.e., those predicates which it implies. In Aristotle's usage, 'A follows B' is equivalent to 'B is below A.' The terms below those which follow a term are then the terms which the terms it follows follow. (And since 'follows' is a transitive relation, the terms following the term in question also follow these terms.)

44b20−24. Here Aristotle fulfills the promise made in 43b36−38.

44b25−37. Aristotle now gives an elegant proof, based on his treatment of deductions, that identical terms occurring in any pairs of groups other than those treated never yield a conclusion.

44b38−45a22. Aristotle closes with an argument that his procedure comprehends all that is worthwhile in any alternative ways of searching for premises which also take account of pairs of contrary or different terms among the various term collections. Relations of contrariety, in particular, were important in the milieu of the Early Academy, and contraries play a major role in Aristotle's own *Topics*. It is likely that his remarks are directed at some actual set of procedures advocated by others, or even by himself at an earlier stage.

His argument is again elegant, resting on two claims: (1) we must look for something the *same*, since what we are looking for is a middle term, and the middle term is what is the same in the two premises; (2) in any event, whenever it is possible to prove something because of relations of contrariety, Aristotle's method will also discover a proof.

45a9−16. This passage as it stands is seriously confused. The case Aristotle is considering is one in which some term *B* that belongs to every *A* is the contrary of some term *G* that *E* belongs to all of. In this case, since *B* and *G* cannot belong to the same thing and *B* belongs to every *A*, *G* therefore cannot belong to *A* and is thus identical to a member of the class *D*; as a result,

Aristotle's method would discover this case too. However, what the text says is not '*G* will be the same as one of the *D*s', but '*B* will be the same as one of the *H*s,' which, if true, would yield a deduction that *A* is true of *no E*. The justification of this offered in lines 13–16 seems to make no sense. Ross brackets the entire passage as an addition by 'a later writer who suffered from excess of zeal and lack of logic,' but if we do so we are left with no treatment for this case. (In 45a12, some manuscripts have 'but to no *G*' rather than 'to no *E*,' and one source has 'but *E* to no *H*.' I do not see how any combination of these can make more sense.)

45a17–22. 'carrying out a superfluous examination': this is a somewhat expansive rendering of the verb *prosepiblepein*, which Aristotle uses only here. 'A different route from the one needed' (*allēn hodon . . . tēs anankaias*): *anankē* here means 'necessary' in the sense 'that without which not' (cf. *Met.* V.5, 1015a20–26). Compare the reference to a 'different route' at 46b24.

Chapter 29

One important difficulty remains for Aristotle's claim that his procedure will find a deduction if and only if a deduction is possible: arguments through impossibility. He maintained earlier in 41a22–b1 that every such argument, insofar as it is deductive, must consist of an argument in the figures. Here, he makes a much stronger claim: every argument through impossibility can be replaced by a 'probative' argument, and vice versa. The consequence would be that proof through impossibility is a completely redundant process. But in A 45, Aristotle seems, instead, to be arguing that there is no alternative to proof through impossibility as the means of completing second-figure *Baroco* and third-figure *Bocardo* (see the Notes on 50b5–9, 51a40–b2).

In the present argument Aristotle really wants to show that whenever a *proof*—a deduction from true premises—through impossibility exists, then there must exist true premises from which a probative deduction of the same conclusion could be constructed. He argues for this by treating the assumption in a proof through impossibility as *independently known* to be false, and then constructing the probative deduction by using the contradictory of that assumption, which must, therefore, be true. But this cannot be applied to the technique of *completing deductions* through impossibility, where the result is not a consequence that contradicts an independently known truth but rather a straightforward inconsistency (assuming *p*, *q*, and *r*, we deduce the contradictory of *q*).

We might try to harmonize Aristotle's views by attributing to him a comparatively sophisticated distinction between proofs through impossibility at the level of the deductive theory itself, and proofs through impossibility relying on deductions established in that theory (see the Notes on 27a14–15). In my opinion, however, it is equally likely that Aristotle's views are simply not fully worked out. See, further, the discussion in B 11–14 and the (perhaps badly confused) remarks in *Posterior Analytics* I.26.

As in A 23, Aristotle follows his treatment of arguments through impossibility with a few general remarks about extending the case to all types of arguments 'from an assumption.'

45a29—b8. Aristotle assumes that every deduction through impossibility must use the contradictory of the intended conclusion, together with one of the premises, to deduce an 'impossibility,' i.e., a statement known to be false. But given the established structures for deductions, it follows that this impossibility must be a statement containing the middle term and that one of the extremes which is not found in the premise used in the original deduction. The contradictory of this 'impossibility' must then be true, and therefore the middle term must fall into one of the three term-classes defined for that extreme. Since we already have a premise about the middle and the other extreme, we need only combine these to produce a deduction; moreover, Aristotle's method is sufficient to have found this deduction in the first place. Aristotle further claims that the process can be reversed to generate a deduction through impossibility wherever there is a probative deduction.

This argument does nothing to establish that the technique of *completion* through impossibility is redundant. At most, it shows that, given the full complement of deductions Aristotle has established, it is always possible to make use of one of these deductive forms directly, rather than constructing a full proof through impossibility.

45b6—7. 'converted': that is, *negated* (one of the many meanings of *antistrephein*: cf. B 8—10). The premise in question is actually the 'impossibility' deduced, not one of the premises from which it is deduced.

45b8—11. Given Aristotle's way of understanding proofs through impossibility, his claim that one of the premises of such a proof is 'put falsely' is correct, provided that we take the premises to be *all* those statements from which the deduction is constructed (the preceding sentence seems to indicate this). Thus, Aristotle regards the deduction through impossibility as really having three premises: the two found in the corresponding probative deduction, together with the denial of the intended conclusion.

45b12—20. As in A 23 (41a37—b1), Aristotle ends his argument with the claim that it can be extended to every kind of argument 'from an assumption.' The two examples he gives, arguments 'according to substitution' (*kata metalēpsin*) and arguments 'according to quality' (*kata tēn poiotēta*) are not discussed elsewhere in Aristotle under those names. The commentators explain the former as arguments resting on a conditional assumption of the form 'If p, then q,' where q is the thing to be proved and p is the 'thing substituted.' The 'thing substituted' is a substitute *subject for argument*: one wants to prove q and so, getting a concession that if p then q, one 'substitutes' p (i.e., makes it the subject of discussion). Compare the analogous passage in A 23, 41a38—b1, where Aristotle says that in *all* these types of arguments 'the deduction comes about in relation to what is substituted' *ho sullogismos ginetai pros to metalambanomenon* (and see also *Top.* II.5, esp. 112a21—23). Arguments 'according to quality' are explained by the commentators as resting on principles typified by

'If this, then *still more likely* that' (as we call them, arguments *a fortiori*). In the *Topics* and the *Rhetoric*, Aristotle frequently lists several types of arguments 'from more and less and likewise' (*ek tou mallon kai hētton kai homoiōs*); the identification is plausible, though not certain. Although we find a subsequent brief discussion of arguments from an assumption in A 44 (with which this passage should be compared), 45b19–20 here shows that Aristotle realized his theory, and even his system of classification for such arguments, was in need of much further work.

The phrase 'when we come to discuss proof through an impossibility' presumably refers to B 14.

45b21–28. Aristotle briefly considers another possible exception to his procedures, somewhat similar to the case of pairs of contrary terms among the term-classes discussed in 44b38–45a22. Suppose that E belongs *only* to Gs and that G is a member of class C (i.e., the things of which A is universally true). It follows that E belongs only to things of which A is universally true. To get from this to the conclusion 'A belongs to every E' as Aristotle does requires a principle something like 'If E belongs only to what A belongs to universally, then A belongs to every E'. It is not at all clear either how to interpret such claims or how to accommodate them to Aristotle's theory of deduction. Apparently similar sentences are found in B 5–7 (58a29–30, 58b9–10, 58b37–38, 59a28–29); later commentators called these deductions through *proslēpsis*, though there is no Aristotelian authority for that use of the term, and no clear indication that Aristotle recognized such a class of arguments. (On this point see the notes on B 5–7.) Given his overall argument, we would expect Aristotle to tell us here how these arguments also may be brought within his procedure; instead, he seems to indicate that they fall *outside* it. It may be that this is a more than usually unfinished note about a problem case which Aristotle never resolved.

This procedure may also have some connection with Aristotle's account of induction: see the Notes on B 23.

45b23. 'by means of the examination for a particular' (*dia tēs kata meros epiblepseōs*): the procedures Aristotle indicates look for common terms in classes C and G or D and G; in the basic procedure as defined in 44a11–35, these are the term-class pairs to be checked when trying to prove particular affirmative or negative conclusions respectively.

45b28–35. As at 49b29–31, these very cursory remarks about possible and necessary conclusions and 'the other kinds of predication' suggest that the arguments of this section were completed before Aristotle had worked out the contents of A 8–22. The only deductions envisioned are those in which the premises are both of the same modality as the conclusion, rather than the complete study of all combinations of modalities given earlier. (And what he says here seems to imply that there are second-figure deductions with two possible premises, contradicting A 17.)

Cases of a predicate which does not belong but is nevertheless capable of belonging, which Aristotle is careful to include here, would actually add nothing at all to the theory of A 8−22.

45b32−34. 'for it was proved': It is quite unclear what Aristotle has in mind here as having been proved, and where he supposes himself to have proved it. Alexander (329.17−29) supposes that Aristotle means to distinguish cases in which a statement is actually false but possibly true (which he calls 'genuinely possible,' *kuriōs endechomenon*) from those which are both true and possibly true; he takes the reference to be to Aristotle's characterization of possiblity in A 13, 32a18−21. Ross says that 'this was shown in the chapters on syllogisms with at least one problematic premise' (that is, the whole of A 14−22); though he does not explain what 'this' is, he evidently takes it to be that a possible conclusion can follow from premises, not all of which are possible. But what Aristotle actually says is that in selecting attributes one should include those which *do not belong but are capable of belonging*; and the treatment of deductions with at least one possible premise in A 14−22 never takes any account at all of this point. Mignucci's suggestion (p. 462) about the meaning of the passage is probably the best: Aristotle is simply noting that in the case of possible premises, we must include in class B, for example, not only things which follow A, but also things which are capable of following it, but do not. But the reference of Aristotle's 'it was proved' is still obscure.

Chapter 30

Chapters 30−31, which provide the grand conclusion to the account of the method for finding proofs that began in A 27, must be understood against the background of Plato's views on 'dialectic' and the proper method for philosophy. Plato accepted two views which Aristotle vehemently rejects: (1) there is a single set of principles from which all the truths about reality may be derived; (2) the procedure of 'division' (as presented in the *Sophist* and the *Philebus*) is the proper method for finding these principles. In addition, Plato held that knowledge of the principles is somehow innate and can be recovered in a way akin to remembering. Aristotle frequently denies that there is any single set of principles, and in some places he links this with denials that there is any single correct approach appropriate to all areas of inquiry. In this Chapter, however, he rather grandiosely offers us his procedure as 'the route' to be followed in all areas whatever. He takes care to make clear just how this is related to his rejection of a universal science, and stresses the role required for observation and the collection of facts. In a closing *tour de force*, he attacks the method of division by arguing that, to the extent that it is of value, it is already included (as 'only a small part') within his own procedure, and that, as a result, he is in a better position to understand it than its own practitioners.

46a5. 'discern' (*athrein*): for the sense of this verb, see *Metaphysics* III.3, 998b1, and *On the Heavens* II.13, 293a29. A passage in the pseudo-Aristotelian *Problems* brings out the meaning well: 'those who are drunk cannot discern distant objects' (872a19).

46a8. 'things that have been strictly proved to belong' (*ek tōn kat' alētheian diagegrammenōn huparchein*): this might be rendered 'things that have been *diagrammed* to belong according to truth.' Translators generally suppose it to mean something like 'from an *arrangement* of terms in accordance with truth' (so Jenkinson). But that would evidently be just an obscure periphrasis for 'from true things.' Aristotle never makes the absurd supposition that different patterns of argument are *valid* in scientific and in dialectical contexts respectively, and in fact he often insists on the reverse. Moreover, he never refers to the terms in a deduction or figure as *diagegrammenoi*. The correct sense comes from the use of *diagraphein* and *diagramma* in connection with geometrical theorems: see, for instance, 41b14, where *diagramma* can only mean 'geometrical proofs.' A striking passage to compare is *Metaphysics* V.3, 1014a35−b3, which refers to 'what are called the elements of diagrams or of proofs in general.'

Aristotle contrasts strict proofs with 'dialectical deductions,' indicating that the basis of the distinction is the epistemic status of the premises on which each rests. Such a view is found elsewhere (for instance, *Topics* I.1, 100a27−b23). However, Aristotle appeals to a different sort of criterion in 24a16−b15 (see the Notes).

46a17−27. Aristotle now recalls his doctrine that each science rests on its 'peculiar principles' (*idiai archai, oikeiai archai*), with no overarching, general principles from which all scientific knowledge can be derived. He says '*the majority* are peculiar' here probably to take account of the 'common principles' (*koinai archai*), which he exemplifies most frequently by the law of excluded middle and certain generalized mathematical claims, that may figure into many different sciences. The status of these common principles is problematic for him: in several places in the logical works (e.g., *Posterior Analytics* I.11, *Sophistical Refutations* 11, *Rhetoric* I.2) he seems anxious to dismiss these as not really principles, at least not in their general forms, but in *Metaphysics* IV he argues that at least the principles of noncontradiction and excluded middle are genuine principles of a science of being as such. This issue is too complex to discuss here.

Aristotle here gives us an especially clear picture of just what his method amounts to. We get the principles of a science by means of experience and his method, as follows. First, experience gives us the 'facts about any subject' (*ta huparchonta peri hekaston*), that is, the collection of all the truths about it. These data constitute a 'collection of facts' or 'history' (*historia*) concerning the subject. We then use this summary to draw up the various term-classes with respect to each term in the science. Application of the procedure to any truth in this *historia* will then yield premises from which to deduce it, *if they exist*. If they do not exist, then (as Aristotle points out here) the procedure will also make that clear. The latter point is of great significance in the light of the theory of demonstration in the *Posterior Analytics*. Aristotle defines a demonstration as a deduction the premises of which meet a number of qualifications, among them being true, 'primary' (*prōtos*) and 'unmiddled' (*amesos*). It is clear from what follows, especially *Posterior Analytics* I.19−22, that this latter term means 'without a middle,' that is, 'lacking a middle term by means of which it can be proved.' It is a peculiarity of Aristotle's deductive theory that a collection of truths (such as an Aristotelian science) may, and indeed under certain fairly general circumstances must, contain statements not derivable from any other combination of statements in the set. Such 'unmiddled' statements cannot be demonstrated, since they cannot even be deduced from other true statements; they must, therefore, be among the principles of the science (*epistēmē*) corresponding to the initial *historia*. (See also the Note on B 16, 65a10−25.)

46a18. 'it is for our experiences concerning each subject to provide the principles' (*tas men archas tas peri hekaston empeirias esti paradounai*): this phrase is grammatically ambiguous, since *empeirias* could be either genitive singular or accusative plural. In the first case, the clause would mean 'it is for experience to provide the principles concerning each subject.' But in the very next sentence, Aristotle gives an example of this, and the relevant experience appears in the accusative case: *tēn astrologikēn empeirian*. Given Aristotle's great propensity for the ellipsis of repeated elements, I venture to infer, both that the verb 'provide' is understood in this second case, and that *empeirias* in the first case is also accusative. Aristotle thus stresses, not just that experience provides us with knowledge of the principles of sciences, but that experience *of the relevant subject matter* provides us with the principles concerning that subject matter.

46a27. 'make that evident' (*touto poiein phaneron*): that is, 'make that *situation* evident,' to wit, that the statement in question cannot be demonstrated. Nothing in Aristotle's preceding discussion explains how his method could make indemonstrable facts *themselves* (as opposed to their indemonstrability) evident. However, his method could indeed make it evident that a statement is not susceptible of proof (if the *historia* and its associated *eklogē* are genuinely exhaustive of all the facts concerning the subject). The question how we come to understand the principles of sciences is discussed—with celebrated obscurity—in *Posterior Analytics* I.19 (though Aristotle's answer is already hinted at in 46a17−22).

46a28−30. The reference is normally taken to be to the *Topics* (perhaps I.14). But there is no discussion in the *Topics* that can plausibly be called a 'more detailed account' of what Aristotle has just gone through, and the discussion of 'how premises are to be selected' in *Topics* I.14 seems very remote from the present subject. Since this sentence intrudes into an otherwise fairly cohesive line of argument in A 30−31, I suggest it may be a later editor's attempt (inspired by merely verbal similarity) at tying together the two passages.

Chapter 31

This Chapter is complementary to *Posterior Analytics* II.5, which evidently refers to it (91b12–14).

46a31. 'Division by means of kinds' (*hē dia tōn genōn dihairesis*) is the procedure given in Plato's *Sophist* and *Statesman*. The person dividing begins by determining some overall genus within which the thing to be defined is included. This genus is then divided into two (or perhaps more) subgenera, and the *definiendum* is assigned to one of these. The process is repeated until a last genus is reached which is identical with the *definiendum*. Aristotle is sometimes criticized for treating this procedure as a rival in some way to his theory of deductions: after all, it may be urged, the two have quite different objectives, and therefore it is no more a valid criticism of division that it fails to prove than it would be appropriate to object that deductions or demonstrations fail to define. But there is a deeper point. Aristotle's real complaint is that division is not a method which leads to the acquisition of *knowledge*: at each step, the divider must 'ask for the initial thing.' Thus, the method cannot produce understanding.

46a32. 'procedure' (*methodos*): to translate this as 'method' obscures the connection with *hodos* ('route'). Aristotle uses *methodos* as a synonym of *hodos* as in 43a21, 45a20, 45b37, 46a3, and later at 46b24, 46b33. Elsewhere, *methodos* often means 'scientific discipline': see the Note on 53a2.

46a36–37. A 'demonstration concerning substance, or what something is' would be a proof of a definition. Aristotle's own views on this subject, as expressed in *Posterior Analytics* II.5–10, are somewhat difficult of interpretation (see Ackrill *1981*), but he seems to reject the notion that definitions or essences are subject to proof.

46a37–39. Aristotle charges the partisans of division with two errors: not only did they miss the true procedure (his), but also they failed even to understand their own.

46b5–7. Here we have a deduction with a disjunctive middle term ('B or C'). Aristotle does not tell us much about how he understands such terms, but there is some evidence available in *On Interpretation* 8 about the comparable case of conjunctive terms.

46b20–22. 'take the universal . . . their extremes': the 'universal' is the term Aristotle has designated A, the 'differences' are the two contraries with which it is divided (B and C), and 'that about which' is the term to be defined (D).

46b24. Those who divide 'follow out their different route in its entirety' (*tēn allēn hodon poiountai pasan*): that is, carry their procedure all the way to its end. (Compare the reference to 'another route' at 45a21). 'Solutions' translates *euporiai*, which is opposed in this sense to *aporiai*: compare *Metaphysics* III.1, 995a29, *On the Heavens* II.12, 291b27.

46b26–37. For good measure, Aristotle notes several other things his deductions can do which division cannot: refute, argue about things other than definitions, and give us knowledge we do not already have. According to the *Posterior Analytics*, demonstrative deduction accomplishes the latter not by showing us new facts, but by giving us explanations.

Chapter 32

Aristotle now begins the last major project of *Prior Analytics* A: explaining how any argument may be put into the forms of the three figures. This project is somewhat comparable to translating natural-language arguments into a formal language. As a result, this section (A32–A44) consists mostly of heuristic devices and explanatory notes, though there is some important theoretical material, especially in 44. (A 45 and A 46 do not fit so clearly into Aristotle's announced goals: see the Notes on them below.) Much of *Prior Analytics* B (especially 23–27) may be a continuation of this project (again, see the discussions below in the Notes).

46b40–47a2. Aristotle promises to tell us how to 'lead back' (*anagein*) or 'break up' (*analuein*) existing arguments into the figures. These two verbs share the prefix *ana*, which suggests either motion upwards or returning back to some starting point. Aristotle has already used *anagein* of the process of completing a deduction, and later in A 45 he uses it of a somewhat more general process of transforming deductions from one figure to another by means of conversions. *Analuein* appears to be synonymous with *anagein*, though its root meaning would suggest decomposing arguments into their constituents in some way. In *Posterior Analytics* I.12, 78a6–8, it appears to designate specifically the search for the premises from which a conclusion can be proved. Since the title 'Analytics' (*ta analutika*) is Aristotle's own and applies to the *Prior* and *Posterior* as a whole, these processes are evidently a primary concern of his.

47a2–5. The summary given here corresponds well to the divisions Aristotle himself indicates in the text of Book A: the first part comprises at least 1–22 (and perhaps 1–26), and its completion is indicated at 43a16–19; the second is announced at 43a20–24 and comprises Chapters 27–30; and the third, which begins here, is declared complete at 51b3–5. But it is possible that much of the material in Book B could also be attached to this third section (see the Notes on B, particularly B 16, B 22–27).

47a5–9. The declaration with which this passage closes is reminiscent of Parmenides.

47a12–13. 'larger parts': that is, premises (rather than terms). 'Universal': in Greek, actually 'in a whole' (*en holōi*).

47a18. 'other useless things' (*alla de matēn*): compare 42a23–24 on 'concealment.'

47a21. '*asked* in this way' (*houtōs erōtēmenous*): Aristotle clearly has a dialectical situation in mind (cf. 24a24–25, 24b10–12).

47a31–40. Recent interpreters have taken this section as evidence that

Aristotle recognized that some valid arguments were not 'syllogistic.' But given the broad generality of application he has tried to show for his account, it would be odd to find such a concession here; and given his definition of *sullogismos*, it is difficult to know what it would mean. In its context, the passage probably has a much less profound sense: 'cases like these' must refer to the examples discussed in the preceding lines, which Aristotle has characterized as arguments in which some premise has been left out. Therefore, he is only saying that some (persuasive?) arguments fail to be deductions as they are presented because certain obvious premises are left unstated. In any event, he does not say that they cannot be accommodated by his methods, but rather, that one should not try to resolve them 'straight off' (*euthus*).

47b1. 'predicated and a subject of predication': in Greek, this is the same verb in active and passive voice (*katēgorēi kai katēgorētai*). Aristotle almost never uses *katēgorein* like this: the passive is normally used with the sense the active voice has here, and the active normally used only of a person uttering a predication.

Chapter 33

In this Chapter Aristotle makes the sensible point that not everything which appears to be arranged as a deduction in the figures really is so. The specific error he is concerned with is usually identified as that of taking an indeterminate premise to be universal. However, the examples he uses to illustrate this point appear, instead, to make it more obscure: each involves a proper name, and Aristotle complicates matters by presenting us with premises in which quantifiers are applied to proper names. Interpreters have, therefore, found the Chapter a source of considerable difficulty; my Notes aim more at indicating what the points of obscurity are than at resolving them. For an insightful recent discussion, see Bäck *1987*.

See Ross's notes for possible identifications of Aristomenes and Mikkalos (who appear in Aristotle as examples only in this passage).

47b21−29. Aristotle locates the problem in his first example in the fact that the (putative) major premise 'Thinkable Aristomenes always is' is indeterminate (lacks a quantifier). However, he says, if we add a universal quantifier to this premise, then it becomes false. Why does Aristotle call it false, rather than nonsensical (as we might be inclined to)? The answer may lie in the fact that the Greek *pas* (like French *tout*) may be used both with sortal terms (like English 'every') and with singulars and 'mass terms' (like English 'all of' or, in the same sense, 'all'). As a result, *pas ho dianoētos Aristomenēs aei estin* could also mean 'All *of* thinkable Aristomenes always is,' which is false for perishable Aristomenes. (Aristotle may have taken note of this distinction: cf. *Metaphysics* V.9, 1018a3−4.)

Mignucci, taking note of this last point, suggests instead that 'Aristomenes' in the second premise is a general term meaning 'person named "Aristomenes.'" Thus, 'Thinkable Aristomenes always is' would mean 'Of the think-able [conceivable?] men with the name "Aristomenes," there will always exist at least one.' This is an ingenious suggestion; but if that is what Aristotle had in mind, why then does he say 'But this is false . . . if Aristomenes is perishable'?

47b23−24.   'Thinkable Aristomenes always is' (*aei gar esti dianoētos Aristomenēs*): while it is usually taken to mean 'Aristomenes *qua* thinkable always exists,' Aristotle just might have in mind also the sense 'Aristomenes is always thinkable.' I have tried to keep the ambiguity in my translation. In-deed, there may even be a sort of pun involved: *dianoētos* can mean 'intended' or 'what is meant,' so that this sentence might mean 'It is always Aristomenes that is meant.'

47b29−37.   Aristotle thinks his second example commits the same fallacy as the first. The reason why 'Musical Mikkalos will perish tomorrow' is not 'universally true' might be that this *sentence* is not always true (if true today, then it was not true yesterday). Or, if the suggestion offered for the last case is plausible, then *ou gar alēthes katholou, Mikkalos mousikos hoti phtheiretai aurion* might mean something like 'it is not true of *the whole of* musical Mikkalos . . .', i.e., part of musical Mikkalos (the plain unmusical man) will remain. Of these two possibilities, the first seems to me more likely: the rather odd grammar of the sentence (word for word, 'it is not true universally, musical Mikkalos that he will perish tomorrow') resembles the sort of construction which in Aristotle often functions like a pair of inverted commas.

Once again, Mignucci takes the argument to involve a use of proper names as a sort of general term: 'musical Mikkalos will perish tomorrow' could mean 'some musician with the name Mikkalos will perish tomorrow,' and of course it does not follow from this that our particular musical Mikkalos will perish tomorrow.

Chapter 34

48a2−15.   Aristotle's first example of terms 'not well set out' is the deduc-tion 'Health necessarily belongs to no illness; every man is susceptible of illness; therefore, health necessarily belongs to no man.' He solves the diffi-culty by substituting terms 'applying to the conditions' (*kata tas hexeis*), i.e., attributive terms like 'healthy' and 'ill,' in place of the corresponding 'condi-tions' (*hexeis*), i.e., abstract singular terms like 'health' and 'illness'. The minor premise then becomes 'Healthy necessarily belongs to nothing ill,' which Aristotle says is false.

Aristotle's example seems to be a modal deduction, with the minor premise equivalent to 'It is possible for every man to be ill' and the major premise and conclusion necessary. According to A 16 (36a7−15), the conclusion from this combination of premises should be *assertoric*: Aristotle ignores this, and instead concedes that a *possible* conclusion might be acceptable. The problem about the setting out of terms really concerns the interpretation of abstract singular terms in predications: 'Health belongs to no illness' might be taken as a statement about two Platonic universals, as a statement about the classes of healthy and ill things, or in some intermediate way. There may be important connections here with Plato's questions about the 'communion of kinds' in the *Sophist*: see Vlastos *1972, 1973a*.

48a15−18.   Aristotle extends his treatment to a parallel second-figure case ('Health cannot belong to any illness; health can belong to every man; therefore, illness can not belong to any man'). His account is cryptically brief: presumably, he thinks it is parallel to the previous example. (If so, he again contradicts his earlier treatment: cf. A 19, 38a14−25.)

48a16.   'mistake' (*pseudos*): this word usually means 'falsehood' or 'false.' However, immediately preceding at 47b40 the verb *diapseudesthai* clearly means 'make a mistake,' not 'state a falsehood' or 'lie.' Compare *Nicomachean Ethics* VI.6 1141a3, 1144a35; *Metaphysics* IV.3, 1005b12, and the Notes on 30a27, 37a22, 48a16, 49a18−22.

48a18−21.   Aristotle is less clear about what the third-figure case is supposed to be. Ross thinks it is 'Health can belong to every man; illness can belong to every man; therefore, health can belong to some illness.' The apparent paradox is then eliminated by the suggested substitution, so that the conclusion becomes the unproblematic 'Some healthy things are possibly ill.'

48a21−23.   These lines (whether Aristotle's or an editor's) reflect second thoughts about the consistency of the doctrine just stated with the rest of Book A. The reference appears to be to 39a14−19, where second-figure *Darapti* with two possible premises is said to yield a possible conclusion.

Chapter 35

48a29−31.   'with a <single> word' (*onomati*): the term *onoma*, 'name,' is used by Plato and Aristotle very much like 'noun' as a grammatical term, but unlike 'noun' it has the ordinary sense 'name' and sometimes the broader sense 'word'.

48a31−39.   The error Aristotle identifies here is not, as generally supposed, believing that demonstration of an unmiddled statement is possible, but mistakenly taking a specific deduction to have unmiddled premises. Otherwise, Aristotle's example is irrelevant: he offers us, not an apparent deduction of an unmiddled statement, but a deduction with an apparently unmiddled *premise*. It is clear that the minor premise of the deduction 'Everything isosceles is a triangle' is unmiddled, since it is a matter of definition. The difficulty is that 'Every triangle has <the sum of its internal angles equal to> two right angles' appears to lack a middle term, even though it is demonstrable (it is, in fact, Aristotle's favorite example of a geometrical theorem; as usual, he states it in an extremely elliptical fashion). This discussion recalls *Posterior Analytics* I.5, which refers to cases of a 'nameless' (*anōnumon*) middle term (74a8) and discusses the same geometrical example.

48a35—37. 'possesses two right angles of itself': in *Posterior Analytics* I.4, the expression 'of itself' (which is an Aristotelian technical usage) is explained as equivalent to 'essentially,' i.e., 'in the definition'; but in the following Chapter 5 it is evidently treated as equivalent to 'just as' or '*qua*.' With this in mind, Ross takes Aristotle to mean that 'there is no wider class of figures to which the <two-right-angle> attribute belongs directly.' But this implies that in a demonstration the middle term must always be *wider* than the minor, which is contradicted elsewhere in the *Posterior Analytics* (cf. I.13, where all three terms of a demonstration are coextensive). The fact is that this is an especially hard case for Aristotle: there is no very plausible way to get the demonstration of this theorem Aristotle knows (cf. e.g., *Metaphysics* IX.9, 1051a24—26) into figured form. Ian Mueller *1974* argues (in my opinion convincingly) that in general, Greek geometrical arguments strongly resist being recast in Aristotle's canonical forms for very fundamental reasons. In the present case, Aristotle must say that there really is a middle term but that it can only be expressed in a 'phrase' (*logos*), though he gives us no idea what that 'phrase' might be (the Greek term would even admit the senses 'sentence' or 'discourse': Ross's strained attempt to supply a middle term shows how extended that phrase may have to be).

Chapter 36

48a40—b2. Although Aristotle generally treats 'belongs to' and 'is predicated of' (or 'is said of') as synonyms, here he distinguishes them, evidently taking the former to be wider in extent than the latter. His claim is that the relationship of predicate to subject in a deductive premise need not be one of predication, though it must be one of 'belonging.' It is clear that Aristotle wants to extend the range of application of his deductive theory to cases which, as he recognizes, cannot easily be treated as categorical sentences. However, it is less clear how he proposes to do that. Mignucci (480—481) proposes that Aristotle here restricts 'predicated' to cases in which the subject term is in the nominative case, while leaving 'belongs' with its customary wide sense in which it can indicate 'any possible grammatical construction for a predicative relation.' Ross (407) says that 'we must take account of the cases of the nouns and recognize that these are capable of expressing a great variety of relations and that the nature of the relations in the premises dictates the nature of the relations in the conclusion.'

These do seem to be descriptions of what Aristotle is trying to do. But it is not at all clear how such an extension is to be justified. Aristotle says that he rests his entire deductive theory on definitions of 'predicated of every' and 'predicated of no' (24b28—30). If he now wishes to extend the notion of a premise to include cases in which the 'predicate' term is *not* predicated of the 'subject,' then what becomes of this theory?

Aristotle does not tell us anything about this, but his examples suggest that he is now willing to admit premises which in some respect *behave like* strictly

categorical sentences, even though they are not. Thus, it is the formal relationships among premises considered as sentences that he is calling attention
to, rather than the semantic basis of those relationships in the relationships of
what their terms denote. It is tempting to see a parallel here to another
passage. In *Posterior Analytics* I.5, Aristotle offers the theorem that proportional
terms are also proportional *alternando* (i.e., if A:B::C:D, then A:C::B:D) as an
example of a theorem that formerly was proved as a different result in different
ways about different subject matters but 'now' is given a 'universal' proof
covering them all (74a17−25). Before the 'universal' proof was discovered,
there were several formally similar statements about proportional numbers,
lines, solids, or times; the formal similarity among these eventually led to the
development of a single proof embracing them all. Similarly, Aristotle here
may be trying to increase the generality of his theory of deductions by explor-
ing other types of premises formally similar to the categorical sentences with
which he began.

48b2−4.   Despite appearances, there is little if any connection between
this sentence and the famous doctrine of the homonymy of 'is' as found in
Metaphysics IV.2, 1003a33−b15, VII.1, 1028a10−31, XI.3, 1060b31−1061a10.

48b4−7.   The example treats the sentence 'There is a single science of
contraries' as having as predicate 'there is a single science *of them*' (*mian einai
autōn epistēmēn*) and as subject 'things contrary to each other' (*ta enantia al-
lēlois*). Ross takes the predicate to be 'that there is one science,' supposing that
Aristotle thinks this is affirmed of 'contraries' by saying, of contraries, that
there is one science of them. But this cannot be right. Aristotle has just
explained that 'belongs' has as many senses as 'is' here, so that, presumably,
we could construct the requisite premise with 'is.' But this would give us
something like 'contraries are there being one science,' which is nonsense.
Instead, Aristotle takes the predicate to have included in it 'of them' (*autōn*).
Thus, what is said to belong to contraries is, not that there is a single science,
but that there is a single science *of them*. There are several objections that can
be raised about this analysis from the standpoint of modern logic, but an
important point that Aristotle does *not* miss (and which Ross apparently does)
is that the predicate in question is *relational*: what is being said about 'contraries' is not 'there is a single science' but 'there is a single science *of those
contraries*.' Aristotle's device of building this into the predicate may not be very
well worked out, but it shows that he was sensitive to the problem.

48b7−9.   'Not in the sense that contraries are a single science of them' (*ouch
hōs ta enantia to mian einai autōn epistēmēn*): this is the received Greek text in
most sources. One of the oldest manuscripts (*n*) and Georgios' Syriac translation add 'are' (*esti*) after 'contraries,' which supports my rendering more explicitly, though the same sense can readily be gotten without it. Ross finds this
unintelligible, and changes the text to *ouch hōste ta enantia mian einai epistēmēn*:
'not so that contraries are one science.' But Aristotle tells us that the *right* way

to understand this premise is as saying 'there is a single science *of them*' about contraries, and we should, therefore, expect the same predicate-term in the first case. It is perfectly in order, in fact, for the first clause to be nonsense: Aristotle's purpose is to argue that the sentence in question is *not* a predication but something else, and to do that he shows that taking it as a predication results in a nonsensical reading. Mignucci (481) gives an interpretation in some ways similar to mine.

Note that even though he claims that it is not a predication, Aristotle says that 'it is true to say' its predicate-term of its subject. This suggests that he is not completely sure how he wants to carry out his own analysis here.

48b10−27.   We now have three examples in which one or both premises are not really predications: Aristotle says one term is not 'said of' (*legetai*) or 'predicated of' (*katēgoreitai*) another. In every case, the conclusion can be interpreted as an assertion of existence, and such statements are quite difficult to put into Aristotle's required canonical form.

48b10−14.   Aristotle's first example of a deduction with nonpredicative premises is clearly intended to be in the first figure. It is perhaps a little clearer how it is supposed to work if we stay close to the Greek word order:

Wisdom is <a> science (*hē sophia estin epistēmē*)
Of the good is wisdom (*tou agathou estin hē sophia*)
Therefore, of the good is <a> science (*tou agathou estin epistēmē*)

Aristotle simply presents the example and observes that neither the minor premise nor the conclusion is a predication. He does not, however, explain how we should understand these premises, if they are not predications, and he does not try to argue that the deduction is a valid one. He defends his claim that the conclusion is not a predication with the observation that 'the good is not a science': this suggests that he takes the minor term to be 'good,' not 'of the good.' The oblique case (in this case genitive) must, therefore, be part of the relevant sense of 'belong' here, so that one way in which X can belong to Y is for X to be 'of' Y. From this, we might suspect that Aristotle is now using 'belongs' in an extremely wide sense, almost like 'is in some relation to.'

One problem with this example is that it is difficult not to take the minor premise and conclusion to be existential ('there is a science/wisdom of the good'). This may not be Aristotle's intent. Ross avoids the existential sense by rendering the deduction as 'wisdom is knowledge, the good is the object of wisdom, <therefore> the good is an object of knowledge.' But this seems to me too highly interpretative to be a translation: the existential reading should not, I think, be foreclosed, and in any event, 'object of knowledge' is very hard to see in Aristotle's Greek.

48b14−19.   Aristotle's next example is something like 'Science is of every contrary or quality; the good is a contrary, and a quality; therefore, science is of the good.' He points out here that both in the minor premise and the conclusion, 'science' is not predicated of anything, although it is in the major premise. Given the discussion in 48b5−6, we might expect him to say that the major term is not 'science' but something like 'there being a science of it.' However, throughout this discussion Aristotle evidently assumes that any expression containing the *word* 'science' must really be an occurrence of the *term* 'science,' regardless of the construction.

48b20−24.   We next get a deduction in which there is no predication at all. It is perhaps significant that both 'science' and 'genus' are relational terms here (a science and a genus are respectively the science *of* something and the genus *of* something).

48b27.   'not said of one another': that is, the middle term is not said of the last nor the first of the middle.

48b27−49a5.   Aristotle now says he will turn his attention to negative cases. His examples are all in second-figure form, probably because the 'predicate' must apply to two different subjects in the same oblique case (and so he needs the premises to share a predicate-term). 'There is no motion of motion' (*ouk esti kinēseōs kinēsis*) seems to be a straightforward negative existential statement. 'There is not a sign of a sign' could be a sort of grammatical remark ('We do not speak of a sign of a sign'), but the parallel with 'There is a sign of laughter' (*gelōtos esti sēmeion*) should incline us towards an existential reading. 'There is opportunity for a god' (*theōi kairos estin*) probably has to be taken as existential.

As before, Aristotle takes terms really to be expressed by their nominative forms, even when they do not occur in this way at all in the argument (as in the example, 'There is opportunity for a god; nothing is useful (and / or needed) for a god; therefore, opportunity is not <the time> needed,' in which, despite the fact that 'god' occurs only in the dative case, Aristotle says the term to choose is the nominative form).

48b34−35.   'through the genus being said about it': commentators beginning with Alexander take this to mean, in effect, 'in the second figure.' The 'genus' is simply the middle term (which, since it is predicated of both extremes, is perhaps analogous to their 'genus). 'About it' (*pros auto*) apparently means 'about the problem,' i.e., about *each* of its terms.

It is worth taking note here of Aristotle's grammatical terminology because these are among the earlier occurrences of such technical language in Greek. He uses the term 'inflection' (*ptōsis*) to designate any inflected form derived from an adjective or noun stem by changing the ending. Our use of the word 'case' in its grammatical sense ultimately descends from this Greek word (by way of the Latin *casus*). However, for Aristotle the nominative form is *not* an inflection: he refers to it, instead, as the 'appellation of the noun' (*klēsis onomatos*). Moreover, included among cases are not only what we would count as oblique cases (genitive, dative, accusative), but also adverbial forms with the ending −*ōs*.

49a2−4. The first three of Aristotle's examples are of relational terms complemented by the dative, genitive, and accusative cases, respectively; the last is just a *non*-relational predicate in the nominative case, here exemplified, not by a predicate in isolation, but by a predicate ('animal') used in an example.

Chapter 37

This little note proclaims its own incompleteness. I translate *katēgoriai* as 'predications' on the basis of parallels with 41a4, 41b31, 45b34 (the sense 'categories' is certainly not appropriate). As in the latter two passages, Aristotle probably has in mind modal qualifications; the call for further study then, presumably, is partly answered by A 8−22. 'Either simple or compound' (*ē haplas ē sumpeplegmenas*): Aristotle does not explain, either here or elsewhere, what 'compound' predicates are, but *On Interpretation* 5 does make reference to a compound *sentence* (*logos . . . sunthetos*, 17a22).

It is conceivable that this note originated separately from the materials immediately preceding it and found its way here in the editorial process (whatever it may have been, and whoever may have done it) which led to the creation of our present text. It describes in broad terms what Aristotle has been talking about in A 34−36, but without acknowledging that he has been talking about it. There are other cases in the *Prior Analytics* in which a detailed discussion of a subject is followed by a briefer and more primitive treatment of the same thing (see, for instance, B 17 and the Notes on it). It is plausible to ascribe these to editorial practice, though we simply do not know enough about the history of the treatises to determine this with any confidence.

Chapter 38

49a11−12. I translate *epanadiploumenon* as 'something *extra* duplicated' to reflect the prefix *epi* + *ana* (Alexander points out that the middle term is already 'something duplicated in the premises': the case in question involves something extra). (The Latin *reduplicatio* captures this.) Aristotle's subject is deductions in which phrases introduced by 'insofar as' or 'because' are added to a predicate. He classes these generally as 'extra predicates' (*epikatēgoroumena*: cf. 49a25): the *epanadiploumena* are those cases of *epikatēgoroumena* in which the extra predicate is identical to that to which it is added.

The 'reduplicative' statements of this Chapter were the subject of much discussion by later ancient and medieval logicians. For a detailed study, see Bäck *1988*.

49a13−14. Because of the ambiguity of the conjunction *hoti*, *epistēmē hoti agathon* could be rendered either 'knowledge *that* it is good' or 'knowledge *because* it is good.' I have tried to reproduce this ambiguity in English rather lamely with 'knowledge *in that* it is good.' (For a rough parallel, compare

24a22−23: *diapherei . . . hoti*, 'is different . . . *in that.*') In *Posterior Analytics* I.13, Aristotle takes some pains to restrict *hoti* to the sense 'that,' using *dihoti* instead for 'because,' but he does not himself observe this distinction elsewhere (even in the *Posterior Analytics*); it clearly will not fit the present context, since Aristotle varies *hoti* here with *hēi* ('insofar as,' *qua*).

49a18.   The expression 'is just a good' (*hoper agathon*), or 'identically a good,' indicates, as Alexander notes, what Aristotle calls 'essential predication': saying of something what it is. This is connected in fundamental ways with the doctrine of 'categories,' or types of predication, elaborated in several places in the treatises: see *Topics* I.9.

49a18−22.   The principal point Aristotle makes in this section applies, as he states it, only to first-figure deductions having an 'extra duplication' in their major premises and conclusions. What he says is that in such cases the extra duplication is to be treated as part of the major extreme, not the middle term, since otherwise we get a nonsensical analysis. In effect, he is glossing 'X is Y in that it is Z' as having the structure 'X, in that it is Z, is Y,' rather than the structure 'X is Y-in-that-it-is-Z.' He does not indicate how we should extend the analysis to other cases besides the first figure.

On the phrase 'incorrect and not intelligible' (*pseudos kai ou suneton*), cf. the Notes on 30a27, 37a22, 48a16 ('and' here means 'i.e.').

49a24.   'goat-stag' (*tragelaphos*): this mythical creature is perhaps Aristotle's favorite example of a nonexistent thing (the point being that the term does indeed have a meaning, so that one can, in a sense, know what a goat-stag is, even though there are no goat-stags to have knowledge of).

49a27−b1.   In this section, Aristotle evidently has in view a more generalized account of the cases involving 'extra duplication' he has just discussed (although he does not actually make this clear). He now distinguishes deductions 'without qualification' (*haplōs*), i.e., in which the predicate of the conclusion is a simple term with no additional qualifiers, from deductions including such an additional expression. His claim that the 'setting (out) of the terms' is not the same in the two cases again resembles his point in 49a11−26, which was just to explain how to set out the terms in reduplicative cases. (Thus, I take *thesis* in 49a27 as if it were *ekthesis*, and not as 'position.')

What Aristotle says is tantalizingly brief, and most of it is really the treatment of a single pair of examples. Consequently, it is difficult to be certain just what he is up to here, but it appears to be a somewhat sophisticated type of relational deduction. The critical point is determining just what the terms of his examples are. He states the terms of the first deduction as 'knowledge in that it is something' (*epistēmē hoti ti on*), 'being something' (*on ti*), and 'good.' Evidently, the deduction he has in mind is the following:

There is knowledge of what is so-and-so in that it is so-and-so;
Being good is being so-and-so;
Therefore, there is knowledge of what is good in that it is good.

Thus, the expression 'being something' (*on ti, ti on*) is a sort of variable here, perhaps best represented as 'being *F*' (see the Note just below on 49a36). Note that here *F* is, in the terms of modern logic, a second-order variable (that is, a variable whose values are predicates, not individuals). The major premise of Aristotle's example is then the second-order statement 'For any *F*, there is knowledge of what is *F* in that it is *F*.' We could then interpret the minor premise as simply the assertion that 'good' is a predicate, so that the entire deduction becomes a matter of instantiating a universal (second-order) statement.

Aristotle contrasts this with the following example:

There is knowledge of what is [so-and-so?] in that it *is*;
What is good *is*;
Therefore, there is knowledge of what is good in that it *is*.

Apparently, 'is' here means 'exists.' (But note that at 43b36—38, Aristotle said that terms which 'follow everything' are useless in the search for deductions.)

If this analysis is on the right track, then what Aristotle is doing in this section is developing a type of generalization of the reduplicative premises considered previously (it is clear that his ideas here are relatively unfinished).

49a28—29.   Aristotle lists three types of cases according to the nature of the qualifier attached to the predicate: (1) the qualification is 'this something' (*tode ti*), (2) the qualification is 'in some respect' (*pēi*), (3) the qualification is 'somehow' (*pōs*). He does not tell us what each of these is, and in fact, he may have no very precise system of classification in mind. The expression *tode ti*, literally 'this here something,' is an Aristotelian coinage which usually indicates a particular sensible individual. Alexander (369.33—370.6) takes it in the present case as equivalent to *ti esti* and supposes that in case (1) the qualification must be part of the essence or definition. He illustrates cases (2) and (3) with the examples 'The healthy is knowable insofar as (*qua*) good' and 'A goat-stag is thinkable insofar as it is nonexistent' (*doxaston hēi mē on*).'

49a36.   'for "being so-and-so" was a symbol for its peculiar being' (*to gar ti on tēs idiou sēmeion ousias*): this puzzling expression makes most sense, I believe, as Aristotle's own explanation of his use of 'being so-and-so' (*on ti, ti on*) as a kind of variable. Aristotle is, thus, telling us something about the *expression* 'being so-and-so.'

49b1—2.   'It is evident . . . particular deductions': Alexander explains this puzzling remark with the suggestion that 'good in that it is good' is a term of lesser extent than 'good' (so that he takes Aristotle's examples to be in some way particular, not universal, deductions). But Aristotle says, not that these deductions are to be regarded as particular, but rather, that particular deductions are (also?) to be treated in this way.

Chapter 39

The point of this little note is to recommend the substitution of single words as terms in place of their expansions into phrases (e.g., as definitions). 'Have the same value' (*dunatai to auto*): the verb *dunasthai*, 'be able,' is also used with the sense 'be worth' (as in connection with coins), and it occurs as early as Herodotus in the sense 'mean' (of words).

Chapter 40

From a modern viewpoint, the difference between 'Pleasure is *a* good' and 'Pleasure is *the* good' is that the former is a predication, whereas the latter is an identity: the occurrence of the same word 'is' in each is a superficial similarity which conceals a diversity of logical form. Aristotle instead treats them as categoricals but with different predicates ('good' and 'the good' respectively). This tells us that he recognized these as different, although it gives us no clues as to how he understood that difference.

Alexander takes the difference between the two examples to be similar to that between using a term in its normal predicative sense and using that term as the name of a species (to modify his example slightly, the following fallacy illustrates the point: 'Every man is an animal, animal is a genus, therefore every man is a genus'). The distinction between '*A* is *B*' and '*A* is the *B*' attracted Plato's attention also (see, for instance, *Hippias Major* 287a−d).

Chapter 41

49b14−32. The distinction made in this section seems clear enough, but its relationship to the rest of *Prior Analytics* A is less certain. Aristotle's concern is the forms '*A* belongs to all of what *B* belongs to' and '*A* belongs to all of what *B* belongs to all of.' His point is that the former need not be interpreted as synonymous with the latter. Alexander says two things about this section, both of them likely correct. First, he connects the discussion with the *dictum de omni* of 24b28−30: '*A* is predicated of every *B*' means 'none of *B* can be taken of which *A* cannot be said'. Next, he links the discussion to the 'prosleptic' premises which appear briefly in B 5−7 (58a29−32, 58b8−10, 58b37−38, 59a28−29). He also informs us that Theophrastus held the difference between the two forms to be purely verbal, both being equivalent to '*A* is true of all of what *B* is true of all of' (379.9−11).

Alexander takes this last form to be equivalent to, or to imply, '*A* belongs to every *B*.' If we suppose it to be a logical truth that any term is universally true of itself, then the inference from '*A* is universally true of whatever term *B* is universally true of' to '*A* is universally true of term *B*' may seem trivial (because *B* is trivially among the terms *B* is universally true of). For Aristotle, however, the status of such identical predications is at least problematic. He rarely uses them as examples; and although he regards their denials ('Some *A* is not *A*') as obvious falsehoods (see B 15), he never states positively that they are themselves true, and might even have viewed them as in some way ill-formed.

49b30−32. 'And if B is said of all of something . . .': more fully, 'if B is said of all of some third thing, then A is likewise said of all of it; but if B is not said of all of this third thing, then A need not be said of all of it.'

49b33−50a4. The crucial factor in interpreting this section is determining just what Aristotle is talking about. Alexander and Mignucci take him to be defending the use of letters in expounding his deductive theory. On that view, the critical point of comparison is between letters and the actual diagrams used in a geometrical proof: each is, strictly speaking, a 'particular thing' (*tode ti*). Now the geometer may make statements in the course of his proof which he knows to be false about the figure in question (e.g., '*AB* is a straight line one foot long'). If it is the falsehood of these assertions about the actual figure that is important here, then the issue would be how a correct proof could rest on what seem to be false premises. Aristotle, however, does not discuss the falsehood of the premises, but rather, the particularity of the figure: the problem is that this particular figure seems to enter into the proof, which purports to be universal. His response that nothing which is not 'as a whole to a part' (*hōs holon pros meros*) enters into a proof is directed at this latter problem: it is universals, or universal premises, that are related to other things as whole to part, and the actual diagram is not so related to anything. (Ross cites *Sophistical Refutations* 178b36−179a8, where it is clear that the issue involves confusing particulars and universals.)

How then does this apply to the use of letters in Aristotle's own proofs of deductions? To see this, we should remember that his proofs of deductions follow the structure common in Greek mathematical proofs, in which the theorem to be proved is enunciated and recapitulated in general language, normally without the use of letters, while letters are introduced in an intermediate step, at the beginning of the proof proper. (This stage of the proof was called the *ekthesis* by later commentators on Euclid.) Evidently, Aristotle's point is that the *actual letters* which he introduces in the course of the proof are not universals in relationships of predication: they are concrete, sensible individuals, just as the diagrams in geometrical proofs are.

Aristotle may have in mind an even closer connection with geometrical proofs if, as is possible, he used letters as part of some diagramming technique (see Einarson *1936*, Rose *1968*). Unfortunately, we have no idea what it might have been. As I have interpreted it, this discussion has no special connection with the procedure usually called 'proof by *ekthesis*.'

49b32. 'of all': the manuscripts add 'A, B, C' here; Ross follows Alexander's text and the Aldine edition in omitting it.

49b33–34. 'any absurdity results . . . setting something out': the phrase *para to ektithesthai ti sumbainein atopon* is grammatically ambiguous. I take *ti* as the object of *ektithesthai* ('setting something out'); other translators take it to modify 'absurd,' giving a sense like 'an absurdity, should one result, is not to be attributed to the setting-out.'

49b35–36. 'calls this a foot-long line, this a straight line, and says that they are breadthless, though they are not' (*tēn podiaian kai eutheian tēnde kai aplatē einai legei ouk ousas*): commentators disagree over whether 'are' (both participle *ousas* and infinitive *einai*) should be taken as existential or predicative. I have opted for the latter course: Aristotle's example clearly concerns a geometer who says things about a diagram that are not strictly true of it (such that a certain line is really straight or really without breadth). The text here is somewhat difficult grammatically and the number of variations suggests it may be corrupt, although I think the point Aristotle is trying to make comes through well enough. To get the sense I do out of Ross's text, I need to treat the first *tēn* as a demonstrative and take the grammar as somewhat elliptical. Barnes omits the first *tēn* and changes the plural participle *ousas* to the singular *ousan*, giving 'this line is a foot long, and straight, and without breadth, when it is not.'

50a1–2. This sentence (*tōi d'ektithesthai houtō chrōmetha hōsper kai tōi aisthanesthai ton manthanonta legontes*) has vexed translators and commentators. The assumption has been that Aristotle is talking about the use of the *procedure* of *ekthesis* here and comparing it to some use of sensory perception in the case of a 'learner,' i.e., a student. But the grammar of the sentence makes it extremely difficult, if not impossible, to get such a sense out of it. Ross makes the inventive suggestion that we read *ton manthanont' alegontes*, 'in taking care of the learner'; but this requires us to read the unusual poetic word *alegontes*, otherwise not found in Aristotle. My translation is grammatically and textually unproblematic, and leads to a simple connection with the argument of the passage: the *expression* 'set out' no more entails that we are really 'setting out' a concrete individual than the *expression* 'perceive' implies actual sense perception. (Compare the English use of 'see' with the meaning 'understand.')

Chapter 42

50a5–10. 'Deduction' here means an extended deduction which may contain subsidiary deductions in several figures. There is no detailed treatment of such complex deductions in Aristotle, though some results are established in A 25 (see 42b1–26).

Chapter 43

50a11–15. Two things about this isolated note suggest the environment of the *Topics*. First, the subject itself recalls that work's division of arguments as they concern definition, peculiar property, genus, or accident. Second, Aristotle twice uses the verb *dialegesthai* in the sense 'argue (to a conclusion),' a usage ubiquitous in the *Topics* but rare in the *Analytics*.

One striking point about this brief text, which is not evident in the translation, is the number of different senses in which Aristotle manages to use the same two words in it. When he announces his subject as 'arguments aimed towards a definition,' the word *logos* is used in the sense 'argument'; a few lines later the same word means 'definition' ('the entire definition'). When he states his subject, 'definition' is *horismos*; by the end of the sentence, at the phrase 'terms in the definition,' he has switched to the term *horos*. He then proceeds to use the word *horos* in the sense 'term' (which is its usual meaning in the *Prior Analytics*).

Chapter 44

50a16−19. This treatment of 'deductions from an assumption' should be studied in conjunction with the earlier discussions in A 23 (41a21−b1) and A 29 (see the Notes on those passages). Aristotle repeats his view that the conclusions of such arguments are really not 'proved by means of a deduction' (*dia sullogismou dedeigmenoi*) but 'consented to by means of an agreement' (*dia sunthēkēs homologēmenoi*: cf. 41a38−b1). Thus, these arguments are deductive only *from* (*ek*) *an assumption*, i.e., deduce from an assumption as a premise: they are not really *deductions* of their ultimate conclusions, but of something else.

50a19−26. 'for example, if someone assumed': In this example, Aristotle uses the language of disputation and dialectic: when the assumption has been agreed upon, the person deducing 'argues' (*dialechtheiē*) the conclusion: the verb *dialegesthai* implies a context of dispute between two parties (see the Note on 50a11−15). Aristotle explicitly says that the desired conclusion 'has not been proved' (*ou dedeiktai*). It is 'necessary to agree' only in the sense that, otherwise, there would be no argument.

The example Aristotle uses here is alluded to several times, in various ways, in the *Prior Analytics* (see 24b20−21 and Note, 48b4−5 and Note, 48b16−17, 69b9−26). The use Aristotle wants to make of the example seems clear enough: in order to show that there is not always a single science for any given pair of contraries, which has as its object both members of that pair, we first secure an agreement that, if there is not a single potentiality or 'power' (*dunamis*) for a pair of contraries, then there is not a single science of them either. There are certain complications about the example itself, however. The deduction whereby it is shown that there is not a single potentiality for every pair of contraries is apparently itself a deduction through impossibility; thus, on Aristotle's analysis, it too is an 'argument from an assumption.' It is at least curious that he should use so unnecessarily complex a case (since it is, in effect, an argument from an assumption *included within* an argument from an assumption).

50a21–23. 'for example, of what is wholesome and what is unwholesome': the majority of translators take *hugieinon* and *nosōdes* here to mean 'healthy' and 'diseased,' which is certainly possible. However, Aristotle evidently regards it as impossible for there to be a single capacity for these contraries in this case, and that is not, at any rate, an obvious absurdity given his views: in several places he suggests that 'every potentiality is of opposites,' and even if this is restricted to 'rational' capacities as in *Metaphysics* IX.2, it appears to be closely associated with the *Prior Analytics'* notion of two-sided possibility (cf. the Note on 32b4–22). And in any event, there is nothing paradoxical whatsoever about holding that the same person may, at the same time, possess both the potentiality for being healthy and the potentiality for being diseased.

We get a much better sense if we take *hugieinon* and *nosōdes* as 'what is *productive of* health,' 'what is *productive of* disease,' as Alexander does (387.1–5; cf. Pacius, 'salubre et insalubre'). The argument to an impossible conclusion is then as follows: if the potentiality (power) of the wholesome were the same as the potentiality (power) of the unwholesome, then the wholesome would have the power of producing disease. But then the same thing would be at once wholesome and unwholesome, which is absurd. I borrow the felicitous translations 'wholesome,' 'unwholesome' from O. F. Owen's 1853 version.

50a27. 'the latter . . . the former': in Greek, 'the latter' is masculine in gender (*houtos*), while 'the former' (*ekeino*) is neuter. The masculine may be explained by the gender of 'deduction,' which actually *follows* it in the sentence.

50a29–38. The 'leading away to an impossibility' (*hē eis to adunaton apagōgē*) is that part of a proof through impossibility in which the 'impossible' conclusion is deduced.

50a39–b4. This note again indicates the unfinished state of Aristotle's views on 'deductions from an assumption' (cf. 45b12–20). The promised fuller treatment is not found in any work known to us.

Chapter 45

According to its last lines (51b3–5), this Chapter brings Aristotle's discussion of the third main subject of Book A (resolving arguments into the figures) to a close. (A 46 is quite clearly an appendix with no close relationship to the projects of the rest of the Book: see the Notes on it.) However, the contents of A 45 are not really part of the project of A 32–44 (explaining how to 'resolve' given arguments into figured form) but instead address a theoretical problem in Aristotle's deductive system: are completions through impossibility necessary? Aristotle explores this by investigating the ways in which one deduction can be transformed into another by way of premise conversions. The location of this material here may result from the fact that Aristotle also calls this procedure 'resolving' (50b30, 33, etc.). An editor may, therefore, have tacked it on here, even though its more natural place would be with the studies in A 23—26.

50b5—9. The subject of the Chapter is not 'resolving' an arbitrary given argument into a figured argument, but 'leading back' a given *figured* argument from one figure into another. In the case of transformations from other figures into the first, Aristotle's procedures are identical to those proofs he uses in A 4—6 which rely entirely on conversions; here, however, he also investigates all possible transformations from one figure to another. Patzig (pp. 46—47) thinks that Aristotle is investigating alternative axiomatizations of this theory, but the closing remarks in 51a40—b2 are not, in my opinion, congenial to this.

51a24—25. 'when this premise . . .': this remark applies to the resolutions of the first and third figures into one another. 'Replaced' (*metatithemenēs*): compare the use of the closely related verb *metalambanein* at 37b15. Aristotle's claim is true only in something of a Pickwickian sense: none of the universal deductions in the third figure is resolved into the third, while *Disamis* in the third figure must have its premises interchanged (51a9—10: 'B must be put as the first term'), so that it is not really the minor premise which is converted in this case.

51a26—27. 'One . . . the other': since third-figure deductions always have particular conclusions, the only second-figure cases Aristotle even considers for resolution into this figure are the two with particular conclusions (*Festino*, *Baroco*).

Chapter 46

This section is not connected in any close way with the remainder of the *Prior Analytics* and in fact shows more kinship with *On Interpretation*.

51b5—8. The contrast between 'not to be this' and 'to be not this' is expressed in Greek as a matter of the position of the word *ou* (*ouk*), 'not,' with respect to the predicate: in 'is not white' (*ouk esti leukon*) the usual denial of 'is white,' the 'not' is attached to the verb, whereas in 'is not-white' (*estin ou leukon*) it is attached to the adjective. The latter sentence is not quite natural Greek: the hyphenated 'not-white' reflects this. I try to avoid the prefix 'non-' when I can, since this suggests a lexical rather than a syntactical distinction that does not exist in Greek. It should *not* be assumed that 'not white' and 'not-white' in my translation perfectly reflect distinctions of *sense* in Aristotle's text, however.

Aristotle's purpose is to show that 'it is not white,' rather than 'it is not-white,' is the denial of 'it is white.' In the *Topics*, he had treated affirmations and their negations as pairs of *predicates*, comparable to contraries or to conditions and their privations. On such a view, 'not-white' is indeed the negation or denial of 'white.' This view affects his understanding of the principles of excluded middle and noncontradiction, which he often states as 'of everything, either the affirmation or the denial is true' and 'an affirmation and its denial cannot belong to anything at the same time.' But in the present Chapter, he, in effect, argues that affirmations and their denials are pairs of *sentences*, or better (in modern terminology) pairs of *open sentences*: sentences in which the subjects are only variables, such as 'it is white' (where 'it' functions as a variable). Compare his views here with *On Interpretation* 10.

51b10–25. The first argument rests on an analogy: 'is able to walk' is to 'is able to not-walk' (*dunatai ou badizein*) as 'is white' is to 'is not-white.' (I translate *ou badizein* as 'to not walk': see the next Note.) Aristotle then argues that 'is able to not walk' is not the same in meaning as 'is not able to walk,' the denial of 'is able to walk,' since 'is able to walk' and 'is able to not walk' can be true of the same individual at the same time. It follows by the assumed analogy that 'is not-white' is not the same in meaning as 'is not white.' (In the course of the argument, Aristotle switches without explanation to the example 'is not good/is not-good'.)

51b18. 'being-able to not walk': here, we find two very similar phrases meaning 'not to walk' (differing only in the word used for 'not': *ou* in one case, *mē* in the other) joined by 'or' (*ou badizein ē mē badizein*). The phrase 'or not to walk' (*ē mē badizein*) has made this sentence difficult for translators. Alexander's text evidently read 'able to walk or not walk' (*dunamenos badizein ē mē badizein*), omitting the first 'not,' but it is difficult to see how this makes sense. Many translators (e.g., Tredennick, Rolfes, Jenkinson/Barnes) simply omit the second 'or not to walk,' while others (Colli, Tricot, Mignucci) try to translate it as it stands. In fact, Aristotle's point is inseparable from a detail of Greek syntax. There are two Greek words for 'not' which are used in different grammatical contexts: *mē* and *ou*. Among other differences, *mē* is the particle normally used to negate infinitives. Even though Aristotle seems rather casual about substituting *mē* and *ou* for one another in many contexts, his usage is very consistent on this point: he rarely uses *ou* to negate an infinitive, and when he does, it can virtually always be explained by grammatical factors not present here (the context is always governed by a verb of saying or thinking). I believe this permits us to understand what is going on in the present passage.

Aristotle has been comparing 'is not white' (*ouk esti leukon*) with 'is not-white' (*estin ou leukon*). Accordingly, here he considers the parallel relation of 'is not one able to walk' (*ouk esti dunamenos badizein*) to 'is one able to not walk' (*esti dunamenos ou badizein*), simply changing the position of the 'not' as before. However, following this transformation strictly results in the anomalous *ou badizein*. Accordingly, Aristotle adds parenthetically *ē mē badizein*: 'or <as we say it> "not to walk"'. I have tried to reflect the difference by translating *ou badizein* with a split infinitive ('to not walk'), which I would like to think captures about the same degree of ungrammaticality in English.

51b24. 'terms in analogous relationships . . .': the Greek phrase is very brief, but the meaning is clear. The term *analogon* really means 'proportional,' but Aristotle sometimes uses it in a broader sense approaching 'analogous,' normally with a four-term analogy in mind ('A is to B as C is to D'). Expressed more formally, his claim here would be 'if A is to B as C is to D and A is different from B, then C is different from D.'

51b31—35. Aristotle's reasoning in this difficult passage may be reconstructed as follows: we have established that 'is not-good' is not a denial; however, whatever is true of another thing is either an affirmation or a denial; therefore, 'is not-good' is a (sort of) affirmation. I take 'an affirmation or denial' here to indicate a sort of disjunctive predicate, as it sometimes does in Aristotle's expressions of the law of excluded middle (*that which* is necessarily true of anything is the complex composed of the affirmation and the denial joined by 'or'). The phrase 'of every single predicate' is in Greek just 'of every single' (*kata pantos henos*), which is clearly an abbreviation. Alexander (401.25—30) takes it to be elliptical for 'of every single (declarative) sentence' (*kata pantos [apophantikou] logou*), which is not, in fact, greatly different from my own reading. The word 'single' is meant to distinguish simple predicates (or statements, on Alexander's interpretation) from those which are complex, i.e., composed of other constituent predicates (or statements). Compare Aristotle's frequent reference to 'single' statements in *On Interpretation*.

51b36—52a24. This account is, in many ways, closely parallel to *On Interpretation* 10—11, although the latter is much more polished and deals with a wider class of cases. As in *On Interpretation*, Aristotle first discusses unquantified cases (51b36—52a14) and then extends the account to quantified, categorical sentences (52a18—24). The unquantified case appears to concern predication of individuals, not indefinite statements, although this is not clear (it is much clearer in *On Interpretation* 10).

52a1. For no evident reason, Aristotle suddenly changes his example from 'good' to 'white.'

52a15—17. In other words, we may replace 'not-*A*' with the privative of *A*, if it has one (e.g., 'unequal' for 'not-equal,' as here). The term 'predication' (*katēgoria*) is here used to designate the opposite of 'privation' (instead of Aristotle's more usual *hexis*, 'possession').

52a24—38. Aristotle now draws a corollary more closely connected with the subjects of the *Prior Analytics*: since affirmative and negative statements are proved in different ways, 'is not white' and 'is not-white' will have different kinds of proofs.

52a28. 'or that it is possible . . . not to be white': Aristotle is giving us examples of genuine negative statements, to be contrasted with 'is not-white,' which he has just argued is really affirmative. But the second example, 'it is possible for an animal not to be white,' is a statement of possibility, and he earlier said that all such statements are really affirmative. Alexander, therefore, interprets the second example as 'it is possible for *no* animal to be white,' i.e., as a necessary universal negative (411.14—24), but this is very strained. Nothing actually turns on this second example: it is at least possible that Aristotle had not settled on his doctrine that possible statements are affirmative when he wrote this passage.

52a31−32. 'first figure': the word 'figure' here means 'mood' (in this case, *Barbara*). I suggest in Smith *1982a* that Aristotle at one time worked with a 'system' consisting of the four deductive forms *Barbara*, *Celarent*, *Camestres*, *Cesare* (see, for instance, *Posterior Analytics* I.21, 82b15−16, 29−31).

52a34−35. Aristotle's text literally reads 'if it is true to call whatever is a man musical, or not musical'; I have supplied the subject 'the thing to be proved'. Ross, who understands the passage as I do, conjectures that *esti*, 'is,' should be *estai*: 'if it is to be true.' But this emendation is not necessary.

52a38. 'the three ways': that is, the three ways of deducing a negative conclusion (see Note on 52a31−32).

52a39−b13. Aristotle now generalizes the material in 51b36−52a14. The relationship between *A* and *B*, and also between *C* and *D*, is materially equivalent to contradiction: exactly one of the pair must be true of anything. '*A* follows *C* and does not convert with it' means 'Everything *C* is *A*, but not everything *A* is *C*.' What Aristotle proves, stated categorically, is that some *A* is *D*, that no *B* is *C*, that every *B* is *D*, and that not every *D* is *B*. In set-theoretic terms, the pairs <*A*, *B*> and <*C*, *D*> both partition the universe, but *C* is a proper part of *A*; it follows that *B* is a proper part of *D*, that *A* and *D* overlap, and that *B* and *C* are disjoint.

The argument pattern discussed here very closely resembles the argument used in *On the Heavens* I.12, 282a14−22.

52b14−34. The 'failure to take correctly the opposites' here evidently rests on a confusion between '*X* is the contradictory of "*Y* and/or *Z*"' and '*X* is the contradictory of *Y* and/or of *Z*.' It is somewhat difficult to follow Aristotle's argument: he, in effect, shows us that a certain line of reasoning leads to an incorrect result and attributes the error to a mistaken principle. (I have tried to make the structure clearer using quotation marks and a few extra phrases; Tricot's translation uses similar devices.)

Aristotle's argument is a sophisticated indirect proof resting on the result just proved in 52a39−b13. Suppose the same situation as in that proof, and take *Z* and *H* to be the contradictories of '*A* or *B*' and '*C* or *D*' respectively. Now make the additional supposition that *Z* is also a contradictory of *A* *alone*, and likewise *H* of *C* alone. Substituting *Z* and *H* for *B* and *D* in the previous result, we get 'everything *Z* is *H*.' Next, take *Z* and *H* to be contradictories of *B* and *D* respectively: then, since we have just shown that *H* follows *Z*, we may substitute *H*, *D*, *Z*, *B* for *A*, *B*, *C*, *D* in the original theorem, giving the conclusion 'everything *D* is *B*.' But the entire argument rests on nothing beyond the premises of the original theorem and the assumption that the contradictory of a disjunctive term is also a contradictory of each of its disjuncts. Consequently, using that principle, we have proved that, in general, if *A* entails *C*, then the contradictory of *A* entails the contradictory of *C*, which Aristotle knows to be false from the previous proof. Aristotle concludes that this principle is erroneous: the contradictory of '*A* or *B*' is not a contradictory of '*A*' or of '*B*' separately.

Given the way he has set the example up, 'A or B' will apply to everything, and thus 'neither A nor B' will apply to nothing. Surprisingly, Aristotle takes no note of this.

52b27. 'we know this': i.e., we have just proved it in 52a39—b14.

52b28—29. 'the consequence was in reverse order': see 52a4—12, 52a39—b14 (and compare *Topics* II.7, 113b15—26).

52b33—34. 'the denials which were taken are two': i.e., Z and H, the 'denials taken,' are each assumed to be *second additional* denials of A and C, in violation of Aristotle's principle (as defended in *On Interpretation*) that there is a single denial of a single expression.

NOTES TO BOOK B

Chapter 1

52b38–53a3. 'We have already': Ross takes this opening sentence to summarize the contents of the whole of Book A, in three divisions: A 4–26 ('the
number of figures . . . of premises'), A 27–31 ('what sorts of things one must
look to . . . any discipline whatever'), and A 32–46 ('the route through which
we may obtain the principles . . . '). But while the first two divisions correspond to Aristotle's own summary in A 32 (46b38–47a1), the third division
planned there is 'how we can lead deductions back into the figures,' which is
the real subject of A 32–44; the third subject mentioned here is actually
treated in A 27–28 (cf. 43a20–21).

53a2. 'discipline' (*methodos*): Aristotle uses this term frequently to designate
both the activity of pursuing scientific inquiry concerning a given subject, and
the results of such a pursuit. Etymologically, *methodos* would mean 'pursuit';
except for later Greek, however, it is mostly used in association with the
pursuit of knowledge and similar activities. In some cases, Aristotle uses it to
include the procedures by which a science is developed (see for instance 46a32
and Note); obviously, our word 'method' is historically connected with this.

53a3–b3. 'Now, seeing that': In this section, Aristotle investigates the
conditions under which a deduction 'deduces several results' (*pleiō sullogizetai*).
He considers two different sorts of cases of this, and it is not fully clear what
they have in common. In 53a3–14, he shows that an additional conclusion can
be derived from many deductive forms through conversions. By contrast, in
53a15–b3 he is concerned with conclusions which are deduced from an original deduction with the addition of another premise. It is difficult to see how
these claims are related to any other projects of the *Prior Analytics*, or how,
exactly, they are related to one another. Conceivably, he is trying to explore
how a collection of deductions fits together in the structure of an entire demonstrative science. This is a subject about which he has comparatively little
to say in either the *Prior* or the *Posterior Analytics*, although he does recognize
its importance. If that is his concern, then it may be relevant to compare this
passage with A 25.

53a3–14. These results are a simple consequence of the conversion rules
of A 3: additional conclusions can be derived from all deductions save those
with *o* conclusions. As commentators observe, this implies that Aristotle was
aware of all the so-called 'subaltern' moods, together with the remaining
fourth-figure moods not already included in A 7, 29a19–29.

53a7−8. 'privative <particular>': Aristotle says only 'privative,' but he must have *o* premises in mind.

53a12. 'this conclusion is different from the previous one': i.e., 'B to no A' is a different conclusion from 'A to no B.' Although this seems too obvious to require mention, Aristotle occasionally speaks as if the converse of a universal negative is the same as it (e.g., B 5, 57a27−29). Since in Book A Aristotle clearly takes them to be different, these may be traces of an earlier position; against such a background, the present sentence would have more point.

53a15−b3. 'This cause': Aristotle now proceeds to give 'another account' of 'deducing several results': literally, to 'discuss them differently' (*allōs eipein*). What follows is not (as some commentators suppose) an alternative explanation of the result he has just proved, but a discussion of a different type of *pleiō sullogizesthai*.

Aristotle tells us that in universal deductions it is possible to prove a variety of conclusions *in the same deduction* by considering various *other* terms which fall under the middle or minor term. (He uses the word 'conclusion,' *sumperasma*, to mean 'minor term'; I translate it here as 'conclusion-term.') Thus, to take his first example, suppose we have the deduction '*A* belongs to every *C*; *C* belongs to every *B*; therefore, *A* belongs to every *B*.' This deduction shows that '*A* belongs to whatever is below *B* or *C*': if we then take some term *D* which is below *B*, we can deduce that *A* belongs to every *D*, etc. In a similar way, he argues that in a universal negative deduction '*A* belongs to no *C*; *C* belongs to every *B*; therefore, *A* belongs to no *B*,' we can deduce additional conclusions *in the same deduction* by taking a term below *B* or *C*. Taken at face value, this implies that all first-figure deductions with the same major premise are the same. It is difficult to understand how Aristotle could call this the 'same deduction' after taking the care he does in A 25 to argue that every *single* deduction is through exactly three terms: surely what we have here is just *another* deduction, with different terms.

There are further difficulties. First, in dealing with the second figure, Aristotle only discusses the case of *Cesare*, with the major premise negative; Waitz notes that his argument cannot be applied to *Camestres*. In addition, as Ross points out, the closing lines (53b1−3) seem to retract the entire point of the section.

It is difficult to be sure what the two cases of 'deducing several' have in common, but one possibility is this: in each case, the same relationship of terms is at least *involved* in the deduction of more than one conclusion. Aristotle tends to identify deductions with their premises, and premises with their terms. Therefore, he may be investigating the question how terms in a given relationship can play a role in more than one deduction. This would be an important part of a study of the entire structures of demonstrative sciences, in which the same premise might appear in several deductions (as in Aristotle's second case), or the same premises might yield conclusions used as premises in different further deductions (perhaps related to Aristotle's first case). Some of the details noted above suggest that Aristotle had not yet worked out his theory of deduction when he wrote these lines.

53a32−33. 'taken as undemonstrated': in the *Posterior Analytics* the term *anapodeiktos* usually means 'not demonstrable,' that is, 'not susceptible of demonstration.' Here, however, it means only 'not deduced from premises' (compare 58a2).

53a40. The deduction 'already formed' (*progegenēmenos*) is the initial deduction '*A* to every *B*, *B* to some *C*.'

53a40−b3. The reference to 'the other figures' is puzzling. Since he has already discussed universal deductions in both first and second figures but only mentioned first-figure particular deductions, it seems most likely that he means 'the same thing goes for particular deductions in the other figures.' But in the second figure, it holds, at best, only for deductions with a negative major premise, which can be converted (and thus not for *Camestres* or *Baroco*); and in the third figure, it does not seem to hold for deductions with particular major premises (*Disamis, Bocardo*).

Chapter 2

Chapters 2−4 form the first of a series of systematic investigations of properties of deductions in all the figures which continues through B 15.

53b4−10. 'Now, it is possible': The general point which Aristotle wants to make in B 2−4 seems straightforward enough: a deduction with true premises cannot have a false conclusion, but it is possible for a deduction with one or more false premises to have a true conclusion. The importance of this result, however, is greater than at first appears. *Posterior Analytics* I.12, 78a6−13, indicate that some of Aristotle's contemporaries probably assumed that a deduction could be discovered by a process of 'analysis,' which amounted to a sort of attempted deduction of the *premises* from the desired *conclusion*. Showing that one cannot infer the falsehood of the conclusion from the falsehood of the premises, or the truth of the premises from the truth of the conclusion, counts decisively against this program.

53b8−10. 'except that': the mention of the distinction between a deduction of the 'why' (*to dihoti*) and a deduction of the 'that' (*to hoti*) is somewhat puzzling here. According to *Posterior Analytics* I.13, a deduction of the 'why' is a full-fledged proof, or demonstration, in which the premises are not only true, but also give the reason or explanation for the conclusion's truth. A deduction of the 'that' is presumably a deduction which fails to be a proof in this sense. Interpreted broadly, this could even include deductions with false premises, and the commentators generally take it so. However, the discussion in the *Posterior Analytics* only concerns deductions with true premises. Aristotle tells us that 'The planets are near; what is near does not twinkle; therefore, the planets do not twinkle' is a demonstration, whereas 'The planets do not twinkle; what does not twinkle is near; therefore, the planets are near' is only a deduction of the 'that,' even though each has true premises: the second, unlike the first, fails to give the cause of its conclusion. (See the Note below on 65a10−25.)

53b10. 'will be explained': this promise is ambiguous, since it might refer either to the claim that a deduction of the 'why' from falsehoods is not possible, or to the general point of B 2−4 that, although a false conclusion may not follow from true premises, a true conclusion may follow from false premises. Commentators have universally taken it in the first way, supposing the reference to be to the concluding lines of the entire discussion (B 4, 57a36−b17). Patzig, while agreeing that the promised explanation is to concern deductions of the 'why' and the 'that,' nevertheless argues in detail that 57a36−b17 is not concerned with that issue at all, and takes the reference to be, instead, to *Posterior Analytics* I.2, wherein Aristotle includes among the conditions a deduction must satisfy in order to be a demonstration the requirement that its premises be true (Patzig *1959*).

Patzig's argument that 57a36−b17 is not an explanation why a deduction of the 'why' cannot have false premises is persuasive, but his identification of the reference is less satisfactory. Aristotle does not *explain the reason* that a deduction of the why cannot be from false premises, either in *Posterior Analytics* I.2, nor anywhere else in the *Posterior Analytics*: this is rather a matter of definition. (If an explanation were wanted, it is not clear what it would need to be: it is like trying to explain why, if the sun makes things hot when it shines on them, that the sun is not the cause of things becoming hot when it is not shining on them.) It is more natural to take the promised explanation as simply the entire discussion in B 2−4 (cf. A 45, 50b9, where 'in what follows' simply refers to the remainder of the Chapter), though 57a36−b17 is also appropriate (see the discussion of that passage below).

53b11−15. 'First, then': taking 53b10 as I prefer, we are given at once half the promised explanation: a false conclusion may not follow from true premises because that would violate the law of noncontradiction.

53b16−25. 'But let it not': this passage is a close parallel to A 15, 34a16−24: having just given a similar argument about inferences using the form 'it is necessary for B to be when A is' (*tou A ontos anankē to B einai*), Aristotle takes care to explain that 'A' cannot be a 'single thing,' i.e., a single statement or premise.

53b26−54a2. 'It is possible': in this first section, Aristotle shows that both premises of any first-figure universal deduction can be false in either sense with a true conclusion.

54a2−b16. 'But if only': Aristotle now treats first-figure cases with one true and one false premise: a wholly false major and a true minor (54a2−18), a partly false major and a true minor (54a18−28), a true major and a wholly false minor (54a28−b2), and a true major and a partly false minor (54b2−16). He gives an explicit definition of 'wholly false' (54a4−6); he clearly means that a universal sentence is 'false in part' if its contradictory is true *and its contrary* *false*, though he does not explicitly say so. If we replace the major premise of a first-figure universal deduction with its contrary, we get the premises of another first-figure deduction having a conclusion inconsistent with the conclusion of the original deduction: for this reason, in the first figure we cannot have the major wholly false and the minor true with a true conclusion. All other combinations are possible, however.

54a8. 'AB as wholly false': here and a few lines later (12−13), Aristotle's language shows another type of abbreviation. In 8, we actually find *tēn de to AB pseudē holēn*: the first article is feminine, the second neuter. Similarly, in 12−13, we have *hē men to BG alēthēs protasis, hē de to AB pseudēs holē*. Ross explains the feminine article as an ellipsis for *hē protasis eph' hēi keitai* ('the premise to which applies') and notes the similar construction in a geometrical example at *Posterior Analytics* 94a31.

54a9−10. 'did not belong' : i.e., 'as we established earlier' (in this case, in A 4).

54a11. 'And similarly': As Ross points out, Aristotle begins the long sentence 54a11−15 intending to end it with 'the conclusion cannot be true,' but actually ends it with 'will be false': this makes the 'neither' (*oud'*) in 54a11 out of place. I omit it in translation.

54a29−30. Aristotle refers to a deduction with a true conclusion as a 'true deduction' even in this case, when one of its premises is false.

54a31−32. 'such species of the same genus as are not under one another': this is the first of a number of examples (continuing through B 3) which Aristotle characterizes by means of the vocabulary of the 'predicables,' as they later came to be called. These are relations which two universals, or classes, may have to one another. In the *Topics*, Aristotle officially distinguishes four: definition (*horos*), genus (*genos*), 'accident' (*sumbebēkos*), and 'property' or 'peculiarity' (*idion*). However, he also makes use of a fifth in that work, the 'difference' (*diaphora*). The term 'species' (*eidos*) in Aristotle sometimes means 'lowest species,' i.e., narrowest universal containing an individual (in this sense, an account of an individual's species would be its definition). Here, Aristotle tends, instead, to treat genus and species simply as universals of greater and lesser generality respectively: if A is a universal contained by B, then A is a species of B and B a genus of A. On such a view, 'genus' and 'species' are relative terms, and the same universal can be both a species and a genus.

54b9. 'which was true' (*hoper ēn alēthes*): that is, this conclusion was the one we initially wanted to show could be true without its premises true. Aristotle uses this way of speaking when (as here) he presents the desired true conclusion as the conclusion of a deduction, even though it is known that not all its premises are true.

54b13−14. The terms 'wisdom' (*phronēsis*) and 'theoretical science' (*theōrētikē: epistēmē* is understood) are the two principal types of intellectual activity recognized by Aristotle (as in *Nicomachean Ethics* VI). A widely established translation for *phronēsis* is 'practical wisdom' (these are, of course, only examples here).

54b17–55b2.   'In the case of particular': the same results are shown to hold for particular deductions, except that it is also possible for the major premise to be wholly false and the minor true (the reason is that the conclusions of *Darii* and *Ferio* in the same terms are not inconsistent with one another). In order, the cases are wholly false major and true minor (54b17–35), partly false major and true minor (54b35–55a4), true major and false minor (55a4–19), partly false major and false minor (55a19–28), and wholly false major and false minor (55a28–b2). The 'particular' is of course the minor premise.

Chapter 3

Aristotle finds every possible combination of truth values of the premises for second-figure deductions consistent with a true conclusion: both wholly false (universals, 55b10–16; particulars, 56a32–b3), one wholly false and one true (universals, 55b16–23; particulars, 56a5–18); one partly false and one true (universals, 55b23–38); both partly false (universals, 55b38–56a4); or the universal true and the particular premise false (56a18–32).

55b7–9.   Ross (432–433) notes a number of reasons why the bracketed parts of this summary do not seem to describe accurately what Aristotle actually does. I follow him in rejecting these words as a later gloss.

55b15–16.   'the same deduction': if the premises of a deduction in second-figure *Camestres* are wholly false, then the premises of a corresponding deduction in *Cesare* are true, and conversely: therefore, for each of these, if the premises are wholly false, the conclusion not only *may* be true, but *must* be. What Aristotle means by 'the same deduction' is not clear: he may mean 'when the premises are wholly false we will have a deduction with the same conclusion.'

55b30.   'when the privative is put in the other position' (*metatithemenou de tou sterētikou*): i.e., with a negative minor rather than major premise. The same use of *metatithenai* follows at 56a4; compare the different sense at 51a24–25.

56a14–15.   'to something white': as Ross points out, this must be taken in the strict sense 'to something but not to everything.'

56a35–36.   'and to some C': as in 56a14–15, this must again mean 'to some but not every.'

Chapter 4

In the first part of Chapter 4 (56b4–57a35) all possible combinations of premise truth-values are again shown to admit a true conclusion: both wholly false (56b9–20), both partly false (56b20–33), one true and one wholly false (56b33–57a9), one true and one partly false (57a9–28). His detailed discussion concerns only the two 'universal' deductions, i.e., those with two universal premises (*Darapti* and *Felapton*): all the particulars are treated in summary fashion (57a29—35).

56b7—8. 'or the reverse': that is, reversing the truth-value assignments to the premises in *each* of the situations just mentioned (true/false, true/partly false).

57a1. After 'the terms . . . are the same,' the manuscripts add the term triplet 'black, swan, inanimate,' which is certainly not the same set of terms as in the preceding example (animal, white, swan). Nor, indeed, could they be: the case needed is third-figure *Felapton* with true major and wholly false minor, so that both extremes need to be universally false of the middle. The trio 'black, swan, inanimate' will work for this purpose if 'swan' is the middle term, since no swan is either black or inanimate and some inanimate things are not black. However, as Ross points out, Aristotle's standard order in stating term-triplets for the third figure (as in A 6) is major-minor-middle, not major-middle-minor as we seem to have here.

There is a similarity between this sentence and 57a8—9, where, because of the symmetry of the premises, the same terms really will serve for two cases (by interchanging major and minor): if the text is not corrupt, then Aristotle has been guilty of a rare oversight.

57a17. 'when the same terms are transposed' (*metatethentōn*): that is, using the same example, but with major and minor terms interchanged. This is still another use of the versatile *metatithenai*: see the Note on 55b30.

57a23—25. 'has been proved': this seems to correspond to the deduction *Felapton*, but it was proved in A 6, 28a26—30, that under the given circumstances, A not only *may*, but *must* not belong to some B. Aristotle may, instead, be referring to 57a1—5, where he gives an example with the required truth values and such that A belongs to some B: if we take this as intended as a strictly particular conclusion ('to some and not to others'), the example might serve.

57a29—35. 'And it is also': Aristotle covers all 'particular' deductions (deductions with one particular premise) with a blanket assertion that the examples used for universal cases can also be used for these. His point depends on the following fact about the third figure: each of the four deductions with a particular premise can be obtained from a universal deduction by replacing one of its premises with the corresponding particular premise (we thus get *Disamis* and *Datisi* from *Darapti*, *Bocardo* and *Ferison* from *Felapton*). Call the two-universal deduction which corresponds in this way to a deduction with one particular premise its *corresponding* deduction, and call the universal premise which corresponds to its particular premise the *corresponding* premise. Then, any model for a corresponding deduction which makes the corresponding premise wholly false makes the particular premise of the deduction false, and any model which makes the corresponding premise false in part makes the particular premise true. Mignucci works through all the details of the correspondence (603—608).

57a36–b17. 'It is evident': Aristotle closes his discussion with a final set of remarks to clarify why a deduction may have a true conclusion and false premises, but not a false conclusion and true premises. The point he addresses is quite precise: even though the conclusion of a deduction with false premises may be true, nevertheless it is not so 'of necessity.' Aristotle supports this with an ingenious argument intended to establish that if A entails B, then it cannot be the case that the denial of A also entails B. (For a detailed study of the passage, see Patzig *1959*.)

What does Aristotle mean by saying that even if the conclusion of a deduction with false premises is true, it is not true 'of necessity'? Obviously, he does not mean 'not necessarily true,' since that would not differentiate such deductions from many with true but nonnecessary premises. A number of commentators take him to mean that the conclusion does not *necessarily* follow in such a case, but Patzig makes clear the hopelessness of this view. Instead, Aristotle surely means the sort of necessity he attaches to any conclusion of any deduction, i.e., 'necessity when certain things are so' or 'conditional necessity' (*tinōn ontōn anankē*); he may also have in mind that the conclusion is not *explained* by the premises in such a case.

Part of the difficulty with understanding this passage is that it is not clear what is wanted here by way of explanation. At one level, it seems sufficient to say that the definition of 'deduction' rules out a deduction with true premises and a false conclusion but not a true conclusion and false premises. This does not, of course, show that cases of the latter sort are in fact possible, but Aristotle's examples do. However, one possible reason for seeking a further explanation might be Aristotle's concern, not simply with deductions in general, but with causal or explanatory deductions (demonstrations).

57b4–17. 'But it is impossible': Aristotle's argument is an intended argument through impossibility using a comparatively sophisticated technique of formal substitution (for a similar case, see *Posterior Analytics* I.3, 72b36–73a6). He first supposes, as a *reductio* hypothesis, that the following are both true:

(1) If A is white, then B is large.
(2) If A is not white, then B is large.

He next says that from premises of the forms

(3) If A is white, then B is large.
(4) If B is large, then C is not white.

we can deduce a conclusion of the form

(5) If A is white, then C is not white.

Next, he states the general principle

(6) If X necessarily is when Y is, then Y necessarily is not when X is not.

Applying (6) to (1), we get

(7) If B is not large, then A is not white.

But this, together with (2) and the inference pattern (3)–(5), gives

(8) If B is not large, then B is large.

Aristotle rejects (8) as impossible, and thus he believes he has deduced an impossibility from the pair (1) and (2).

Some commentators have suggested that the 'impossibility' deduced is not really impossible at all. Łukasiewicz (*1957*, 49–51) pointed out that as a thesis of propositional logic, thesis (8) ('If not-p then p') is simply equivalent to p, and thus proving that a proposition follows from its own denial is proving that very proposition. Moreover, Aristotle himself knows of, and even uses, arguments having this form. Vailati *1911* notes that Plato's argument against Protagoras' 'man the measure' doctrine in the *Theaetetus* and the proof of Euclid IX.12 have this structure; Mignucci points out that an argument in Aristotle's own *Protrepticus* (fr. 2) does also (614–615).

It is of course conceivable that Aristotle might in one place argue in accordance with a principle and (through inadvertence, inconsistency, or a change of mind) explicitly deny that same principle in another place. However, there is an important difference here. It is not as clear that (1) and (2) are jointly possible in application to *explanations*. We may express this difference by substituting 'since' for 'if' in (1) and (2):

(1ʹ) Since A is white, B is large.
(2ʹ) Since A is not white, B is large.

If we interpret 'Since p, q' as 'If p then q, and p,' then obviously (1ʹ) and (2*) cannot simultaneously be true (since that would entail 'A is white and A is not white'). Now, Aristotle clearly does not have this sort of argument in mind. However, we might take (1ʹ) and (2*) as assertions about different occasions: on one occasion the reason why B is large is that A is white, while on another the reason is that A is not white. Now, (6) may be regarded not just as a rule of inference, but as a principle of explanation: if p explains q, then q being false explains p being false. It would follow from this and (1ʹ) that B not being large explains A not being white. The inference (3)—(5) can be given a similar reading (if p explains q and q explains r, then p explains r). If this is what Aristotle has in mind, then (8) does become absurd, since it asserts that the reason why B is large is that it is not large.

57b10. 'the first': the text reads 'A' (i.e., the letter alpha), which as Ross notes can be interpreted as the numeral 'one.'

57b17. 'just as if by means of three terms': the deduction (3)—(5) involves three terms. We get an argument of the same form containing only two terms by substituting *A* for *B* and *B* for both *A* and *C*.

Chapter 5

The subject of Chapters 5–7, 'proving in a circle' or 'proving from one another,' is closely connected with the argument in *Posterior Analytics* I.3 against the possibility of a 'circular' proof of the principles of a science from one another in some fashion (there appears to be an explicit reference to these chapters at 73a6–20). In the *Posterior Analytics*, Aristotle discusses a chain of deductions in which *p* is deduced from *q*, *q* from *r*, and finally *r* from *p*. The position which he attacks was, evidently, that in such a 'circular' case *all* of *p*, *q*, and *r* were proved in virtue of their being deduced from each other. Aristotle's objection is threefold: (1) invoking his requirement that the premises of a proof be epistemically prior to the conclusion, we would get the absurd result that a proposition is prior to itself; (2) such a procedure amounts to deducing a proposition from itself, and thus, anything whatever would admit of this sort of 'proof'; (3) in any event, the procedure can only be applied to a narrow and unimportant class of cases. It is in reference to (3) that Aristotle appeals to the present discussion in *Posterior Analytics* I.3.

The exact relationship of 'circular' proof as defined here to the circular argumentation of *Posterior Analytics* I.3 is not as straightforward as at first appears: in B 5–7, the procedure is not a matter of deducing propositions from one another in a circle, but rather of constructing a deduction of one of the premises of a deduction from the conclusion and the *converse* of the other premise. But with some speculation, we may imagine how Aristotle might have been led from one case to the other. The simplest case of a circular deduction would be two propositions which can be deduced from one another. But although Aristotle implicitly recognizes such cases in the conversion rules for *i* and *e* statements, he refuses to call these deductions (see the Notes on 40b35–36). And, in any event, obviously no circularly proved set of principles for a science can be constructed on this model. Let us, therefore, suppose that every deduction has (at least) two premises. But since no deduction is possible in which *both* the premises can, in turn, be deduced from the conclusion, the next possibility would be a deduction either premise of which could be deduced from the conclusion and the other premise. However, an investigation of all deductions in the figures shows that this can never happen. If we suppose him to have gotten to this point, Aristotle may then have asked: is anything *close* to this situation possible? A simple modification is replacing 'and the other premise' by 'and *the converse of* the other premise': and here we find that under some circumstances such circular deductions are possible. (For a fuller discussion of this interpretation, see Smith *1986*.)

Apart from these formal questions about proof theory, something like deduction in a circle plays a role in Aristotle's conception of change in the sublunary world, where processes often follow a circular path: see, for instance, *Posterior Analytics* II.12, 95b38−96a7, and *On Generation and Corruption* II.10−11.

There is no suggestion that Aristotle thinks of circular deduction as some sort of transformation which preserves validity, like those studied in B 11−13, so that one could use it to get new deductions from old. What Aristotle actually does is investigate each deduction in the figures, determining when a circular deduction works.

57b18−21. 'Proving in a circle': the *kai* in the phrase *to kuklōi kai ex allēlōn deiknusthai* is epexegetical: *to kuklōi deiknusthai* and *to ex allēlōn deiknusthai* are different names for the same process. (Compare *Posterior Analytics* I.3, 72b17−18: *endechesthai gar kuklōi ginesthai tēn apodeixin kai ex allēlōn.*) The definition would apply to a single deduction of a premise from the conclusion and the converse of the remaining premise, but it seems more likely that by a circular proof, he means an extended structure in which every premise also appears as a conclusion. Such a structure must contain six statements and six deductions. Let $p, q \vdash r$ be the original deduction and let 'conv(p)' denote the converse of p (note that conv(conv(p)) $= p$). The full-fledged circular proof structure will then be:

(1) $p, q \vdash r$
(2) $r, \text{conv}(q) \vdash p$
(3) $q, \text{conv}(r) \vdash \text{conv}(p)$
(4) $\text{conv}(p), \text{conv}(q) \vdash \text{conv}(r)$
(5) $\text{conv}(r), p \vdash \text{conv}(q)$
(6) $\text{conv}(q), r \vdash p$

Application of the transformation to (6) then gives us (1) again.

Aristotle refers to circular deduction here in a way that indicates that the expression (or expressions: see above) were in current use in his time, perhaps in the Academy. *Posterior Analytics* I.3 makes it clear that there were partisans of some sort of circular deduction as a method of proving everything, including the first principles themselves (we do not know who they were: for conjectures, see Smith *1986*).

57b25. Ross brackets 'because' (*hoti*) here, supposing it to have the meaning 'that' and finding it ungrammatical.

57b32−35. Terms 'convert' if they are universally true of each other (or, in the case of a set of three terms, pairwise convertible). Note that if A and B are convertible terms in this sense, then the sentence *AaB* is also 'convertible' in the sense that it and its converse *BaA* are both true. (Of course, it is not convertible in Aristotle's usual sense.)

57b33. 'undemonstrated' (*anapodeiktos*): see the Note above on 53a32−33.

57b35−58a12. 'But in the case': Aristotle considers a deduction in *Barbara* and proves that such a deduction can be built up into a complete circular deduction, in which every premise is also a conclusion, if and only if its terms all convert with one another. The strategy of the proof appears unnecessarily complex but is not. Aristotle begins with a deduction

(1) *AaB, BaC* ⊢ *AaC*.

He also assumes that a circular deduction of each premise is possible:

(2) *AaC, CaB* ⊢ *AaB*
(3) *BaA, AaC* ⊢ *BaC*

Now, both the premises of the original deduction have occurred as conclusions. However, two new premises have been introduced: *CaB* in (2) and *BaA* in (3). Applying the circular-proof transformation to (3) and (2) respectively gives:

(4) *BaC, CaA* ⊢ *BaA*
(5) *CaA, AaB* ⊢ *CaB*

At this point, every premise occurring in any of these deductions has also occurred as a conclusion, with the single exception of *CaA* in (4) and (5). An appropriate circular transformation of either (4) or (5) yields the needed result:

(6) *CaB, BaA* ⊢ *CaA*.

58a15−20.   'And it also results:' it is a matter of the definition of circular proof that the conclusion is used in proving each of its premises, but Aristotle probably makes this remark here in light of the results he is aiming at in *Posterior Analytics* I.3 (cf. 73a4−6).

58a27−29.   'the same premise': this remark sheds some light both on Aristotle's concept of a statement or proposition and on the conversion rules: if an *e* premise is *the same premise* as its converse, then conversion inferences are not deductions because nothing *different* follows in them. But this is not always Aristotle's view: cf. 58b25−27, 59a10−14, and the Note on 53a12. The point of the remark is also obscure: the reason there is no deduction when the circular transformation is applied is that both premises are negative. Aristotle may mean that even after conversion, *AeB* is *still* negative, so that the problem of two negatives is not alleviated.

58a29−30.   'Instead, one must take': this 'premise' is the first example of what later commentators designated a 'prosleptic' premise (relying on 58b9: see the Note below). Their general form is: 'A belongs to all/to none/to some/ not to all/ of what B belongs to all/to none/to some/not to all of.' Sixteen such forms are possible; though some are equivalent to categoricals (e.g., 'A belongs to all of what *B* belongs to all of' is equivalent to *AaB*), most are not. Aristotle arrives at the form in an obvious way. The circular transformation applied to *AeB, BaC* ⊢ *AeC* gives the two negative premises *BeA, AeC*, from which nothing follows. Aristotle therefore asks: what else would it take to get *BaC* from these? The 'prosleptic' premise is simply *constructed* as exactly what we must assume about *B* and *A* to get the desired conclusion. Aristotle never develops a theory of such statements, but recent writers have: see Lejewski *1961*, Kneale *1975*.

58a36−b12. 'In the case': in discussing particular deductions, Aristotle appeals to the rule that a universal conclusion must have universal premises to rule out circular deductions of their universal premises. But he has just allowed the deduction of the affirmative premise of a negative deduction; and in the present case the required 'prosleptic' premise can readily be constructed ('What belongs to some of *C* belongs to all of *B*').

58b1. 'both premises become particular': but in this case the relevant premises (i.e., the conclusion and the particular premise) are already particular, before either is converted. By 'conversion' Aristotle may just mean (loosely) the entire process of converting a premise and trying to use it with the original conclusion to construct a deduction.

58b9. Between 'universal deductions' and 'that is,' some manuscripts add the phrase 'cannot be, but it can be by means of an additional assumption' (*ouk esti, dia proslēpseōs d'estin*). Since this has limited authority and seems not to make sense, Ross rightly condemns it. It is the only place in which the term *proslēpsis* ('additional assumption') is used of one of Aristotle's noncategorical premises: thus, the designation 'prosleptic argument' seems not to be Aristotelian. And even if the passage is Aristotle's, *proslēpsis* has no special connection with these premises: the verb *proslambanein* is frequently used elsewhere of all sorts of 'additional assumptions,' including the additional steps required to complete an incomplete deduction (cf. 58b25−27, 59a11−13, 61a20, 61b7).

Chapter 6

58b15−18. 'the positive cannot be': this reluctance to get an affirmative conclusion from negative premises is not reflected in 58a29−32 above.

58b21. Ross brackets 'and to no *C*,' though the phrase has reasonably good authority, on the grounds that *BeC*, the conclusion of the original deduction, is *already* assumed. But it is Aristotle's usual practice to mention both premises.

58b25−27. The 'premise taken in addition' (*proslēphtheisēs*) apparently is the converse of the desired conclusion (*BeA*), from which the conclusion follows at once. The use of *proslambanesthai* here shows that the term is not at all associated with noncategorical premises (cf. 61a20, 61b7, and the Note on 58b9).

58b27−29. 'the same reason . . stated previously': that is, at 58a38−b2.

58b35−38. 'for it results': Aristotle's remark here about two negatives would also seem to apply to the first-figure case (*Celarent*), despite the treatment in 58a26−32.

Chapter 7

58b39−59a3. 'when both the premises are taken as universal': Aristotle again rejects getting a universal with a particular premise.

59a8−14. 'For let A belong': this passage is striking in several respects. Aristotle begins with the deduction *AaC*, *BiC* ⊢ *AiB* and, converting the major premise, gets the premises *CaA*, *AiB* for a circular deduction. *CiB*, the converse of the original minor premise, then follows through *Darii*: but Aristotle, taking care to distinguish an *i* sentence from its converse, says that *BiC* has *not* been proved, even though it necessarily follows (which apparently contradicts the definition of 'deduction' at 24b18−20). He then says that it must be 'supposed in addition' (*proslēpteon*) that 'if this belongs to some of that, then that other also belongs to some of this' in order to get the conclusion, and that as a result, the circular deduction no longer rests only on *CaA*, *AiB*. Most striking is the 'additional assumption' of a basic conversion rule: this would describe what happens in most of the completions in A 4−7.

59a32−41. It is difficult to make sense of the bracketed passage on several points, and Ross accordingly rejects it. The greatest difficulty is the statement that, in the first figure, circular proof with a negative deduction comes about through the third figure. Evidently, this is meant to apply only to the 'prosleptic' proof of the minor premise of *Celarent*: Ross makes the plausible suggestion that it is based on a superficial similarity between 'what this belongs to none of the other belongs to all of' and third-figure deductions. The reference to incompleteness is also surprising, since this is the only mention of that concept outside A 1−22.

Chapter 8

59b1−11. Converting as defined here is a transformation performed on existing deductions (cf. 61a21−25 below). 'Replacing' (*metatithenai*) the conclusion is, as we immediately learn (59b6−11), 'converting' it, which means substituting either its contrary or its contradictory for it. (Compare 51a24 and the use of the related verb *metalambanein* at 37b15, 40a34, 56b8.) Aristotle's procedure here is sometimes seen as the derivation, from a deduction p, q ⊢ r, of another deduction p, not(r) ⊢ not(q) or not(r), q ⊢ not(p) (see Patzig *1968*: 152−154). The justification offered in 59b3−5 does appear to recognize the logical validity of such a process; however, Aristotle includes among the pairs of 'contraries' corresponding *i* and *o* statements, which of course are not inconsistent with each other. (At A 15, 63b27−28, Aristotle notes that the 'opposition' of these is merely verbal.) Moreover, the actual procedure of B 8−10 never appeals to this justification. Instead, Aristotle first performs the transformation, taking the 'converse' of the conclusion and one of the premises, and then notes whether these new premises yield the 'converse' of the remaining original premise. The summary at the end of the account (61a5−16) suggests that he is not *appealing* to a rule for deriving deductions but rather attempting to *establish* one by investigating all possible cases. It is worth noting the similarity between 'conversion' and circular proof: in each case, we take an existing deduction and try to get from it a deduction of one of its premises (perhaps transformed) from the conclusion and the other premise (each perhaps transformed). However, in circular proof it was the premise, not the conclusion, which was 'converted,' and 'converted' had a different meaning.

Aristotle gives no explanation of why this procedure of 'conversion' is important. I would speculate that it is dialectical in origin: to convert an opponent's argument is to 'turn it around,' rejecting its conclusion, and thereby rejecting one of its premises (compare the similar definition of converting in *Topics* VIII.14, 163a32−36).

59b11−20. 'For let A': Aristotle's treatment of first-figure *Barbara* exemplifies his approach to all cases. Beginning with a deduction *AaB*, *BaC* ⊢ *AaC*, he first pairs the contrary *AeC* of the conclusion with each premise in turn. The pair *AaB*, *AeC* are the premises of a second-figure deduction which yields *BeC*, the contrary of the original premise *BaC*. However, the pair *AeC*, *BaC* are third-figure premises which yield only *AoB*, the contradictory of the original major premise *AaB*. As the first case makes clear, Aristotle is using his knowledge of deductions in the figures to make inferences, not relying on a logical rule of the sort Patzig supposes.

59b39−60a1. 'conclusion that falls short': i.e., is only the contradictory (not the contrary) of the other premise.

Chapter 10

60b15−18. 'either it is necessary . . . conversion': here, 'conversion' means what it does in A 4−7. In completing deductions, Aristotle always tries first to convert so as to get first-figure premises. The deduction considered here is *Darapti*: *AaC*, *BaC* ⊢ *AiB*. 'Contrary' conversion gives either *AoB*, *AaC* or *AoB*, *BaC*. In the first case, the premises are in the second figure. In the completions of A 5−6, Aristotle always tries to convert second- and third-figure premises so as to get first-figure premises: with *AoB*, *AaC* this gives *AoB*, *CiA*, two particular premises. The second pair *AoB*, *BaC* is already in the first figure, but the universal premise *BaC* is 'about the minor extreme'; this also holds for the first pair. As Aristotle notes, he has proved (in A 4−6) that in a deduction in the first or second figure with *only* one universal premise, the universal must be the major premise.

60b28. 'this is the way . . .': i.e., it must be the major premise that is negative.

Chapter 11

61a18−21. 'A deduction through an impossibility': Aristotle here defines the subject which he investigates in Chapters 11−13. His definition implies that his subject is not the general technique of proof through impossibility, but a transformation which can be applied to existing deductions in the figures. There is a sort of formal similarity between this transformation and both circular proof and 'conversion': in each, we begin with a deduction p, $q \vdash r$ and produce another $f_1(r)$, $f_2(p) \vdash f_3(q)$, where f_1, f_2, f_3 are transformations applied to categorical premises (including conversion, 'contrary' conversion (or contradiction), 'opposite' conversion, and identity). Note that deduction through impossibility as here defined, unlike circular proof and 'conversion,' is a logically valid rule of inference. Aristotle's examination, however, appears, at least in part, intended to *prove* its validity rather than apply it. These Chapters should be compared with A 23, 41a21−b1, A 29, and A 44, 50a29−38.

61a21−27. By 'the way of taking premises is the same' (*hē autē lēpsis amphoterōn*) Aristotle means that the premise pair produced in a 'conversion' always corresponds to an identical pair produced in a deduction through impossibility, as the example (61a27−31) illustrates. The difference between 'conversion' and proof through impossibility may be seen as dialectical: conversion is a response to a deduction already constructed by someone else, whereas a deduction through impossibility is a way of generating an argument originally. Compare this account with A 23, 41a23−32; A 44, 50b32−38; B 14, 62b29−38. Note that for Aristotle, that statement the contradictory of which is deduced is not a premise of the *deduction*, though it is a premise of the *argument*.

61a27−31. 'For instance, if A': this example, which is supposed to show that there is a deduction through impossibility corresponding to every 'conversion,' is unclear on one point. Suppose that we have a deduction AaC, $CaB \vdash AaB$. Aristotle has shown that this may be 'converted' either contrarily, giving AaC, $AeB \vdash CeB$, or oppositely, giving AaC, $AoB \vdash CoB$. Aristotle appears to be saying that there is a deduction through impossibility corresponding to *each* of these: one in which the assumption is AeB and one in which it is AoB. It is true, of course, that either of these leads to a contradiction with CaB. However, when we appeal to the 'impossibility' to conclude the 'opposite' (*antikeimenon*) of the assumption, we get AiB and AaB respectively. Aristotle may, at one time, have erroneously thought that a proof through impossibility of the first sort could actually establish, not AiB, but AaB: cf. *Posterior Analytics* I.26. (Note, incidentally, that by Aristotle's reckoning, these deductions through impossibility are in the *second* figure: the figure of a deduction through impossibility is the figure of its contained deduction.)

61a34−62b24. In the remainder of 11−13 Aristotle follows a set order of investigation. For each figure, he asks, in turn, how a deduction through impossibility may be constructed in that figure for a given categorical sentence type. He answers this by determining how the contradictory of the given categorical type may appear as a premise in the figure in question. However, Aristotle investigates possible deductions using the *contrary* of the intended conclusion as an assumption as well as the contradictory. In each case, he determines two things: (1) if the contained deduction is in the given figure, which premise (major or minor) should the assumption be? (2) should one assume the contrary or the contradictory of the conclusion? Aristotle's discussion is easier to follow if it is borne in mind that he consistently uses 'assume' (*hupotithenai, hupokeisthai*) or 'set down' (*keisthai*) of the premise used as *reductio* hypothesis and 'take' (*lambanein*) of the other premise. (In many cases, he uses no verb: I have filled in the blanks in accordance with his practice.)

The details of his investigation suggest that although he has *stated* the general logical principle on which proof through impossibility rests, he regards that principle as in need of a proof, which he gives by examining all possible cases.

61a35−b10. 'A universal positive': Aristotle considers two possible ways of deducing *AaB* through an impossibility: assuming its contradictory *AoB* or its contrary *AeB*. Neither of these can serve as the minor premise of a first-figure deduction; *AeB* can serve as the major premise, but deducing a contradiction only gives us the falsehood of *AeB*, not the truth of *AaB*. (His argument is curiously elaborate and indirect: why not say straightaway that assuming *AeB* will not work for this reason?)

61a38−39. 'from whichever side' (*hopoterōthenoun*): i.e., from the side of the predicate term (*CaA*) or from the side of the subject (*BaD*).

61a40. 'for in this way': to get a first-figure deduction with *AxB* as a premise, we must add either a major premise *CxA* or a minor premise *BxD*.

61b11−19. Aristotle's treatment of *i* conclusions in the first figure is representative. He shows: (1) we may use the contradictory assumption (*e*) as the major premise of *Celarent* or *Ferio*; (2) we cannot use the contradictory assumption as the minor premise; (3) we cannot use the contrary assumption (*o*) at all. He notes in summary that 'it is the opposite [sc. contradictory] which must be assumed [rather than the useless contrary].'

61b19−33. 'Next': the next case, that is, proving an *e* conclusion.

61b24−30. 'And if the contrary': if, in trying to prove *AeB*, we assume its contrary *AaB*, we may indeed come up with a first-figure deduction having a false conclusion, but the falsehood of the assumption *AaB* does not entail the truth of the desired *AeB*. Once again, Aristotle goes by a roundabout path to show this.

62a2−8. 'But when this has been proved': this difficult text is aimed at showing that we cannot prove an *o* conclusion with an *i* assumption. This would appear to be a mistake: Aristotle normally holds that an *e* sentence entails its subcontrary, so that proving *AeB* is sufficient for proving *AoB*. His objection here is that this will, in effect, go too far in a case in which *AoB* is strictly true, i.e., *A* belongs to some but not every *B*. Making the *i* assumption will 'reject what is true in addition,' that is, the implicit *i* sentence. With somewhat convoluted reasoning, Aristotle adds that the *i* assumption cannot lead to an impossibility because then it would be false, but we have supposed in this case that it is true. It is hard to see how to make this fully coherent: his point should be that it is not *necessary* to suppose the 'contrary' in this case, even if it is sufficient.

In 62a4−5, I read *ou para tēn hupothesin sumbainei to adunaton* ('[neither] does an impossibility follow as a result of the assumption'), with the majority of manuscripts, rather than Ross's conjecture *ouden para tēn hupothesin sumbainei adunaton* ('nothing impossible follows as a result of the assumption'). Aristotle often uses the phrase 'the impossibility' (*to adunaton*) without implying that some particular impossibility is being referred to (as in 'by means of an impossibility,' *dia tou adunatou*). Compare the analogous use of 'the necessity' (*to anankaion*) to mean 'the conclusion' even when there is no conclusion. The sense is 'an impossibility, *if there is one*, does not follow. . . .' Manuscript *n*, which has *oude* rather than *ou*, actually supports this better: 'the impossibility does not *even* follow as a result of the assumption.'

62a9−10. 'not to belong to some': on the expressions 'not to every' (*mē panti*) and 'not to some' (or 'to some not': *tini mē*), see e.g., 27a36−b3 and the associated Note. It is impossible to reproduce in English the important fact that the 'not' in one case comes *before* the term of quantity and in the other case *after* it.

62a11−19. 'It is evident': this passage gives two very different sorts of reasons for always assuming the contradictory rather than the contrary of the desired conclusion in a deduction through impossibility. First, Aristotle makes the logical point that only in this way does showing the assumption false always entail that the desired conclusion is true. His second point, however, is a matter of what is 'accepted' (*endoxon*): the term is an important one from the *Topics*, where it is defined to mean something like 'reputable' or 'received' (in common use, it means 'famous'). Aristotle's point seems to be that people, in general, will accept the inference from rejecting the contradictory of a statement to asserting that statement, though the same does not hold for the statement and its contrary.

Chapter 12

62a36−37. 'the same as in the case of the first figure': that is, no conclusion will be possible (cf. 61b17−19).

Chapter 13

62b25−28. Aristotle's summary of his discussion of deduction through impossibility indicates that at least one of his main concerns is to show that in such deductions it is the contradictory, not the contrary, which must be assumed. From our perspective, it is part of the *definition* of *per impossibile* deduction that the contradictory is what is assumed. This points to the fact that much of Aristotle's terminology derives from an existing dialectical practice. Argument through impossibility was a well established practice in philosophical and mathematical circles. However, to judge by the present discussion, some aspects of that practice were (as Aristotle discovered) indefensible on logical grounds. In concluding that one must assume the contradictory, not the contrary, of what one wants to prove through impossibility, he is recommending a refinement in a received procedure.

Chapter 14

62b29−38. This account may be compared with A 23, 41a21−b1, and A 44, 50a29−38. For the sense of 'familiar' (*gnōrimos*), see *Posterior Analytics* I.1−2 (compare also the Notes on B 16). This remark applies to the conclusion of the deduction itself (i.e., of the entire deduction in the probative case, or of the contained deduction in a deduction through impossibility). The point is that we do not even need to know in advance what the conclusion of a probative deduction is (since it is deduced from the premises), whereas we must know in advance that the 'conclusion' of the contained deduction is false. The remark that deduction through impossibility applies equally to negative and affirmative statements is not trivial: *Posterior Analytics* I.26 seems to associate it with negative statements only (cf. 63b19−21).

62b32. 'More precisely': this translates *men oun*, which as Ross says here 'introduces a correction.'

62b35−36. 'believe in advance' (*prohupolambanein*): the majority of translators take this word to mean 'assume in advance,' and LSJ lists only that and closely related meanings (significantly, all their citations are from Aristotle). But *hupolambanein* usually means 'believe' or 'conceive,' not 'assume' (cf. 64a9 below). Other occurrences of *prohupolambanein* in Aristotle (*Posterior Analytics* I.1, 71a12; *Rhetoric* II.21, 1395b6, 11; *Poetics* 25, 1461b1) concern understanding or believing something beforehand. In the *Poetics*, Aristotle is talking about how a poet's words are to be understood, and quotes a criticism of those who *start out* with an improbable interpretation; in the *Rhetoric*, the subject is really what people *already believe* (i.e., their prejudices); and in the *Posterior Analytics*, Aristotle is discussing what one must 'know in advance' (*proginōskein*) in scientific instruction. The present passage, in fact, closely parallels the *Posterior Analytics*. What Aristotle is talking about is not whether one need make an *assumption* beforehand, but whether one need *have any belief* about whether one's premises are true. Rolfes's translation is similar to mine ('man braucht nicht im voraus zu *wissen*, daß [der Schlußsatz] gilt oder nicht gilt'), although 'know' ('*wissen*') is probably too strong.

62b38−63b21. 'Everything concluded': The remainder of B 14 is a more elaborate proof of the claim made in A 29, 45a23−b11, that probative proof and proof through impossibility are interchangeable.

62b40. 'through the same terms': the Aldine edition adds 'but not in the same figures' here.

63a1. 'the true conclusion' (*to alēthes*): that is, 'the conclusion which is true' (on Aristotle's analysis, the 'conclusion' *deduced* in a proof through impossibility is the *false* conclusion of the contained deduction). This sentence could be paraphrased 'when the contained deduction in a proof through impossibility is in the first figure, then the corresponding deduction with true premises will be in the middle or the last,' and similarly for other cases.

63b12–13. 'it is also possible': the text here seems to me to be corrupt. Some manuscripts read 'it is also possible to prove each of the problems through the same terms probatively and through an impossibility.' Now, what Aristotle has just shown is that whenever a conclusion has been deduced through impossibility, then that same conclusion could also have been deduced probatively using the same terms: thus, 'and through an impossibility' seems not to give the right sense and Waitz and Ross accordingly reject it. But while the troublesome phrase cannot be right, the result of omitting it is, at any rate, a rather elliptical sentence. (The phrase might, in fact, be a corrupt form of the needed supplement: perhaps *hōs kai dia tou adunatou?*)

63b16–18. 'the same deductions . . . by means of conversion': the 'conversion' meant is the procedure of B 8–10.

63b19–21. 'separated off': i.e., proof through impossibility is not limited to proving any particular type of categorical sentence.

Chapter 15

63b22–30. A deduction 'from opposite premises' is a deduction having as its premises some statement and its opposite (either contrary or contradictory). Premises of this sort will, of course, have the same subject and predicate respectively, and thus the premise pair will have only two distinct terms: the middle and a single 'extreme.' If a deduction is possible, it will be in either the second figure (with the common predicate as middle) or the third (with the common subject as middle). In his opening statement, Aristotle presents a surer understanding of opposites than found in B 8–10 (*i* and *o* statements are at once dismissed as merely 'verbal' opposites). The Chapter also seems to be largely independent of B 1–14.

Aristotle does not say what the purpose of these investigations is. They may be related to the dialectical game of the *Topics* in which the goal is to drive one's opponent into a contradiction (cf. 64a33–37 below), and there may also be some connection with the contents of B 2–4 (cf. 64b7–27). The most evident connection, however, is with the discussion of inconsistent beliefs in B 21.

63b31–39. Aristotle's argument here is curiously indirect: it would be simpler just to point out that opposite premises cannot occur in the first figure since the middle term must occur as subject of one premise and predicate of the other, from which it would follow that all three terms of the deduction would have to be the same.

64a11. 'converted in respect of the terms' (*epi tōn horōn*): cf. 64a40−b1, 64b3. The qualification may be intended to differentiate the sense of 'convert' from that in B 8−10.

64a16−17. The case in which 'the terms below the middle' (i.e., the extremes) are 'as a whole to a part' includes premises like 'Every science is good/ Medicine is not good,' which are not opposites. However, since medicine is 'part' of science, Aristotle replaces the second premise with the associated particular premise 'Some science is not good.'

64a33−37. 'We should take note': this passage suggests that the investigation of deductions from opposite premises has some sort of dialectical importance. It might be asked: whoever would try to argue from blatantly inconsistent premises like these? Aristotle answers: we can get the same result by deducing one of the premises from other things, or we might (as explained in *Topics* VIII.1) get our respondent to accept them if he is inattentive or we are skillful.

64a37−b6. 'And since': this passage is somewhat out of place. The point is that there are six possible opposite-premise combinations: *ae, ao, ie* and (by 'converting' the premises) *ea, oa, ei*. Ross assumes that Aristotle is talking specifically about the second figure, which leads to some difficulties in understanding the passage. But all Aristotle probably means is that these six are all the relevant combinations, and that he has investigated all six for both figures, even though he does not explicitly mention all of them in 63b31−64a32. He does appear to omit *ei* and *ie* cases, though he has discussed *Festino* implicitly at 64a12−13, *Ferison* at 64a27−30.

64b7−8. 'as was explained earlier': in B 2−4.

64b9−10. 'contrary to the subject' (*enantios . . . tōi pragmati*): *pragma* could mean 'thing' or 'fact' as well, and those senses might not be out of place here given that Aristotle regards the law of noncontradiction as a general truth about *things*. However, all he probably has in mind here is the much humbler point that the predicate deduced is contrary to (or at any rate inconsistent with) the *subject term* of the conclusion, as in his examples.

64b11−13. 'from a contradiction': Aristotle's point is that a pair of opposed premises constitutes a 'contradiction' (affirmation-denial pair), and the two parts of such a contradiction cannot simultaneously be true. The mention of subject terms takes account of the additional cases in which we have, not two exact contradictories or contraries, but premises in which the subject term of one is a part of the subject term of the other. (I thus take *kai* in *kai tous hupokeimenous horous . . .* as epexegetical.)

64b13−17. The 'trick arguments' (*paralogismoi*, 'paralogisms') Aristotle has in mind here are evidently arguments through impossibility. The sense in which deductions from opposite premises are 'contrary' has just been explained (64b11−13). The example 'not odd if it is odd' *may* be connected with a Greek proof of the incommensurability of the diagonal: see the discussion of the next Chapter. It may also be important to note that the most celebrated paradoxical arguments of Greek philosophy (Zeno's arguments about motion) took the form of arguments through impossibility.

64b17–27. The arguments to self-contradictory conclusions discussed here almost certainly have their home in the environment of dialectical refutation: as Ross observes, Plato's dialogues contain many examples. Aristotle distinguishes three cases: (1) getting the contradiction from a single deduction, (2) assuming one part of it and getting the other through a deduction, (3) getting both parts through deductions. The first case, which evidently involves a deduction having a premise with a complex and self-contradictory predicate such as 'white and not white,' may appear to be a merely formal possibility, but *Posterior Analytics* I.11, 77a10–21, seems to concern just such arguments (this is a difficult text to make sense of). The remaining two cases are those of 64a33–37. In 64b23 after 'belief' most sources add 'and not belief,' which would make Aristotle's example illustrate taking a contradictory 'straightaway.' However, as the example is developed it clearly illustrates case (2), in which one contradictory is 'taken' and the other obtained through deduction. It would be quite in harmony with Aristotle's practice to use 'take in addition' (*proslambanein*) of an additional premise like this, but not in connection with a self-contradictory premise such as 'every science is belief and not belief.' I accordingly follow Ross in rejecting these words.

64b24. 'the way that refutations are effected': this might be a reference to 62a40–b2.

Chapter 16

64b28–30. The traditional Latin translation for the subject of this Chapter (in Greek *to en archēi aiteisthai*) is *petitio principii*, 'asking for the starting point'; 'begging the question,' its traditional English 'translation,' bears only a remote similarity to Aristotle's phrase (and in my opinion, it is really nonsensical in modern English). Aristotle has in mind an argumentative or dialectical situation in which one participant is required to prove something proposed (the 'initial thing': *to en archēi, to ex archēs*). The proof is to be constructed by asking questions of the other participant. Aristotle clarifies the sense of the phrase by adding an explanatory 'or taking' (*kai lambanein: kai* is epexegetical): as he tells us in A 1, 24a22–25, the difference between dialectical and demonstrative premises is that the dialectician asks while the demonstrator takes (cf. Mignucci, 661–662). 'Asking for the initial thing' in its most straightforward form is, then, just putting the very thing to be proved to one's respondent as a question. To judge by Aristotle's remarks, here and elsewhere, the phrase was a term of art from early on in the history of institutionalized dialectic.

I have elected to translate *aiteisthai* with 'ask' rather than the more conventional 'postulate.' 'Ask' is what *aiteisthai* means in ordinary Greek; indeed, our use of the word 'postulate' simply descends from the Romans' use of Latin *postulare* ('ask') as a translation of this very verb in such contexts as Aristotelian dialectical terminology and subsequent philosophical and mathematical usage. Thus, to translate as 'postulate' is, in a way, not to translate but to encode.

One other point about the translation: the phrase 'to grasp its family, so to speak' translates *hōs en genei labein*. Most translators take the word *genos* (here in the dative *genei*) to be the technical term 'genus' and thus interpret the phrase as something like 'to grasp it in its genus' (whatever that may mean) or 'speaking generally'; indeed, Bonitz 150b32−33 gives this passage as the sole authority for such a meaning in Aristotle. But *en genei* is an ordinary Greek expression meaning 'related to' or 'in the same family as'; I have so taken it here.

64b30−34. 'several ways': compare this account of types of failure to demonstrate with the definition of 'demonstration' in *Posterior Analytics* I.2. Note that here Aristotle distinguishes between being 'prior' and being 'more familiar' or 'better recognized' (*gnōstoteron*). The latter term is often translated 'better known,' but it is clearly intended here as a synonym for *gnōrimōteron* ('more familiar') in the *Posterior Analytics*.

64b34−65a37. 'However, since some things': both the content and the purpose of this discussion of 'asking for the initial thing' are difficult to determine with certainty. We may divide the argument into three sections: 64b34−65a9, 65a10−25, and 65a26−37. In the first, Aristotle gives us a general definition of *to ex archēs aiteisthai*; in the second, he discusses the application of this to deductions in first-figure *Barbara*; and in the third, he expands the discussion to apply to deductions with negative premises or in other figures. It is the second of these sections which raises the most difficulties, both as to its overall meaning and with respect to textual details. We can, however, form a reasonable interpretation of it if we first understand the sections which surround it.

The definition Aristotle gives is 'trying to prove through itself that which is not familiar through itself' (*mē to di' hautou gnōston di' hautou tis epicheirei deiknunai*). He later varies 'not familiar through itself' with 'not clear through itself' (65a25), and the immediately preceding sentence gives us 'not of such a nature (*pephukos*) as to be recognized (*gnōrizesthai*) through itself' as another equivalent. This is, as noted above, the language of the theory of demonstration in the *Posterior Analytics*, and it is specifically tied to Aristotle's own view that there *are* certain things which are 'familiar through themselves' and not in need of, or susceptible of, demonstration. It is somewhat surprising to see this offered as a general definition of 'asking for the initial thing,' given the meaning of that expression in dialectical practice. It is also difficult to imagine what 'trying to prove something through itself' would be. Would that simply consist of *asserting* it, or perhaps asserting it together with the claim that it needed no proof? But in that case it is hard to see how the question of 'asking for the initial thing' comes up as a question about an argument. We would have to suppose our demonstrator to say, when asked to prove X, 'There is no need to prove X; it is of such a nature as to be evident through itself.' It seems quite beside the point to respond to this with 'But you are asking for what it was required to prove.'

The critical point, I think, is that 'asking for the initial thing' is typically a matter of *surreptitiously* introducing the thing to be proved among the premises. This can be done in several ways, e.g., by substituting synonyms for the terms in the conclusion and hoping that our opponent will not notice. As a dialectical criticism, the point of 'you are asking for the initial thing' is something like this: 'you are supposed to be deducing the required conclusion from *other* premises, not just asking me to concede it.' Consequently, it embraces not only the blatant case in which the one putting the questions just turns the intended conclusion into a question and asks for it, but also, cases in which the questioner asks something which, to put it somewhat loosely, no one would concede who would not already concede the conclusion.

And this is precisely where the problem for analysis arises: how are we to describe such cases? There is no sharp line between blatantly asking for the desired conclusion, asking for it in a disguised form, and asking for something which, on reflection, we might regard as equivalent to it, or equally hard to swallow. What Aristotle offers us here is a general characterization of what *can* legitimately be asked for, employing his own notion of the 'priority' of one premise to another: there are some things which, on his view, are *by nature* prior to others, and it is an error to ask someone to concede what is posterior in trying to prove what is prior. Thus, in 64b38−65a1, Aristotle distinguishes the blatant case of asking 'directly' (*euthus*) for the conclusion, but the fact that he says nothing more about it suggests that he considers this merely a possibility and not the interesting case.

But there is another aspect to this discussion. Many details make it clear that Aristotle has circular proofs (in the sense defined in B 5) in mind. In modern use, the expressions 'arguing in a circle' and 'begging the question' are roughly interchangeable, which may contribute to our own inability to see that these are, for Aristotle, completely different things. A circular deduction for him is an extended structure of deductions in which each premise also appears as a conclusion; 'asking for the initial thing' is, instead, a dialectical matter. However, Aristotle himself associates the two closely by arguing in *Posterior Analytics* I.3 that those who try to prove everything using circular demonstrations are really just 'asking for the initial thing.' He tells us, there, that circular proof is just proving that 'when A is, then A is' (73a4−6, 72b32−35); he uses almost exactly the same words about cases of 'asking for the initial thing' here in 65a7−9. The connection is confirmed in 65a10−25, where the cases of 'asking for the initial thing' studied turn out to be identical in form to the circular deductions of B 5.

Now, what Aristotle seems to be doing here is the converse: treating at least a large number of cases of 'asking for the initial thing' as circular deductions. We can, I think, make sense of this if we remember his initial characterization of 'asking for the initial thing' as 'trying to prove through itself what is not naturally proved through itself.' The only plausible case of such an attempt which emerges from Aristotle's account is just exactly the circular demonstrator's attempt at proving things from one another. Thus, two cases of 'asking for the initial thing' emerge: the blatant or 'direct' case, and the case of the circular demonstrator. It is, in fact, not unreasonable to suppose that these are the only cases possible. Suppose p is prior to q and that it is natural to prove q from p, but nevertheless, possible to use p in deducing q. This can only happen if p and q can be used in deducing one another, i.e., in a circular demonstration.

65a4−7. Commentators generally take Aristotle's reference to 'those who think they draw proofs that there are parallels' to concern attempts to prove the parallel postulate: for discussions, see Heath *1926*, I.191; Ross 462−463. Although the verb *graphein* literally means 'draw,' Aristotle frequently uses it to mean 'prove' in geometrical contexts (see the Notes on 46a8 and 41b14). I try to capture the sense that a diagram is probably always presupposed with the (perhaps intemperate) translation 'draw proofs.'

65a10−25. There are difficult questions about the language in this passage, but the overall argument seems clear enough. Aristotle considers two cases. In the first, the putative demonstration is the deduction

(1) $AaB, BaC \vdash AaC$.

If one of the premises, for instance AaB, is 'equally unclear' as the conclusion AaC, then this fails to be a demonstration. But Aristotle now adds a second possibility: suppose that B and C 'convert,' so that we also have as a premise

(2) CaB.

We then have a deduction in *Barbara* together with the converse of one of the premises. Accordingly, we can also deduce the other premise:

(3) $AaC, CaB \vdash AaB$.

Note that this is exactly the pattern of a 'circular proof' as discussed in B 5. Aristotle tells us that in this case, the would-be demonstrator is 'asking for the initial thing.' Similarly, if BaC should be 'equally unclear' as the conclusion, then (1) would fail to be a demonstration. However, if A and B should convert, so that we also have as premise

(4) BaA,

then it is also a case of 'asking for the initial thing.' Aristotle tells us that this is
'for the same reason' (65a3). By analogy with the first case, this must mean that
(4) and the conclusion AaC permit the deduction

(5) $BaA, AaC \vdash BaC,$

again in circular-proof fashion.

But while the argument of this passage seems clear enough, Aristotle's language raises problems in a number of points. The following Notes address
these one by one.

65a14−15. 'one belongs to the other' (*thateron thaterōi huparchei*): this
phrase, and its companion 'A follows B' in 65a22−23, are difficult to understand. Aristotle defines three cases in which 'asking for the initial thing' arises:
(1) B is the same as C, (2) B converts with C, (3) 'one belongs to the other.' In
65a21−23, where the argument is exactly parallel, he instead presents the
cases corresponding to (2) and (3) as subcases of the case corresponding to (1):
'A [is] the same as B because A either converts with or follows B.' In each
instance, Aristotle's third case (or second subcase) seems absurdly wide: 'B
belongs to C' is simply the premise itself, in the first example, as is 'A follows
B' in the second, and one term's following another is hardly a plausible reason
for calling them identical.

Ross undertakes to solve the problem in 65a15 by reading *enhuparchei*, 'belong in,' i.e., 'be essentially predicated of,' which just may have been what
Philoponus read (so Mignucci: 'l'uno è presente nella definizione dell'altro').
He then must treat 'follows' in 65a22 as equivalent to this and regard both as
indicating a sort of 'partial identity.' But this is really of no help. Aristotle
would have to be saying that if B is essentially predicated of C, then using
BaC as a premise to deduce AaC is 'asking for the initial thing,' and by
these standards many (perhaps all) of his paradigm demonstrations would be
ruled out.

The evidence indicates, instead, that Aristotle is in each case thinking only
of identical or convertible terms. First, as noted above, the argument closely
parallels the discussion of circular demonstration, which is only possible for
convertible terms. Second, when Aristotle offers a reprise of his results a few
lines later in 65a28−29, he only mentions identity. Even if we do take essential
predication to indicate a kind of partial identity, it is convertibility that is
critical to Aristotle's argument; and partially identical terms are not convertible. We must, therefore, suppose that each of these problematic phrases
somehow expresses identity. The phrase 'one belongs to the other' might,
with strain, be taken to mean '*each* belongs to the other'; 'follow' would then
need to be elliptical for 'follow each other,' which is not very plausible. It is, I
think, impossible to accept Hintikka's argument (*1973*, 53−55) that *hepesthai*
sometimes expresses equivalence, congenial as this would be.

65a17−19. 'if he converted it' (*ei antistrephoi*): like Tricot and Rolfes, I take 'convert' to have a transitive sense here. In the phrase 'as it is, this prevents him, but not the type of argument,' many commentators take 'this' to be 'the fact that *BaC* does not convert.' But there is no such fact: the very case in view is the case in which *B* and *C* are identical or clearly convertible. Instead, what Aristotle means is that it is only the arguer's failure to convert (that is, take *CaB* as a premise) that prevents him from deducing *AaB*, not anything about the actual relationship of the terms. The meaning of 'the type of argument' (*ho tropos*) is probably something vague like 'the way the argument works.'

'if he did this, he could do what was stated': that is, if he converted *BaC* to get *CaB* and deduced *AaB* from this and *AaC*, then he would be able to carry out 'what was stated' in B 5 in the account of circular deductions. The phrase continues with an explanation of what 'what was stated' is (*kai* is epexegetical). 'Convert through three terms' means 'as the result of a deduction (which requires three terms)': cf. 57b17. The majority of interpreters suppose, instead, that 'what was stated' refers to the definition of 'asking for the initial thing' in 64b36—38. But while Aristotle certainly agrees with that, I believe the reference to B 5 is his immediate point.

65a26—35.   This section extends the account of asking for the initial thing to other deductions and other figures. Aristotle is obviously relying on the results of B 5—7 (for a very full discussion of the details, see Mignucci, 666—673).

65a29.   The phrases 'the same things . . . to the same thing,' 'the same thing . . . to the same things,' which summarize the discussion of 65a10—25, are clear in meaning and establish that it is identity and convertibility that are in question in that section. Note that Aristotle here seems to equate coextensionality or convertibility with identity.

65a30.   'in both ways': i.e., either with the convertible terms both as predicates or with them both as subjects.

65a35—37.   'Asking for the initial thing': This remark appears to have been tacked on to the discussion (but cf. A 30, 46a8—10).

Chapter 17

65a38.   This Chapter concerns a type of objection which may be voiced to a proof through impossibility: 'the falsehood does not follow because of this' (*ou para touto sumbainei to pseudos*). It is clear, again, that the phrase is not Aristotle's coinage but part of the currency of his day: his purpose here is to accommodate it in his deductive theory, and also to recommend a more precise sense for it, much as he does with 'asking for the initial thing' in the previous Chapter. Aristotle first takes note that this objection may properly be used only in criticizing proofs through impossibility, not in attacking direct deductions which happen to have negative conclusions or in rejecting a statement by proving its contradictory.

65b1–4. 'For unless the argument had come to a contradiction': this is a rather expansive translation of *mē antiphēsas*, 'unless having contradicted.'

65b3–4. 'it does not suppose what it contradicts': that is, a probative argument does not include a supposition which is then contradicted by the conclusion of a 'leading away to an impossibility.' The text is uncertain at this point: I have followed Ross's *ou gar tithēsi ho antiphēsin* and taken the subject of both verbs to be 'the argument.' Other well attested readings, however, include 'it does not suppose the contradictory' (*tithēsi tēn antiphasin* and 'the person who is going to contradict does not suppose it' (*ou gar tithēsi ho antiphēsōn*).

65b8. 'assumption': I use this translation here, and at 65b14, 66a2, 66a8, for *thesis*. When Aristotle makes frequent use of the word *hupothesis* in a passage, he occasionally omits the prefix *hupo*, and *hupothesis* occurs in this Chapter with considerable frequency: 65b11, 14, 22, 28, 32, 34, 66a3, 12. Compare the similar use of *keisthō* for *hupokeisthō* at B 12, 62a23.

65b9–12. This final account of the 'not because of this' phrase shows the important issue. In a deduction through impossibility, an assumption is rejected because *it* leads to an impossibility if assumed. But, in general, there will be several premises to a deduction; and a deduction through impossibility does not, strictly speaking, tell us which of its premises to reject, but only that we cannot maintain them all. We might then say that the deduction through impossibility permits us to deduce the denial of any of its premises by retaining the remainder. The objection 'not because of this' introduces a restriction on this move: we cannot use a deduction through impossibility to prove the denial of one of its premises unless no impossibility follows from the *remaining* premises. Thus, Aristotle here adopts a position broadly similar to modern relevance logic.

65b13–21. Aristotle's first case is simply the importation into the argument of an unrelated deduction of an impossibility (presumably by importing its premises). For the sense of 'unconnected' here, cf. A 25, 42a21. Heath *1949*, 30–33, sees in the example a reference to an alternative proof of incommensurability. Such a proof may well have existed; but if that is what Aristotle has in mind, then evidently he regarded it as fallacious. It seems to me much more likely that the example he has in mind is purely fanciful. Presumably, he envisions someone who, first, assumes that the diagonal of a square is commensurable with its side; then, imports one of Zeno's arguments against motion, bringing it to its impossible conclusion; and, finally, concludes that the assumption of commensurability is false since an absurdity has been deduced. The reference to the *Topics* is probably to *Sophistical Refutations* 5, 167b21–36, as Ross suggests.

65b21–32. Aristotle's second case concerns assumptions which are, in fact, 'connected' (that is, by a middle term) to the impossibility deduced, but nevertheless not the 'cause' of it. He allows that an assumption connected in this way with the impossible consequence may still fail to be the 'cause' of it. Therefore, the initial criterion, which amounted simply to being linked to one of the terms of the premise to be rejected through a chain of terms, is too broad and needs refinement. We get a refined criterion in 65b32−40: each of the terms of the assumption must be connected with the impossible conclusion in 'the appropriate way.' Again, this is reminiscent of the efforts of modern relevance logicians to find a formal criterion (such as variable-sharing) for relevance.

66a1−15.   This passage indicates the unsettled condition of Aristotle's thought on his subject. Conceding that even his revised criterion may fail, he tries for a final improvement, which amounts to saying that 'not because of this' means 'the assumption is merely a superfluous premise in the deduction.' The fit between this and the technical definition appealing to connections through middle terms is not spelled out, and it is not clear how it should or could be. It is also not clear that Aristotle's position is fully consistent with B 4, 57a40−b17.

66a13−15.   For discussions of the mathematical example, see Heath *1949*, 29−30, and Mignucci, 679−681.

Chapter 18

66a16−24.   A 'false argument' (*pseudēs logos*) is a deduction with a false conclusion; Aristotle's point is that in every such argument there must be a 'first' or 'highest' false premise from which the false conclusion results. Although related to the preceding discussion, this note does not depend on it and seems, in fact, to reflect a more primitive understanding. Especially significant is the assumption that in every argument with a false conclusion there is a single 'first falsehood': this seems completely oblivious of the difficulties Aristotle has just gone through in trying to define the 'relevant' falsehood in a deduction through impossibility. We may also note that letters are used in this section to denote premises, not terms as in B 17. In view of these details, I suspect that B 18 is an earlier study of the same question.

66a17.   'from two premises': the Greek text is actually 'from *the* two premises,' which might mean 'from the two premises as explained in the account of the figures.'

Chapter 19

66a25−32.   This section and the one following are unusual in the *Analytics* in that they concern argumentative (or disputational) technique rather than proof. B 19 is reminiscent of *Topics* VIII, but it clearly presupposes the contents of *Prior Analytics* A. The term *katasullogizesthai*, 'be argued down' or 'be defeated in argument,' occurs nowhere else in Aristotle or other classical authors.

'Allowing the same thing twice' does not mean agreeing to the same premise twice, but rather conceding two premises with a term in common.

66a32. 'what argument we are defending' (*pōs hupechomen ton logon*): literally, 'how we are defending the argument.' The term 'defend' (*hupechein*) is a technical term of dialectic, indicating the opposite argumentative role to 'attack' (*epicheirein*): see *Topics* VIII.3, 158a31 (and cf. *Posterior Analytics* I.12, 77a40–b15). Note that *epicheirein* occurs in the next sentence (66a34).

66a37. 'without middles' (*amesa*): that is, premises should not be presented for acceptance in an order which makes it apparent that their terms form a chain.

Chapter 20

66b4–17. This Chapter gives a further application of Aristotle's deductive theory to argumentative practice (the assimilation of refutations to deductions indicates his aim of generalizing as far as possible). Here, something which 'gets an affirmative response' amounts to an affirmative premise, something which 'gets a negative response' to a negative premise. This usage makes sense in a dialectical context, since premises are always put as questions admitting a yes or no answer. In defining a refutation (*elenchos*) as 'a deduction of a contradiction,' the term 'contradiction' (*antiphasis*) probably has the sense 'contradictory of some assertion' (i.e., which one's opponent has maintained).

66b4. 'when . . . i.e.': the *kai* in *pote kai pōs echontōn tōn horōn* must be epexegetical if it is to make any sense.

66b9–10. 'what is proposed': i.e., 'proposed for refutation.' The Greek, *to keimenon*, is equivalent to *to prokeimenon* (Aristotle occasionally drops a prefix from a compound verb like *prokeisthai*).

66b16–17. 'the determination of a refutation and of a deduction are the same': 'determination' (*dihorismos*) might be taken to mean something like 'distinction' or even 'account.' It frequently means 'definition,' but that sense will not work here: Aristotle does not mean that 'refutation' and 'deduction' are synonymous, but that the results proved earlier about deductions also apply to refutations (presumably because a refutation is a *species* of deduction).

Chapter 21

In this Chapter, Aristotle wants to explain how it is apparently possible for someone to have both knowledge and ignorance about the same thing at the same time, in violation of the law of noncontradiction. His answer rests on a distinction of three kinds of cases of knowing. This Chapter should be compared with the discussion of 'ignorance with respect to a disposition' in *Posterior Analytics* I.16–17. The subject here is an important one for Aristotle. In *Metaphysics* IV he tries to argue that no one can have beliefs which contravene the law of noncontradiction; here, he tries to explain what appear to be examples of just such contrary beliefs. Perhaps more important still is the connection with the problem of 'weakness of will,' that is, the paradoxical fact that we sometimes seem to act consciously in disregard of our considered best judgments. Aristotle's discussion of this problem in *Nicomachean Ethics* VII (= *Eudemian Ethics* VI) recalls the present discussion in a number of its details and should be compared with it (see in particular VII.3).

66b18−34.   Aristotle's opening reference to 'falling in error in connection with the position of terms' (*en tēi thesei tōn horōn apatōmetha*) strongly recalls the subject of A 33, which is 'being deceived . . . by the resemblance of the position of the terms' (*apatasthai . . . para tēn homoiotēta tēs tōn horōn theseōs*: 47b15−17). What Aristotle discussed there were arguments which appear to be deductions because the terms in them appear to be in relationships of predication although they are not. Here, he evidently resumes his earlier discussion of types of deception or error in reasoning. If indeed B 21 is a continuation of A 33, its otherwise intrusive appearance in Book B would be explained.

The principal difficulty with which Aristotle is concerned is this: Suppose that there are two sets of premises from which a certain conclusion can be proved, and suppose that someone believes the premises in one set but disbelieves those in the other. If we suppose that knowledge of what is demonstrable is just knowledge of premises from which it can be demonstrated, it then seems to follow that this person simultaneously knows and does not know the same thing.

66b20−23.   'the same thing . . . several things primarily': A belongs to B 'primarily' or 'first' (*prōtos*) if AaB and there is no term C such that AaC and CaB (or in other words, AaB is 'without a middle term,' *amesos*). For more on this see *Posterior Analytics* I.15. Aristotle treats 'belonging of itself' (*kath' hauto*) as equivalent to this. In *Posterior Analytics* I.16−17, he distinguishes cases of inferred ignorance involving unmiddled and nonunmiddled premises respectively. Here, he may only wish to rule out the possibility that any of the premises in the example is itself known or believed on the basis of a deduction.

66b22−30.   Aristotle envisions two cases: In each, we suppose that AaB, AaC, BaD, and CaD are all true, so that we can deduce AaD with either B or C as middle term. In each case, suppose also that someone correctly believes AaB, BaD, and CaD, but mistakenly believes AeC (and therefore is in a position to deduce both AaD and AeD from premises he believes). The difference between the two cases is that in the first (66b22−26), the terms B and C are not 'from the same series' (that is, neither BaC nor CaB), whereas in the second case (66b26−29) they are (and in particular BaC). The term 'series' (*sustoichia*) means 'sequence of terms each of which is universally true of its successor.'

66b30−31.   'Based on these premises': the puzzle Aristotle raises here applies to both the previous cases. Aristotle's answer appears in 67a8−26.

66b34−67a5.   Aristotle first responds to his problem by arguing that certain types of inconsistent beliefs are indeed impossible. In the case of terms not from the same series, 'the first premise is taken as a contrary,' so that the person in question would simultaneously have and not have the same belief, which is impossible.

Evidently, Aristotle regards the premises *AaB* and *AeC* as somehow contrary to one another, although it is not clear how. One suggestion is the following: He rephrases *AeC* as 'A belongs to none of what C belongs to' and *AaB* as 'A belongs to what B belongs to.' Now, given *CaD* and *BaD*, we can take D as an instance both of 'what C belongs to' and 'what B belongs to.' This would bring the discussion of this case more into line with the subsequent discussion of the *Meno* argument and universal *versus* particular knowledge (it is not clear why Aristotle could not offer the same solution for this case as he does for the later one).

The argument in the *Meno* rests on a puzzle in Plato's *Meno* (80d−e) which purports to show that we cannot seek either what we know (for we already have it) or what we do not know (for we could not tell if we found it). Aristotle refers to this problem more than once in developing his theories of knowledge: see *Posterior Analytics* I.1, 71a29−30, and the discussion in Ferejohn *1988*.

67a5−21.   Knowing the universal while failing to recognize one of its instances (e.g., because we do not even know that *this* particular exists) does not entail self-contrary beliefs, since there are two ways in which we can have knowledge of all of something. This distinction closely corresponds to that made in *Posterior Analytics* I.1.

Several times in this passage, Aristotle uses an idiom that is ambivalent between 'know' in the sense of *connaître* and know in the sense of *savoir*: 'know x, that . . .' (e.g., *oide to G, hoti duo orthai*, 'he knows C, that it is two right angles,' or similarly *agnoein to G hoti estin*, 'he does not know C, that it exists'). I have tried to preserve this ambiguity with a somewhat barbarous English construction. (The same locution is found a number of times in Plato's *Meno*, e.g., 71a5.)

67a12−13.   'ignorant that C exists': more literally, 'not-knowing C, that it is' (*agnoein to G, hoti estin*).

67a20.   'contrary states of knowledge': in Greek, simply 'contrary [knowledges]' (*tas enantias*, with the governing noun *epistēmas* clearly implied). I have tried to supply a more idiomatic English rendering. We might almost borrow a modern philosophical idiom and say 'contrary epistemic states.'

67a21−26.   Applying this distinction to solve the problem in the *Meno*, we see that the advance knowledge required is only universal knowledge, never knowledge of particulars. This section very closely resembles *Posterior Analytics* I.1, 71a17−b8: see McKirahan *1983* for a discussion.

67a27−30.   Aristotle here distinguishes two different types of knowledge of particulars: 'contemplating' them (*theōrein*) and knowing them 'in virtue of their peculiar knowledge' (*tēi oikeiāi <epistēmēi>*). 'Contemplation' or 'reflection' is in Aristotle associated with demonstrative science. It should be remembered here that, for him, the objects of science are unchangeable, unlike sensible particulars.

67a29−30. 'be in error about the particular' (*apatasthai de tēn kata meros*): this is Ross's conjecture (the manuscripts have *tēi*). He suggests that 'the particular' is 'the particular error' (*tēn kata meros apatēn*), noting that the verb *apatasthai* often takes its cognate noun as direct object, as at *Posterior Analytics* I.5, 74a6. However, it could also mean 'the particular knowledge' (in contrast to 'the universal' a few words earlier), in which case it would be an 'accusative of respect' ('in respect to the particular knowledge').

67a30−38. Aristotle now returns to the initial case of two inconsistent beliefs resting on deduction, offering his solution to the puzzle at 66b30−34). In this case, it is a failure to 'reflect simultaneously' (*suntheōrein*) that accounts for the apparent possession of contrary beliefs: the person in question knows that *AaB* and that *BaC*, but simply does not consider them together, and as a result, the inference to *AaC* is not made. It is, therefore, possible for this person to believe the contrary of *AaC*. The case given here seems to be exactly parallel to that in 66b34−67a5: the distinction, evidently, is that here the person's error is not a matter of holding two contrary beliefs, but rather two beliefs of different kinds (a universal belief and a particular belief).

67a38−b11. In addition to the distinction between universal and particular knowledge, Aristotle now distinguishes between possessing and exercising (*energein*) knowledge. These two distinctions are independent of one another: universal and particular knowledge can each be either exercised or possessed but not exercised (elsewhere, Aristotle refers to the latter as 'potential' knowledge). In the present case, he recognizes two instances of exercising knowledge, viz., the actual perception of sensible objects and the actual making of inferences (which apparently is automatic once the premises are 'considered together'). The failure to make the inference from 'Every mule is infertile' and 'This is a mule' to 'This is infertile' is a failure of the latter kind.

The distinction between knowledge as possessed and knowledge as exercised is a favorite theme for Aristotle (see e.g. *On the Soul* II.1, 412a10−11; *Metaphysics* V.7, 1017a35−b6, XIII.10, 1087a15−16; *Topics* V.2, 130a19−22; *Nicomachean Ethics* VII.3, 1146b31−33; *Eudemian Ethics* II.9, 1225b11−14).

67b12−26. This section does not further the discussion in the rest of B 21, although it does concern a relationship between beliefs and facts and the possibility of someone having inconsistent beliefs. It appears to reflect a less thorough familiarity with the issues than the preceding discussion; the call for further discussion at the end (67b26) may indicate that it is an earlier essay. The phrase 'the essence of good' (*to agathōi einai*: literally, 'the to be for good') is an Aristotelian usage with the approximate sense 'what it is to be for good' (for Aristotle, a definition of something is an 'account of its essence').

Aristotle's real concern here is the relationship between beliefs about identity and beliefs about predication. To begin with, he tells us that believing that being good is being bad is believing that being good is *identical to* being bad (and thus not a matter of believing that one is predicated of the other). He then argues that one cannot believe that *A* is identical to *B* without also believing that *B* is identical to *A*, appealing to an analogue of a deduction with convertible terms. Finally, he asserts that, in effect, inferential relationships are the same in belief and thought as in fact: if a set of premises entails a conclusion, then believing the premises entails believing the conclusion.

I have taken the example of believing that the essence of good is the essence of bad as merely an arbitrary example, with no further significance (Aristotle often uses concrete terms in discussions: cf. B 4, 57a36–b17). It seems probable, however, that Aristotle has in mind some type of situation in which it is argued that a person has inconsistent beliefs as a result of thinking that the same thing is simultaneously good and bad (which could perhaps form the basis for an argument in Platonic fashion that this person confuses the nature of goodness with the nature of badness). This, in turn, may lend further support to the suggestion of a relationship between this passage and Greek discussions of the problem of weakness of will.

Chapter 22

The miscellany of results in this Chapter may be intended to function as lemmas for the last five Chapters of the Book (B 23–27); otherwise, their provenance and purpose are somewhat obscure. Many of the results established here are established elsewhere in more complete form, and there are several puzzling or erroneous passages. B 22 thus appears to be an early fragment, written before the full study of deductions in Book A had been completed.

67b27–68a3. Here, as in B 5–7, Aristotle explores the result of supposing that one of the premises of a deduction is 'convertible.' However, the term 'convert' now has a different sense: a premise is said to 'convert' here if its converse (the result of exchanging subject and predicate terms) is also true (evidently, Aristotle has only true premises in view). If an *a* premise converts in this sense, then its terms convert in the sense of B 5–7 (that is, are coextensive). However, all (true) *e* premises convert in this way. As a result, the present notion of conversion appears to be not fully thought out, suggesting that the passage may be an earlier attempt at the same study given in B 5–7.

Aristotle first (67b27–32) shows that either premise of a deduction in *Barbara* (e.g. *AaB, BaC ⊢ AaC*) can be deduced from the converse of the conclusion together with the other premise:

(1) With the minor premise: *BaC, CaA ⊢ BaA*
(2) With the major premise: *CaA, AaB ⊢ CaB*

This result is, of course, identical with that established in B 5. Next (67b32–68a3), he turns to the case of 'not belonging' (i.e., a deduction *AeB, BaC ⊢ AeC* in *Celarent*), announcing that this is 'likewise.' Now, what Aristotle said initially was that when the extremes convert then the middle must convert with either of them. We would accordingly expect him to mean here that if the extremes of *Celarent* convert, then each of the premises must also: that is, that the converse of either premise can be deduced from the converse of the conclusion and the remaining premise. But Aristotle proved in B 5 that this is false: only the major premise can be so derived.

Aristotle's actual account is problematic. He first shows that the converse of the *conclusion* can be derived by converting the *major premise*:

(3) $BaC, BeA \vdash CeA$

The deduction in (3) is second-figure (*Camestres*). The next case is difficult to follow and textually corrupt. Its first sentence appears in several forms: 'If B converts with C, then A also converts <with it>' (manuscripts A^1, B^1, G); 'if C converts with B, then it also converts with A' (A^2, B^2, n^2); 'and also if C converts with B' (n^1). The second of these, which is the most common reading, implies that we can get *CeA* (the converse of *AeC*, the original conclusion) by using the converse of *BaC*. But neither the pair *CaB, AeB* nor the pair *CaB, BeA* gives this conclusion. The first reading is ambiguous, since it does not say what A converts with, but since this construction usually means 'with the last term that occurred in the dative case' it would probably be C. But this is then the same case as the second reading. Ross, instead, combines both readings for 'if C converts with B, then A will also convert <with it>,' thus giving the deduction *CaB, AeC* ⊢ *CeA* (fourth-figure *Camenes*). Ross also finds a problem in the third case. The deduction is clearly *CaB, CeA* ⊢ *BeA*; but although Aristotle explicitly uses the converse of the minor premise (*CaB*), he only mentions the use of the converse of the conclusion (*CeA*). Ross accordingly inserts *kai* in 67b38 to get 'and if *in addition* (sc. to C converting with B, from the previous case) C converts with A.' He thus arrives at the following three deductions:

(3) $BaC, BeA \vdash CeA$ (*Camestres*)
(4) $CaB, AeC \vdash CeA$ (*Camenes*)
(5) $CaB, CeA \vdash BeA$ (*Camestres*).

Ross then must explain Aristotle's remark (68a1−3) that only the last of these 'begins from the conclusion,' i.e., has the conclusion (or its converse) as a premise: (4), after all, has the conclusion itself as a premise. According to Ross, Aristotle means that only the last uses the *converse* of the conclusion as a premise, as the two affirmative cases do.

This interpretation is strained in several respects. To begin with, (4) is a fourth-figure deduction, and even though Aristotle may recognize all the deductions in the fourth figure, he virtually never appeals to them. In addition, Ross's interpretation of 68a1−3 is unnatural: wanting to say 'does not begin with the *converse* of the conclusion (though perhaps with the conclusion itself),'

Aristotle says 'does not begin with the conclusion.' It is also difficult to see either (3) or (4) as illustrating the claim that 'if the extremes convert, then the middle must convert with respect to each.' Since it is hard to imagine Aristotle writing this passage after having written B 5–7, I suggest that he wrote it before he had worked out all the details of his deductive system and that his second case simply contains a mistake: the received text, which gives the invalid *CaB, AeB* ⊢ *CeA*, is what Aristotle intends.

There are two further arguments for this: First, Aristotle seems to accept the similar invalid inference *CaB, AeB* ⊢ *AeC* in the *Posterior Analytics*, indicating that traces of an imperfect understanding of his own deductive theory persist in the treatises (see the discussion in Smith *1982*). Second, and more speculatively, we may make a good guess as to Aristotle's strategy here. Attempting to apply the conversion procedure of 67a27–32 directly to *Celarent* gives the premise pairs *CeA, BaC* and *CeA, AeB*; neither of these yields the converse of the other premise. Accordingly, he asks: what else might work? He notes that by converting one premise, he can get the converse of the conclusion:

(3) *BaC, BeA* ⊢ *CeA*

Next, he tries to do the same with the other premise, erroneously thinking that this works also:

(4) *CaB, AeB* ⊢ *CeA*

Finally, he notes that the first premise of (4) together with its conclusion yield the converse of the other premise:

(5) *CaB, CeA* ⊢ *BeA*

68a3–16.   Bearing in mind that two terms are such that one or the other, but not both, belongs to everything if and only if they are contradictories of each other, we may restate the two results proved here as: if *A* and *C* convert with *B* and *D* respectively, and *A* is the contradictory of *C*, then *B* is the contradictory of *D* (68a3–8); if *A* and *C* are the contradictories of *B* and *D* respectively, and *A* converts with *C*, then *B* converts with *D* (68a11–16). Pacius observed that the example, which in the manuscripts appears between these two results as 68a8–11, actually illustrates the *second* point. I follow Ross's text in transposing these lines.

68a16–25.   Aristotle appeals to the result proved here shortly afterwards (68b24–27). The remark in 68a20–21 that 'B will be said of all of those things of which A is said *except for A itself* (*plēn autou tou A*) is puzzling. Mignucci notes Kirchmann's suggestion that Aristotle may not regard convertibility as a criterion for identity of terms (699); but even if that is so (as it probably is), it is irrelevant here, since the question is precisely one of extension (and cf. the Notes on 65a14–15, 65a29). Since Aristotle is generally reluctant to treat terms as predicated of themselves, it may be that he means 'B is predicated *just exactly* what A is predicated of, with the exception of A itself, of which B is also predicated'; but against the supposition that he wants to avoid 'self-predications' is his remark in the preceding sentence that B is predicated of itself. Ross suggests instead that B is not predicated of A (though coextensive with it), because A is the genus of B (but Aristotle does not indicate such a restriction).

68a25–39. The terms 'preferable' (*hairetōteron*) and 'more to be avoided' (*pheuktoteron*) played a major role in dialectic as Aristotle knew it; *Topics* III.1–3 is a collection of principles for determining what is preferable to, or more to be avoided than, what. This is related to the larger study of argument in two quite different ways. First, as *Topics* III.4–6 shows, Aristotle noted that results concerning these terms could be generalized to apply to any relative terms. Second, choice-worthiness and its opposite may be important to Aristotle because of his understanding of 'practical reasoning,' or reasoning concerned with means and ends and leading to action. According to *Nicomachean Ethics* VI.2, pursuit and avoidance play the same roles in practical reasoning as affirmation and denial in theoretical reasoning, suggesting a greater importance than at first appears for studies like the present one.

Aristotle's language in this section is frequently highly abbreviated; I have filled it out in what I think are fairly obvious ways, but the reader should beware.

68a26. 'preferable in the same way': that is, preferable *to the same degree*.

68a39–b7. This example, which simply illustrates the point made in 68a25–38, recalls the many erotic examples of Plato's dialogues.

Chapter 23

B 23–27 form a continuous investigation of several argumentative terms: 'induction' or 'leading up to' (*epagōgē*), 'example' (*paradeigma*), 'leading away' (*apagōgē*), 'objection' (*enstasis*), 'likelihood' (*eikos*), 'sign' (*sēmeion*). Aristotle's purpose is to bring 'absolutely any form of conviction whatever arising from whatever discipline (*haplōs hētisoun pistis kai hē kath' hopoianoun methodon*) under the umbrella of the deductive theory of A 1–22. As such, these Chapters form a natural continuation of A 1–44. The terms Aristotle discusses were all evidently part of a technical vocabulary of rhetoric established before he began to write: his purpose here is not to define these terms for the uninitiated, but to show how they may be fitted into the account of deductions in the figures.

68b15. The term *epagōgē* is traditionally translated 'induction' (from its Latin cognate *inductio*). There are strong reasons for preserving this tradition: 'induction' is a technical term with Aristotle, the sense of which must be determined from his use; it is historically important that *epagōgē* is the Greek ancestor of 'induction'; and the term is deeply entrenched in the secondary literature. With this said, the reader should beware of reading associations from the subsequent history of philosophy into Aristotle's word, at least without careful consideration of what he says. The correct sense would be better captured by 'leading up,' or possibly 'introduction.' Ross's survey of the uses of *epagōgē* (481−484) is still the best.

It is a bit surprising to find Aristotle speaking of a 'deduction from induction' (*sullogismos ex epagōgēs*). Elsewhere, he presents deduction and induction as the two possible types of argument and sharply separates them (see A 25, 42a3−4 and *Topics* I.12, VIII.2; *Rhetoric* I.2, 1356a35−b11). But the overall project of these latter sections of Book B is the assimilation of 'absolutely any form of conviction whatever' to the theory of figured deductions: now we see just how far Aristotle intends to carry this. Ross calls B 23 a '*tour de force* in which A. tries at all costs to bring induction into the form of syllogism,' (486) and says (I think correctly) that it was produced by an Aristotle 'filled with enthusiasm for his new-found discovery of the syllogism' (50).

68b15−27. Aristotle's argument here presupposes that *epagōgē* is a process of bringing forward each of a number of individual cases and establishing the same thing about each. He describes this as a sort of proof of *AaB* from *AaC* and *BaC* together with the premise that *only C* is *B*; therefore, *B* and *C* convert, and by the result established at B 22, 68a16−25, *AaB*. The process of induction must be thought of, not as the inference to *AaB*, but as the process of bringing up the cases one by one (thus, in 68b15, Aristotle distinguishes between the deduction from *epagōgē* and *epagōgē* itself: the deduction takes place *after* the induction has established *AaC*).

The requirement that induction deal with all the particulars or all the cases is probably one Aristotle inherited from the rhetorical tradition, rather than one of his own suggestions. Here, he takes it for granted that 'induction is through them all' and tries to show that under that assumption, the inference is sound. On a related point, the term *C* in his example actually does not correspond to any predicate: it is, rather, 'composed of every one of the particulars.'

68b21−22. The phrase in parentheses seems to assume what is to be proved, i.e., that *AaB*. Ross, noting that one manuscript reads 'for every bileless thing *C* is long-lived,' suggests 'for every *C* is long-lived,' while Tredennick rejects the phrase. Neither of these is very satisfying (there is no textual support for the rejection, and Ross's proposal gives us a somewhat unusual construction *pan gar to acholon G* where we would normally expect Aristotle to say *pan gar to acholon to G*). Tredennick may be right, but I offer the following speculation: Aristotle does not say that C comprises all of the *long-lived* things, but all of the *bileless* things. As a result, the *epagōgē* in this case must operate by considering, one after another, each of the *bileless* things, every one of which then is found to be long-lived (by observation) and known to be bileless (by selection). Thus, what Aristotle is saying with the troublesome phrase is this: since, as a matter of fact, everything bileless is long-lived, it will result that in selecting bileless things for consideration we are also selecting long-lived things. When we have exhausted the entire class of bileless things (so that we know that B does not 'extend beyond' C but converts with it), we are in a position to infer that whatever is bileless is long-lived. This interpretation is also supported by the reading of manuscript *n*, which has 'the particular long-lived *things*' (plural) at 68b20.

A long tradition faults Aristotle's apparent supposition here that induction must rely on a study of *all* individual cases (so-called 'perfect induction'). But we can interpret 'all cases' in two ways: either as an examination of every *individual* falling under a certain predicate or as an examination of every separate *kind* falling under it. Aristotle does not tell us explicitly which he has in mind, but his biological example lends itself best to the latter interpretation (it would, accordingly, be every bileless *species*, not every individual bileless animal, that we would have to include in our survey, and this is not an unreasonable requirement). Later, in B 24, we read that *epagōgē* proves from 'all the individuals' (69a17: *ex hapantōn tōn atomōn*). But Aristotle frequently uses *atomon* to mean 'species having no subspecies' (cf. *Posterior Analytics* I.23, 84b15; II.5, 91b32).

68b24–27. 'it has been proved earlier': at 68a16–25. The 'extreme' here is the term to which the 'same things' belong.

68b30–37. Aristotle here links up his assimilation of *epagōgē* to the figure-theory with his theory of the cognition of indemonstrable first principles through induction in *Posterior Analytics* II.19, at the same time getting at least a sort of characterization in the same terms of his customary distinction between what is more familiar 'to us' and what is more familiar 'in itself' or 'by nature' (for which see, among other passages, *Posterior Analytics* I.2, 71b33–72a5; *Physics* I.1, 184a16–25; *Metaphysics* VII.3, 1029b3–12; *Nicomachean Ethics* VI.3, 1139b34–36). Since the account of *Posterior Analytics* II does not assume anything like experience with every particular, some details must be supplied to bring the two accounts into harmony; this is a thorny problem which I cannot address in any useful fashion in these Notes. (See Hamlyn *1976*, Engberg-Pederson *1979*, McKirahan *1983*.)

Chapter 24

68b38–69a19. Reasoning by example as Aristotle here presents it has the following structure: we wish to prove that *AaC* and do so by first taking *D*, which is like *C* in some way and where it is familiar that *AaD*. We now take another predicate *B* such that both *BaC* and *BaD*; we 'infer' *AaB* from *AaD* and *BaD* (and perhaps other examples as well); and finally we deduce *AaC* from *AaB* and *BaC*.

The critical point here is the inference from *BaD* and *AaD* to the generaliza-tion *AaB*. This, in fact, is much closer to the modern sense of the term 'induction' (inferring a generalization from one of its cases) than the process Aristotle defines as *epagōgē*, the more so since Aristotle allows that several examples might be used. However, he indicates two points of distinction between example and induction: (1) reasoning by example does not consider all cases, (2) reasoning by example 'connects the deduction to the extreme' while *epagōgē* does not. We can make sense of this if we suppose that *epagōgē* is used to find demonstrations. It will follow that in establishing *AaB* by *epagōgē*, where *C* is the class of things selected because they are *B* and then observed to be *A*, our ultimate purpose is to *deduce* the conclusion *AaC* from the premises *AaB*, *BaC*. In the case of an example, however, the purpose is to establish what amounts to another particular case: we want to prove that war with the neigh-boring Thebans would be evil for the Athenians, and so we first offer a familiar example (the war of the Thebans with their neighbors the Phocians was an evil for them) to establish the principle 'war with one's neighbors is an evil' and then apply this to the particular case at hand.

Aristotle's example of an example is one of the few passages in the *Analytics* for which an absolute date (after 353 B.C.) has been suggested on historical grounds (see Ross 22, 488).

69a14–19. The part-whole relations Aristotle mentions here are all rela-tions of 'middle term' (i.e., 'term that does not appear in the conclusion') to 'minor extreme' (predicate of the conclusion). In a straightforward deduction in Aristotle's standard case (*Barbara*), the middle term is to the minor as whole to part; in induction, according to the analysis of B 23, it is as part to whole. In an argument through example, however, it is logically coordinate with the minor extreme, since both are parts of (fall under) the major term but neither is part of the other. The sense in which argument through induction 'proves the extreme to belong to the middle from all the individuals' is spelled out in B 23, 68b15–29, where it is the *major* extreme that is so proved to belong. (On 'individuals' in 69a17 see the notes above on B 23.)

To 'connect' (*sunhaptein*), as Aristotle uses the term here, is to link up two terms by means of a middle term; B 23 emphasizes the fact that *epagōgē* does not do this in order to show its role in establishing unmiddled premises. On the account just given, an example is really a device for producing conviction in the major premise of a deduction, which is then, in turn, used to establish another conclusion. Thus, in order to establish that war with neighbors is an evil, we use the example of the war of the Thebans with the Phocians; having established this, we then use it as major premise to deduce the conclusion that war with the Thebans is an evil for the Athenians. Since there is a deduction, there is a middle term which 'connects' two extremes.

One minor puzzle remains. Aristotle says that *epagōgē* does not, and *para-deigma* does, connect the *deduction* with the 'extreme.' This may simply be a loose usage, but it is just possible that *sullogismos* here means 'minor term';

Aristotle sometimes uses *sullogismos* to refer to the conclusion (*sumperasma*) of a deduction, and he sometimes uses *sumperasma* to mean 'minor term' (e.g., *Posterior Analytics* I.11, 77a21).

Chapter 25

69a20−36.   The term *apagōgē* is as difficult to translate as its cousin *epagōgē*. The traditional English rendering is 'reduction,' but this invites confusion with *anagōgē*. The process Aristotle defines involves leading the argument away from one question or problem to another more readily resolved (thus I opt for 'leading away').

As defined here, *apagōgē* is a matter of finding premises from which something may be proved. Aristotle says that this constitutes *apagōgē* under two circumstances: (1) the major premise is 'clear' and the minor premise is at least as convincing as the conclusion; (2) there are 'fewer middles' of the minor premise than of the conclusion. Criterion (1) is epistemic, while (2) is proof-theoretic: both are included in *Posterior Analytics* I.2 among the requirements which the premises of a demonstration must satisfy. For this reason, I have translated *epistēmē* here as 'scientific understanding,' the technical sense it carries in that treatise. (In the example which follows immediately I revert to the briefer 'science.')

69a28−29.   'for it is closer . . . did not have scientific understanding': the text here presents some problems. Most manuscripts give the text as *enguteron gar tou epistasthai dia to proseilēphenai tēn AG epistēmēn proteron ouk echontas*. Ross puts a comma after 'science' (*epistēmēn*), which would give the sense 'for it is closer to scientific understanding because of taking in addition the knowledge of AC, which we previously did not have.' Since the entire point is to *establish* knowledge of AC here, this seems absurd; accordingly, Ross changes 'AC' to 'AB.' The sentence would then say that we get closer to a scientific understanding of AC ('Justice is teachable') by 'taking the knowledge' of AB ('Justice is a science'). But this does not seem to illustrate what Aristotle has just said. The definition of *apagōgē* supposes that 'the first clearly belongs to the middle': we may, I think, take this to mean that the major premise AB is scientifically known. However, neither the minor premise BC nor the conclusion AC are known. Under those circumstances, if the minor premise BC is 'more convincing' than the conclusion AC, then assuming *that minor premise* brings us closer to scientific understanding because the assumption made is more convincing. On Ross's interpretation, we must assume AB, but Aristotle presents this premise as already 'clear' (and thus there is no need to 'assume' it). It is also unclear to me how we get 'closer' to science on Ross's view: closer than what? My translation keeps the text as it is, but punctuates after *proseilēphenai* ('taking in addition'). Pacius' text, *proseilēphenai tēi AG tēn BG* ('assuming BC in addition to AC'), would support essentially the same interpretation; Waitz adopts this, and Tricot and Rolfes give different renderings of it. However, this has less manuscript authority and does not give a good sense (it makes Aristotle appear to treat the conclusion to be proved as a sort of assumption).

69a35−36. 'when BC is unmiddled': Aristotle supposes that the major premise AB is 'evident,' and takes this, in turn, to mean both 'without a middle' (*amesos*) and 'familiar in itself.' If, in addition, the minor premise also is without a middle, then both premises of the deduction are indemonstrable first principles, and therefore the deduction is a demonstration producing scientific understanding.

Chapter 26

The subject of objections (*enstaseis*) is treated in *Rhetoric* II.25 and mentioned in the *Topics*, *Sophistical Refutations*, and *Posterior Analytics*: evidently, this was a technical term of rhetorical theory before Aristotle. (*Posterior Analytics* I.4, 73a32−34, I.6, 74b18−21, and I.12, 77b34−39 are worth comparing here.) An objection in this sense is an attack on one of the *premises* of an argument: attacking an argument by giving a counterargument against its conclusion is 'refutation' (*elenchos*: see B 20) or 'counterdeduction' (*antisullogismos*: see *Topics* VIII.8). Although Aristotle's initial definition suggests that an objection is simply a statement either contrary or contradictory to a premise, the evidence of the *Rhetoric* and later passages in the present Chapter indicate that what Aristotle is talking about is something comparable to an 'enthymeme': a statement such that either the contrary or the contradictory of the premise objected to follows from it with another obvious but unstated premise.

69a39−b1. The statement that a premise 'either cannot be particular at all, or not in universal deductions' is puzzling: it is, of course, true that a universal deduction must have only universal premises, but it is quite opaque how this differentiates objections from premises in an interesting way (an objection also can only be particular *in objection to* a universal premise).

69b1−8. The 'two ways' are clear enough, but the restriction to two figures is more difficult to understand: this is one of the reasons Ross concludes that B 26 'suffers from compression and haste.' Aristotle assumes that if the objection is universal in form it must be deduced in the first figure, while if it is particular it must be deduced in the third. Ross explains this by supposing that the objection is actually brought against a premise which is itself already the conclusion of a deduction and that, for some reason, Aristotle requires the objection to give a deduction in the same figure as that original deduction: otherwise, he says, the explanation 'opposites are concluded only in the first and third figures' makes no sense. However, he himself points out that on this interpretation the reference to the third figure makes no sense either, since contradictory statements cannot be deduced in that figure.

It may be impossible to straighten out Aristotle's thought in this Chapter, but it seems to me relevant that his discussion revolves, to some extent,

around the problem of *finding* an objection. The objection found is a premise
which shares one term with the premise objected to, and has a new term in a
relationship to it determined by the type of premise objected to and the type
of objection (contrary or contradictory) desired. Looking for a premise in this
way recalls the procedures of A 27−28 (44a11−35); and there, Aristotle found
premises for universal conclusions in the first figure and for particular conclusions in the third. The only exceptions are second-figure *Camestres* and fourth-
figure *Bramantip* as alternatives for *e* and *i* conclusions respectively; and Aristotle says that the first requires a 'prior deduction' (*ek prosullogismou*, 44a22−23)
and that the second is a 'converted deduction' (*antestrammenos sullogismos*,
44a31). He thus assigned a special priority to the four deductions *Barbara*,
Celarent, *Darapti*, *Felapton*, as the ones to which one should look in searching
for premises. In view of his further requirement that it should be immediately
evident that the contrary or the contradictory of the initial premise follows
from the objection stated (cf. 69b32−36 below), the remarks in A 28 about
Camestres and *Bramantip* probably disqualify them here.

69b8−19.   In these examples, the objection itself is really the *major premise*
of a deduction from which the contradictory or contrary of the premise attacked follows. The minor premise is supposed to be something obvious,
and therefore unstated. For an affirmative premise, Aristotle's two cases are:
(1) objecting contrarily, we find a term *C* such that *CaB* is obvious and object
that *AeC* (and *AeB* follows in *Celarent*); (2) objecting contradictorily, we find a
term *C* such that *BaC* is obvious and object that *AeC* (*AoB* then follows in
Felapton). For a negative premise, the cases are identical except that the objection itself (i.e., the major premise) is of the form *AaB*.

69b19−28.   Though Aristotle's language here is highly compressed, and as a
result obscure, his point is clear enough. The objection sought is to be a
premise having as one term the *predicate* of the premise attacked; Aristotle
defines its relationship to the other premise, which depends on the nature of
the objection. The way in which Aristotle describes the procedure comports
well with the methods of A 28: from among those which the predicate belongs
to all of (or to none of), we search for a term which belongs to all of the subject
(or to which the subject belongs to all of).

69b28−32.   'Those premises': this may give a clue as to why Aristotle
considers only first- and third-figure arguments for objections: the two procedures he has defined (one for universal and one for particular conclusions)
can be applied both to affirmative and to negative premises simply by changing the major premise sought from *e* to *a*.

69b32−36.   'And in addition': This suggests that Aristotle avoids the second figure partly because he regards it as not yielding sufficiently obvious
deductions. The phrase 'because C does not follow it' is ambiguous: 'it' could
be either A or B. On the first possibility, the case is objecting to *AaB* by stating
CeA (where *CaB* is evident); on the second, the objection is *CeB* and the
unstated premise is *CaA*. Ross opts for the first interpretation on the grounds

that it is in this way less obvious what the unstated premise must be. But in A 28 the second-figure deduction in *Camestres* (which corresponds here to the second case) is said to require additional argument.

69b35−36. 'turn aside': Aristotle uses the verb *ektrepesthai* of pursuing a wrong approach to a problem or a wrong line of inquiry (cf. *Physics* I.8, 191a26, 191b32.

69b36−37. Ross, following Susemihl, rejects this sentence as out of place and inconsistent with the contents of B 27.

69b38−70a2. This closing note attests to the unfinished state of B 26. The commentators note that these other types of objections correspond to the last three of the four enumerated in *Rhetoric* II.25; the first of the four, 'from the thing itself' (*aph' heautou*), corresponds closely to the type of objection treated in B 26, as Ross notes. Since the fourth type of objection is described as 'judgments on the part of famous men' (*hai kriseis hai apo gnōrimōn andrōn*), I have translated *kata doxan* as 'according to reputation' rather than 'according to opinion.'

Chapter 27

70a3. Ross, noting that the Chapter begins somewhat abruptly and, unlike B 23−26, without a summary definition of its subject, transposes a sentence here from 70a10. But despite what Ross says, the subject of the section is not enthymemes (the word *enthumēma* occurs only once in it), but signs and likelihoods. This is confirmed by the references to it from the *Rhetoric* (I.2, 1357b21−25; II.25, 1403a4−5, 1403a10−12), which all concern signs and likelihoods.

The distinction between a likelihood (*eikos*) and a sign (*sēmeion*) is that they are defined by different sorts of criteria: a premise is a likelihood if it is 'well-known' or 'accepted' (*endoxos*), which, as the *Topics* makes clear, is a matter of the attitudes of belief people have towards it. A sign, by contrast, is defined as such by its role in a kind of deduction. As with Aristotle's other definitions, this is not intended to explain the term for those (like us) who are ignorant of its meaning, but to accommodate it in the deductive theory of the figures. The examples later in the Chapter make it clear enough what a sign is: it is just a statement predicating *A* of *B*, offered in support of the claim that *C* is predicated of *B*. For instance, wishing to establish the statement 'This woman is pregnant,' one might say, 'This woman has milk.'

70a5−6. Note that the examples here concern conduct typical of people who have certain emotional attitudes towards others and provide a basis for inferring those attitudes: we infer that X loves Y because X shows affection for Y, we infer that X is envious of Y because X hates (expresses hatred for) Y. I have slightly expanded the translations to reflect this.

70a9−10. 'Enthymemes' (*enthumēmata*) are discussed at length in the *Rhetoric*. The term is a difficult one to render without prejudice, meaning something like 'reason' or 'thing that makes one believe.' However, since it plays no important role in the *Prior Analytics*, its full elucidation may gratefully be foregone here.

70a11−24. The main point of the Chapter is to classify all occurrences of signs in terms of the figures. Aristotle distinguishes three cases: (1) we offer *BaC* as a sign for *AaC* when it is true that *AaB*; (2) we offer *AaC* as a sign for *AaB* when it is true that *BaC*; (3) we offer *AaC* as a sign for *BaC* when it is true that *AaB*. In case (1), the conclusion actually follows from the sign and the (unstated) other premise. In (2), the conclusion does not follow, although *AiB* does, and in any event, the argument resembles the pattern in *epagōgē*. In (3), neither the conclusion nor anything else follows from the premises. All three examples that he offers are plausible as rhetorical or forensic arguments; Aristotle is presumably trying to show that even though (3) is widely used, it should not be.

70a24−28. A sign is a stated premise with an unstated partner: if we actually state the second premise, we are not offering a sign but giving a deduction. (But as we see in the next passage, it is not really a deduction in cases (2) and (3).)

70a28−38. The crucial difference between the three cases is their deductive status. 'Nonbinding' (*lutos, lusimos*) means 'refutable' (cf. the use of the verb *luein* in *Metaphysics* XII.10, 1075a31, 33). Aristotle is saying that if the premises of a sign of type (1) are true, then no objection can be brought against it, since it is a proof, whereas even if the premises in cases of types (2) and (3) are true the conclusion may fail to be and so may possibly be refuted. 'The truth, then, can occur in all signs' probably means only that in each case the conclusion *may* be true when the premises are.

70b1−6. Aristotle ponders two alternative ways of distinguishing between signs and 'evidences' (*tekmēria*). The latter is a legal term, amounting to 'proofs' (a *tekmērion* constitutes conclusive evidence for something, while a *sēmeion* is merely an indication). The 'middle' here is the sign in case (1) above: the actual sign *is* the middle term, as having milk is a sign of being pregnant. In the other cases, the sign in this sense is not the middle term for premises in the relevant figure. Aristotle here wonders whether it is the term itself, or the entire deduction, which should be called 'sign' or 'evidence.'

70b7−38. This terminal section, on 'recognizing natures' (*phusiognōmonein*), seems to have no very close connection with the *Prior Analytics*. It might have been included (or appended by an editor) because this skill also formed part of the orator's bag of tricks. However, the discussion never refers to the other themes of the *Prior Analytics*. It seems more likely, therefore, that this passage found its place here only because it is concerned with certain physical states as *signs* of states of character. The art of physiognomonics was evidently established before Aristotle's time, in the fifth century: Alexander of Aphrodisias (*De Fato* 6) recounts an anecdote of an encounter between Socrates and the physiognomonist Zopyrus. A pseudo-Aristotelian (but probably Peripatetic) treatise with the title *Physiognomonics* has come down to us. As both this passage and that treatise make clear, the gist of this 'art' was a system of associations between anatomical characteristics and traits of character, based in large part on purported associations found in animals.

70b11. 'passions' (*orgai*): the word *orgē* in Aristotle (or generally in Greek) usually means 'anger,' but it also can mean 'strong emotion'; the use of the plural here, which is comparatively uncommon in Aristotle, together with the context, make 'passions' a good English version (cf. Tricot's French 'passions').

70b11–31. Aristotle concedes that physiognomonics could indeed work under certain restricted circumstances, to wit: (1) natural affections (*phusika pathēmata*) 'change' body and soul together; (2) each condition has one and only one sign; (3) we can determine both the affection and the sign peculiar to each animal species. The reasoning then proceeds as follows: If there is some affection which naturally belongs to all animals of a certain species (but only incidentally to animals of other species), then by (1) there must be some unique bodily sign associated with this affection; and by (2), this must be the unique sign associated with that affection wherever it is found. Aristotle does not appear to have any quarrel with (1), which evidently rests on the observation that there are naturally determined 'signs' (expressions) of various emotions. He also does not question (2), though his language suggests that he is merely accepting it for the sake of argument. What he does, instead, is raise difficulties about making use of (3) in those cases in which a species has more than one natural trait. The suggested solution, a sort of method of differences, is straightforward enough.

70b19. 'affection' (*pathos*): Ross notes that here this would have to denote the 'sign,' i.e., the bodily characteristic, rather than the affection of character (which is what *pathos* means throughout the rest of the passage); accordingly, he rejects this occurrence of the word. But Aristotle is perfectly capable of such a switch in word meaning within a passage: compare A 43 and the associated Note.

70b21. 'a man': Ross brackets the article before *anthrōpos*, evidently because he thinks the sense would otherwise have to be 'man in general,' i.e., every man without exception. But in connection with *estai*, 'is possible,' this is not very different from 'some men are brave,' which is what Aristotle means here.

70b32–38. This note offers a schema for physiognomonic explanations using the theory of figured deductions, in the style common throughout B. There is nothing here that Aristotle might not have said, but also nothing beyond an obvious application of Aristotle's techniques to the case in question.

APPENDIX I
A LIST OF THE
DEDUCTIVE FORMS IN
PRIOR ANALYTICS A 4–22

I list below the various premise pairs which Aristotle shows to yield a conclusion in A 4–22. Each deduction or premise-pair is accompanied by a textual citation and a brief indication of the way in which Aristotle proves the existence or nonexistence of a deduction for that case. As a convenience, I include the traditional mood names for premise pairs which correspond to them. Some modal-premise combinations corresponding to these pairs do not yield conclusions, and some of the modal pairs which yield conclusions do not correspond to named pairs. Question marks indicate points in which Aristotle's text is difficult to interpret. Readers who wish more detailed accounts should consult the table given by Ross and the studies of Becker, McCall, and Wieland.

The largest part of list is taken up with modally qualified forms. Here, I use **A** to indicate 'assertoric' premises (those with no modal qualifier). In discussing combinations of one assertoric and one necessary premise, Aristotle frequently takes it for granted that an assertoric conclusion can be deduced and only proves that a necessary conclusion cannot be. I indicate these by noting that he gives a 'proof that *not* **N**.' 'Modal conversion' means the conversion of a possible affirmative premise into its corresponding negative, or vice versa. Many of Aristotle's proofs rely on the use of conversion to bring about a previously established modal deduction. I indicate this by giving the figure and the modal qualifications of the premises. Thus, 'conversion to I **NA**' means 'conversion leading to a first-figure premise pair with necessary major premise and assertoric minor.' Aristotle often says that a given proof proceeds 'likewise' or 'as before,' and it is sometimes quite unclear what he intends. I have left many of these remarks unresolved.

The traditional names for the incomplete forms actually encode instructions for carrying out proofs. The first letter of the name (B, C, D, F) indicates the first-figure form to which the proof appeals; 's' following a vowel indicates that the corresponding premise (always an *e* or *i*) is to be converted (*conversio simplex*); 'p' following 'a' indicates 'conversion by limitation' (*conversio per accidens*) of a universal premise, i. e., conversion into a particular premise (*a* into *i*, *e* into *o*); 'r' indicates proof through impossibility; and 'm' indicates that the premises must be interchanged. (Other letters, such as 'l' and 'n,' have no significance.) Thus, the name *Camestres* tells us that a proof that an *e* conclusion follows from an *a* major premise and an *e* minor may be constructed by converting the first premise (*Camestres*) and interchanging the premises (*Camestres*), giving the first-figure form *Celarent* (*Camestres*), then converting the conclusion (*Camestres*); and, that a proof through impossibility is also possible (*Camestres*).

NONMODAL (ASSERTORIC) DEDUCTIONS

FIGURE I (A 4)

AaB, BaC ⊢ *AaC*	*Barbara*	complete (25b37−40)
AeB, BaC ⊢ *AeC*	*Celarent*	complete (25b40−26a2)
AaB, BiC ⊢ *AiC*	*Darii*	complete (26a23−25)
AeB, BiC ⊢ *AoC*	*Ferio*	complete (26a25−27)

FIGURE II (A 5)

MeN, MaX ⊢ *NeX*	*Cesare*	conversion (27a5−9)
MaN, MeX ⊢ *NeX*	*Camestres*	conversion, impossibility (27a9−15)
MeN, MiX ⊢ *NoX*	*Festino*	conversion (27a32−36)
MaN, MoX ⊢ *NoX*	*Baroco*	impossibility (27a36−b3)

FIGURE III (A 6)

PaS, RaS ⊢ *PiR*	*Darapti*	conversion, impossibility, *ekthesis* (28a17−26)
PeS, RaS ⊢ *PoR*	*Felapton*	conversion, impossibility (28a26−30)
PaS, RiS ⊢ *PiR*	*Datisi*	conversion (28b7−11)
PiS, RaS ⊢ *PiR*	*Disamis*	conversion, impossibility, *ekthesis* (28b11−15)
PoS, RaS ⊢ *PoR*	*Bocardo*	impossibility, *ekthesis* (28b17−21)
PeS, RiS ⊢ *PoR*	*Ferison*	conversion (28b33−35)

DEDUCTIONS WITH ONE OR MORE MODALLY QUALIFIED PREMISES

NN: (A 8: All forms except *Baroco* and *Bocardo*, 29b36−30a5)

FIGURE I

N*AaB*, N*BaC* ⊢ N*AaC*	*Barbara*	[complete]
N*AeB*, N*BaC* ⊢ N*AeC*	*Celarent*	[complete]
N*AaB*, N*BiC* ⊢ N*AiC*	*Darii*	[complete]
N*AeB*, N*BiC* ⊢ N*AoC*	*Ferio*	[complete]

FIGURE II

N*AeB*, N*AaC* ⊢ N*BeC*	*Cesare*	conversion
N*AaB*, N*AeC* ⊢ N*BeC*	*Camestres*	conversion
N*AeB*, N*AiC* ⊢ N*BoC*	*Festino*	conversion
N*AaB*, N*AoC* ⊢ N*BoC*	*Baroco*	*ekthesis* (30a6−14)

FIGURE III

N*AaC*, N*BaC* ⊢ N*AiB*	*Darapti*	conversion
N*AeC*, N*BaC* ⊢ N*AoB*	*Felapton*	conversion
N*AiC*, N*BaC* ⊢ N*AiB*	*Disamis*	conversion
N*AaC*, N*BiC* ⊢ N*AiB*	*Datisi*	conversion
N*AoC*, N*BaC* ⊢ N*AoB*	*Bocardo*	*ekthesis* (30a6−14)
N*AeC*, N*BiC* ⊢ N*AoB*	*Ferison*	conversion

N + A:

FIGURE I (A 9)

N*AaB*, *BaC* ⊢ N*AaC*	*Barbara*	*ekthesis* (30a17−23)
N*AeB*, *BaC* ⊢ N*AeC*	*Celarent*	*ekthesis* (30a17−23)
AaB, N*BaC* ⊢ *AaC*	*Barbara*	proof that *not* N through impossibility and through terms (30a23−33)
AeB, N*BaC* ⊢ *AeC*	*Celarent*	proof that *not* N through impossibility and through terms (30a23−33)
N*AaB*, *BiC* ⊢ N*AiC*	*Darii*	*ekthesis* (30a37−b2)
N*AeB*, *BiC* ⊢ N*AoC*	*Ferio*	*ekthesis* (30a37−b2)
AaB, N*BiC* ⊢ *AiC*	*Darii*	proof through terms that *not* N (30b1−6)
AeB, N*BiC* ⊢ *AoC*	*Ferio*	proof through terms that *not* N (30b1−6)

FIGURE II (A 10)

N*AeB*, *AaC* ⊢ N*BeC*	*Cesare*	conversion to I N*A* (30b9−13)
AaB, N*AeC* ⊢ N*BeC*	*Camestres*	conversion to I N*A* (30b14−18)
AeB, N*AaC* ⊢ *BeC*	*Cesare*	[no argument]
N*AaB*, *AeC* ⊢ Be*C*	*Camestres*	conversion to I **AN**; argument that *not* N through impossibility, terms (30b20−40)
N*AeB*, *AiC* ⊢ N*BoC*	*Festino*	conversion to I N*A* (31a5−10)
N*AaB*, *AoC* ⊢ Bo*C*	*Baroco*	that *not* N through terms (31a10−15)
AeB, N*AiC* ⊢ Bo*C*	*Festino*	that *not* N through terms (31a15−17)
AaB, N*AoC* ⊢ Bo*C*	*Baroco*	that *not* N through terms (31a15−17)

FIGURE III (A 11)

N*AaC*, *BaC* ⊢ N*AiB*	*Darapti*	conversion to I N*A* + *ekthesis* (31a24−30)
AaC, N*BaC* ⊢ N*AiB*	*Darapti*	conversion to I N*A* (31a31−33)

N*Ae*C, *Ba*C ⊢ N*Ao*B	*Felapton*	conversion to I **NA** + *ekthesis* (31a33−37)
*Ae*C, N*Ba*C ⊢ *Ao*B	*Felapton*	conversion to I **AN**; terms (31a37−b10)
*Ai*C, N*Ba*C ⊢ N*Ai*B	*Disamis*	conversion to I **NA** + *ekthesis* (31b12−19)
N*Aa*C, *Bi*C ⊢ N*Ai*B	*Datisi*	conversion to I **NA** + *ekthesis* (31b19−20)
*Aa*C, N*Bi*C ⊢ *Ai*B	*Datisi*	conversion to I **AN**; terms (31b20−31)
N*Ai*C, *Ba*C ⊢ *Ai*B	*Disamis*	that *not* **N** through terms (31b31−33)
N*Ae*C, *Bi*C ⊢ N*Ao*B	*Ferison*	'same as before' (31b35−37)
*Ao*C, N*Ba*C ⊢ *Ao*B	*Bocardo*	that *not* **N** through terms (31b40−32a1)
*Ae*C, N*Bi*C ⊢ *Ao*B	*Ferison*	terms (32a1−4)
N*Ao*C, *Ba*C ⊢ *Ao*B	*Bocardo*	terms (32a4−5)

PP:

Figure I (A 14)

P*Aa*B, P*Ba*C ⊢ P*Aa*C	*Barbara*	complete (32b38−33a1)
P*Ae*B, P*Ba*C ⊢ P*Ae*C	*Celarent*	complete (33a1−5)
P*Aa*B, P*Be*C ⊢ P*Aa*C		modal conversion (33a5−12)
P*Ae*B, P*Be*C ⊢ P*Aa*C		modal conversion (33a12−17)
P*Aa*B, P*Bi*C ⊢ P*Ai*C	*Darii*	complete (33a23−25)
P*Ae*B, P*Bi*C ⊢ P*Ao*C	*Ferio*	complete (33a25−27)
P*Aa*B, P*Bo*C ⊢ P*Ai*C		modal conversion (33a27−34)
all *i/o−a/e* combinations		rejected by terms, conversion to previous cases (33a34−b17)

Figure II (A 17)

all forms rejected		failure of P*e* conversion (36b35−37a31)
P*Ae*B, P*Aa*C		rejected by several arguments, terms (37a32−b10)
all other forms		rejected by terms (37b10−16)

Figure III (A 20)

P*Aa*C, P*Ba*C ⊢ P*Ai*B	*Darapti*	conversion (39a14−19)
P*Ae*C, P*Ba*C ⊢ P*Ao*B	*Felapton*	conversion (39a19−23)
P*Ae*C, P*Be*C ⊢ P*Ai*B		modal conversion (39a26−28)
P*Aa*C, P*Bi*C ⊢ P*Ai*B	*Datisi*	conversion (39a31−35)
P*Ai*C, P*Ba*C ⊢ P*Ai*B	*Disamis*	conversion (39a35−36)
P*Ae*C, P*Bi*C ⊢ P*Ao*B	*Ferison*	conversion (39a36−38)
P*Ao*C, P*Ba*C ⊢ P*Ao*B	*Bocardo*	conversion (39a36−38)

P*AeC*, P*BoC* ⊢ P*AiB*		modal conversion (39a38−b2)
P*AoC*, P*BeC* ⊢ P*AiB*		modal conversion (39a38−b2)
all forms with two particulars		rejected by terms (39b2−6)

P + A:

FIGURE I (A 15)

P*AaB*, *BaC* ⊢ P*AaC*	*Barbara*	complete, *ekthesis* (33b33−36)
P*AeB*, *BaC* ⊢ P*AeC*	*Celarent*	complete (33b36−40)
AaB, P*BaC* ⊢ P(*AaC*)	*Barbara*	proof through impossibility (34a34−b2)
AeB, P*BaC* ⊢ P(*AeC*)	*Celarent*	proof through impossibility; terms (34b19−35a2)
AaB, P*BeC* ⊢ P(*AaC*)		modal conversion (35a3−11)
AeB, P*BeC* ⊢ P(*AaC*)		modal conversion (35a11−20)
all forms with minor *BeC*		rejected by terms (35a20−24)
P*AaB*, *BiC* ⊢ P*AiC*	*Darii*	complete (35a30−35)
P*AeB*, *BiC* ⊢ P*AoC*	*Ferio*	complete (35a30−35)
AaB, P*BiC* ⊢ P(*AiC*)	*Darii*	through impossibility (35a35−40)
AeB, P*BiC* ⊢ P(*AoC*)	*Ferio*	through impossibility (35a35−40)
AaB, P*BoC* ⊢ P(*AiC*)		modal conversion (35b5−8)
AeB, P*BoC* ⊢ P(*AoC*)		modal conversion (35b5−8)
all forms with minor *BoC*		rejected by terms (35b8−14)
all forms with two particulars		rejected by terms (35b14−22)

FIGURE II (A 18)

P*AeB*, *AaC*	(*Cesare*)	rejected 'as before' (37b19−23)
AaB, P*AeC*	(*Camestres*)	rejected 'as before' (37b19−23)
AeB, P*AaC* ⊢ P(*BeC*)	*Cesare*	conversion to I **AP** (37b24−28)
P*AaB*, *AeC* ⊢ P(*BeC*)	*Camestres*	[conversion] (37b29)
AeB, P*AeC* ⊢ P(*BeC*)		modal conversion (37b29−35)
P*AeB*, *AeC* ⊢ P(*BeC*)		modal conversion (37b29−35)
all forms with two affirmatives		rejected by terms (37b35−38)
P*AeB*, *AiC*	(*Festino*)	rejected 'as before' (37b39−38a2)
AaB, P*AoC*	(*Baroco*)	rejected 'as before' (37b39−38a2)
AeB, P*AiC* ⊢ P(*BoC*)	*Festino*	conversion (38a3−4)
AeB, P*AoC* ⊢ P(*BoC*)		modal conversion (38a4−7)

FIGURE III (A 21)

AaC, P*BaC* ⊢ P(*AiB*)	*Darapti*	conversion to I **AP** (39b10−16)
P*AaC*, *BaC* ⊢ P*AiB*	*Darapti*	conversion to I **PA** (39b16−17)
P*AeC*, *BaC* ⊢ P*AoB*	*Felapton*	conversion to I **PA** (39b17−22)
AeC, P*BaC* ⊢ P(*AoB*)	*Felapton*	conversion to I **AP** (39b17−22)
AaC, P*BeC* ⊢ P(*AiB*)		modal conversion (39b22−25)
AeC, P*BeC* ⊢ P(*AoB*)		modal conversion (39b22−25)

AiC, P*BaC* ⊢ P*AiB*	*Disamis*	conversion to I **PA** (39b26−31)
P*AaC*, *BiC* ⊢ P*AiB*	*Datisi*	conversion to I **PA** (39b26−31)
P*AiC*, *BaC* ⊢ P(*AiB*)	*Disamis*	conversion to I **AP** (39b26−31)
AaC, P*BiC* ⊢ P(*AiB*)	*Datisi*	conversion to I **AP** (39b26−31)
P*AeC*, *BiC* ⊢ P*AoB*	*Ferison*	conversion to I **PA** (39b26−31)
AeC, P*BiC* ⊢ P(*AoB*)	*Ferison*	conversion to I **AP** (39b26−31)
P*AoC*, *BaC* ⊢ P(*AoB*)	*Bocardo*	through impossibility (39b31−39)
all forms with two particulars		rejected through terms (40a1−3)

P + N:

FIGURE I (A 16)

N*AaB*, P*BaC* ⊢ P(*AaC*)	*Barbara*	'as previous' (35b37−36a2: cf. 34a34−b2)
P*AaB*, N*BaC* ⊢ P*AaC*	*Barbara*	complete (36a2−7)
N*AeB*, P*BaC* ⊢ *AeC*	*Celarent*	through impossibility (36a7−17)
P*AeB*, N*BaC* ⊢ P*AeC*	*Celarent*	complete; cannot be done through impossibility (36a17−24)
N*AaB*, P*BeC* ⊢ P(*AaC*)		modal conversion (36a25−27)
N*AeB*, P*BeC* ⊢ P*AeC*		modal conversion (36a25−27)
P*AaB*, N*BeC*		rejected by terms (36a27−31)
P*AeB*, N*BeC*		rejected by terms (36a27−31)
N*AeB*, P*BiC* ⊢ *AoC*	*Ferio*	through impossibility (36a34−39)
P*AeB*, N*BiC* ⊢ P*AoC*	*Ferio*	not **A**, proof 'as before' (36a39−b2)
N*AaB*, P*BiC* ⊢ P(*AiC*)	*Darii*	not **A**, proof 'as before' (36a39−b2)
all forms with universal **P** minor		rejected by terms (36b3−7)
all forms with universal **N** minor		rejected by terms (36b7−12)
two particulars or indefinites		rejected by terms (36b12−18)
P*AaB*, N*BiC* ⊢ P*AiC*	*Darii*	'as before'
N*AaB*, P*BoC* ⊢ P(*AiC*)		(35*b* 28−30)
N*AeB*, P*BoC* ⊢ *AoC*		(35*b* 30−31)

FIGURE II (A19)

N*AeB*, P*AaC* ⊢ P(*BeC*) ⊢ *BeC*	*Cesare*	conversion to I **NP** for **P**; through impossibility for **A** (38a16−25)
P*AaB*, N*AeC* ⊢ P(*BeC*) ⊢ *BeC*	*Camestres*	'same as previous' (38a25−26)
P*AeB*, N*AaC* ⊢ *BeC*	(*Cesare*)	rejected by terms, detailed argument (38a26−b4)
P*AaB*, N*AeC*	(*Camestres*)	same as previous (38b4−5)
N*AeB*, P*AeC* ⊢ *BeC*		modal conversion and conversion to I **NP** (38b8−12)
P*AeB*, N*AeC* ⊢ *BeC*		'likewise' (38b12−13)
all *aa* forms		rejected by terms (38b13−23)

NAeB, PAiC ⊢ BoC	*Festino*	'same as universal' (38b25−27)
NAaB, PAoC		rejected by terms (38b27−29)
all forms with two affirmatives		rejected 'as before' (38b29−31)
NAeB, PAoC ⊢ BoC		modal conversion (38b31−35)
all forms with two particulars		rejected by terms (38b35−37)

FIGURE III (A 22)

NAaC, PBaC ⊢ P(AiB)	*Darapti*	conversion to I NP (40a12−16)
PAaC, NBaC ⊢ PAiB	*Darapti*	conversion to I PN (40a16−18)
PAeC, NBaC ⊢ PAoB	*Felapton*	conversion to I PN (40a18−25)
NAeC, P(BaC) ⊢ AoB	*Felapton*	conversion to I NP (40a25−32)
NAaC, PBeC ⊢ P(AiB)		modal conversion (40a33−35)
PAaC, NBeC		rejected by terms (40a35−38)
NAiC, PBaC ⊢ PAiB	*Disamis*	conversion to I PN (40a40−b3)
PAaC, NBiC ⊢ PAiB	*Datisi*	conversion to I PN (40a40−b3)
PAiC, NBaC ⊢ P(AiB)	*Disamis.*	conversion to I NP (40a40−b3)
NAaC, PBiC ⊢ P(AiB)	*Datisi*	conversion to I NP (40a40−b3)
PAeC, NBiC ⊢ PAoB	*Ferison*	conversion to I PN (40a40−b3)
PAoC, NBaC ⊢ P(AoB)	*Bocardo*	through impossibility? (40a40−b3)
NAoC, PBaC ⊢ AoB	*Bocardo*	through impossibility? (40b3−8)
NAeC, PBiC ⊢ AoB	*Ferison*	conversion to I NP (40b3−8)
NAiC, PBeC ⊢ PAiB		modal conversion (40b8−11)
PAiC, NBeC		rejected 'as before' (40b10−12)

APPENDIX II
DEVIATIONS FROM
ROSS'S (OCT) TEXT

The following list gives all the places in which I follow a different reading from Ross's edition (published both as part of his commentary and as the Oxford Classical Text: see the Bibliography). My policy has generally been to err on the side of conservatism: in no case do I propose any conjectural readings, and when I deviate from Ross it is most often because I think I can give a good sense to a phrase he finds problematic. In one instance (43a10), I have relied on Williams *1984* in correcting Ross's apparatus.

In general, I give my reasons for adopting these readings in the Notes on the relevant passages. However, there is one systematic difference which must be explained here. Aristotle uses two idioms for expressing particular (*i* and *o*) categorical sentences. The more common form contains the definite article in the dative singular (e.g., 'A belongs *to some B*,' τὸ A τινὶ τῷ B ὑπάρχει); the less common form differs only in that the article is in the genitive plural ('A belongs *to some of the Bs*,' τὸ A τινὶ τῶν B ὑπάρχει). There is considerable variation between these two constructions in the manuscripts. Ross notes that τινὶ τῶν is not only less common but also virtually absent from Alexander's citations; since he also regards it as less in accordance with Aristotle's metaphysical views than τινὶ τῷ, he goes to great lengths to excise it, reading τινὶ τῷ if there is even the slightest manuscript authority for it. But even under these standards, he is sometimes forced to retain τινὶ τῶν (e.g., 33a27, 37a5, 18; cf. 44a17 and 44a20). It does not seem to me consistent to say, as Ross does, that τινὶ τῶν is not the sort of phrase Aristotle would prefer and then hold that the two phrases are equivalent in sense. It is also possible that there is a significant difference in sense: we sometimes find near unanimity in the manuscripts in reading τινὶ τῶν in passages associated with the procedure of *ekthesis* (six such occurrences are found in A 2, 25a15−26, all well-attested and all rejected by Ross). It is possible that this is a deliberate choice on Aristotle's part, since proof through *ekthesis* seems to depend on regarding the subject term of a sentence as a multitude in some way (Philoponus so took it). I have accordingly restored τινὶ τῶν wherever it is clearly supported by the majority of the sources Ross relies on (manuscripts A, B, C, and *n*).

At	For	Read
24b17–18	[ἢ διαιρουμένου]	ἢ διαιρουμένου (retain)
24b29	[τοῦ ὑποκειμένου]	τοῦ ὑποκειμένου (retain)
25a15	μηδενὶ τῷ Β	μηδενὶ τῶν Β
25a16–17	μηδενὶ τῷ Β	μηδενὶ τῶν Β
25a21	τῷ Β . . . τῷ Α	τῶν Β . . . τῶν Α
25a22	τῷ Β	τῶν Β
27a10	τὸ Ξ τῷ Ν	τῷ Ξ τὸ Ν
30b16	οὐδενὶ τῷ Β	οὐδενὶ τῶν Β
31a9	τῷ Γ . . . τῶ Γ	τῶν Γ . . . τῶν Γ
31b1	τῷ Β . . . τῷ Β	τῶν Β . . . τῶν Β
33a14	τῷ Β	τῶν Β
33a15	τῷ Γ	τῶν Γ
33a23	[τέλειος]	τέλειος (retain)
35b4	[ἢ μὴ ὑπάρχειν]	ἢ μὴ ὑπάρχειν (retain)
36a34	τῷ Β	τῶν Β
36a36	τῷ Γ	τῶν Γ
36a38	οὐδενὶ τῷ	οὐδενὶ τῶν
36b5	[πρὸς τῷ μείζονι ἄκρῳ]	πρὸς τῷ μείζονι ἄκρῳ (retain)
37a13	τῷ Α	τῶν Α
37a14	τῷ Β	τῶν Β
37a28	οὐ . . . ἀλλὰ	οὐ μόνον . . . ἀλλὰ καὶ
38a22	τῷ Γ	των Γ
38a24	τῷ Γ . . . τῷ Γ	τῶν Γ . . . τῶν Γ
39a18	τῷ Γ	τῶν Γ
39a19	τῷ Β	τῶν Β
39a34	τῷ Β	τῶν Β
39b14	τῷ Β	τῶν Β
43a10	τρόπων	πτώσεων
44a20	τῷ Ε	τῶν Ε
44a28	τῷ Ε	τῶν Ε
45a9	τῷ Θ	τῶν Θ
45a10	τῷ Ε	τῶν Ε
45a29	τῷ Ε	τῶν Ε
45a30	τῷ Ε	τῶν Ε
45a32	τῷ Ε . . . τῷ Η	τῶν Ε . . . τῶν Η
45a40	τῷ Ε	τῶν Ε
45b26	τῷ Ε	τῶν Ε
48b7–9	οὐχ ὥστε τὰ ἐναντία [τὸ] μίαν εἶναι [αὐτῶν] ἐπιστήμην	οὐχ ὡς τὰ ἐναντία τὸ μίαν εἶναι αὐτῶν ἐπιστήμην
50a2	τὸν μανθάνοντ᾽ αλέγοντες	τὸν μανθάνοντα λέγοντες
52a34	ἔσται	ἔστι
57b25	[ὅτι]	ὅτι (retain)
58a30	τῷ Γ	τῶν Γ

58b20−21	[τῷ δὲ Γ μηδενὶ]	τῷ δὲ Γ μηδενὶ (retain)
62a4−5	οὐδὲν παρὰ τὴν ὑπόθεσιν	οὐ παρὰ τὴν ὑπόθεσιν
	συμβαίνει ἀδύνατον	συμβαίνει τὸ ἀδύνατον
65a15	ἐνυπάρχει	ὑπάρχει
67b30	ἀντιστρέψει	ἀντιστρέφει
67b37	τὸ Α	τῷ Α
67b38	τὸ Γ καὶ πρὸς	τὸ Γ πρὸς
68b21−22	πᾶν γὰρ τὸ Γ	πᾶν γὰρ τὸ ἄχολον
69a28	τὴν ΑΒ	τὴν ΑΓ
70a9−10	(transposed to 70a2−3)	(leave in place)
70b19	[πάθος]	πάθος (retain)
70b21	[ὁ] ἄνθρωπος	ὁ ἄνθρωπος (retain article)

Glossary

Translations in boldface type are the English renderings I have normally followed for the associated Greek terms. The same English term is sometimes associated with more than one Greek term (e.g. **possible**), and different English terms are sometimes given for the same Greek term (e.g. *logos*). The reasons for these choices are scattered through the Notes (I try to collect the appropriate references under the Index entries for the terms in question). In the translation, context sometimes requires deviating from the translations given in the Glossary. Translations given in lightface roman type (e.g. syllogism) are not used in my version but are found in other translations or in the secondary literature: I include them here, with reference to the corresponding term in my translation, for the reader's convenience.

Translation	*Greek Term*
accepted	*endoxos*
admit	*dechesthai*
affirmation	*kataphasis*
affirmative	*kataphatikos*
agree	*homologein, sunchōrein*
agree in advance	*prodihomologein*
agreement	*homologia*
all	SEE **every**
argue	*dialegesthai*
argument	*logos*
ask	*aitein, aiteisthai; erōtan*
ask for the initial thing	*to ex archēs aiteisthai*
assertion	*phasis*
assume	*hupotithenai, hupokeisthai*
assumption	*hupothesis*
attack	*epicheirein*
beg the question	SEE **ask for the initial thing**
belief	*hupolēpsis*
believe	*hupolambanein*
believe in advance	*prohupolambanein*
belong	*huparchein*
case	*ptōsis*
collection of facts	*historia*

239

complete (adjective)	*teleios*
complete, be completed (verb)	*teleiousthai, epiteleisthai*
completion	*teleiōsis*
concealment	*krupsis*
conceive, conception	SEE **believe, belief**
conclude, come to a conclusion	*perainein*
conclusion	*sumperasma*
condition	*hexis*
connect	*sunhaptein*
connected	*sunechēs*
contemplate	*theōrein*
contingent	SEE **possible**
contradict	*antiphanai*
contradiction	*antiphasis*
contrary	*enantion*
conversion	*antistrophē*
convert	*antistrephein*
deduce	*sullogizesthai*
deduction	*sullogismos*
defend	*hupechein*
definition	*horismos, logos* (SEE 50a12, *175*)
demonstrate	*apodeiknunai*
demonstration	*apodeixis*
denial	*apophasis*
determinate	*dihōrismenos*
determination	*dihorismos*
determine	*dihorizein*
dialectic, dialectical	*dialektikē, dialektikos*
difference	*diaphora*
discipline	*methodos*
discourse	*logos*
divide	*dihairein, dihaireisthai*
division	*dihairesis*
ecthesis, ekthesis	SEE **setting-out**
enthymeme	*enthumēma*
error, be in error	*apatē, apatasthai*
essentially	*en tōi ti esti*
establish	*kataskeuazein*
evidence	*tekmērion*
evident	*phaneros*
examination	*epiblepsis, episkepsis*
examine	*epiblepein, episkopein, skopein*
example	*paradeigma*
experience	*empeiria*

extreme	*akron*
every; to every	*pas*; *panti*
false	*pseudēs*
falsehood	*pseudos*
familiar	*gnōrimos, gnōstos*
familiar through itself	*di' hautou gnōstos*
figure	*schēma*
follow	*akolouthein, hepesthai*; things that follow, *ta hepomena*. SEE ALSO result
for the most part	*hōs epi to polu*
genus	*genos*
get answers	*punthanesthai*
goat-stag	*tragelaphos*
hypothesis	SEE assumption
imperfect	SEE incomplete
impossible, impossibility	*adunatos, adunaton*
in relation to	*pros*
incidentally	*kata sumbebēkos*
incomplete	*atelēs*
incorrect	*pseudos* (arguments or inferences)
indemonstrable	*anapodeiktos*
indeterminate	*adihoristos*
individual	*atomon*
induction	*epagōgē*
inflection	*ptōsis*
initial, the initial thing	*to ex archēs, to en archēi*
inquiry	*skepsis*
interval	*diastēma*
lead back	*anagein*
lead to an impossibility	*agein/apagein eis to adunaton*
leading away	*apagōgē*
likelihood	*eikos*
main	*kurios*
major (extreme)	*meizon (akron)*
method	SEE route
middle	*meson*
minor (extreme)	*elatton (akron)*
necessarily	*anankaion*
necessary; of necessity	*anankaios, anankē; ex anankēs*
necessary when these things are so	*toutōn ontōn anankaios*
necessity	*anankē, to anankaion*
negative	*apophatikos*
nonbinding	*lusimos, lutos*

objection	*enstasis*
of itself	*kath' hauto*
opinion	*doxa*
oppose, be opposite to	*antikeisthai*
opposite	*antikeimenos*
particular (of premises)	*kata meros, en merei, epi merous*
particulars (individuals)	*ta kath' hekasta, ta kata meros*
peculiar	*idios*
perfect (adjective or verb)	SEE complete
petitio principii	SEE asking for the initial thing
positive	*katēgorikos*
possible	*endechomenos, dunatos*; be possible *endechesthai, enchōrein*
potential	*dunatos*
predicate, be predicated (verb: usually passive)	*katēgoreisthai*
predication	*katēgoria*
prefix	*prosrhēsis*
premise	*protasis*
previously stated, previously mentioned	*proeirēmenos*
principle	*archē*
prior deduction	*prosullogismos*
privative	*sterētikos*
probability	SEE likelihood
probative, probatively	*deiktikos, -ōs*
problem	*problēma*
procedure	*methodos*
propose	*proteinein*
proposition	SEE premise
prove	*deiknunai*
prove in a circle	*to kuklōi deiknusthai*
put	*tithenai*
quality	*poiotēs*
recognize natures	*phusiognōmonein*
refutation	*elenchos*
refute	*anaskeuazein, aposterein*
replace	*metalambanein*
reputable	SEE accepted
resolution	*analusis*
resolve	*analuein*
result (verb)	*sumbainein*
route	*hodos*
say of	*legesthai* (in passive voice)

science, scientific understanding	*epistēmē*
select	*eklambanein, eklegein*
selection	*eklogē*
self-evident	SEE **familiar through itself**
sentence	*logos*
series	*sustoichia*
set out	*ektithenai, ekkeisthai*
setting out	*ekthesis*
sign	*sēmeion*
species	*eidos*
subject	*hupokeimenon*
substitute	*metalambanein, metatithenai*
substitution	*metalēpsis*
suppose	*tithenai, keisthai* (passive voice)
syllogism, syllogize	SEE **deduce, deduction**
take	*lambanein*
take in addition	*proslambanein*
taking	*lēpsis*
term	*horos*
treatise	*pragmateia*
true	*alēthēs*
true of (verb)	*alētheuesthai*
undemonstrated	*anapodeiktos*
universal	*katholou*
unmiddled	*amesos*
without qualification	*haplōs*

Bibliography

This Bibliography makes no pretensions to completeness; it is a listing of the secondary literature, editions, and translations cited. For a more comprehensive listing, consult the bibliography in Mignucci *1962*.

BOOKS AND ARTICLES ON ARISTOTLE AND THE *PRIOR ANALYTICS*

Ackrill, J. L. *1963*. *Aristotle's Categories and De Interpretatione*. Oxford: Clarendon Press.

————. *1981*. "Aristotle's Theory of Definition: Some Questions on *Posterior Analytics* II.8−10." 359−84 in Berti *1981*.

Bäck, Allan. *1987*. "Philoponus on the Fallacy of Accident." *Ancient Philosophy* 7: 131−46.

————. *1988*. *On Reduplication*. Munich: Philosophia Verlag.

Barnes, Jonathan. *1975*. *Aristotle's Posterior Analytics*. Clarendon Press.

————. *1976*. "Aristotle, Menaechmus, and Circular Proof." *Classical Quarterly* 26: 278−92

————. *1981*. "Proof and the Syllogism." 17−59 in Berti *1981*.

Becker, Albrecht. *1933*. *Die Aristotelische Theorie der Möglichkeitsschlüsse*. Berlin: Junker. Reprinted Darmstadt: Wissenschaftliche Buchgesellschaft, 1968.

Berti, Enrico. *1981*. *Aristotle on Science: the "Posterior Analytics."* Padua: Antenore.

Bocheński, Innocentius M. *1970*. *A History of Formal Logic*. Translated by Ivo Thomas. Second Edition. New York: Chelsea.

Brunschwig, Jacques. *1981*. "L'objet et la structure des *Seconds Analytiques* d'après Aristote." 61−90 in Berti *1981*.

Burnyeat, Myles. *1981*. "Aristotle on Understanding Knowledge." 97−139 in Berti *1981*.

Clark, Michael. *1980*. *The Place of Syllogistic in Logical Theory*. Nottingham: University of Nottingham Monographs in the Humanities.

Corcoran, John. *1972*. "Completeness of an Ancient Logic." *Journal of Symbolic Logic* 37: 696−702.

————. *1973*. "A Mathematical Model of Aristotle's Syllogistic." *Archiv für Geschichte der Philosophie* 55: 191−219.

————. *1974a* (editor). *Ancient Logic and Its Modern Interpretations*. Dordrecht: D. Reidel.

————. *1974b*. "Aristotle's Natural Deduction System." 85−131 in Corcoran *1974a*.

244

_____. *1974c.* "Aristotelian Syllogisms: Valid Arguments or True Generalized Conditionals?" *Mind* 83: 278–81.

Einarson, Benedict. *1938.* "On Certain Mathematical Terms in Aristotle's Logic." *American Journal of Philology* 57: 34–54, 151–72.

Engberg-Pedersen, Trols. *1979.* "More on Aristotelian *Epagoge.*" *Phronesis* 24: 311–14.

Evans, J. D. G. *1977. Aristotle's Concept of Dialectic.* Cambridge: Cambridge University Press.

Ferejohn, Michael. *1988.* "Meno's Paradox and *De Re* Knowledge in Aristotle's Theory of Demonstration." *History of Philosophy Quarterly* 5:99–117.

Frede, Michael. *1974.* "Stoic vs. Aristotelian Syllogistic." *Archiv für Geschichte der Philosophie* 56: 1–32.

Freeland, Cynthia. *1986.* "Aristotle on Possibilities and Capabilities." *Ancient Philosophy* 6: 69–90.

Geach, Peter T. *1972. Logic Matters.* Oxford: Basil Blackwell.

Hamlyn, D. W. *1976.* "Aristotelian Epagoge." *Phronesis* 21: 167–84.

Heath, Thomas L. *1926. The Thirteen Books of Euclid's Elements.* Second edition. Cambridge University Press.

_____. *1949. Mathematics in Aristotle.* Oxford: Clarendon Press.

Hintikka, Jaakko. *1973. Time and Necessity: Studies in Aristotle's Theory of Modality.* Oxford: Clarendon Press.

Kneale, Martha. *1975.* "Prosleptic Propositions and Arguments." 189–207 in S. M. Stern, A. Hourani, and V. Brown, eds., *Islamic Philosophy and the Classical Tradition: Essays Presented to Richard Walzer.* Columbia, S. C.: University of South Carolina Press.

Kneale, William and Martha. *1962. The Development of Logic.* Oxford: Clarendon Press.

Lear, Jonathan. *1980. Aristotle and Logical Theory.* Cambridge: Cambridge University Press.

Lejewski, Ceslaw. *1961.* "On Prosleptic Syllogisms." *Notre Dame Journal of Formal Logic* 1: 158–67.

Łukasiewicz, Jan. *1957. Aristotle's Syllogistic from the Standpoint of Modern Formal Logic.* Second edition. Oxford: Clarendon Press.

McCall, Storrs. *1963. Aristotle's Modal Syllogisms.* Amsterdam: North-Holland Publishing Company.

McKirahan, Richard. *1983.* "Aristotelian Epagoge in *Prior Analytics* II.21 and *Posterior Analytics* I.1." *Journal of the History of Philosophy* 21: 1–13.

Mueller, Ian. *1974.* "Greek Mathematics and Greek Logic." 35–70 in Corcoran *1974a.*

Owen, G. E. L. *1959.* "Logic and Metaphysics in Some Early Works of Aristotle." 163–90 in I. Düring and G. E. L. Owen, editors, *Aristotle and Plato in the Mid-Fourth Century* (Göteborg).

Patzig, Günther. *1959.* "Aristotle and Syllogisms from False Premises." *Mind* 68: 186–92. Reprinted as 196–203 of Patzig *1968.*

_____. *1968*. *Aristotle's Theory of the Syllogism*. Translated by Jonathan Barnes. Dordrecht: D. Reidel.

Rescher, Nicholas. *1964*. "Aristotle's Theory of Modal Syllogisms and Its Interpretation." 152–77 in *The Critical Approach to Science and Philosophy*, ed. Mario Bunge. New York.

Rose, Lynn E. *1968*. *Aristotle's Syllogistic*. Springfield, Ill.: Charles C. Thomas.

Smiley, Timothy. *1973*. "What Is a Syllogism?" *Journal of Philosophical Logic* **2**: 136–54.

Smith, Robin. *1982a*. "The Syllogism in *Posterior Analytics* I." *Archiv für Geschichte der Philosophie* **64**: 113–35.

_____. *1982b*. "What Is Aristotelian Ecthesis?" *History and Philosophy of Logic* **3**: 113–27.

_____. *1983*. "Completeness of an Ecthetic Syllogistic." *Notre Dame Journal of Formal Logic* **24**: 224–32.

_____. *1984*. "Aristotle as Proof Theorist." *Philosophia Naturalis* **21**: 590–97.

_____. *1986*. "Immediate Propositions and Aristotle's Proof Theory." *Ancient Philosophy* **6**: 47–68.

Solmsen, Friedrich. *1929*. *Die Entwicklung der aristotelischen Logik und Rhetorik*. Berlin: Weidmann.

Vailati, Giovanni. *1911*. "A proposito d'un passo del Teeteto e di una dimostrazione di Euclide." 516–27 in his *Scritti*. Florence. Reprinted Florence: La Nuova Italia, 1980.

Vlastos, Gregory. *1972*. "The Unity of the Virtues in the *Protagoras*." *Review of Metaphysics* **25**: 415–48. Reprinted with revisions as 221–65 of Vlastos *1973b*.

_____. *1973a*. "An Ambiguity in the *Sophist*." 270–308 in Vlastos *1973b*.

_____. *1973b*. *Platonic Studies*. Princeton: Princeton University Press.

Waterlow [Broadie], Sarah. *1982*. *Passage and Possibility: A Study of Aristotle's Modal Concepts*. Oxford: Clarendon Press.

Wieland, Wolfgang. *1966*. "Die aristotelische Theorie der Notwendigkeitsschlüsse." *Phronesis* **11**: 35–60.

_____. *1972*. "Die aristotelische Theorie der Möglichkeitsschlüsse." *Phronesis* **17**: 124–52.

_____. *1975*. "Die aristotelische Theorie der Syllogismen mit modal gemischten Prämissen." *Phronesis* **20**: 77–92.

_____. *1976*. "Probleme der aristotelischen Theorie über die Schlüsse aus falschen Prämissen." *Archiv für Geschichte der Philosophie* **58**: 1–9.

_____. *1980*. "Die aristotelische Theorie der Konversion von Modalaussagen." *Phronesis* **25**: 109–116.

Williams, Mark F. *1984*. *Studies in the Manuscript Tradition of Aristotle's Analytica*. Königstein: Verlag Anton Hain.

TRANSLATIONS, EDITIONS AND COMMENTARIES

[Aldina]. *1495–98. Aristotelis opera graece* . . . [First printed edition of Aristotle's works.] Venice: Aldus Menucius.

Alexander [of Aphrodisias]. *1883. Alexandri Aphrodisiensis in Aristotelis analyticorum priorum librum I commentarium*. Ed. M. Wallies. *Commentaria in aristotelem graeca* II.1. Berlin: Georg Reimer.

Ammonius. *1890. Ammonii in Aristotelis Analyticorum Priorum Librum I Commentarium*. Ed. M. Wallies. *Commentaria in Aristotelem Graeca* IV.6. Berlin: Georg Reimer.

Barnes, Jonathan. *1984. The Complete Works of Aristotle: The Revised Oxford Translation*. [The translation of the *Prior Analytics* included is a revision of Jenkinson *1928*.] Princeton: Princeton University Press (Bollingen Series).

Bonitz, H. *1870. Index Aristotelicus*. Berlin. Reprinted Graz: Akademischen Druck- u. Verlangsanstalt, 1955.

Colli, G. *1955. Organon. Introduzione, traduzione e note di G. Colli*. Turin.

Gohlke, P. *1953. Aristoteles, Die Lehrschriften, herausgegeben und übertragen und in ihrer Entstehung erläutert von P. Gohlke. Mit einer Einleitung über Aristoteles und sein Werk*. Bd. II.2: *Erste Analytik*. Paderborn: F. Schöningh.

Jenkinson, Arthur J. J. *1928. The Works of Aristotle Translated into English* [the 'Oxford Translation'], vol. I. [Only the translation of the *Prior Analytics* is by Jenkinson]. Oxford: Clarendon Press.

Mignucci, Mario. *1961. Gli analitici primi: Traduzione, introduzione e commento di Mario Mignucci*. Naples: Luigi Loffredo.

Owen, Octavius Friere. *1853. The Organon, or Logical Treatises of Aristotle, with the Introduction of Porphyry*. Literally translated, with notes, syllogistic examples, analysis and introduction. 2 vols., London: Henry G. Bohn (Bohn's Classical Library).

Pacius, J. *1596. Aristotelis organon graece et latine* . . . Geneva. Reprint Frankfurt/Main: Minerva, 1967.

Philoponus, John. *1905. Ioannis Philoponi in Aristotelis analytica priora commentaria. Commentaria in aristotelem graeca* XIII.2.

Rolfes, Eugen. *1921. Lehre vom Schluß, oder Erste Analytik (Organon III). Übersetzt und mit Anmerkungen versehen von Eugen Rolfes*. Hamburg: Felix Meiner.

Ross, W. D. *1949. Aristotle's Prior and Posterior Analytics. A revised Text with Introduction and Commentary*. (Reprinted with corrections 1957, 1965.) Oxford: Clarendon Press.

————. *1964. Aristotelis Analytica Priora et Posteriora*. (Oxford Classical Text: Ross's text, with a Preface and Appendix added by L. Minio-Paluello.) Oxford: Clarendon Press.

Tredennick, Hugh. *1938*. *The Organon, I: The Categories, On Interpretation, Prior Analytics*. [Translation of *Prior Analytics* alone is by Tredennick.] Cambridge, Mass.: Harvard University Press (Loeb Classical Library).

Tricot, J. *1971*. *Organon III: Les premiers analytiques*. *Traduction nouvelle et notes par J. Tricot*. (New edition: first edition 1936.) Paris: J. Vrin.

Waitz, Theodor. *1844*. *Aristotelis organon graece*. *Novis codicum auxiliis adiutus recognovit, scholiis ineditis et commentario instruxit Theodorus Waitz*. Leipzig: Hahn.

Index Locorum

249

General Index

Index entries in boldface type are terms used in Aristotle's text; those in light type are subject entries only. Reference to the Introduction and Notes is by page number in italics, while reference to Aristotle's text is by Bekker line number or book and chapter (e.g. A23).

Academy, Platonic *153*, *193*.
accepted (*endoxos*), of premises 24b12, 62a13, 62a16, 62a18−19, 70a3−4, 70a7, 70b4−9, *108*, *200*, *226*.
Ackrill, J.L. *160*.
addition (*proskeisthai*) 30a1.
affirmation (*kataphasis*), type of categorical sentence *xvii*; every affirmation has a denial, 51b34−35; 'not-good' a kind of affirmation, 51b35; treated in *Topics* as type of predicate, *177−78*.
affirmative (*kataphatikos*) *xvii*; one premise of every deduction must be affirmative 41b6−7, *124*; affirmative conclusion only from two affirmative premises 38a36−38, 41b27−31, *137*; particular affirmative indeterminate *116−17*; possible premises affirmative in form 25b19−25, 32b1−3.
Alexander of Aphrodisias *105*, *110*, *115*, *126*, *133*, *135*, *168*, *170*, *172*, *173*, *179*.
analysis, as deducing premises from conclusion *185*.
Analytics (as title) *161*.
Aristomenes (name used as example) *162−63*.
ask 1 (*erōtan*), of dialectical presentation of premises 24a27, 66a37, 39; of arguments 47a21−22; demonstrator does not ask but takes 24a24; ask for more things than necessary 42a39; for premises without conclusion 66a26; for useless things 47a18; dialectical premise asking (*erōtēsis*) of a contradiction 24a25, *108*, *148*.
ask 2 (*aitein*, *aiteisthai*) division asks for what it ought to prove 46a34−35, 46b11.

ask for the initial thing (*to ex archēs aiteisthai*) 41b8−9, 14, 20−21, B16, *142−44*, *204−9*; definition 64b36−38; occurs in Platonic Division *160*.
assertion (*phasis*) = **affirmation**, and its denial 37a12, 51b20−21, 52b22−24, 62a13−14, 63b34−35; initial assertion (= **assumption** in a deduction through impossibility) 65b20−21; the opposite assertion (= contradictory) 34b31.
assume (*hupotithenai*, *hupokeisthai*) *xxix−xxx*, 25a19, 27a8, 35, b1, 19, 28b27, 29a6, 34a40−41, b5, 36a11, 15, 38−39, 36b37 (*keisthō*), 38a24−25, 39a38, 42a27, 45b2, 52b24, 61a28, 31, 37, 40−41, b8, 11 etc. (freq. in B11−13); assuming the subject 43b2; when something false but not impossible is assumed, result is false but not impossible 34a25−33; terms assumed 24b25−26; SEE ALSO **assumption**.
assumption (*hupothesis*) 28a7 etc. (*thesis* at 65b8, 14, 66a2, 8: SEE *210*); proof or deduction from an assumption 40b25−29, A44, *155*, *175−76*; deduction from impossibility as from assumption 41a21−37; types of these 45b15−20, 50a39−b4, cf. 41a37−b1; every deduction probative or from an assumption 40b25, *140*; every deduction from an assumption about the thing substituted 41a38−9; the initial assumptions 24a30−b10; contradictory of assumption made 34b28−31; deducing universal problems from an assumption by means of the examination for a particular 45b22−35; deductions from

determine (*dihorizein*) 24a11, 25b26,
32b23, 34a34; with respect to time
34b8, 34b18.
development of Aristotle's theory *xiii*.
diagrams *173, 207*.
dialectical arguments 65a37, *205*; premises 24a22–b15; exchanges *108*;
refutation *204*; treatise on dialectic
(= *Topics*) 46a29–30.
dictum de omni et nullo 24b26–30, *111, 146,
172*, cf. 33a3–5.
direct SEE probative.
discipline (*methodos*) 53a2, 68b12, *183*.
division (*dihairesis*), Platonic *xiv, 157, 160*;
Aristotle's criticism A31; 'small part' of
Aristotle's procedure 46a31–32; weak
deduction 46a32–33.
draw (*graphein*) in sense 'prove' 65a5,
207.
duplication (something extra duplicated,
to epanadiploumenon) 49a11–26.

Einarson, Benedict *112, 114, 147, 173*.
ekthesis, in Greek geometrical proofs
173; SEE ALSO setting out.
Eleatics *115*.
Engberg–Pedersen, Trols *221*.
enthymeme (*enthumēma*) 70a9, *226–7*.
error (*apatē*), be in error, be deceived
(*apatasthai*) *215*; because of failure to
take opposites correctly 52b14–34; in
connection with beliefs B21, *213–15*;
because of resemblance of position of
terms A33; because of something necessary resulting 47a31–40; because
terms have not been set out well A34;
from trying to set out term as word
A35; error contrary to universal knowledge a deduction 67b11; in accordance
with middle term 67a31–32; in case of
particular premises 67a8–10; about
terms from same series 66b26–30;
67a38, 67b10; of the partisans of Division 46a37–39, *160*.
essence, of bad and good 67b12–26.
essentially (*en tōi ti esti*), predicated essentially 43b7, *151*.

evidence (*tekmērion*), difference from sign
(*sēmeion*) 70b1–6, *227*.
example (*paradeigma*) B24, *221–22*; difference from induction 69a16–19.
excluded middle, law of 52b22–24,
62a13–15, *158, 178, 179*.
existential instantiation *112*.
extreme (*akron*) *xviii–xix*; definition in
first figure, 25b36–37; in second
26b36–37, 39; in third 28a13–14.

fallacy SEE error.
false conclusion from true premises impossible 53b11–25.
false in part 54b3 etc., cf. 53b29; 'wholly
false' 54a4–6.
falsehood does not follow because of this
B17.
familiar (*gnōrimos*) 68b35–36, 40, 69a16,
221; in *Posterior Analytics 205*.
Ferejohn, Michael *214*.
figure (*schēma*) *xviii–xix*; definition of
first figure 26b33; of second 26b34–36;
of third 28a10–12; determination of figure in leading back 47a40–b14;
recognized by position of middle term
47b13–14; in sense 'mood' 51a31–32,
180.
first-figure deductions, assertoric A4; with
necessary and assertoric premises A9;
with two possible premises A14; with
possible and assertoric premises A15;
with possible and necessary premises
A16.
for the most part (*hōs epi to polu*)
25b14–15, 32b4–22, *126–27*.
formal model for Aristotle's theory
xix–xxi.
Forms, Platonic *123*.
fourth-figure deductions recognized
29a21–27, *118*.
Frede, Michael *xi, 111*.
Freeland, Cynthia *127*.

Geach, Peter *ix, xvii, 114*.
genus (*genos*) *187*.
geometrical examples 41b14–22,
48a33–37, 66a14–15, 67a13–26.

versal by means of examination for
particular 45b22—35; particular, universal knowledge 66b32—33, *214—15*;
67a18—19, 20 (*tēn kath' hekaston*).
particular (2) of individuals: (2a) *to kath'
hekaston*: 43a27, 43a39—40, 67a18—20;
sensible particular *121*; induction is
from particulars 68b20, 28; (2b) *ta en
merei, ta kata meros*: 67a23—24, 27, 39;
(2c) *tode ti*: 48a38, 49a28—29 ('this
something'), 49b34, *171, 173*.
Patzig, Günther *xvi, 110, 112, 114, 115, 121,
150, 177, 186, 190, 196, 197*.
peculiar (*idios*), premises peculiar to a
science 46a17; peculiar premises arise
from experience 46a17—21; of predicates *151*.
per se SEE **of itself.**
perceptible (*aisthēton*) what is individual
and perceptible 43a27, 43a39—40.
perfect induction *221*.
petitio principii SEE **asking for the initial
thing.**
Philoponus, John SEE John Philoponus.
Phocians 69a1, 5, 10, *222*.
Plato *105, 106, 157, 164, 204, 219*.
positive (*katēgorikos*), synonym of **affirmative** (q.v.) *112*.
possible (*endechomenon, dunaton*), **is possible** (*endechesthai, enchōrein*) of premises
25a2, 31—32, etc.; definition 32a18—20,
124—25; different senses 25a37—40;
conversion of possible premises
25a39—b25; possible premises affirmative in form 25b19—25, 32b1—2;
affirmative, negative possible premises
convert 32a29—35; distinction between
dunaton and *endechomenon 123, 131*; consequence of something possible not
impossible 34a5—24; consequence of
false but not impossible assumption not
impossible 34a25—34, 34b1—2; necessary called possible equivocally
32a20—21; denial of possible premise a
disjunction 37a24—26, *135—36*; for the
most part and indeterminate 32b4—13;
possibility not according to determination 33b30 etc., *125, 131, 134*; 'is
possible' arranged similarly to 'is'

25b22, 32b2, *126*; senses in which possibility must be understood 34a12—15.
potentiality (*dunamis*) *175—76*.
practical wisdom *188*.
predicables *187*.
predicate, simple and complex 49a6 *169,
179*.
predicate (*katēgoroumenon*) extra predicate (*epikatēgoroumenon*) *169*.
predicate (verb: *katēgoreisthai*), definition
of 'predicated of every/none'
24b28—30, cf. 30a1—2; active/passive
voice distinguished 47b1—2; relation of
terms in deduction not always predication, A36; opposite of 'reject' 63b36.
predication and identification *172*; identical predications *173*; essential *170*.
predication i.e. type of sentence *172*.
predication (*katēgoria*) in sense 'kind of
predication' 41a4, 41b31, 45b34—35, *170*
(cf. **problem**); opposite of **privation**
52a15—16, *179*; reversed in predication
57b19.
preferable (*hairetōteros*) 68a25—39.
prefix (*prosrhēsis*) 25a3.
premise (*protasis*) *106—9*; sentence affirming or denying something about
something 24a16—17; demonstrative,
dialectical, and deductive 24a17—22,
107—8; dialectical premise asking of a
contradiction 24a25, *148*; demonstrative
premise taking of one part of a contradiction 24a23—24; deductive premise
24a28—29; universal, particular, indeterminate 24a18—22, 25a4—5; meaning
of indeterminate premises *107*; indeterminate equivalent to particular
29a27—29; one premise of deduction
must be like conclusion 32a10—12,
41b27—31; premises actually taken
35a4, 13—14, 37b32—33, 38a32—33,
b7—8, *133*; nothing follows from single
premise 34a17—19, 40b35—36, *131, 140*;
as what is proposed *151*; procecure for
finding, *152*.
principle (*archē*) 53a2—3; common and
peculiar 46a17, *158*; how to obtain the
principles concerning any subject
A27—28; in *Posterior Analytics 149*;

Aristotle's
Prior Analytics
translated by
Robin Smith
was set in
Caslon
by
Andresen Typographics

Caslon
is a classic
"old style" typeface
based on designs by
William Caslon
(1692–1766)